BIG BETS

© 2011 BY SOUTHERN COMPANY
ALL RIGHTS RESERVED
PUBLISHED 2011

FIRST EDITION
2ND PRINTING

PUBLISHED BY
SOUTHERN COMPANY
30 IVAN ALLEN JR. BOULEVARD NW
ATLANTA, GEORGIA 30308

ISBN-13 978-0-615-46486-2

LIBRARY OF CONGRESS CONTROL NUMBER | 2011925378

BOOK DESIGN BY BURT&BURT

PRINTED IN THE UNITED STATES OF AMERICA
100% RECYCLED PAPER

BIG
BETS

DECISIONS AND LEADERS
THAT SHAPED SOUTHERN COMPANY

DUB TAFT & SAM HEYS

Southern Company, 2011

The switch house at Tallulah Falls Dam in 1913; switchgears inside early powerhouses were massive metal-enclosed structures. *GPC Archives*

Surveyors at Cherokee Bluffs: The site on the Tallapoosa River responsible for inspiring a dream that set the course of history for both Alabama Power and Southern Company. Martin Dam (at right) was completed at the bluffs in 1927. *APC Archives*

THIS STORY BEGINS WITH A DREAM conceived a century ago. Retracing the origins of the first big idea that resulted in Southern Company's formation will lead you to a point on the Tallapoosa River known as Cherokee Bluffs. This bucolic retreat once was accessible only to those who could trek wilderness trails that snaked around rocky cliffs and over rough terrain. From atop the highest ridge, hikers could enjoy panoramic views of verdant-rich forests and surrounding hills. From inside the gorge, overnight campers could catch hearty catfish in the deep holes and swim in cool waters that gushed over rugged rapids at the narrow points before stretching out to rest lazy and smooth as silk.

In 1911, a visionary entrepreneur came to Alabama and, within moments of his first visit, dreamed of building a colossal dam at Cherokee Bluffs. James Mitchell was more than a dreamer. He was a gifted engineer who already had developed and operated electric railways and giant hydro power projects on several continents. He could make big things happen through his immense physical and creative energy and his connections to international investment bankers. To transform secluded Cherokee Bluffs into a 40,000-acre lake would require the labor of several thousand construction workers and carpenters, roadway and railway builders, woodsmen and sawmill hands, using what today would be considered primitive drills and pumps, cranes and concrete mixers, explosives and stone crushers. The project's scope was so challenging that the dam—stretching 2,000 feet across and rising 168 feet above the riverbed—would create the world's largest artificial reservoir when eventually completed in 1927. A big dream.

But Mitchell's dreams were not limited to this one impoundment on the Tallapoosa. He also planned to build a series of dams and powerhouses on the Coosa and other great rivers of Alabama. And he conceived a grand-scale transmission system to connect these waterpower facilities to cities and communities throughout Alabama and then to interconnect Alabama's power lines with those in neighboring states. He envisioned an electric supply system and a regional grid that could serve energy markets across the Southeast.

In essence, James Mitchell dreamed Southern Company. The plans he set into motion, the organization he put together, the money he raised, the talent he attracted, the passion he poured into this dream, all represent the first big bet for Southern Company.

Big bets are pivotal decisions leaders must make when the stakes are high. Bets that can make or break their company and their personal legacy. Bets that decide which path an enterprise will take at critical crossroads. Bets that shape and reshape its destiny. Mitchell's bet was on the creation of a new type of electric system—one that could stand up successfully in a region investors avoided, one that would build a market for power as hydro dams were being constructed, one that could help transform an impoverished region and uplift it into the light of a New South economy.

Mitchell lived to see one of his many dams completed in Alabama—but not the one that sparked his dreams at Cherokee Bluffs. By the time the first sunrise flared across that new reservoir in the Deep South, Mitchell himself lay in a cold, silent grave in the far, far North. He was killed, some would say, by his work—by the boldness and sheer size of it, by the superhuman force and energy he put behind it, by the harpies and caustic critics who rose against it, by the impossible odds and obstacles he had to overcome because of it. Dead at age fifty-four, he paid the supreme sacrifice for his demanding work and daring dreams.

But those dreams did not die with James Mitchell. They were passed to others who caught his vision—other dreamers, builders, and leaders who, in time, would put together, city by city, state by state, the electric system and organization that eventually would become Southern Company. This is the story of that company's evolution, the turning points in its history, the events, crises, ideals, and principles that forged its character. This also is the story of the individuals who guided the enterprise through its critical formative years and the leaders who followed in their footsteps. This is the story of the decisions they faced, the dreams they pursued, the troubles they encountered, and the big bets they made.

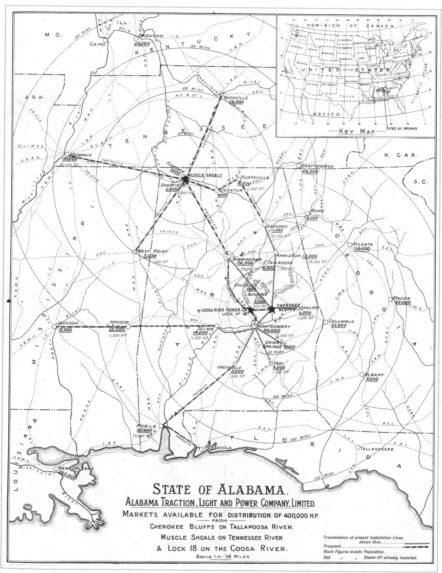

James Mitchell's map of a potential power market, which he used to attract British investors and create the first holding company in Southern Company's lineage. At right, Mitchell in his prime ca. 1918.
APC Archives

WHAT MITCHELL STARTED

THE FIRST TIME THEY SET EYES ON HIM, Henry C. Jones and William Patrick Lay knew they had at long last found the man they had been seeking. James Mitchell was an experienced, reputable developer of big projects, a rugged man of impressive physical and mental strength. He was outgoing, articulate, and immediately likable.

"He was a man of action if ever there was one," said Jones.

"Electrified with vigor, energy, and determination," Lay recalled.

Jones and Lay had been searching several years for financial backing of their proposed hydroelectric plants in Alabama. Their separate journeys led them to the New York offices of Paul Brady, an associate of George Westinghouse and a promoter who was instrumental in the start-up of many early power projects. Westinghouse and Brady got in touch with Mitchell and told him about the prospects down South. An established name in the rapidly changing field of electric energy, Mitchell had made his fortune developing hydro dams and electric tramways in South America and was now scouting the globe for attractive new opportunities.

The year was 1911. William Howard Taft, the heftiest president ever, was in the White House continuing the enlightened policies of his predecessor and sponsor, Theodore Roosevelt. The nation was in what would become known as the Progressive Era—a time of great reforms in labor, wage, food, and drug laws, an age that gave birth to the National Park Service, a period of rising social consciousness and receding "robber baron" abuses. It was an epoch of rapid technological advancements—the dawn of man's flight, the advent of automobiles produced on an assembly line, and the spread of central station power plants, bringing greater industrialization and affordable electricity to more and more people.

America was coming of age. But sadly, the South was not. Chiefly agrarian and lagging in industry, it seemed stuck in the previous era and dependent more than ever on cautious northern capital. Only a few southern developers were able to finance the huge plants needed to fire up the region's economic engines. And in the very heart of Dixie, home of abundant hydro resources—some of the nation's greatest—Alabama was having trouble getting anything started.

Enter Mitchell with access to British money. In the fall of 1911, his travels brought him to Georgia to evaluate potential projects on the Savannah River. He explored the shoals known as Clark's Hill, north of Augusta, and deemed it uneconomical to develop at the time. His next stop was Alabama. It was a defining moment for the state and for the group of utilities that would emerge from his visit.

MITCHELL'S INITIAL VISIT AND DREAM

It was a brisk but sunny November morning when Mitchell stepped off the train in Dadeville, made his first call on Jones, and asked if they could ride out immediately to have a look at a place known as Cherokee Bluffs. A man of action.

"I had sought such a man as Mr. Mitchell for years," said Jones. An electrical contractor, Henry C. Jones headed a group struggling to develop hydroelectric projects on the Tallapoosa River, a sizable stream in east-central Alabama that joins the Coosa River above Montgomery to form the Alabama River.

Jones and his partners had searched several years before finding a developer for the area's only dam—one of modest size, only 8,500 horsepower, located three miles above the town of Tallassee. Cherokee Bluffs, seven miles above that point, was a challenge to reach. Mitchell and Jones used a horse and buggy to cross the hilly trails and made their final approach on foot. Mitchell's excitement swelled when he saw water gushing over a solid-rock bed between two mountain walls that jutted upward to a height of 160 feet or more—a natural site for a dam, capable of impounding what Jones called a "stupendous volume of water."

Jones pointed out benchmarks placed on both sides of the river by K. F. Cooper's survey team and discussed the preliminary site studies, but he fell silent when he realized his guest was forming his own preliminary plans. For a few moments, Mitchell stood apart from Jones on the ridge, taking it all in. He liked what he saw, was thrilled by it. He had seen similar formations in the mountains of South America. He knew what could be created at this place, and he knew how to build it. Patiently watching, Jones knew the man was visualizing things, but he wouldn't know until later just how big that vision was.

On the return trip, they discussed other projects, perhaps the work of Frank Washburn, president of the American Cyanamid Company and head of a group trying to develop an enormous site on the Tennessee River at Muscle Shoals in northwest Alabama. Jones and Washburn had jointly created the Alabama Interstate Power Company with the idea that their two projects might be coordinated someday. When Mitchell asked about state laws and water power rights, Jones referred him to Massey Wilson, a former state attorney general who had prepared land titles for Jones. Not knowing that Wilson recently had moved out of state, Mitchell took the train to Montgomery and made a cold call at the offices of Tyson, Wilson & Martin in the downtown National Bank Building. Instead of Wilson, he found a young partner, Thomas W. Martin, in the office that day.

Theirs would be an unlikely alliance. Mitchell was a man of commanding size—nearly six feet, 180 pounds, with the demeanor and dress of an aristocrat, the ruggedness of a rugby player, and a voice resonating with energy and authority. By comparison, Martin was tiny—little more than five and a half feet, maybe 130 pounds, with the looks of a schoolboy and voice of a genteel southerner. Yet Martin soon found Mitchell to be "pleasant and agreeable and of great personal charm," and Mitchell found Martin to be experienced in legal matters of immediate interest.

Alabama leaders were eager to attract capital, explained Martin, and had passed legislation in 1907 offering waterpower developers a ten-year tax exemption and other incentives. Planning groups and partnerships had been formed for all the major streams, and Martin knew many of the players. But very little was coming from their efforts other than surveys and studies, since most were unable to raise enough money to build their projects. Like most of the South, Alabama was still struggling. The industrial revolution had practically passed the region by because most northern bankers were reluctant to risk investments in a region viewed as backward and economically retarded. The South's first major hydro projects were built in the Carolinas, and a few were being constructed in Georgia. But Alabama's vast hydro potential was practically untapped.

Mitchell retained Martin's services to help pull together additional research and then traveled to Wetumpka and Gadsden to meet with several other developers, including William Patrick Lay. None of the early pioneers had worked harder for their projects than Lay, who in 1906 organized the first company bearing the name of Alabama Power. A steamboat captain, engineer, and promoter, Lay was passionate about the Coosa River and had helped organize the Coosa-Alabama Improvement Association in 1890 to champion the building of locks and dams needed to open the river to navigation through a 142-mile stretch of shoals and rapids between Wetumpka and Greensport. Of most interest to Mitchell, Lay had obtained congressional approval, in 1907, to construct a dam at a site known as Lock 12. For six years, Lay had pursued investors from New York, Boston, St. Louis, Montreal, and "anywhere, O Lord!" Many times, just as he thought he was finally getting financial backing, "it would all go up in smoke." Most recently, Lay had signed an option with A. B. Leach and Company of New York, but, because he had been disappointed too many times before, he kept searching for a backup. He finally found one standing in his doorway: James Mitchell.

"Well do I remember the November morning when I first met him," he recalled. "He seemed to be almost electrified with vigor, energy, and determination. In addition to all of these splendid qualifications, Mr. Mitchell was affable, pleasant, and easy of approach." Lay eagerly rolled out his maps and took Mitchell to see several of the sites, including the clearing he had made at Lock 12, on the Coosa near the town of Clanton.

Next, Mitchell turned his attention to the Tennessee River. Near Sheffield, he met with Washburn and one of his partners, J. W. Worthington, to explore Muscle Shoals, where rapids and rocks stretched the river a mile wide at some points. Aside from opening the river to navigation, a dam at Muscle Shoals could produce the enormous volume of electricity needed to make nitrates at a factory Washburn wanted to build. Worthington, president of the Sheffield National Bank and an advisor to the Tennessee River Improvement Association, wanted the site built because it would expand his region's economy like nothing yet seen in the South.

During the next few weeks, Mitchell studied every aspect of Alabama's watersheds and prospective power markets, meeting with political leaders, landowners, and other hopeful developers. He took Lay, Martin, and others on some of the excursions, bouncing around dirt roads in horse-drawn buggies and climbing rocky hills where there were no trails. Alabama had some of the richest hydro resources in the country, but fifteen different groups had acquired sites, rights, and lands at practically every point that could be developed economically.

"Some of these projects are so conflicting with each other," Mitchell told Martin, "it's impossible for them to be developed separately. It would be nothing short of financial disaster for me to enter this field unless we can consolidate all these interests under a broad and comprehensive plan." That plan's cornerstone was an option to buy Cherokee Bluffs, which Mitchell secured November 14, one day before receiving a reassuring message from W. C. Church, a nationally known hydraulic engineer and builder of more than sixty waterpower dams. When Church described Cherokee Bluffs as "the most satisfactory large power [project] that has ever gone through this office," Mitchell knew he had a crown jewel.

Finalizing a plan for dams, transmission lines, and interconnections, Mitchell sketched his dream onto a map of the region, a map he could use in a prospectus to raise millions of dollars to build such a system, a map that would inspire the creation of a southeastern power market Southern Company would one day serve. "There is no record to indicate that anyone had ever made so bold a plan," Martin later wrote.

By December, Mitchell's initial work was done. He was ready to leave Alabama, hop a train to New York, and purchase a ticket aboard a Cunard ship, the quickest passage across the Atlantic, promising to get travelers to London within eight to ten days. The fast friends he had made in Alabama wondered if they would ever see him again. Some called him a crazy, redheaded Englishman. Or was he a Yankee or Scotsman? Or perhaps a Canadian or a South American? No one was quite sure. But they would soon learn that he was all of these, a man of the world who had just stepped into their lives and was about to transform their world forever.

MITCHELL'S MANY CAREERS

Before he came to the South, James Mitchell already had accomplished more than many business pioneers achieve in their entire careers. Indeed, he seemed to have lived multiple lives. Born June 19, 1866, in Pembroke, Ontario, Mitchell came from Scot ancestry and poor farming parents. In 1868, the family moved across the border and settled in Milton, Massachusetts, where Mitchell's four brothers and four sisters were born. A tall, thin, freckle-faced boy, Mitchell displayed exceptional abilities in mathematics and had such a thirst for knowledge that his classmates often wondered "how one redhead could carry all he knew." In preparing for college, he passed examinations to enter Harvard. But on his schoolmaster's advice, Mitchell instead went to work in 1882 for Charles L. Bly, of Boston, a firm that built instruments for the emerging fields of electricity and telecommunications. After two years, Mitchell joined the Thomson-Houston Electric Company—forerunner of General Electric—where he made volt and ampere meters and invented what was possibly the first automatic circuit breaker. His aptitude for experimental work and his precision brought him to the attention of company founder and inventor extraordinaire Elihu Thomson and his associate E. W. Rice, for whom Mitchell helped build some of the industry's first electric railway motors.

"He was always the first one on the job in the morning and the last to leave at night," said W. N. Walmsley, who trained in the shop under the young taskmaster. "To the poor young boys who had no practical knowledge of the operation of a machine shop, he was kindness itself—if the boy showed any interest in his work. . . . Those, however, who did not apply themselves, very soon found themselves out of that department."

Mitchell matured into an attractive young man with a thick shock of auburn hair, piercing blue-green eyes, and the mental and physical stamina of a leader who exhibited the work capacity of three people. So it was no surprise when he was placed in charge of the entire railway department. Called to Denver once by a company having troubles just prior to its railway system's grand opening, Mitchell went straight to the car barn without changing his clothes, tore apart the engine, worked through the night, dashed to the hotel to wash up, donned his "Prince Albert" suit and top hat, and went off to pick up the mayor for the ceremonies.

After assignments in Chicago and California, Thomson-Houston asked Mitchell to go to Brazil in 1890 to install a special electric railway line up a mountainside near Rio de Janeiro. Rice said he wanted Mitchell for the job because he was an "indefatigable worker" who "demonstrated an unusual engineering ability and adaptability in meeting unexpected situations and people." Mitchell stayed in Brazil for the next sixteen years, selling and installing steam and hydro plants while making infrequent trips to London for project financing and to New York to visit family and recuperate. Once, during an epidemic in Rio de Janeiro, he contracted yellow fever. Another time, he came home with tuberculosis but recovered and returned to work after a few months in the Adirondacks.

A quick study of Portuguese, Mitchell so endeared himself to the Brazilians that they talked about him for years as "one of the great Americans" who, through fair dealings, helped cement friendships between the two countries. "A super amount of energy radiated to all of those about him," noted engineering consultant Hugh L. Cooper, who worked alongside Mitchell in building a dam for São Paulo Tramway, Light & Power Company. That project also gave Mitchell the opportunity to work for F. S. Pearson, a renowned engineer who developed projects on three continents. After completing São Paulo's dam and powerhouse, Pearson asked Mitchell to stay on as general manager from 1900 to 1905 and then help him organize Rio de Janeiro Tramway, Light & Power.

By 1907, Mitchell was exhausted and ready to leave South America. When Walmsley, his former employee at Thomson-Houston's shop, arrived at the harbor to replace him, Mitchell threw his arms around his neck, proclaimed him "savior," and explained, "I've wanted for so long to have a rest, but did not feel free to leave until I had a successor and had time to go fully into detail with him." After an initial stay in Washington, D.C., Mitchell moved his family to London and told his wife, daughter, and son he was retiring, that his pioneering days were over. He felt far older than his forty-one years; illnesses and the pace of his work had taken their toll.

His adventures might have ended there, but after rest, recuperation, and recreation, Mitchell regained his strength and began traveling again. Returning from a trip to the Amazon, he connected with an old acquaintance, Sir Edward Mackay Edgar of Sperling and Company, a London investment house. Also a native Canadian, Edgar had organized big hydroelectric projects before moving to London to join the prestigious house of Sperling, bankers for major investments across the globe. Known as the "man with a load of millions," Edgar put together international deals in cotton, iron, steel, shipbuilding, and energy developments, including financings for Mitchell's South American projects. Knowing those investments paid off largely because of Mitchell's abilities, Edgar jumped at the chance to send Mitchell to Russia, Japan, Mexico, and the United States in search of new investment opportunities. It was Edgar who asked Mitchell to investigate hydro sites along the Savannah River. And it was Edgar whom Mitchell most wanted to see after the Alabama excursion. Across the cold Atlantic in December 1911, Mitchell sailed for England with map and prospectus and dream in hand.

MARKETING THE DREAM

The heart of London's financial district was three blocks north of the River Thames, where the Stock Exchange and the esteemed Bank of England anchored the corners of Threadneedle, Moorgate, and Old Broad streets. Clustered around these giants were investment houses supported by Corinthian, Gothic, and neoclassic columns rising like fortresses of the British Empire. London was still the "sun in the financial solar system" in 1911 and would remain so until after the forthcoming Great War.

On Moorgate Street, behind iron gates extravagantly embellished with a leaf motif, stood Basildon House, headquarters of Sperling and Company. Inside its halls, Mitchell pitched his proposed Alabama projects, paying special homage to Cherokee Bluffs as "an exceptionally favorable site, capable of generating energy ten hours daily at a hundred thousand horsepower." Edgar and his investment counselors were attentive and interested. Though positively inclined toward the South, the British knew full well the risks inherent in building an expensive enterprise in advance of a market for its product.

Mitchell pointed to Tennessee Coal, Iron, and Railroad Company and the expanding markets for iron and steel: "Within eighteen miles of Birmingham alone are huge deposits of iron, coal, and limestone—all three prerequisites for the steel industry. This is the only place where such a condition exists in the United States." He also mentioned the Coosa Valley's large bauxite deposits and the potential of nitrate fertilizer production through his association with Washburn and the American Cyanamid Company. Unfolding his map, Mitchell traced the network of transmission lines he envisioned and described the region's growing economies.

"Within a radius of two hundred miles of these power sites are found the most important cities of Tennessee, Georgia, Alabama," he explained, "and important cities in Illinois, Missouri, Kentucky, Arkansas, Mississippi, and

Florida. New Orleans is three hundred miles distance and, when deemed advisable, can be served by the company's circuits, as well." It was enough for Sperling and Company to ponder, so Mitchell was invited back in succeeding days to stand up to questioning and work out a financial plan.

Edgar wanted to back Mitchell's big bet and convinced his associates that the risks were somewhat mitigated by having one of his "most trustworthy and loyal colleagues" in charge of their investment. Sperling and Company agreed to underwrite the venture but stipulated that the holding company be incorporated in Canada. Memories of fortunes lost in America's 1907 panic were still fresh, making Canadian securities much easier to market to British investors.

To create the Canadian holding company, Mitchell tapped the services of Lawrence Macfarlane, Sperling's legal representative in Ontario. He, too, was caught in Mitchell's spell, marveling at how he "attacked the complicated problems with his wonderful energy and ability and in an incredible short space." Macfarlane would join Mitchell's board and handle many of the new company's legal and financial matters from Montreal. Incorporated January 5, 1912, Alabama Traction, Light & Power Company, Ltd., became the first holding company in Southern Company's lineage of predecessors.

Upon returning to New York, Mitchell used personal funds to cover expenses while waiting for the company's first bond issue to be marketed. From his hotel room, he dispatched a stream of telegrams to Martin regarding deeds, surveys, and property negotiations. On February 1, Mitchell received a cable reporting that A. B. Leach and Company had passed the deadline for exercising its option on Lay's Coosa River holdings. Like others before it, Leach's bid had fallen through. Two days later, Lay was in New York signing a new agreement with Mitchell.

On March 1, Montreal Trust Company issued $6 million in bonds for Alabama Traction, Light & Power, all but a small portion being bought by English investors. Mitchell immediately began closing on the options he held and negotiating for other properties not yet in hand. Within four months of his arrival in Alabama, the enterprise was under way.

BUILDING A START-UP COMPANY

Opening an office in New York's financial district at 100 Broadway, Mitchell began recruiting the best engineering minds and managerial talent he could find. At the top of his list were Eugene A. Yates and Oscar G. Thurlow, who became chief engineer and design engineer, respectively. Yates was a Rutgers University graduate who helped design and construct the East River tunnels in New York City and hydroelectric projects in Canada. Thurlow was a Massachusetts Institute of Technology whiz who designed bridges, tunnels, and dams in Connecticut, Pennsylvania, New York, Puerto Rico, and Washington, D.C. Both also had worked on engineering projects in Alabama.

For his lead electrical engineer, Mitchell hired his younger brother, W. E. Mitchell, a graduate of Massachusetts Institute of Technology. He followed in Mitchell's footsteps to take on General Electric (GE) assignments in New York, Brazil, California, and Nevada. Others on the first team were A. C. Polk, a Virginia Military Institute graduate hired as resident engineer to oversee construction, and W. W. Freeman, a high-ranking officer with the Edison Electric Illuminating Company of Brooklyn, who served as a vice president and general manager. Frank Washburn and J. W. Worthington were asked to remain in charge of two subsidiaries—Washburn as president and general manager of Alabama Interstate Power Company and Worthington as president of the Muscle Shoals Hydro-Electric Power Company. Mitchell planned to consolidate these and other subsidiaries into Alabama Power, but Martin advised they be kept separate until all land purchases and legal claims were resolved. Washburn would later manage Alabama Power's operations while serving as its president from late 1913 through February 1915. In return, Mitchell supported Washburn's plans for building a nitrates plant. Worthington conducted economic studies for Mitchell and served as the company's chief lobbyist in Washington through 1915.

Two other important early players were Reuben A. Mitchell and Sydney Z. (S.Z.) Mitchell, who owned the Alabama Power Development Company and whose assets included a 2,000-kilowatt project at Jackson Shoals, a steam plant under construction in Gadsden, and other power projects in Alabama. The Mitchell brothers [no relation to James] were born and raised in Tallapoosa and Coosa counties, but while Reuben spent his entire life in Alabama, S.Z. left the South, developed projects for the Edison Company on the Pacific Coast, and became a national energy developer and financier. In 1905, he was named president of Electric Bond & Share (EBASCO), a GE subsidiary, where he excelled at fixing underperforming utilities and municipalities and keeping them healthy with ongoing engineering, financial, and consulting support. Because it often traded initial services for a minority ownership or share of bond offerings, EBASCO accumulated a fat portfolio of utility securities from across the country.

James Mitchell needed the Alabama properties held by the Mitchell brothers, but S.Z. proved to be a tough negotiator who wanted a piece of Alabama Traction. S. Z. Mitchell previously had put together his own syndicate to help develop Alabama power projects and, before selling anything to Alabama Traction, had to buy out the interests of two other partners—William P. Bonbright & Company and Colonial Securities Company. Bonbright had even attempted to undermine James Mitchell's start-up plans by sending a representative to Sperling to advise Edgar to stay out of Alabama because others were interested in developing the state's water-power resources. Edgar ignored the warning and remained loyal to his friend. But it took until July of 1912 to strike a deal for Alabama Power Development, and Mitchell had to pay a "handsome, if not extravagant," price. Because much of the transaction was handled in the form of a stock swap, S. Z. Mitchell became a sizable stockholder, secured a seat on Alabama Traction's board, and agreed to take a percentage of its future bond issues. Reuben became a vice president and director of Alabama Power.

Those negotiations were still in play when James Mitchell and Lay met in Martin's office May 1 for the final closing on Lay's properties. It was an important moment for the old steamboat captain who was seeing his six-year effort now bearing fruit. He couldn't let the formal occasion pass without a few emotional words, concluding with, "I now commit to you the good name and destiny of Alabama Power Company. May it be developed for the service of Alabama." Mitchell responded by prophesying how a new Alabama and a new South would emerge stronger and richer from their enterprise.

"To make money is all right; to build industry is fine," said Mitchell. "But to build an industry that saves mankind from toil which it can well be spared, that reduces the labor and drudgery of women, that provides leisure for education and culture—truly is a much finer thing." The ceremony made a permanent impression on Martin, who would retell the story throughout his career. If he had ever questioned Mitchell's motives before, those doubts were laid to rest. Shortly after that meeting, Martin became the firm's general counsel and dedicated himself to Mitchell's big bet, knowing what it would mean for Alabama if the man could build but one of the many projects planned.

Later in May, Mitchell brought the new team together in a small room in Montgomery's 1116 Bell Building—the company's first office before moving to Birmingham that fall. Outlining an amazing twenty-year plan, Mitchell reviewed the map and proposed transmission lines, explaining how they would develop the sites in logical sequence, coordinate dams in different watersheds to conserve and use water to its maximum, interconnect the powerhouses, and expand the electrical system into adjoining states to interconnect with other utilities across the Southeast. "Within twenty years," he predicted, "we will develop 600,000 horsepower at a cost in excess of $100 million."

"What a dream!" Martin thought. "What a dream, when coal was selling for 90¢ a ton at Birmingham!" Some team members may have wondered if it were possible to raise that kind of money, but all were aware they had signed up for the opportunity of a lifetime.

Mitchell was eager to get construction started. More than eager, he was getting impatient. He had hoped to be moving dirt and blasting rock at Cherokee Bluffs by now and had been visiting the area to buy land between stops in Montgomery, Birmingham, and New York. He became buddies with Nora Miller, a colorful, "splendid-spirited" landowner who had funded all community projects in the county and knew every resident. The "mother of Cherokee Bluffs" took a liking to Mitchell, invited him into her home, and drove him around in her big car to help secure vital locations on the river. Things had been falling into place nicely until, suddenly, Cherokee Bluffs seemed snake-bit with trouble upstream and down.

Upstream at Buzzard Roost Shoals, Benjamin Russell of Alexander City had started work on a small dam in an area that would be flooded by Mitchell's project. Russell filed an injunction to stop the company, and Mitchell called him to New York to work out a solution. After several conferences and talks over dinner or on the way to the theater, Russell softened. "While perfect strangers before this meeting, and on opposite sides of the fence," he said, "I very soon recognized his keen perception, his ability to get at the core of things quickly, to sort out the wheat from the chaff. And because of his frankness, his fairness, and broad-gauged kindly manner, he early in the conference gained and held my utmost confidence and respect." Back in Birmingham and Alexander City, Martin finalized the agreement and continued the courtship.

The trouble downstream was a different story. There were two obstacles: a dam and a cotton mill that would be affected by the altered flow of water from the proposed hydro plant. Satisfactory arrangements were worked out with the dam's owner, but the other party—Mount Vernon–Woodberry

Cotton Duck Company—ran chief engineer Eugene Yates and his survey crews out of the area with a restraining order. Alabama laws gave Mitchell the power of eminent domain, so after several attempts to strike a deal, Martin began condemnation proceedings and secured a favorable court ruling. But when Mount Vernon–Woodberry decided to take the case to the U.S. Supreme Court, Mitchell threw up his hands. It could be years before the high court took up the matter. In fact, it would be 1916 before the Supreme Court heard the suit and decided in Alabama Power's favor.

Cherokee Bluffs had been key to Mitchell's interest in Alabama. It was to be one-third the price per kilowatt of the average hydro project. It was Mitchell's first love in Alabama, the ideal project he pitched in London and featured in his prospectus to investors. But it was time for a change in strategy. Cherokee Bluffs would have to wait. Visiting a disappointed Nora Miller, Mitchell gave her a silver trowel in recognition of her support and promised that she would use it in laying the dam's cornerstone one day.

Mitchell turned his attention to Lock 12 and had good reasons to do so. Political debates were blocking Congress from issuing new dam permits, and a 1914 deadline attached to Lay's original permit for Lock 12 was two years away. Earlier, Martin and Macfarlane had reviewed the laws and determined the dam could be completed after the deadline without fear of losing the permit. But the company couldn't afford to take that risk given hot debates bubbling in Washington over waterpower rights. The clock for Lock 12 had been ticking for five years, and Mitchell decided he should get the dam built before the second quarter of 1914, when the clock would stop.

BUILDING THE FIRST DAM

To construct Lock 12, Mitchell turned to one of New York's leading contractors—the MacArthur Brothers, hired on a "cost, plus fixed fee" basis, with a bonus for completing work ahead of schedule. Alabama Power provided direction and supervision. Those responsibilities went to Yates, the company's chief engineer, and other members of his team—Thurlow, Polk, and W. E. Mitchell.

To redirect the river during construction, a cofferdam of timbers, boulders, gravel, and clay was erected halfway into the water on one side of the river, then curved into a wide U-turn and extended back to shore. The area inside the cofferdam was drained, and the foundation and first stage of the dam were constructed. Then the cofferdam had to be torn down and the process repeated on the other side before the two sections could be connected and the powerhouse constructed. Next, tons of concrete were poured to raise the structure to required heights, and flap gates were dropped into place, closing culverts so the reservoir would fill.

A simple enough plan—on paper. In reality, Yates and his team were challenged in every way imaginable while dealing with a construction company that didn't always see things eye-to-eye. Roads had to be carved out of the hills, labor camps built for housing, and kitchens assembled for feeding up to 2,500 workers. Nearly 600 acres of heavily wooded areas had to be cleared and saw mills erected to cut timber into boards. Railroad tracks had to be laid, 45 trestles of an existing railroad rebuilt, a rock quarry operated, and a 100-ton crane hauled in to maneuver the turbines and generators. More than 125,000 cubic yards of sand and gravel were shipped in along with 200,000 barrels of cement and 175,000 cubic yards of rock. The work was backbreaking and dangerous, involving heavy equipment, hundreds of hand tools, timbers, and dynamite. There were fatalities and injuries, attended to by medical services contracted from nearby towns.

The legal work was as massive as building the dam itself. There were titles and grants of landowners to acquire and verify; design-change approvals needed from the government; and condemnations to activate under eminent domain. Consolidations of stocks, bonds, notes, and indebtedness also were needed from dozens of acquired properties.

Underwriting the project was even more challenging. The dam was hardly half finished before a war erupted thousands of miles away among countries in the Balkans, sending ripples across Europe and halting the flow of British sterling to Alabama. When Mitchell returned to London in the summer of 1913, he was shocked at what he found.

"Liquidation in all lines has been going on at a terrific rate, and it is useless to talk of placing any securities here at the present moment," he wrote to Freeman, asking him to seek funds from S. Z. Mitchell. Freeman received a cold rebuff from S.Z. and was told that EBASCO was legally obligated to take on additional bonds only in conjunction with Sperling. S.Z. made it clear he would neither furnish funds nor make it easy for Alabama Traction to get funds from his own banking sources—a response that raised questions about the EBASCO chief's loyalties and motives.

"Defer unnecessary payments," ordered James Mitchell from London, "and defer all work which is not likely to be immediately remunerative." Insisting that Freeman send letters daily with updates on the situation,

Mitchell investigated the idea of forming a joint syndicate to raise money outside of Sperling, but following what were called "settling days" in the London markets, Sperling was able to place the next bond issue for Alabama Traction. S. Z. Mitchell also came through with his portion.

Money remained tight the rest of 1913. When James Mitchell saw a December report that Lock 12 might be $300,000 over budget, he returned to Alabama, inspected the site, and complained loudly about the contractor, the slow pace, wasted money, poorly fitted penstock gates, and other "badly executed" work. "It is perfectly manifest that none of the men in authority now employed at Lock Number 12 have ever had any experience in connection with the construction or operation of a hydroelectric plant of such magnitude," Mitchell told Washburn. Two months later, after Washburn attacked the problems with urgency and efficiency, Mitchell received a report that major construction was finished, laborers were leaving the camps, and only the finishing touches remained. By spring, the bricking, ironwork, electrical, and mechanical work was completed in time for unit 1 of Lock 12 to begin operating April 12, 1914.

Better news was emerging from England's financial markets. Edgar sent word he would come visit and expressed an "unusual degree of optimism and confidence in the future." The Bank of England's rates had been reduced, and Mitchell told Washburn, "We're now in a position to raise funds for almost any project we may bring up and to any reasonable extent. We're all getting along in years. So we want to get to work on a big scale as soon as possible."

FIGHTING THE WATERPOWER WARS

Even before work started on Lock 12, Mitchell was helping Washburn advance his plans for a nitrates plant, which required tremendous amounts of electricity. When plans for Cherokee Bluffs and Muscle Shoals were delayed, Mitchell flagged Lock 18 on the Coosa as the next-best site, since it could be developed without government assistance, even though Congress still had to authorize the permit. While Washburn was seeking funding for his nitrates plant from Mitchell's friends in London, Worthington was working through the Alabama delegation to secure a dam permit for Lock 18.

Getting a license approved by Congress was a formidable task, given the growing waterpower war—political debates over what level of ownership, tax, or controls federal or state governments should place on hydro plants. Licensing came to a halt as one group defeated all bills that regulated developments and another group defeated all bills that didn't include regulation. Advocates for government control depicted private hydro developers as green octopus monsters wrapping tentacles around the nation's power plants, industries, and homes in an attempt to form a "waterpower trust." Some groups claimed the nation's waterpower assets were already in the hands of ten groups led by GE, a giant believed to be indirectly controlled by J. P. Morgan. Furthermore, Alabama Traction was said to be one of GE's pawns, based on EBASCO's prominent shareholder position and S. Z. Mitchell's board membership.

Against all odds, the Lock 18 bill made it through the Senate on August 16, 1912, and the House on August 22. The victory was short-lived, however, since President Taft vetoed the measure two days later because it didn't include a federal tax provision. "I think this is a fatal defect in the bill," the president noted in his message back to Congress, "and that it is just as improvident to grant this permit without such reservation as it would be to throw away any other asset of the Government."

Taft's veto was inevitable, coming less than three months before the election when he needed to show proof that he was not a pawn of private business. The president was smarting from a scandal caused when his secretary of the interior had given away public land to a Morgan-led syndicate, and he was under fire from his former sponsor, Teddy Roosevelt. Three weeks before Taft's veto, Roosevelt had accepted a third-party presidential nomination in an evangelistic convention in Chicago, during which he called for the new Progressive Party to bring about greater conservation and social justice as part of his "square deal" promise to the nation.

After hearing pleas from a delegation led by Alabama senator John H. Bankhead, Taft said he would reconsider his Lock 18 veto if the principle of taxation were preserved and recommended the group work something out with the secretary of war. Mitchell sent Freeman and Worthington to see the secretary, and Worthington reported, "The secretary of war stood ready to do most anything that we might request, if the company would agree . . . to the federal government's right and power to regulate . . . and also that a toll be paid to the government." Both requirements would compromise his company's strongly held views on "state rights," so Mitchell let the opportunity pass.

By this time, Washburn had secured $4 million in financing from Sperling and was ready to build his nitrates project in Canada, where cheap power from Niagara Falls was abundant. Mitchell tried to keep him in

Alabama by offering to supply electricity temporarily from Lock 12 while working on a new proposal for Lock 18. But Washburn needed primary power and lots of it. Reviving the Lock 18 bill looked unlikely. Things were falling apart for private hydro developers, a few of them having already decided they could live with some level of federal control.

In the end, almost everyone lost in the waterpower battle of 1912. Alabama and the nation lost an important industry; Mitchell lost the opportunity to build another hydro project; Alabama Traction lost its bid to develop Muscle Shoals in conjunction with the government; Taft lost the election; Roosevelt lost his luster and command of center stage; and the Republican Party lost much of its liberal wing. Alienated from the conservative camp, splintered Progressive Party members began aligning their votes with Democrats. The waterpower wars, meanwhile, would continue for eight more years. No new dam permits would be issued until passage of the Federal Water Power Act of 1920.

SURVIVING BANKRUPTCY THREATS

Financial crisis continued to be a recurring theme for Alabama Traction, but two events brought Mitchell's enterprise seriously close to ruin. The first was a malaria scare, the second a war that completely shut down international financial markets.

Malaria had been an ongoing problem throughout Alabama's history, and residents of present-day Clanton began to panic as the vast lake filled at nearby Lock 12. In 1914, hundreds of people filed lawsuits, claiming malaria-carrying mosquitoes were breeding in the impounded water. When damage claims climbed above $3 million, Mitchell's general counsel, Tom Martin, assembled the best lawyers in the state and prepared an extensive defense. At the end of the first all-day planning session, most of the attorneys left convinced there was no hope of avoiding bankruptcy. Refusing to accept that view, Martin searched for a star witness, traveled to Washington, D.C., and solicited the aid of the world's greatest authority on malaria—Dr. William Crawford Gorgas, surgeon general of the U.S. Army, known for his efforts to eradicate yellow fever and malaria in Havana and Panama. A native of Alabama, Gorgas agreed to help Martin and returned to his home state to inspect the lake and surrounding communities.

During the first trial, held in Columbiana in February 1915, Gorgas explained in simple terms the various types of mosquitoes, their habits, breeding places, and life cycles. And he talked about his personal experience as a farm boy in Bibb County, Alabama, far from any large body of water, where there had always been trouble with mosquitoes and malaria. "The new reservoir is not causing their trouble," he claimed, pointing to old buckets, barrels, and other breeding places found close to the homes of those suing the company. Convinced by the doctor's testimony, the jury returned a verdict in favor of Alabama Power, and as soon as several other cases received the same verdict, the remaining lawsuits were dismissed.

Martin's gratitude was so abounding he later dedicated a power plant to Gorgas, persuaded a nearby community to name its town in his honor, wrote papers on his achievements, and lobbied for thirty-five years to have the doctor inducted into the New York University Hall of Fame for Great Americans, which finally occurred in 1951.

Simultaneous with the threat of "mosquito lawsuits," another financial disaster was heating up in Europe. On July 28, 1914, when Austria-Hungary declared war on Russia, the London Stock Exchange shut down and remained closed the rest of the year. In August, when England entered the Great War, funding for Alabama Traction dried up. Forced to disband his construction organization, Mitchell seized upon every signal that the conflict would soon end, but all hopes of an early settlement were abandoned following the digging of the first trenches along the Western front.

Unable to meet its obligations or raise funds to extend power lines to new customers, Mitchell's team tried to persuade contractors and creditors to accept notes payable a year later for material and machinery. But Alabama's whole economy was looking bleak. The price of cotton, the South's only dependable money crop, dropped to less than half the cost of production, which had a negative domino effect on many other business lines. Alabama Power's suppliers couldn't float the money, and creditors wanted their notes secured by bonds from the holding company. Even though Mitchell threw his personal savings into his company's treasury, Alabama Traction missed an interest payment on bonds for the first time.

"We realized that the war was likely to be a long one," recalled Martin, "and that the company had to abandon its financing program of obtaining funds from England." To issue Alabama Power bonds that could be marketed to U.S. investors, however, Alabama Traction had to be released from financial restrictions included in its charter. While Mitchell returned to London to seek that relief, Martin convinced creditors the company would pay its bills if given more time. In case Mitchell's mission proved unsuccessful, however, Martin prepared papers to begin bankruptcy proceedings on short notice.

In Sperling's London offices, Mitchell painted a bleak picture for Edgar. It certainly wasn't the only bad news the bankers had been hearing. Fortunes were being swept away across the globe. Edgar called a meeting of the major bondholders to hear Mitchell's proposal: defer for three years any interest on their bonds, cancel certain provisions of the trust deed, and allow Alabama Power to issue securities in America that would have priority over the Alabama Traction bonds. The concessions were unprecedented. But the alternative was the death of Alabama Traction.

S. Z. Mitchell sent a proxy to the meeting, a lawyer who sat on the sideline, watching and waiting, neither voting for nor against the proposal. Was EBASCO expecting to add another prize to its portfolio of utilities at receivership prices? That question remained unanswered because James Mitchell's integrity again carried the day. The British investors voted to approve the plan and amend the trust deed. Friend or foe? Sometimes both, S. Z. Mitchell remained an anomaly in the company's history. His cards may not have always been on the table, but he continued to be a powerful board member and a valuable funding source. Before new bonds could be issued, James Mitchell still was in desperate need of cash, and S. Z. Mitchell helped arrange a loan of up to $5 million. In addition to his normal fee, the EBASCO chief asked for certain favors: whenever possible and appropriate, toss a few contracts and equipment purchases to GE. This prompted Mitchell to reassure his Westinghouse friends, "We are under no obligation, nor does the [EBASCO] press us in any way. Placing our orders will be dictated solely by what the management conceives to be in the best interest of our company."

The loan bridged the financial gap until Alabama Traction could consolidate its smaller companies into Alabama Power, which in turn could sell its first securities in the U.S. market. That step came one month after winning the first mosquito trial. "We couldn't possibly have continued to function," said Martin, "unless we had won those suits." Martin also had learned the value of trusting relationships and was "forever indebted to those citizens of England, who were willing to stake millions of dollars upon their faith in the future of industry in the Deep South and in the ability and integrity of James Mitchell and the other officials of the company."

MANUFACTURING THE FIRST CUSTOMERS

It is hard to imagine the leap of faith required to start an unproven enterprise, investing millions of dollars without confirmed customers. But that is essentially what Mitchell did. When he began constructing the first dam, he didn't have a single customer, so he and his team had to "manufacture" them by the time they manufactured the first kilowatts.

The first customers were those inherited from the transfer of Alabama Power Development Company's properties July 28, 1913, making Alabama Power officially an operating company. But it was a modest start—only three industries and several hundred residents in Talladega. "The getting of new business has proved to be more difficult than was originally anticipated," Mitchell admitted in his first annual report. By 1914, the numbers didn't look all that much better, but Mitchell was able to report "a more favorable outlook," having set up a new business department managed by Theodore Swann, a colorful and energetic engineer with previous sales experience in West Virginia. Swann secured contracts with coal mine and cotton mill operators, many of whom had to be convinced they should replace their mechanical equipment with machines driven by electricity. He also sold "secondary" power to steel mills and other industries during times they couldn't generate their own.

By the time Lock 12 was on-line, the company also had secured its most important wholesale customer, the Birmingham Railway, Light & Power Company. Mitchell had been desperate to get the contract, since it would be his largest and was mentioned in his prospectus. W. W. Freeman held several polite and pleasant negotiating sessions with the customer, but he was never able to close the deal. Mitchell finally turned to Martin, who proved more adept at maneuvering between competing political interests in Birmingham and a fiery-tempered general manager who preferred another power supplier. In getting the contract, Martin earned his credentials as a negotiator and strategist, and Mitchell began seeking his advice on issues beyond legal matters, naming him a vice president in 1915 and involving him more frequently in managing the company's operations.

Mitchell also "manufactured" customers through attempts to build up Alabama's economy by reinvigorating old industries and backing the start-up of new ones, an endeavor aided by the hostilities in Europe. Using his English connections, Mitchell secured war-related orders and helped organize the Anniston Steel Company, Southern Manganese Company, and Anniston Ordnance Company. During the war boom, Alabama also profited from expanded coal, iron, textiles, and a new industry. The state's first graphite mine opened in 1915, but there were thirty-nine operating by 1918.

To help supply the increasing electricity load, Alabama Power added a fifth unit at Lock 12 and built a steam plant near coal fields on the Black Warrior River. The plant's first 20,000-kilowatt unit was completed in August 1917, but that was the last major plant Mitchell could finance once his access to capital and his prices were frozen by wartime restrictions. When America entered the conflict in April 1917, interest rates soared, and the price of labor and materials doubled and tripled. With earnings barely covering fixed costs and new loans impossible, Mitchell had to cut construction and ask new customers to pay for their own transmission line extensions.

Throughout the war, Alabama Power's steam plants were constantly called into service even though they had been built as backup power to hydro. Coal prices shot up, and shortages began appearing, resulting in a nationwide "coal famine" in the winter of 1918, exacerbated by severe weather, transportation problems, and labor strikes. President Woodrow Wilson ordered shutdowns of factories not engaged in urgent war work, but because of its location next to coal fields, the Warrior steam plant was allowed to operate when hydro capacity couldn't meet the load. The crisis spurred Alabama Power to buy 15,000 acres of coal lands to secure future fuel supplies.

Toward the war's end, when Mitchell sensed that soon he would be losing large electricity users, he began looking for ways to retain as much of Alabama's industry as possible. He promoted the state's steel and iron goods in other regions of the country and looked for opportunities to convert the ordnance works into factories for consumer goods. He also started looking east to the growing energy market in Georgia. Henry Atkinson, chairman of the Georgia Railway & Power Company, had initially called on Mitchell in October 1917 for up to 20,000 kilowatts of capacity. At the time, Alabama Power's generation was fully committed, but Atkinson and Mitchell began discussing the idea of building a generating unit in Alabama and shipping the power to Georgia. "Coal by wire" was a novel idea, but it would be cheaper than hauling coal to a new plant in Georgia.

Mitchell and Atkinson had their engineers start drawing up plans for an Alabama-Georgia transmission line connection. Mitchell's team also was conducting planning sessions with eight other southeastern utilities, discussions which led to greater coordination and interconnections among their systems. So in addition to accelerating industrial development in the South, the wartime economy advanced the idea of a southeastern grid, the type Mitchell had envisioned when he first drew up his map and made plans to develop Alabama's hydro resources to supply power across the region.

MITCHELL'S DECISION AT MUSCLE SHOALS

The Great War had yet another dramatic impact on Mitchell's company. It forced him into a decision that changed the fate of Muscle Shoals and ended his dream of developing giant hydro dams when he acquired the Muscle Shoals Hydro-Electric Power Company in 1912. The regional map that Mitchell had shown to potential European investors depicted the potential of hydro resources at Muscle Shoals to be so large that power could be transmitted 200 miles in all directions to Tennessee's largest cities, Memphis and Nashville, and all the way to Paducah, Kentucky. The site was critical to his overall plans for Alabama Traction, but the project's scope was so challenging, Mitchell knew it could be undertaken only in partnership with the government.

The U.S. Army Corps of Engineers agreed with that view because the profusion of rapids, reefs, towheads, and other obstructions at Muscle Shoals had challenged navigation through that stretch of the Tennessee River since the age of pioneers and explorers. When the Corps of Engineers invited power companies to submit proposals for a business-government development in 1913, Mitchell sent engineers Yates and Thurlow to Muscle Shoals to conduct studies and put together a plan. The army engineers had envisioned building four small dams, but Mitchell's team showed it would be more economical and efficient to build two large ones that would generate more than twice the capacity of the government plan.

Thurlow explained that the Tennessee River flow during six or seven months of the year was sufficient to produce 500,000 horsepower but was inadequate the rest of the year. The difference could be made up by coordinating Muscle Shoals operations with those at the dam Mitchell planned at Cherokee Bluffs. "The proposed combination is unique and produces a power situation the equal of which is not to be found east of the Mississippi River, except at Niagara," said Thurlow. The Corps of Engineers liked the proposal and recommended it to Congress. But the same waterpower debates that impacted Lock 18 also doomed Muscle Shoals. No immediate action on the proposal was taken by Congress in 1914, nor in 1916 after new government studies again recommended Mitchell's plan.

The Great War in Europe interceded to change Muscle Shoals's destiny. America suddenly needed a domestic source of nitrates for military explosives, and producing nitrates required massive amounts of electricity. President Wilson appointed a board composed of his war, agriculture, and interior secretaries to review proposals from across the country and select a site for two nitrates plants. Lobbying for favored locations was so intense that a decision was not announced until October 1, 1917.

Mitchell had joined state officials in promoting Muscle Shoals for the proposed factories and joined in celebrations when that site was selected. But the party soon ended when the War Department was not open to a joint development with Alabama Traction. The government wanted Mitchell's properties but was unwilling to reimburse him for approximately $500,000 invested in them.

Mitchell and Martin made several attempts to negotiate a fair price, while also sharing surveys, plans, and engineering drawings developed by the company. But on Valentine's Day 1918, the War Department served notice it was preparing to "condemn the property" and value it only as farmland. Rather than take the matter to court, Mitchell offered the site as a gift. "In times like these," he wrote the chief of engineers February 18, "(our) consideration must be secondary to the urgent need of the nation . . . for war nitrates, and we have accordingly determined to donate our lands to the government for this purpose." Secretary of War Newton D. Baker thanked the company for its "generous and public-spirited action." And eventually, the U.S. Treasury forwarded a check for $1 as a token payment. As Martin prepared deeds of conveyance and final terms of the donation, Mitchell tried to insert some right of protection in case the development didn't proceed according to plans. But the government insisted on unconditional transfer, and that is how it was turned over.

For more than a year, northwest Alabama boomed with construction of two nitrates plants, the dam, and a coal-fired steam plant at Sheffield. Even at a frenzied pace, the power facilities could not be completed in time, so the War Department worked out an agreement with Alabama Power to build a generating unit at the company's nearest steam plant, ninety miles to the southeast on the Warrior River, at what later would be named Plant Gorgas. Using one of the existing Gorgas foundations saved the government precious time, so Alabama Power provided the site and designs, as well as the construction crews to build the unit and string a transmission line to Sheffield. The War Department financed the project but gave the company

example. Martin negotiated interconnections with southeastern power executives and signed the first interchange contract with the Georgia utility February 5, 1920. By that time, Mitchell's health had declined further, and he began spending all his time at his residence on Long Island. Realizing the moment had come to step down, Mitchell offered his resignation. The board elected Martin president of both Alabama Power and Alabama Traction, Light & Power on February 16 but retained Mitchell in the chairman role.

On Thursday, July 22, 1920, following a second massive stroke at his Long Island home, James Mitchell died. He was fifty-four years old.

Telegrams and messages from across the nation and abroad poured into Alabama Power offices. "His personality was possessed of that quality which men call magnetism," said John B. White, an engineering consultant from New York. "His fairness was proverbial," wrote Macfarlane from Montreal. "He is mourned here by a host of friends," wrote Edgar from London. The messages filled a twenty-eight-page issue of the company's newsletter with stories of his integrity and generosity of spirit, his vitality and vision, his boldness and brilliance.

"He could visualize a contemplated enterprise with intense vividness, and his penetrating mind could see the completed work in all its symmetry and beauty," wrote Reuben Mitchell. "A creative genius," added Martin. "Indeed, he considered that he had done something for mankind in building a great enterprise where none existed before." And a resolution from Alabama Power's board concluded: "His failing health was largely due to the tremendous efforts required by the work he had undertaken. Those who knew him best realize that in his passing, he paid the supreme sacrifice to the industry to which his life was dedicated."

LESSONS LEARNED

James Mitchell arrived in Alabama fifteen years after George Westinghouse had built his hydroelectric plant at Niagara Falls, sent power more than twenty miles away to Buffalo, New York, and demonstrated to all how the industry was going to evolve in the twentieth century. Using alternating current over high-tension wires, electricity could be generated at remote central power stations and transmitted great distances. No longer would electricity belong to the privileged few. It was possible to bring it to industry and business. It was possible to bring it to the general public.

The Electric Age would bring about great transformations in business, in society, in lifestyles, and in the very way people thought about the electric industry itself. In 1911, power generation in the South was still a local community affair. Steam units rarely served customers beyond the city limits; dynamos were operated by isolated businesses; and only a limited number of large hydro plants were being developed. In most cities, electricity was being used for street lighting and urban trolleys, by a few factories, and in homes of only the most affluent. The dream of affordable, abundant electricity was still only a dream. And the idea of great power developments in Alabama was still only an idea. Some eight years later, it was a reality.

Mitchell looked beyond conventional wisdom and constraints of the times. The plans he mapped out in Alabama were a quantum leap over the paths many other pioneers were following in the early years of electricity. He blazed a new trail altogether, envisioning a series of hydro projects so great he would have to market electricity throughout the state and region. Mitchell's map and the vision behind it became the first "big bet" for Southern Company, its later creation made possible by the boldness of Mitchell's dream. He had conceived that dream within two weeks of his first visit to Alabama, before he had raised the first investment dollar, purchased the first piece of land, generated a single kilowatt of electricity, and even before a market existed for power on the scale he imagined possible.

Among the early lessons learned was that, to be commercially successful, an enterprise of this scope would have to build its own market as it was constructing itself. This placed Alabama Traction, Light & Power—the first holding company in Southern Company's lineage of predecessor companies—on a path of actively leading, not following, the economic expansion of the region it served. And this strategy of developing a market from the ground up and assuming an active role in bringing about the Southeast's industrial awakening would become a Southern Company tradition.

To become successful, the start-up company also learned it had to rapidly build strengths in the fields of engineering, finance, law, public policy, and corporate leadership.

Mitchell recruited the industry's best engineers. They were needed to design the large dams and solve the problems of transmission and distribution that manufacturers had not yet figured out for the type of system he was creating. The talented people he brought together in Alabama would become inventors themselves, designing technologies from lightning arrestors to automated switching stations, conducting pioneering work in power dispatch, and integrating a variety of generating sources into a common system. The technical solutions and superior designs taught the company the essential value of keeping engineering expertise at the center of its core strengths.

Access to money got the company started but became even more critical to keeping it going. Mitchell's team learned how quickly financial resources could dry up and bring a great venture to a halt. His leaders also learned that the reputation of the company and its people could make the difference between gaining access to capital and being denied. Mitchell's integrity and the confidence of his British backers pulled the company through its early crises. But something more would be needed to ensure its future. The building of large-scale central generating stations was already beginning to transform electric utilities into one of the nation's most capital-intensive industries. Future requirements of the company would demand a different approach to raising money, a broader base of bondholder and stockholder support, a far more sophisticated financial structure, and a level of expertise in finance that did not yet exist inside the company. All that would have to be developed.

Legal, legislative, and regulatory challenges facing Alabama Traction seemed almost insurmountable. Once, while acquiring companies and land titles and fighting lawsuits, Mitchell commented, "We have retained practically all the lawyers in the valley." Even that would not be enough. The company's future may have been charted in the boardroom, but it increasingly would be derailed in courtrooms, legislative chambers, and public opinion arenas. After Lock 12 was built, Mitchell's hands were almost completely tied by these obstacles. Utility regulation was still in its infancy, evolving from control by local franchises and state enactments to regulation by state public utility commissions. Federal regulation was still a foreign concept. But Westinghouse's technology had suddenly made "waterpower" enormously valuable, and both conservationists and public power proponents feared the prospects of leaving those powers in the hands of private interests and state governments. Despite "state rights" arguments, federal regulation would be inevitable. The company learned it needed not only an effective legal presence at local and state levels, but a persuasive voice in national policy-making debates. That need would only grow as dozens of new laws impacting utility operations stacked up in the years ahead.

More than anything else, Mitchell's enterprise required strong leaders—not just good managers but people with intelligence and character, people who were flexible and creative in their thinking, people who when knocked down had the fortitude to get up and keep going, people who were committed to doing great things for their company and community. Most important, Mitchell needed people with vision, leaders who had faith in the future of the South and the company, who could see the market's potential, and who would be willing to stake their careers and fortunes on a big idea. Those were the types of leaders he recruited.

Mitchell bet everything on his big idea—his energies, his abilities, his fortunes, and ultimately his life. He had forced it to take shape and become a sound investment, shepherded it through a critical start-up period, and guided it through several political and financial crises. With his death, the challenges were passed to Martin and his team of southern pioneers—the challenge to finish the great constructive work started in Alabama, the challenge to build a southeastern network of utility systems, the challenge to ensure the future of Southern Company by collecting on Mitchell's big bet.

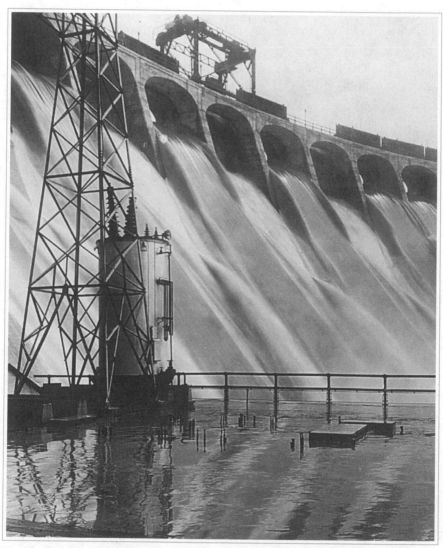

View of spillways from the transformer deck at Martin Dam in 1928. Its namesake, Thomas W. Martin, expanded Alabama Power statewide and created a new holding company that brought together the subsidiaries of the future Southern Company. At right, Martin ca. 1920. *APC Archives*

WHAT MARTIN FINISHED

TOM MARTIN DASHED DOWN THE MARBLE steps of Basildon House and scampered into the backseat of a car on Moorgate Street in the heart of London's financial district. "Queen Anne's Mansions," he called to the driver. "Victoria Street at St. James."

Martin's spirits had just been lifted by the success of his meeting with Sir Edward Mackay Edgar and a team of Sperling and Company investment managers. They sealed their agreement with a handshake instead of a written contract, not a typical business practice for Martin the lawyer, but awfully appealing to Martin the southerner, for whom a gentleman's word was as good as gold. Martin had come to respect Edgar's word—a confidence dating back to a trusting relationship that company founder James Mitchell had established with Edgar and his investors when they provided seed money for Alabama Traction, Light & Power in 1912. The British had shown Mitchell inordinate flexibility during several crises plaguing Alabama Traction in the start-up years. Now, in 1924, they were extending their liberal support to Martin as he was preparing to boldly reshape the holding company he had inherited from Mitchell.

beginning to merge with larger ones or were looking for potential partners to finance big construction projects. Other holding companies across the country were buying up both municipal and utility systems and paying hefty prices for the poorly funded and healthy alike. Many other combinations were being inspired by a new idea hyped in government and industry circles—a concept called "superpower," the notion that great savings could be generated by grouping the nation's electric resources into "superpower zones" through interconnecting grids.

To make his mark in this rapidly changing and competitive environment, Martin had to act with speed and sureness. Aboard the *Olympic*, heading toward the New York harbor, he felt a great sense of urgency and exhilaration about what he was about to do. He would complete the work that Mitchell had started in Alabama, but he would take Mitchell's big bet an important step further by bringing the southeastern power market together under the common ownership of a multistate holding company. He would call it Southeastern Power & Light. If anyone were going to develop a "superpower" in the Southeast, Martin thought, it should be him.

THE MAKING OF TOM MARTIN

Above all else, Thomas Wesley Martin was a loyal disciple of the South and a passionate champion of his home state. He was born August 13, 1881, in Scottsboro, Alabama, where his great-great-grandparents of English ancestry had settled in the early days of the nineteenth century. His father became the state's attorney general in 1889 and moved the family to Montgomery, thus exposing his children to statesmen, lawyers, and business leaders who debated the politics, problems, and promises of Alabama.

Martin and his younger brother by one year, William Logan Jr., attended public schools in Montgomery and prepared for college at Starke University School, near the state capitol. Professor John Metcalfe Starke was a disciplinarian who believed in old values. Martin aspired to Starke's intellect and integrity and embraced his formula for success: "work and more work." The professor also was a natural role model because he was small, about 125 pounds, and had the courage to stand down men twice his size. Perhaps small-framed Martin saw in Starke the ability to achieve great status in the community despite one's physical stature. Martin overcompensated for being undersized physically by excelling in everything mentally and receiving the school medal for excellence.

After graduation, Martin studied law for a year at the University of Alabama and spent the summer of 1900 traveling through New England with friends selling stereoscopic equipment and images. The industry and prosperity he saw firsthand in the North made him painfully aware of the poverty within his home state. Upon returning to Montgomery, he enrolled in a business school, continued his study of law privately, and passed the bar a year later.

While taking up practice with his father in Montgomery, Martin served as a court reporter on the side, the experience teaching him much about the state's laws. In 1903, he was appointed assistant to Attorney General Massey Wilson and later served as assistant attorney general. No doubt, those first appointments were aided by family connections, his father having revised the State Code of Alabama and served on several commissions appointed by the governor. The senior William Logan Martin was so revered he won a state legislature seat with no campaign other than his announcement and was chosen Speaker of the House in January 1907, two months before tragically dying of pneumonia. When his body lay in state in the very spot occupied by the body of Confederate President Jefferson Davis years earlier, it seemed that all of Alabama mourned his loss and praised his legacy, which probably nourished Tom Martin's own desire to be of special service to his state. But family needs would have to come first. At age twenty-six, Tom Martin found himself head of the household, which included his mother and two of his sisters. At the time, William Logan Jr. was a cadet at West Point.

The month following his father's death, Martin joined forces with Massey Wilson in setting up a new law practice, which later became Tyson, Wilson and Martin, when John R. Tyson, former Alabama Supreme Court chief justice, joined the team. The firm became an advocate of progressive state laws, including those promoting hydro project investments, and Martin gained valuable experience preparing legal filings for several potential developers, which led to his association with Alabama Traction and Alabama Power. In joining that group as general counsel in 1912, Martin saw an opportunity to become part of a venture that could do something splendid for his struggling state.

"As Alabama grows, so will the company," James Mitchell had repeated many times. What had been a motto for Mitchell became a mantra for Martin. He worked hard for Mitchell's big bet and impressed him with quick thinking, sound reasoning, and an ability to find a reserve of power to throw into action to help retrieve a lost cause. Under Mitchell's example and the first half of the twentieth century and even larger than what Mitchell had contemplated—2,000 feet long and 168 feet high, holding back 72 billion cubic feet of water. Among other challenges, a camp for 3,000 workers had to be built; 40,000 acres cleared of timber, brush, and debris; 1,600 graves moved to higher ground; railroad track and trestles raised; and a 100-foot-high bridge constructed. When completed in 1927, the lake—named for Tom Martin—would become the world's largest artificial reservoir. Aside from its efficiency in building dams, powerhouses, and transmission systems, Dixie Construction provided another advantage important to Martin. Being Alabama-based, it hired workers from the region and purchased most of its materials and supplies within the state, thus pumping money back into local communities.

Martin looked for every means possible to boost the state's economy and generate new customers. "Next to the manufacture of power itself," he was fond of saying, "our greatest manufacture must be of customers." To attract the large customers, Martin set up a new industries division under a young engineer, Thomas D. Johnson, who placed ads in national journals, created exhibits and booklets for trade shows, and conducted studies to promote the state's resources. "Some eastern cotton mill executives knew little about Alabama," noted Martin, after participating in one of the tours. "They were inclined to consider it a foreign country." Initially targeting textiles, the recruiting effort produced its first victory in 1922, when Pepperell Manufacturing Company decided to establish a branch at Opelika. By 1924's end, Alabama Power had more than forty cotton mills on its lines, and the economic development campaign was expanded to include iron, steel, paper, rubber, canning, and a wide range of other industrial customers.

Martin also "manufactured" rural customers, who typically were last to be served by electric utilities because of the expense of extending lines to reach them. Alabama Power's first rural transmission line, installed in 1920, provided power to only ten farms and a cotton gin in Madison County. Six years and nearly 5,000 agricultural customers later, the company was recognized as having the nation's best rural electrification program. Among other projects, Martin funded research to develop new electric applications for the farm, donated thoroughbred Herefords to stimulate cattle and dairy industries, established fish hatcheries, and funded a new process for making insecticides to control boll weevils, which were threatening to destroy the cotton industry. Many of Alabama Power's rural and urban customers also became investors. Believing customer ownership of the company's securities would win support and cooperation needed from the public, Martin created an investment department and, by 1925, had more than 100,000 preferred stockholders in the state.

The expansion to other southeastern markets started in fall 1921, when Alabama Power completed its first transmission line connection to Georgia, the spare kilowatts arriving at a critical moment, in the middle of a drought that affected the Southeast. Thanks to interconnections already established with Georgia's neighboring utilities, a five-state transmission grid was in place as soon as the Alabama-Georgia line became energized October 23. As a result, Martin was able to wheel power all the way to the Carolinas, the states suffering most from the drought. When power shortages overwhelmed Alabama Power's supply, Martin eventually secured the lease of capacity available from a war-surplus coal plant that had been sitting idle in Sheffield, Alabama, since the Armistice. Over the next decade, Alabama Power continued to lease the plant and wheel half the energy to adjoining states. As a result, Martin became the natural leader for bringing about greater power coordination in the Southeast.

Stronger cooperation and interconnections among southeastern utilities also were stimulated by a 1920 report, produced by engineering consultant Eugene Yates. Estimating savings of $112 million over ten years, the study led to the 1923 formation of an eight-utility operating committee whose representatives met regularly to discuss common problems and compare operating data. W. E. Mitchell, who served on the committee for Alabama Power, credited the group with facilitating power exchanges during emergencies and improving each company's operating economies. Yet, he reported, it was impossible for independent companies to conduct the type of full-scale system planning and joint projects advocated in the Yates Report.

"These early interconnection agreements were significant and important," Martin conceded. "But we realized that maximum benefits will never be attained without complete integration. And that will be possible only through common ownership." Martin had the vision and leadership required to bring about that integration, and he was ready to pull various power interests together under the umbrella of common ownership.

CREATING SOUTHEASTERN POWER & LIGHT

Alabama Power was serving only the state's northern portion in 1922, when Martin sent Dixie Construction superintendent Milo S. Long to check out added Moss Point and Pascagoula, extending service to every municipality on the Mississippi coast.

In fall 1925, work crews from Dixie Construction Company completed the final stretch of a transmission line from Alabama's northwest corner to Iuka, a sleepy little Tishomingo County town, which suddenly came alive as Mississippi celebrated what Governor Whitfield termed the state's "declaration of industrial independence." With banners, bunting, bands, and badge-bearing committeemen bustling about, a crowd of 7,000 consumed two tons of smoked barbecue.

For the next two years, competition with Couch remained ferocious, and bidding wars resulted in service areas being inefficiently intertwined, particularly in the northeast. Realizing this situation wouldn't work in the long term, boards of the competing companies authorized property swaps in what was called the "northeast-southwest exchange." Mississippi Power gave up southwest properties like McComb and Magnolia in exchange for Mississippi Power & Light's "Columbus group," which included wholesale contracts for Tupelo and West Point, as well as retail service to ten other northeast communities. The deal, negotiated by Barry in 1927, allowed Eaton to consolidate his territory into the state's entire eastern half from the Gulf Coast to the Tennessee border. Within that service area, more than sixty new cities and towns were added to Mississippi Power lines during the next two years and another nineteen in April 1930 with the purchase of Mississippi Utilities Company.

What began in 1925 as one utility in Gulfport was transformed, five years later, into an integrated system serving 175 communities throughout east Mississippi.

EXPANDING TO SOUTH ALABAMA AND FLORIDA

Martin thought utilities in south Alabama and along the Florida Panhandle could be placed under a common roof—a subsidiary created August 11, 1924, called Consumers Power Company and changed three months later to Gulf Electric Company, perhaps after Martin realized a Michigan utility already claimed the former title. At the time, Yates's team was negotiating the purchase of properties in Pensacola, Florida, and a dozen Alabama municipalities, including Eufaula and Enterprise, being served by a group called the Georgia-Alabama Power Company. Within another fourteen months, utility systems from Mobile to Panama City, Florida, would be housed under the Gulf Electric banner.

To run these new operations as general manager, Martin and Yates selected one of their most versatile players, Wells M. Stanley, who had worked in almost every department of Alabama Power. A native of Pierre, South Dakota, Stanley had spent most of his childhood in Huntsville and was manager of the Huntsville Light, Railway, and Power Company when Alabama Power bought that system in 1914. He stayed in that role until being promoted to oversee Birmingham operations in 1917. Two years later, as manager of the Northern Division, he solved operating and commercial problems so well his organization became a model for the company's other divisions.

In fall 1924, Stanley was dispatched south to secure agreements from city leaders who had to approve franchise transfers from Georgia-Alabama Power, and in November, he reported to Yates—"four approved the contracts, two said no, one invited me back for another presentation, and another had strong leaders waging campaigns against the transfer." During the next three months, he sorted out all those problems while scouting dozens of other cities in Alabama and Florida.

The Pensacola situation was particularly complex and required a study by Chester Bingham, one of Martin's legal counsels and later treasurer of Alabama Power, to analyze the properties that had emerged from Pensacola Street Car Company and the Pensacola Electric Light and Power Company, incorporated in 1884 and 1887, respectively. Many reorganizations later, these utilities ended up as Pensacola Electric Company and the Escambia County Electric Light & Power Company. Although both were now under common ownership, Pensacola Electric was being operated under a receivership, having defaulted on bonds in 1920. To gain a clear title, negotiations had to be conducted with a court-appointed receiver, city and county leaders, bondholders, and the management firm contracted to operate the electric equipment. Purchase of the Pensacola properties closed on February 10, 1925, and within a few months Yates and Stanley had contracts with Andalusia Light & Power, eight of the Georgia-Alabama Power cities, and several other southeast Alabama franchises, including the prized Mobile Electric Company—all of which were consolidated into Gulf Electric.

During 1925, Yates also worked out a deal to buy the Florida and Alabama utility systems served by Houston Power Company. Since all franchise transfers had to be renegotiated with each individual city, Yates told

Stanley to repack his bags: "I want you to acquire all towns west of the Chattahoochee River in both Florida and Alabama which are on these lines. There are about thirty-four towns that we have got to give attention to." For the rest of the year, Stanley turned up in every community along the coast, making presentations and dashing off frequent updates to Yates on contracts closed, offers submitted, options secured, agreements signed, elections successful, elections failed, elections pending, franchises signed, and others delayed or simply labeled "no activity at this time."

Stanley closed so many prospects that double taxation became a problem for Southeastern Power & Light and necessitated the creation of a separate Florida subsidiary. Because Gulf Electric was Alabama-based, it had to pay an Alabama tax on the equity investments in Florida, plus a Florida tax on the property values themselves. Martin made the logical decision to consolidate the Alabama properties of Gulf Electric within Alabama Power and create Gulf Power to house the Florida acquisitions. Incorporated in October 1925, Gulf Power Company received a certificate to do business in Florida on January 15, 1926. Three weeks later—February 6—Gulf Power officially became an operating public utility with the acquisition of Chipley Light and Power Company. During March, Gulf Power assumed operations in Panama City, St. Andrews, Bonifay, Graceville, Millville, and Lynn Haven. Then, on May 31, the Pensacola properties were merged into the new company.

To head Gulf Power, Martin selected a Floridian, Francis Carter, a Pensacola lawyer and judge who had handled legal work for many of the purchases. Carter was a short-term, part-time president, taking the position only because Stanley would run operations as his vice president and general manager. To serve as his assistant general manager, Stanley brought in someone who would years later become company president—Lansing T. Smith Jr., superintendent of Alabama Power's Northern Division. Together, they negotiated more franchises and privately owned utilities in Florida while attending to twenty scattered generating facilities, all with limited potential but providing needed service to ice plants, lumber mills, electric transit systems, and other customers in communities along the Panhandle.

Stanley and Smith soon learned that life on the coast could be hazardous. Less than four months after consolidation of the Pensacola operations into Gulf Power, the region was hit with a hurricane that slammed downtown with twelve-foot tidal waves and destructive 120-mile-per-hour winds. Gulf Power's generating plant at Barracks and Main streets operated through part of the storm as Stanley and the crew watched their autos disappear beneath the swirling bay waters. After wood from a lumber mill across the street started battering the building, they shut down the plant just as one of the giant smokestacks gave way.

The following morning, September 20, Stanley dashed off a report to Yates: "After midnight, winds grew steadily stronger. At 5:30 a.m., believe storm was at its worst although at this moment wind is 108 miles per hour.... With thirty men and tools promised us from Dixie Crews at Flomaton, think we will be able to restore partial service eight or ten hours after storm quits, providing daylight is available. Property damage is severe. . . . As all communication is cut off, thought I would get these few lines to you by the noon train. Written in haste."

To rebuild the system and restore service, 600 workers from Dixie Construction and other companies in Alabama, Georgia, and Mississippi worked for two months. Stanley reactivated the damaged and inefficient plant in Pensacola but put it on standby in mid-December 1926 as soon as Polk's crews could cut a transmission line through swamps and forests from Flomaton to Pensacola and construct a substation in Pensacola's Brentwood area to link Gulf Power to cheaper, more reliable hydro power from Alabama.

Early the next year, Stanley and Smith expanded Gulf Power's service to DeFuniak Springs, Valparaiso, Niceville, and Camp Walton. And in June 1927, they learned their part-time president was eager to give up his position after complaining to Martin that Stanley's frequent absences required him to "execute documents and take some small part in certain business matters." Dispelling any notions about assuming the type of role Eaton was playing in Mississippi, Carter pleaded to Martin: "May I ask that you give consideration to the question whether the business is not now in such condition that you will consent to my resignation in order that an active president may be installed."

"The west Florida situation is moving rapidly," Martin replied, "If you can stay, I'll adjust the situation during the early part of 1928." By that time, Gulf Power had new contracts for additional cities in west Florida, and the Alabama properties of Gulf Electric and Houston Power were consolidated into Alabama Power. Carter's resignation was accepted, but having Stanley in charge of operations allowed Martin the luxury of not needing to install a full-time president. So in addition to his duties as president of Southeastern Power & Light and Alabama Power, Martin served as president of Gulf Power through 1931.

FORMING GEORGIA POWER COMPANY

Talks with the Georgia utilities did not get serious until fall 1925, even though Martin had been studying such a union much earlier. Georgia was the biggest market in the region and would make an ideal combination with Southeastern because of the diversity of load and stream flows that could be added to the total system. Assistant chief engineer Carl James sent Martin and Yates a September 1925 study that estimated the potential savings: 1926–$900,000; 1927–$500,000; 1928–$600,000; 1930–$1.2 million; 1935–$400,000. "The combined loads are so significant," James said, "when Cherokee Bluffs and Lock 18 are built, the system will immediately absorb their total output. And it will be more economical for Georgia to build its plants when the load can absorb it likewise. It's better to have the system built with large installations and their total load absorbed as soon as they come on line rather than done in stages separately."

Through interconnections, power exchanges, and planning meetings, Southeastern had established a good relationship with Georgia Railway & Power Company chairman Henry Atkinson and its president, Preston Arkwright. Martin knew the Georgia system was overdeveloped on hydro and underdeveloped on steam generation. Some years, it couldn't supply its load; other times, excess hydro ran to waste. But in 1925, a drought was pushing the Atlanta-based utility to the point of disaster. Rainfall was nearly 40 percent below normal—the lightest ever recorded in seven southern Appalachian states, according to the U.S. Geological Survey. Crops failed, rivers dropped to their lowest levels, and small streams, wells, and springs dried up. Available steam plants in the region ran at full capacity for nearly five months, and for the first year in Alabama Power's history, more electricity was generated from steam than hydro.

Georgia Railway & Power's hydro capacity was down 60 percent, and Atkinson was taking as much electricity from Alabama Power as the lines could handle. Still short, he had to begin rationing power August 21—transferring city water pumping loads to night hours, restricting cotton gins to three days per week and Sundays, cutting back on trolley service, and curtailing power to customers. Adding to those problems, Atkinson had reached an impasse in financing the company he had shepherded for thirty-four years.

The Georgia utility had evolved from a long series of street lighting, gas, railway, and electric services in Atlanta before Atkinson combined forces in 1912 with developers to finish building the challenging Tallulah Falls Dam in north Georgia. As Atlanta boomed, Atkinson raised millions for new power plant construction and began extending service beyond the city. But high interest rates and restrictive mortgages were bringing the company near the point of financial ruin even before the 1925 drought hit. Needing a minimum of $10 million annually for new expansions, Atkinson was suddenly trapped in a corner. Having exhausted the ability to issue any new securities, his only option was to renegotiate leases and mortgages, restructure the company, and issue new securities—a plan that was getting little interest from his investors.

Martin offered a better solution: join Southeastern Power & Light, a proposal that appealed to Atkinson and his two largest stockholders, Randal Morgan and C. Elmer Smith. Morgan was chairman of United Gas Improvement Company (UGI), a national conglomerate that obtained its major shares in 1903 when a stock-swap deal brought Atlanta Gas Light into Atkinson's operations. Smith was a power project developer who became the largest stockholder in 1912 when his holdings—including the Tallulah Falls Dam—merged with the reorganized Georgia Railway & Power. Atkinson, Arkwright, and Smith were quick to see the advantages of joining the Southeastern holding company, but to secure Morgan's approval, Martin had to make several trips to UGI's Philadelphia offices. When an agreement finally was reached in early January 1926, the Atlanta newspapers praised it as a $250 million merger "assuring the region an industrial progress without limits and making impossible a recurrence of recent power famines." With Atkinson's endorsement, the merger received stockholder approval, bringing the Georgia utility into the Southeastern system on April 1. As part of the agreement and because of the strength of their leadership, Atkinson continued as chairman and Arkwright as president.

Before the ink was dry on the contract, Yates and Barry were scouting out other Georgia opportunities. By June 1926, forty-two additional cities and towns—including Macon, Brunswick, and Athens—were brought into the circle, and that number quickly doubled. "Rome, Vidalia, Macon, Athens, Milledgeville, Brunswick," reported *Snap Shots*, the employee newspaper. "Almost every week brings more announcements of the purchase of electric generating plants or distribution lines in Georgia."

That fall, Arkwright gave employees an impressive update: "On the first of January of this year, we served eighty towns with electric service. Today, we are serving or preparing to serve in Georgia 158 cities and towns. This union of the electrical companies of Georgia means more for the state, I believe, than anything which has happened in recent years."

The scattered Georgia utilities initially continued to operate under existing names as separate subsidiaries of Southeastern, with Atkinson and Arkwright providing supervisory control. But as the acquisitions multiplied, it made sense to merge them all under the name of Georgia Power Company. That consolidation agreement, finalized November 16, also was praised by local editors, who saw the benefits of improved services and industrialization opportunities for their towns through a national ad campaign and publicity handled through Southeastern's New York office.

Under the holding company's simplified financial structure, Georgia Power was able to secure capital at much lower interest rates. Additionally, the improved financial picture allowed the company to complete the North Georgia hydro group—six dams built in stair-step fashion on the Tallulah and Tugalo rivers, the waters of one reservoir becoming the tailwaters of the other, creating what was viewed as the most completely developed continuous stretch of river in the United States. "Separated, each company has to maintain capacity for its own peak; united, we get the use out of that machinery over longer hours of the day," said Arkwright in praising the merger. "Sound economies come for the companies running as one: they can do business with less capital, lower fixed charges, less operating expenses per unit of service."

As the Georgia operations grew more complex, Martin sent one of his top officers, W. E. Mitchell, to Atlanta to serve as general manager. Mitchell, who later became Georgia Power president, took two of his key Alabama managers with him—J. M. Oliver, operating engineer, and C. B. McManus, northern district manager. Oliver became Georgia Power's operating manager and eventually progressed to the position of executive vice president. McManus became superintendent of district operations and later served as president of both Georgia Power and Southern Company. As Georgia Power spread across two-thirds of the state, Mitchell's team managed the growing territory by creating four divisions—Atlanta, Athens, Rome, and Dublin—with smaller district offices reporting to them. Augusta became the fifth division in 1928, upon Southeastern's acquisition of utilities in that area.

Polk's Dixie Construction crews were so busy interconnecting Georgia cities and refurbishing systems that Martin created Empire Construction Company in mid-1927 just to handle the engineering and construction work in Georgia. Also that year, two additional Alabama-Georgia interconnections were completed, giving Georgia Power access to more energy during the 1927 dry season, which proved to be almost as bad as the 1925 drought. This time, however, Georgia experienced no brownouts or power rationing.

"You would not even know that a drought existed," Arkwright reported to a group of bankers in Boston the following spring. "The reason was that the two companies were then under common control by the Southeastern Power & Light Company and were operated all through the year in accordance with the method that was most efficient and economical for the systems as a whole. The result was that we had conserved our power resources and were therefore able to carry ourselves through the drought without curtailment or disturbance to our power customers." The seeds planted by the Yates Report in 1920—the promises of greater reliability and efficiencies through coordinated operations and planning—were bearing plentiful fruit.

CREATING SOUTH CAROLINA POWER

The opportunity to expand into South Carolina probably emerged from Martin's negotiations with Randal Morgan on the Georgia situation, since Morgan's company, UGI, also had controlling interest in several Charleston electric, gas, and railway properties. Within a few months of the Georgia agreement, Martin had a man in Charleston "quietly checking out the new business prospects." By 1927, a new deal was cut with UGI, and South Carolina Power Company was incorporated. The acquisitions included Charleston Gas Light Company, Charleston Edison Light & Power Company, Charleston Consolidated Railway & Lighting Company, and Charleston Consolidated Railway Gas & Electric Company. All these properties were reorganized and consolidated into Southeastern's new South Carolina subsidiary during 1927's first quarter.

As soon as the Charleston deal was in place, Yates sent his experts to analyze every aspect of the operations and report on what worked, what didn't, and what it would take to bring everything up to Southeastern standards. From that evaluation, he told Martin there were three areas that needed serious attention: "one, reduce railroad operating expenses; two, reduce steam production expenses; and three, get more business." One of the oldest cities in America, Charleston had enjoyed expansion during World War I, then suffered a period of recession and readjustment but was "filling out" again. The city not only had been a world port for two and a one-half centuries, it also operated naval station docks erected during the war.

Ash Collins, Alabama Power's commercial manager and inventor of the Reddy Kilowatt character, reported favorably on the docks and railroad operations and the outlook for new industry. However, utility merchandising was "far below what they should be for a town of that size, an estimate of only 150 electric refrigerators." His recommendation: Hire a home economist and several salesmen to start a "strong commercial program." Meanwhile, Polk opened a Charleston office of Dixie Construction to refurbish, replace, renovate, and rebuild—a familiar routine fine-tuned during the foregoing acquisitions. By 1927's end, Southeastern had made more than $1.1 million in improvements and additions to its South Carolina assets.

To head the utility during its initial year of operation, Martin turned to a politically savvy lawyer, Benjamin A. Hagood, whose name meant something to local opinion leaders. Then in 1928, Stuart Cooper—a vice president who previously had headed UGI's local operations—served as interim president until Martin could move F. P. (Pat) Cummings into the role that November. A native New Yorker, Cummings received his early training with GE and the Henry L. Dougherty Company before joining Alabama Power in 1915 as operating superintendent. Following stints as efficiency engineer and commercial manager, he became a vice president for Southeastern in 1926, responsible for overseeing the New York office and helping to negotiate acquisitions. He had, in fact, conducted the initial evaluations on the South Carolina properties and directed a major expansion effort that included the purchase of the Edisto Public Service Company, the Augusta-Aiken Railway and Electric Company, and the Georgia-Carolina Power Company. Those acquisitions added fifteen counties southwest of Charleston and along the South Carolina-Georgia border to South Carolina Power's territory and included the Stevens Creek Hydroelectric Plant on the Savannah River and two smaller hydro plants near Aiken. The Augusta-Aiken and Georgia-Carolina deals also benefited Georgia Power, bringing Augusta and twenty-seven municipalities and towns into its service area.

As president, Cummings pursued contracts with other South Carolina towns and expanded service to sixty communities by year-end 1928, when L. A. Magraw, vice president and general manager, sent him a holiday message: "We have this day accepted franchises from the towns of Reevesville, Furman, Harleyville, Smoaks, Eutawville, Scotia, and Ehrhardt." South Carolina Power was no longer a one-city utility. Within two years, it had grown to a respectable size, serving a 10,000-square-mile territory.

CONSOLIDATED OPERATIONS AND MARTIN LEGACIES

By 1929, Martin had collected on Mitchell's big bet and a few of his own. In creating Southeastern Power & Light, he had designed the financial, legal, and organizational foundation on which to build one of the nation's larger and more successful utility groups. Larger than the footprint of today's Southern Company, Southeastern's territory extended across 140,000 square miles—from Charleston in the east to central Mississippi in the west, from the Tennessee border in the north to the Gulf Coast in the south.

Martin had put that system together through "work and more work." While he and his team were negotiating the largest number of acquisitions in the company's history, they also were building dams and steam plants, stringing hundreds of miles of new wire, and refurbishing vast numbers of inadequate, outdated systems. Southeastern delivered reliable electricity while reducing rates, almost without exception, by 10 to 60 percent.

Through integrating their operations, Southeastern's subsidiaries achieved great savings. The low-cost plants could be operated continuously to serve a diversity of base loads across the region, and the older, high-cost units could be reserved for peak periods and emergencies. Substantial economies also came from joint planning of future investments and introducing a diverse fuel mix. Coal generation, for example, was shipped to Georgia by wire from the Gorgas plant in Alabama until it became economically feasible in 1929 to build Plant Atkinson near Atlanta.

Power pooling, economic dispatch, and other concepts were created or enhanced by some of the industry's best engineering talents working within a separate subsidiary—Southeastern Engineering Company, an organization to provide technical, legal, planning, and other specialized services at cost to all subsidiaries. To coordinate financing requirements, Martin formed the Southeastern Securities Company, which gave the utilities access to equity, improved their credit ratings, and enabled them to borrow money at lower interest rates. Southeastern Securities also promoted customer ownership. When $117 million in financing was needed, employees sold almost 70,000 shares of preferred stock in 1927, the year Alabama Power also was able to sell bonds at 4½ percent, compared with its first bond issue in 1915 at more than 12 percent.

Among other achievements, Martin's rural electrification program was extended throughout the system, resulting in Southeastern stringing 1,155 miles of rural lines by 1929. Martin also introduced the concepts of materials management, volume purchases, and sharing inventories. He created efficiencies and savings but caused great changes within the organizations being brought together. Martin met little resistance to these changes, partly because he was delivering solutions to problems but also because his leadership and technical team were exported to help run each of the subsidiaries—Sweatt to Mississippi, Stanley to Florida, Cummings to South Carolina, and W. E. Mitchell, McManus, and Oliver to Georgia.

But Martin's legacy was far greater than the series of plants, transmission networks, and companies he put together. By extending to all the subsidiaries a model for recruiting new industries, he enabled many remote communities to participate in the economic boom of the Roaring Twenties. Towns across the service territory benefited from national ad campaigns and promotions through Southeastern's New York office, which helped fuel economic development across the Southeast.

"The South has entered a period of advancement which gives promise of bringing it on a parity with, if not above, other sections of the country in industry and agriculture," Martin told his stockholders in 1927, citing a U.S. Department of Commerce report showing manufacturing in the Southeast growing faster than the national average and hydroelectric power expanding at more than twice the national rate. That year, the load of Southeastern's newly acquired properties increased nearly 10 percent, primarily to serve new cotton mills, wood-product plants, railroads, mines, foundries, quarries, brick plants, and chemical plants. And in 1928, that growth doubled when the territory added nearly seventy new factories. A great industrial migration into the region was beginning to take place—the roots of what later would become known as the "economic miracle of the South."

Martin was said to have managed with "forcefulness, foresight, and fairness." In spite of his slight stature and usually soft voice, he "filled every room he entered," dominating conversations with his bright mind and almost never losing an argument. Some saw him as dignified with unassuming humility; others thought him austere and possessing an enormous ego. But even his worst critics would agree that he was a man of remarkable intellect, courage, and integrity. Once, an engineer buying rights of way told him that land in one area could be had for $5 an acre. When Martin learned it was worth "about $25," he told the employee, "Then we'll pay $25."

The work force was in awe of him. "He was one of the largest little men I ever knew," said one employee. Martin built up the esteem of his labor force, giving workers a greater view of themselves and their mission of service. "We are servants of the public," he told them, "not cringing servants, but servants who perform a great work and who are entitled to a fair wage and fair treatment, just as it is incumbent upon us to give good service and treat the public fairly."

That philosophy inspired loyalty and high morale, motivating employees to go the extra mile to achieve implausible growth. By 1929, Southeastern was serving more than 280,000 customers in five states. Martin had pulled together many of the markets on Mitchell's map and assembled the sixth-largest utility group in the United States. More important, Martin built an organization so efficient that even the Federal Trade Commission later would compliment its engineering, construction, economics, and management and describe its integrated operations as "almost ideal."

MARTIN'S BATTLES AT MUSCLE SHOALS

Martin's many achievements were all the more remarkable considering the consuming interest he had to devote to a new battle for Muscle Shoals, the Tennessee River area that Martin's company had donated to the government to support World War I defense efforts. After the war, Congress began debating what to do with the government's properties at Muscle Shoals, which included an almost-completed steam plant and half-completed Wilson Dam—named for President Woodrow Wilson. Between 1921 and 1933, no fewer than 138 separate congressional bills would attempt to deal with Muscle Shoals. No topic outside of Prohibition commanded as much attention, and practically every candidate in the South proclaimed a position on the matter. Martin was pulled into the center of that battlefield to protect his company's interests against politicians, public power groups, and the richest tycoon in America.

More than anyone else, industrialist Henry Ford was responsible for placing Muscle Shoals in the national spotlight when he tried to buy the assets for $5 million, promising to manufacture automobiles, tractors, aluminum, textiles, and steel there and build a seventy-five-mile-long city— "larger than Detroit." The Tennessee Valley went wild with rumors that Ford would create a million jobs, employ Alabama's entire work force, and give away a free ton of fertilizer with each new Model T sold in the United States. "I Want Ford to Have Muscle Shoals" buttons were peddled in the streets, and endorsements came flooding in from many groups.

The War Department considered Ford's proposal unacceptable, as it required a 100-year lease, an exemption from the fifty-year limits of the

Federal Power Act of 1920, and a government obligation to finish Wilson Dam and another hydro plant upstream at about half what the Corps of Engineers calculated it would cost.

When Martin read Ford's proposal, he was shocked to see it included unit 2 at Plant Gorgas, the one financed by the government during wartime that Alabama Power was leasing and trying to buy according to the government's agreement with the company. Upon failing to persuade Ford to strike the Gorgas provision from his bid, Martin had no choice but to jump into the arena with Ford. On February 15, 1922, he made a counterbid so superior that he published a side-by-side comparison. Ford's offer would require $65 million in additional appropriations from Congress; Alabama Power's would require none. Ford would pay no state or federal taxes; Alabama Power would pay both. Ford would pay no return on the $17 million already spent on Wilson Dam; Alabama Power would give the government 100,000 horsepower of electricity free as a return on those investments. Ford would not be regulated by federal and state commissions; Alabama Power would. The list continued for two pages, but for many the facts didn't matter. Martin couldn't compete with the hero worship heaped on Ford.

The feud with Ford lasted from 1922 to 1924. Martin finally prevailed in getting the government to honor its commitment to sell his company the Gorgas unit, and after Wilson Dam was completed, he was able to lease its power output because Alabama Power owned the only transmission lines in the area. However, Martin was never able to work out a purchase agreement for Muscle Shoals assets despite being joined by southeastern utilities making joint bids over several years.

Each proposal's defeat was enabled by the untiring efforts of Nebraska senator George Norris, the person most determined to turn Muscle Shoals into a public power project. As chairman of the committee to which various Muscle Shoals bills were referred, Norris was friendly to neither Ford nor Martin, vowing no *private* company would get control of Muscle Shoals. "That applies to any damn corporation," he said. "I don't care if it's Ford's or any other."

In fall 1924, about the time Martin was creating Southeastern Power & Light, Ford suddenly withdrew his offer, transforming the Muscle Shoals situation into a private versus public power debate. During the next eight years, Norris led the charge for public power, Martin the charge for private. Early on, it appeared Martin might have an edge. Congress generally opposed the federal government owning and operating public utilities. In spring 1925, Alabama senator Oscar Underwood called for leasing Muscle Shoals's facilities to private interests, and his bill made it through both houses of Congress and to the final stage of a conference committee. That fall, a Muscle Shoals Inquiry Commission appointed by President Calvin Coolidge also recommended leasing the assets. And the following spring, a joint committee of Congress favorably recommended the bid Martin organized with thirteen utilities to create both power and fertilizer companies to lease and operate the facilities.

In every instance, the proposals were blocked by Norris, who turned his venom on Martin and what he called the "power trust." Based on a conspiracy theory that a group of monopolies led by General Electric and J. P. Morgan were trying to gain control of "every electric light bulb in the country," Norris and his supporters launched a congressional investigation in 1925 of practically every private utility in the nation. Conducted by the Federal Trade Commission, the probe criticized private utilities' accounting methods, political influence, business practices, and ethics. But mostly, the reports raised concerns about the rate at which holding companies were buying up utilities across the country and operating outside of state regulation. Using every finding from the investigation to his advantage, Norris gained victories for his Muscle Shoals proposals in 1928 and 1931, but both bills were struck down by presidential vetoes.

By that time, Martin confessed, "The federal foot was already in the door." Although he didn't give up the fight for Muscle Shoals, Martin had other distractions that commanded his attention—a new fight with a group that looked eerily like a "power trust."

LESSONS LEARNED

The 1920s brought enormous change. In addition to birthing rum-runners, speakeasies, and stock speculation, the Jazz Age restored the nation's prosperity and created mass markets for automobiles, movies, radios, and all types of new electrical appliances. The electric utility industry expanded in every way—technologically, territorially, and structurally. Through better engineering, new generators churned out more than three times the kilowatts of units built a decade before. The carrying capacity of new high-voltage transmission lines advanced even faster. The improvements made it possible to transmit electricity from remote powerhouses to city centers, from urban to rural areas, from one state to another, spreading the output of larger and larger generators over greater and greater distances.

These advancements gave birth to electric supply networks—interconnections that allowed regional utilities to interchange power, coordinate planning, and solve power supply problems the nation had experienced during the war years. In turn, networks stimulated consolidations of all types—smaller utilities merging with larger, municipals forming partnerships with private power or joining their ranks, and interconnected utilities forming loose federations. Inevitably, the changes produced larger and larger holding companies.

The lesson learned above all others during this era was that the plump promises of network economies could not be achieved without full integration of interconnected systems. And full integration of utility operations was not possible without common ownership. The experience of utilities operating in the Southeast was typical. Following the landmark Yates Report in 1920, they hastened to build interconnections and work out coordination agreements. But as independent companies, they had to continue evaluating interactions and planning investments as if operating in isolation. By coming under Southeastern Power & Light's umbrella, they could operate as if they were a single utility—sharing capacity and reserves freely, planning investments jointly, and sharing the benefits of serving a greater diversity of power users with a greater diversity of power generators operating in different time zones and rainfall regions.

Throughout the nation, other approaches to organizing networks were proposed and widely debated. In 1921, the U.S. Geological Survey released a study that spawned what was called the "superpower" craze. Consulting engineer William S. Murray, who directed the study, proposed creating an integrated network extending from New England to Washington, D.C., an area called the Superpower Zone. The promise of 40 percent savings fired imaginations. Another report debated during the same decade was the Giant Power plan, which would give the federal government control over planning for both generation and transmission. While Superpower and Giant Power weren't formally adopted, they remained topics of discussion for decades. The notion of superpower zones, in particular, stimulated greater utility interconnections. Ultimately, the secret to delivering the savings promised in Murray's report was revealed by the Tom Martins of the industry, who simply integrated more and more operations under the holding company structure.

Another lesson of the 1920s was that electricity and the economy were becoming inseparable. The Electric Age was coming to bloom, transforming industry and commerce, transforming household chores and agriculture, transforming the way people worked and lived across the nation. Nowhere was that demonstrated more clearly than in the South, where access to low-cost electricity finally opened the floodgates of economic development. "The South is the nation's last industrial frontier," Martin told audiences as he was putting together Southeastern Power & Light. "The South is now in the midst of her youthful strength. Her greatest growth is ahead."

Martin's vision was to build the keystone for unlocking those opportunities—a reliable, economical power supply network. "Power is woven inseparably in the social and industrial fabric," he said. "It is even to a greater extent basic to the immediate future of the South." By combining low-cost power with an aggressive industrial development strategy, Southeastern accelerated the South's economic engines, which brought greater progress and higher standards of living to the region. Supported by research and dozens of special reports and economic studies, Martin's industrial recruitment program became a national model and a key component of what would eventually become Southern Company's growth strategy for decades to come.

One other important lesson learned in creating Southeastern Power & Light was that success in a competitive environment required taking enormous risks—big bets made with courage and bold actions. When he started Southeastern in 1924, Martin was serving fewer than ninety cities and towns in Alabama. Little more than five years later, he had expanded operations to more than 1,100 communities. He and his team moved at jet-age speed during a Model-T era. In those five short years, Southeastern Power & Light established the benefits of a coordinated and integrated system so strongly that these companies would never operate independently again. The energy markets outlined on Mitchell's map had been assembled into a utility federation that would endure the test of time. Even after eight decades of changes, all but one of the subsidiaries would remain under a common umbrella, operating much the same way as when Martin put them together during the 1920s.

"A Citizen Wherever We Serve" captured a commitment Southern Company upheld throughout its history. In the 1920s, the Georgia Power band led parades across the state as the company expanded. At right, early leaders Henry Atkinson (top) and Preston Arkwright. *GPC Archives, Kenan Research Center at the Atlanta History Center, GPC Archives*

CITIZENS FOREVER

PRESTON ARKWRIGHT, AN UPRIGHT, look-you-in-the-eye leader who could fill a room just by the way he carried himself, never stood taller than the day he stepped to the podium of the city auditorium at Atlantic City, New Jersey, in June 1927. He was fifty-six years old and had already been an electric utility president for a quarter-century. He knew his business, and he knew his role. It was as if all the years before—all the selling, all the negotiating, all the talking to employees—had been preparation for this moment. This was his stage and his time, and he was about to tell the rest of the fledgling electric utility industry who he was, whom he worked for, and what they all could become.

Only fifteen years earlier, the reach of Arkwright's business—Georgia Power Company—did not extend beyond Atlanta's suburbs. Now, Georgia Power served approximately two-thirds of its state. A new day had dawned. Less than two minutes into his speech, he told the several hundred people attending the annual National Electric Light Association convention what he wanted them to understand.

"Our business is different from nearly all other businesses that I know," he said in his deep, resonating voice. "When we go to a place, we go not as tourists. Not as transients. Not as drummers. Not as temporary residents. Not as promoters. Not as tenants. . . . When and where we go, we build. We construct works of permanent character that can never be moved away. Our first act on arrival constitutes a declaration that we have selected that particular place in which to become a citizen, not just for an hour, not for just a day, but always."

The South of the 1920s still owned little of permanence, other than its vast fields and forests and the heart of its people, who continued to struggle to scratch out a living on the land and overcome the lingering shadow of a war they had fought and lost more than sixty years before. Against this hard-scrabble tableau, Arkwright wanted to make it clear his company was an immovable object, a permanent fixture, not a "drummer," the itinerant peddler who would appear suddenly on a horse-drawn wagon or traverse the dusty roads of the South with pots and pans on his back.

Arkwright explained to his audience the meaning of being "a citizen wherever we serve," a tagline inserted on all Georgia Power advertising after he coined the term in a 1926 speech. "We place individual representatives in each town and each city to which we go, and there they must live, becoming themselves part of the citizenship of the community. . . . We enter intimately into all the life of the community, into all the homes and all the stores and all the industries and all the activities. There is no other business that does it so generally, so intimately as this business of ours."

Arkwright saw 1927 as a defining time in his company's history. In a quarter-century, he had seen Georgia Power evolve from a small operation, marketing the revolutionary force of electricity to doubting customers, into the largest company in the state. The public now thirsted for more and more electricity, and Arkwright saw more spiraling growth ahead. He believed it was time to define for all what kind of company Georgia Power would be. Its values would be the values of Arkwright and Henry M. Atkinson, the company's founder and chairman, and would be stamped proudly on the company's forehead. A month earlier, Arkwright had told the Georgia Power sales department: "We will make the best company in the Southeast right here in Georgia, and we will build up every town and county in the state where our lines run." Afterward, he was ready to tell the rest of America.

"We don't run a main store in one place and branch stores in another to which we send out goods when they get a little shopworn, out of style, or stale," he said in Atlantic City. "We don't give one character of service to the big city and a different character of service to the small town. . . . We serve the rich and the poor—all alike—with the same quality and adequacy of service and at the same rates. The kilowatt of the poorest of our customers is just as good a kilowatt as money can buy."

Arkwright's speech established a vision for utilities throughout America, a rock thrown into the ever-swelling lake of a burgeoning growth industry, its ripples felt coast to coast. Many utilities requested a copy of his speech; others requested him to speak. "It is the clearest and best interpretation of this business of ours that I have ever heard," wrote Anna Belle Turner, of Central Hudson Gas & Electric Corporation in New York.

The utility industry was still discussing Arkwright's message when he outlined an equally compelling vision for "Building Georgia," a speech delivered in late August 1927 to the annual Georgia Press Association convention, a critical audience of newspaper editors. He took with him the Georgia Power band, which normally heralded the coming of electricity as it marched into a town but, on this trip, would play at the convention barbecue and on the Putnam County Courthouse lawn in Eatonton.

Arkwright told the editors the state should decentralize its industry base, pointing to well-researched statistical charts as he talked. Industry was mainly concentrated in Georgia's larger cities at that time, but Arkwright said increasing electrification could enable industry to locate in smaller cities and towns, near raw materials and local labor. He argued that the dominant factor in determining prosperity was the availability of power. "A network of transmission lines is one of the most important factors in bringing about decentralization of industry," he said.

Georgia remained essentially an agricultural state in the 1920s, its wealth based largely on farm production and land values. Arkwright told the editors that the arrival of industry—with its greater tax base, rising land values, and increased local business—would not only raise tax revenue for improved education and other cultural advances but also create a local market for farm products, as well as off-season employment for farm laborers. "Seventy-five percent of Georgia's population lives in rural districts, either on farms or in communities of less than 2,500 people," he said. "How can they have proper educational facilities? Under present conditions, the land won't support it."

neighbors, producing a "separate population with a distinctive demography" and an economy still dominated by a single commodity.

But by 1920, the king—cotton—was nearly dead. Soil exhaustion had eroded the lower South's rich farmland, and the boll weevil threatened to devour what was left. Staple agriculture had not only strangled the South's farmland and stifled its cities' growth but had also begun to sap the spirit of its proud people, slowly, one day at a time, through the backbreaking chores of their rural existence. At its most basic level, the South was a region still running on animal energy.

Enter electricity and its near-mystical powers to both kill and illuminate, as well as its power to change. Enter the merchants of change. Enter the greatest invention of the twentieth century.

PARTNERS IN PROGRESS

Exactly a year after his "Citizen Wherever We Serve" speech, Arkwright returned to Atlantic City for the 1928 National Electric Light Association (NELA) convention, where he was elected president unanimously, moving up from first vice president. *Snap Shots*, Georgia Power's monthly newspaper, called it "the highest honor electric and power companies could bestow." Already forty years old, the NELA was the foremost electric industry association, the forerunner of the powerful Edison Electric Institute. In the 1920s, southerners were rarely elected president of any national group, but Arkwright had stepped up to the platform and never blinked. It was nearly impossible not to like him. He told the 1928 convention, "I long to be of some use."

Arkwright made himself useful immediately, traveling that month to Pasadena, California, in the first of twelve visits during the next eleven months to speak at every NELA divisional meeting across America. "No doubt other presidents of the NELA have done as much, but at least in regard to traveling, none of them can have done any more," he told the Southern Division in Asheville, North Carolina, on May 9, 1929, in a speech entitled "The South's Symbol of Hope." Southern utilities, he explained, "weren't always well thought of, even in this territory. We were too big. Our people weren't used to it; our people had no wealth; our people were suspicious of aggregations of capital. . . . We had to grow big. It takes a strong man to help one less strong. It takes a big service agency to do a big job."

Arkwright was the strong, clear voice of Georgia Power's ideology, but he was only half of its leadership team. The other half was Henry Atkinson, founder and chairman. Rarely have two men with such common values and vision found such a compatible business partnership. They were, however, an unlikely pairing. One was a southerner whose father-in-law was a Confederate general, the other a New Englander and the nephew of an abolitionist who helped finance the raid on Harper's Ferry. But both were offspring of a new, postwar America, and their partnership was born when both were still in their twenties—in the early 1890s, when Arkwright became attorney for Atkinson's first utility. They connected quickly, drawn like moths to light. They saw the future the same way—bright and large enough to leave a footprint.

Born in Brookline, Massachusetts, in 1862, Henry Atkinson quickly became "Harry." His family had come ashore from England two centuries earlier with the Puritans. His grandfather was a minuteman in the American Revolutionary War, and his father was a pioneer cotton manufacturer. Harry Atkinson was sent to the private schools of Boston and then on to Harvard, where he excelled in both football and academics. Upon graduation, like so many of his well-born eastern contemporaries, Atkinson went west. He found land that looked promising but, after more than a year, eventually left discouraged. He showed up in Atlanta in 1886, a wandering cowboy searching for roots. He chose Atlanta because of his father's business connections or because he was still trying to be a pioneer. If he were seeking an economic frontier, he found one—and an opportunity to make a difference.

When Atkinson arrived in Atlanta, smoky oil lamps lighted most of the city streets, and mules or horses pulled streetcars. Initially a banker, backed by northern capital, Atkinson loaned money to the would-be builders of the New South. He would make a fortune in banking, cotton, and real estate. He studied the possible future of electricity in Atlanta for two years before buying, in 1891, a company that owned a few streetlights but supplied no electricity for residential or commercial lighting. Total capacity of the utility was one megawatt.

In 1902, after winning a street railway struggle dubbed "The Second Battle of Atlanta" against businessman and Atlanta society darling Joel Hurt, Atkinson became chairman of the new, consolidated Georgia Railway & Electric Company, financed largely by Boston stockholders. Now with a larger and fast-growing company, Atkinson needed Arkwright to be more than his lawyer, so he made him president. Within a decade, their company had grown so fast that its name would change again, to Georgia Railway & Power, after acquiring the huge Tallulah Falls hydro project and merging with other utilities, including Morgan Falls, just north of Atlanta.

Atkinson was a capitalist, and his faith in the South's industrial potential exceeded that of most of his contemporaries. No one dreamed more boldly or worked more tirelessly to develop Georgia. In his lifetime, he would bring an estimated $200 million into the state to finance various projects. He once said, "When anyone asks me what my business is, I am glad to reply, 'Public service.'" Without service, Atkinson believed "there can be no satisfaction in the business career. The mere making of money is the poorest business a man can follow." He told employees to "be right in everything you do."

Atkinson realized Arkwright was better suited to be the company's public face. Born in 1871 to an English father and Ohio-born mother, Arkwright saw his first electric light at a circus—exhibited and showcased like the wild animals captured and subdued by man. His father, Thomas Arkwright, had worked under a machinist in England, but when his apprenticeship ended, he fled England's class society to see what he could make of himself in America. He started a foundry outside Savannah, Georgia, and eventually built a cotton factory, operated by steam. He named his first son "Preston" for the English town he had left behind for better opportunity.

Young Preston was packed off to St. Joseph's Academy in Sharon, Georgia, at age eight and would graduate from Savannah's Chatham Academy as valedictorian. Only three years later, he was the University of Georgia's salutatorian, receiving both bachelor's and law degrees in 1891. He then married into one of Georgia's prominent political families and went to work in the family's law firm in Atlanta. It was from there that he began representing Atkinson's first utility, Georgia Electric Light Company. Through the ups and downs of an infant company struggling to survive, the two men's respect for each other deepened. Together, they would electrify Georgia.

THE NIGHT THE LIGHTS WENT ON IN GEORGIA

No one really knew how dark it was until the lights came on. Electricity had done nothing for rural America—except by its absence, which left farm families to days of drudgery and evenings of fumbling around, unable to see. With no indoor plumbing, they fetched their water several times a day from a well or the creek down the hill. To cook or warm themselves, they cut down trees, splitting and gathering the wood daily. To keep their food from spoiling, they stored it in a cellar, a springhouse, or a box filled with ice. They washed their clothes in an iron pot and farmed from dawn to dusk, often with the most rudimentary implements. They milked cows by lantern and hope—hoping the lantern would not be kicked over by the cow and burn down the barn and then hoping the milk would not spoil before the dairy picked it up. When nightfall arrived—if they were not so exhausted they went straight to bed—they relaxed in the shadows thrown from kerosene lamps. They arose the next morning, still in the dark, to start their ordeal all over again.

For farm women, electricity would eliminate hauling wood to keep a fire in the stove and summer days of canning, baking, and ironing in a kitchen so hot they could barely breathe. It would eventually vanquish the wash-day marathon of putting clothes in a big tub of warm water with lye soap, rubbing the clothes on a washboard, beating them on a battling block, rubbing them some more, putting them in a pot to boil, rinsing them in three different tubs of water—all hauled from the well—and hanging them out to dry before the afternoon rains came.

When the lights came on—finally—farmers kept flipping the switch or yanking on the pull-chain. They couldn't believe it. They refused to turn them off until late at night, fearful they might disappear as suddenly as they had appeared. Later, when daytime electrical service arrived, some farmers refused to return to their fields that afternoon. It was a holiday.

To the liberators went the spoils of gratitude. "They liked us. We were a blessing. We were very welcomed," said Lawrence Shadgett, a senior Georgia Power operations engineer then. "I remember in Dawson County, just north of Atlanta, the people were only getting lights from six o'clock at night until two or three o'clock in the morning. . . . We built a line from Cumming up the highway to Dawsonville. As soon as it was built, the people were so happy they had a barbecue in celebration." And the men who built the twenty-three miles of rural line to serve 144 homes were the guests of honor. Dawsonville did not have railroad, telephone, telegraph, sewage, or a water system, but it had electricity.

VALUE SYSTEMS IN LOCKSTEP

The reception Georgia Power received in Dawsonville was happening all over Georgia. Once the company became part of Southeastern Power & Light in

1926, its growth skyrocketed. In the first six months, forty-two cities and towns were brought into the company. Within less than a year, the number of communities served doubled. Then in 1927, Atkinson and Arkwright created a Rural Lines Division, as Southeastern Power & Light CEO Tom Martin had long been a champion of rural electrification. If the do-it-all Arkwright was bothered by having an additional boss in Birmingham, he did not show it publicly. The acquisition by Southeastern greatly strengthened Georgia Power financially, and Arkwright became a strong proponent of the holding company system, testifying before Congress in 1930 of its effectiveness.

The similarities shared by Arkwright and Martin were a major reason the takeover went so smoothly. Both were lawyers drawn into electrification of the South by moneyed outsiders with great vision. Each was the southern half of his respective partnership. However, Arkwright came from a more privileged background. Also, Martin did not make as strong a first impression as the upbeat Arkwright, whose external buoyancy and easy sense of humor made him seem more approachable. "He was very imposing—a fine-looking, upright, and strong man. . . . He could talk about anything, anytime, with anybody," said Shadgett.

Regardless of their personalities, Arkwright's and Martin's value systems were in seeming lockstep. Both were entrepreneurial, altruistic, and committed to improving their home state and the lives of others. Most important, their views of what an electric utility should look like were mirror images. They believed that, next to the manufacture of electricity, a utility's second-most important product was the manufacture of customers—whether through industrial development, appliance sales, or rural electrification. As more rural lines were built, for example, Georgia Power sent rural-service engineers to help farmers develop water and irrigation systems, feed mills, sweet potato curing plants, and milking machines.

Both men treated employees with absolute deference. Arkwright spoke to employees whenever he saw them and addressed them as "Mr.," "Mrs.," or "Miss," regardless of their rank or stature. He would promptly see any employee who wanted to talk to him. That was a standing policy. "The employees in this company stand first," he said. "They stand above the interest of the public. They stand above the interest of the stockholder. . . . If we have capable, devoted, industrious, contented, happy employees, they will do a better job for the customer, and we will do it more successfully for the proprietor."

Arkwright gave employees a common currency to take on the job every day, essentially telling them, "This is how we will operate, this is how we will live." For a rapidly expanding company, that external identity was critical. Internally, he worked to create a family culture within the company, which was often referred to as "Uncle George" by employees. And he made sure union employees were part of the family.

Georgia Power established collective bargaining long before it was law—an unusual stance in the South then—and would eventually become the largest union employer in the state. Initially, Atkinson's and Arkwright's utility was "strictly a nonunion shop" and anyone joining a union would be fired. But when the company made rules forbidding the wearing of union buttons and associating with organizers after a favorable arbitration decision, Arkwright saw the relationship between management and employees quickly deteriorate and decided to recognize the union—with a 20 percent increase in pay. "We entered into contracts . . . because of a change in our own convictions," said Arkwright, who once commented he would join a union if his position afforded him the opportunity. "I believe the men can do more for their own interest, and more for my company's interest, if they are banded together in a strong union," he said.

Arkwright had such a reputation for fairness that he was chosen in 1937 by the owners of the three Atlanta newspapers and their union pressmen as the sole arbiter of a prolonged labor dispute, his eventual decision being accepted without question by both sides. He later was appointed chairman of the Atlanta Labor Mediation Board. At one time or another, the press, public, and politicians all tried to persuade Arkwright to run for governor or mayor. But he chose to lead Georgia Power instead. He knew where he was meant to serve.

In 1945, at age seventy-four, Arkwright was elevated to chairman of Georgia Power, the position having been vacant since Atkinson's death in 1939. Despite his age, he remained CEO, passing the presidency to longtime general manager W. E. Mitchell, the brother of James Mitchell, who had founded Alabama Traction, Light & Power. He was still on the job when he died in 1946. He had left the office on a late-November morning to go to Emory Hospital for treatment of a chronic bronchial ailment. Four days later, Monday, December 2, he died of pneumonia, just three months after the death of his wife, Dorothy. Arkwright's funeral was held December 4; all Georgia Power offices and stores in Atlanta were closed that day until after the 11:30 a.m. service.

interchanged power. Martin had met Cobb at industry meetings but didn't know him personally. With a few frosty words, Cobb turned Martin's world upside down.

"Mr. Martin, I want you in my office Friday morning at eight," said Cobb without any polite, preliminary chitchat. "I just acquired control of your company."

"What do you mean you've acquired?" asked Martin, scrambling to make notes and retrieve train schedules from his desk files.

"My associates and I control considerable shares of your company," came the unnerving response, "and we're holding most of your warrants." Option warrants granted the holder a right to purchase shares of common stock. They usually were issued with bond securities but could be detached, traded separately, or converted to common stock at a hefty premium.

"Let's make it nine-thirty," Martin suggested after checking train departure and arrival times.

"That's fine," Cobb answered. "See you then. Good-bye." The line went dead.

Martin's head was spinning. He was not entirely blind to the dangers of swimming in the holding company ocean, but still the call was a shock. He thought he had protected his company from this type of raid. In setting up Southeastern Power & Light, the board had been careful to deposit slightly more than 25 percent of the company's voting stock into a trust with Martin and W. H. Hassinger as voting trustees. A board member and friend, Hassinger was an entrepreneur who made his fortune developing Alabama's iron and steel industries and had put up funds needed to preserve Southeastern's management continuity for at least ten years. The trust arrangement should have provided ample protection against another investor gaining controlling interest. The two largest stockholders were Electric Bond & Share (EBASCO), owning nearly 15 percent, and United Gas Improvement Company, with 7.1 percent. Almost all other shares were widely distributed. If someone had been buying up major chunks of Southeastern's stock and warrants, Martin hadn't been warned. His transfer agent was a bank in Birmingham, not a Wall Street insider.

Martin also may not have been monitoring trading activity on his option warrants. Because they were widely held, warrants would make a very inconvenient takeover device. They had to be purchased on the New York Curb Exchange, where their values fluctuated daily with the price of the company's common stock. For the warrants to be converted to stock, the holder had to pay an additional $50 a share. Martin was beginning to realize that someone with deep pockets was willing to pay a princely sum to gain control of his utilities. Someone with very deep pockets indeed.

MEETING COBB AND "ASSOCIATES"

The holding company waters had been growing treacherous throughout the 1920s. Trawling the deep was a new breed of fish—the investment bankers. They were very different from the builders, engineers, and entrepreneurs who created and operated the traditional utility business. The bankers were not interested in actually running operating companies since those profits were limited by regulation. Rather, they were after the big bucks that came with underwriting utility securities, earning commissions and fees when calling in old stocks and bonds and issuing new ones. With an inside track, they could also augment profits by actively trading in the very stocks they were handling, manipulating both the buy and sell side.

These bigger fish had grown fat feeding on the utility consolidations frenzy happening across the nation as small operating companies expanded, merged with larger ones, or fell under the banner of a parent firm. Now these financial adventurers were creating holding companies themselves—not the type Martin ran, but rather a type of "investment trust" holding company created to accumulate shares of many utility stocks into what became the leveraged mutual funds of their times. The value of these investment trusts went far beyond the actual securities they held because they could issue their own trust-fund stock and use their financial power to bring about new mergers, which, of course, required issuing new securities to sell to a growing speculative market. These financiers sat on utility boards and developed tight networks of associates that resulted in more and more utilities being concentrated into fewer and fewer hands.

Who were the "associates" helping Cobb gain control of Southeastern Power & Light? Martin couldn't be sure, but he knew that Cobb was tightly connected to Bonbright & Company, an investment house that underwrote $1.6 billion in utility securities between 1924 and 1929. Martin himself had used Bonbright to issue Southeastern's first $10 million bond sale in 1925. In lieu of a cash fee, Bonbright had accepted 100,000 option warrants as a commission. But that was nearly four years ago, and Martin had not used Bonbright's services since. Still, he knew its reputation. The firm was headed by two inspired financing strategists—Alfred Lee Loomis and his brother-in-law Landon K. Thorne. Practically unknown when they took control of Bonbright in 1920, Loomis and Thorne became Wall Street superstars by 1929. They worked the market from every angle, amassed an impressive portfolio of utility stocks, and formed their own investment holding company, brazenly named American Superpower Corporation.

Martin wondered if Loomis and Thorne had been keeping an eye on his growing operations. Had the Bonbright boys been holding onto their Southeastern stock options since 1925 and possibly accumulating more warrants over the counter? Had they been buying up his common stock through American Superpower? Or had they cut a deal with a few other investors who held large blocks of Southeastern's shares?

The possibilities haunted Martin on the long train trip to New York that Thursday evening. He wasn't sure what type of predators he might face the following morning. Although Bonbright topped the list of possible culprits, other clever players were probably involved in the takeover scheme. Cobb, Loomis, and Thorne sat on many boards and had powerful friends in the utility and banking communities, including the "House of Morgan," known to follow big money like a shark follows a trail of blood in deep waters.

Throughout the night, Martin tossed and turned in his Pullman sleeper and rehearsed alternate lines of defense. He had a sharp legal mind and the self-assurance of a successful CEO. If it came down to it, he knew how to put up a hell of a fight in boardroom and courtroom chambers. By the time he hailed a cab at Penn Station and headed for Cobb's office at 20 Pine Street, just one block north of the stock exchange, Martin was ready for battle.

As it turned out, a fight was not what Cobb had in mind. He greeted Martin dressed as if going to a formal affair—starched black suit, white piping on his vest, pearl stickpin in his tie. In the most formal and imperial manner, he showed Martin proof of the warrants and the number of shares that he and his associates now held or controlled. Cobb didn't reveal all his cards, but it soon became clear that Bonbright was the mastermind behind the scheme and Cobb was simply a front man for several powerful players who held all the aces.

Martin would learn later about the roles played by these other big fish. Meanwhile, he was boxed into a corner. Surprisingly, Cobb did not threaten his victim with commonplace takeover language. Instead, he used a bear-hug tactic, talking in terms of an alliance. They would bring their empires together by creating a new holding company. They would call it Commonwealth & Southern Corporation—with Cobb as chairman and

Martin as president. Martin also could continue as president of his Southeastern group, which would become a subholding company under the new umbrella. The combination would offer something unique to a financial market already mad over utility stocks. It would unite the strengths of the North and South. The diversity of regions and the diversity of economies, industries, and customers across eleven states would transform their two kingdoms into a formidable new contestant in the holding company game.

An alliance. A new utility giant. That's the way it would be communicated to the world, that's the way it would be pitched to stockholders, and that's the way Commonwealth & Southern would be sold to Wall Street. The plan had a certain face-saving wrapper. It might even have been appealing if presented under different circumstances. Cobb was almost inviting Martin to enter into a partnership. Almost—excepting the fact that Cobb held the upper hand and controlled how things would be done. "You will be president," came across as an order, not a request. That icy treatment offended Martin, and his blood boiled each time Cobb turned his nose down at him. Known to elevate snobbishness to new heights, Cobb had a haughty manner and a penetrating stare, a look embellished by a childhood injury that gave his right eyelid a slight droop. He wore the blemish as a badge, an asset useful in unnerving both opponents and subordinates throughout his climb to the top.

Despite the regal appearance, Cobb came from quite humble beginnings as the son of a Boston minister called to Grand Rapids, Michigan, where Cobb completed school and took his first job as a clerk. Working his way up the ranks of Grand Rapids Gas Light Company, he became a protégé of company president Henry D. Walbridge. When Walbridge teamed up with utility pioneer Anton G. Hodenpyl in the early 1900s, Cobb helped them put together utility projects in five states. Then after the two partners split in 1911, Cobb dumped his mentor and stuck with Hodenpyl, becoming chairman of the operating committees for several of his electric, gas, and transportation subsidiaries. Cobb also helped Hodenpyl and a new partner, George E. Hardy, consolidate several properties in Michigan to form Consumers Power Company, which, with Cobb as president, became one of the nation's leading utilities. In 1924, the Hodenpyl-Hardy assets were brought together under a new holding company, Commonwealth Power Corporation, which Cobb also ran. At one point, he was president of seven operating companies, and after Hodenpyl retired, Cobb eventually gained control of the entire empire by ruthlessly squeezing out Hardy.

Cobb's empire continued to expand under the tutelage of his New York bankers. In May 1928, Bonbright brought Commonwealth Power together with Penn-Ohio Edison to form a new holding company called Allied Power & Light. Allied's stock was on the market for little more than six months before a quarter of its shares were scooped up by another player in the Southeastern takeover. It was called United Corporation, a new firm that Bonbright also helped create, this time in a joint venture with J. P. Morgan & Company and Morgan's Philadelphia affiliate, Drexel & Company. Like everything else it did, the "House of Morgan" entered the utility market in a big way. Within one year, United became the nation's largest holding company, attaining a capitalization twenty times greater than U.S. Steel, one of Morgan's many other creations.

Bonbright, American Superpower, United, Morgan, and Drexel were all parties to the plot for creating Commonwealth & Southern (C&S). As front man, B. C. Cobb could run the operations and was given a seat on the boards of United Corporation and American Superpower. Meanwhile, his "associates" were manipulating the mergers needed to form C&S.

The takeover happened something like this: Bonbright and American Superpower collected nearly 240,000 of Southeastern's option warrants, and United, Morgan, and Drexel gained control of Commonwealth by buying up shares of Allied stock. United also bought controlling interest of Martin's second-largest stockholder—United Gas Improvement Company, headed by Randal Morgan, who also sat on American Superpower's board. Southeastern's largest stockholder, EBASCO, also may have been a willing party to the takeover, if not an active player. S. Z. Mitchell and C. E. Groesbeck, chairman and president of EBASCO, respectively, served on several boards affiliated with Bonbright, including American Superpower. In fact, EBASCO was American Superpower's largest shareholder, so Mitchell would have been an approver, if not initiator, of its major strategic moves. Three of these players—Randal Morgan, Mitchell, and Groesbeck—were directors of Southeastern Power & Light. So in addition to being embarrassed and enraged by the takeover, Martin had reasons to feel betrayed.

His company had been kidnapped, entrapped in an elaborate web. But under the circumstances, Martin was being given a decent deal. So he checked his temper and began to negotiate. Cobb expected it. He would not have wanted to keep him if Martin had not been a strong CEO. Too, Cobb needed cooperation, not a proxy fight. The plan to create C&S represented a bet worth millions for his financial backers, so Cobb made a few symbolic concessions. Martin secured several board seats for representatives from his Southeastern group and leadership positions for some of his key officers. In the months that followed, he also was able to exert some influence on the C&S organizational structure and on how subsidiaries would be managed.

The organization date was May 23, 1929. The state of incorporation was Delaware. No lavish celebration marked the occasion. No champagne flowed. But the "partnership" of C&S was officially under way. American Super-power, United Corporation, EBASCO, and United Gas ended up holding 30 percent of all voting shares of the senior securities; the balance would be sold and widely distributed among more than 180,000 stockholders. Among those first named to the new board of directors were the ace-holders—Bonbright's Loomis and Thorne, EBASCO's Mitchell, and United's president, George Howard.

As Cobb predicted, the new company was a hit. Newspapers praised it, both in the North and South—"the largest charter ever filed in the state of Delaware," reported the *New York Times*, pointing out that C&S had an authorized capital stock of 62 million shares. The "alliance" represented more than 2 million kilowatts of generating capacity owned and another 300,000 kilowatts under lease or contract. While 75 percent of the operating revenues came from electricity, the companies were attractively diversified with gas properties throughout most of the territories and a portfolio of other assets, including coal mines in three states, seventeen heating plants, twenty-six water-pumping plants, forty ice plants, and twenty-six railway systems. C&S had all the trappings for becoming the new darling of Wall Street.

HIGH FLYING BEFORE THE FALL

The merger news created the desired buzz. Southeastern's common stock, already trading at more than $90 per share, jumped nearly $7 on the day of the announcement and was soaring above $126 a share within two months. Commonwealth Power's and Penn-Ohio Edison's stock prices also shot up. Holders of large blocks of these stocks were the first to be extended private offers to convert their investments to the new common stock. Martin's shareholders would receive 4½ C&S shares for each Southeastern share, plus an option warrant giving them the right to purchase 2¼ additional shares of the stock at $30 each in the future.

In advance of the first public issue, brokers started hyping C&S stock, as many as twenty plugging it daily in *Wall Street Journal* ads. No fewer than seven ads on the front page included a "Commonwealth & Southern" banner on June 4, the day the stock first traded on the Philadelphia Exchange, selling initially at $26⅞. Two days later, when listed on the New York Curb Exchange, it was trading at $31. The following week, Cobb and Martin extended to all stockholders of their holding companies a stock-trade offer identical to the terms of the earlier private offer. That announcement, together with news of Morgan's consolidation of three other major utilities in upper New York, pushed half a dozen utility stocks to record prices. And on June 14, C&S set a new single-day record for stock trading on the New York Stock Exchange—586,800 shares changed hands. By the first week of September, 95 percent of the Southeastern, Commonwealth, and Penn-Ohio shares had been exchanged for C&S stock, with the number of shares issued reaching nearly 30 million. The financial houses were collecting hefty commissions on the creation of C&S.

But the sunny days were soon clouded by storms descending upon the nation's financial markets. The timing for launching the new company could not have been worse. Warning signs of a weakening economy had been there all year, and after peaking in September, stock prices started a steady decline in October. Savvy stockholders began to fret and pull money out of the market. Worries turned to panic October 24—Black Thursday—a day investors sold 13 million shares. The street's most influential bankers scurried to J. P. Morgan & Company offices, across the street from the exchange. Between emergency conferences at noon and again at 4:30 p.m., financial leaders conducted press conferences to calm Wall Street's fears. And they tried to prop up the market by buying volumes of shares, similar to the strategy Morgan used to arrest the 1907 financial panic.

But this panic was different. Millions of new securities had been issued during the euphoric years. Gambling in the stock market had become a national disease, the flurry fed by a liquidity boom of historic proportions. Cash was everywhere, interest rates were low, and money was easy. Thousands of investors bought stocks on margin, paying as little as 10¢ on the dollar, the kind of speculation that doubled stock prices within a year and sucked in many small-time savers and first-time stock buyers across the country. Having never experienced a bear market, correction, or panic before, newcomers were intoxicated by the financial bubble that kept pushing their stock prices up, up, up near the point of delirium.

When the bubble burst and the bell rang to close trading on Black Thursday, an eerie roar surged from the exchange floor—a mixture of groans, boos, and sighs of relief so loud they could be heard by a despairing crowd gathered in the streets outside. The *New York Times* described the weird sound as "chords from a primitive requiem." Some traders cried, their faces streaming with perspiration; some walked around dazed, their hands full of still unexecuted orders; others laughed and jumped about hysterically. Working into the night, several thousand clerks finished tabulating the day's transactions and confirmed that a rally before close had recovered some of the losses. The news helped cheer the brokers somewhat, and the next morning other bankers joined to keep propping up the battered stocks. U.S. Steel and the American Can Company demonstrated their faith by declaring a special $1 dividend on their shares, and President Herbert Hoover issued a statement reassuring the nation that "the fundamental business of the country . . . is on a sound and prosperous basis."

But a dark curtain of doubt had moved across the nation. More sober minds contemplated the president's remarks over the weekend and decided to call in their sell orders on Monday morning. By Tuesday, October 29, nothing could stop the collapse. More than 16 million shares changed hands—a record that would stand for thirty-nine years. Speculators who had bought stock on margin were forced to liquidate their holdings at any price. Millions of these orders hit the floor simultaneously, sending both good and bad stocks into the tank.

Martin was in New York that day, so he probably watched from his office window as frightened investors gathered outside the exchange, anxious for the latest news from inside because tickers were running hopelessly hours behind. Many nervous young men spilled into the streets, choking off traffic, their hats pulled across furrowed brows, hands thrust inside pockets, grim lines of fear creeping across their faces. It is likely that these events made an indelible impression on Martin and helped shape how he would later view his own company.

Cobb, however, was not in the office. On "Tragic Tuesday," he was relaxing at a fishing and hunting club on Bras Coupe Lake north of Ottawa—unofficial vacation headquarters for favored executives. When he received word of the market collapse at the clubhouse, he didn't flinch. The news wasn't entirely unexpected. He had cautioned his overenthusiastic executive team during the recent growth frenzy to stay realistic and never call the company's stock safe in spite of its soundness. "Let's not make any promises," he reminded them in his 1929 New Year's message. "Let's not make any promises, for promises are sometimes broken." Knowing millions of promises were being broken across the nation, Cobb decided to stay at the lodge. No need to rush back to New York. The news about his companies and personal investments could wait. The crash might delay things a bit while the market settled down. It might require him to tweak his strategy for C&S. But it wouldn't derail his plans.

For two more ghastly weeks, the market continued to plummet. By November 13, $30 billion in stock market values nationwide had been wiped out. C&S stock landed at $10. Some well-known high-rollers killed themselves, several jumping to their deaths from offices and hotels. One New York utility president gassed himself. Most seasoned investors, like Cobb, counted their losses and plotted ways to regain their fortunes. Many first-time investors approached 1930 still dazed in disbelief. The decadent decade of the twenties had come to a crashing, crumpling collapse.

THE POSTCRASH MERGER

The basic premise for C&S survived the crash. If anything, Cobb would argue, the "market correction" reinforced the advantages of a strong network of companies and may have shaped the company's next dramatic move to fully consolidate its operations. Cobb and Martin merged all their intermediate holding companies into C&S and dissolved Southeastern Power & Light, Allied Power & Light, Commonwealth Power, and Penn-Ohio Edison. That may have been a strategy planned all along, but more likely the decision was in response to government investigators, who were pointing fingers at investment trusts for contributing to inflated stock prices leading up to the crash. Utah senator William H. King deemed the trusts guilty of "criminality" for having issued stocks without support of sufficient underlying assets or earnings. "Many corporations have . . . increased their stock issues without reasons and without justification," he claimed, "expecting to unload them, as unfortunately has been done, upon a credulous, hysterical, if not intoxicated public." For whatever reason, C&S was transformed in very short order from something that looked initially like an investment trust into something that looked much like a traditional holding company.

Cobb and Martin sent the merger plans to investors January 7, 1930, and by the end of March completed the last of the stockholder meetings required to approve the restructuring. The merger would save money and create a more efficient, simpler corporate structure, they told stockholders. It also would allow them to consolidate three separate generation and transmission subsidiaries into one unified engineering and construction organization serving subsidiaries in all eleven states. Called Allied Engineers, this group was headed by Eugene A. Yates, who had been Southeastern's vice president and general manager.

The restructuring resulted in the operating companies reporting directly to the parent company, but their operations were coordinated along regional lines. The Northern Group included five operating utilities. Three were formerly part of Commonwealth Power: Consumers Power Company, serving 640 cities and towns in the greater part of lower Michigan; Central Illinois Light Company, centered around Peoria, Springfield, and surrounding communities; and Southern Indiana Gas and Electric Company, serving 23 cities including Evansville. Two Northern Group utilities were formerly part of Penn-Ohio Edison: Ohio Edison Company, based in Akron and serving 145 other Ohio communities; and Pennsylvania Power Company, centered in New Castle and serving more than 80 cities and towns in the region.

The Southern Group included the Tennessee Electric Power Company, based in Chattanooga and serving 328 communities in the southern and central portions of the state, and the five operating utilities formerly making up Southeastern Power & Light—Alabama Power Company, Georgia Power Company, Gulf Power Company, Mississippi Power Company, and South Carolina Power Company, collectively serving more than 1,100 cities and communities in the Southeast. F. P. (Pat) Cummings, one of Martin's executives, was named "sponsor" of the Southern Group, an executive function for coordinating C&S practices, policies, and services among the six companies.

At the time of the merger, there were 165 separate companies residing within the various business units of C&S. Many were small companies that had been purchased and merged into the larger utilities. Others were formed as a legal means to finance projects or buy real estate, rights of ways, and franchises. Dozens were nonfunctioning and could be removed from the charts. As part of their effort to simplify the corporate structure, Cobb and Martin eliminated sixty subsidiaries in 1930 and dissolved more than forty others during the next two years.

This type of cleanup and simplification made the organization easier to manage and further reduced costs. It also helped separate C&S from a host of other holding companies that were giving utilities a bad name. Even before the crash, the questionable practices of this new breed were being targeted by a series of Federal Trade Commission (FTC) investigations. Congress grew increasingly fretful about the rapid rate at which holding companies were still growing. Sixteen of the larger ones had gained control of 80 percent of the nation's electric generating capacity by 1929, and the top three would control four of every five operating utilities by 1932. Some of these holding companies ruled like absentee landlords over properties widely scattered across the country. In bidding for new acquisitions, they had paid unrealistic prices, often three or more times book value—motivated by, the FTC said, "the desire for commercial expansion, greed, or personal ambition to become dominating factors in the industry."

FTC reports showed how some holding companies stacked up pyramids of intermediate subholding companies and subsidiaries and issued dozens of different types of securities with unequal voting rights, so investors often were confused about where their securities ranked in the pecking order of investment risk. These parent firms also inflated profits by marking up billings between subsidiaries.

By contrast, C&S set up a simple structure, eliminated intermediate subholding companies, and issued only three classes of securities: bonds, preferred stock, and common stock. Most important, C&S billed all service company expenses to the various business units at cost. Martin ran his Southeastern Engineering group that way and championed the policy until it was adopted by Cobb and the C&S board. Undoubtedly, the way Cobb and Martin set up their new organization was greatly influenced by the crash and by the FTC investigation still under way at the time of the merger.

C&S UNDER MARTIN AND COBB

His wounded pride somewhat bound and healed, partly aided by flattering press reports on the new company and its president, Martin put his energy and enthusiasm into his new role. He was a devoted disciple of the holding company system and often preached its advantages and values, and he filled scrapbooks with news clippings and speeches made by Owen D. Young, the charismatic head of General Electric who often glorified the mission, contributions, and positive attributes of the nation's holding companies.

That is how Martin liked to view his own company, providing a noble service to his customers, state, and region. He had high hopes that C&S would duplicate on a grander scale what James Mitchell had put together with Alabama Traction, Light & Power and what he had put together with Southeastern Power & Light. A larger holding company could mean more efficiencies, lower costs, faster economic development, and greater service. Those were his aspirations for C&S when he took an apartment at the Plaza Hotel and began dividing his time between New York and Birmingham.

For the next two years, Martin would wear many hats. In addition to his C&S position, he continued to serve as president of Alabama Power and Gulf Power. And he paid close attention to his former Southeastern operations. With Tennessee Electric Power added to the network, the Southern Group became the nation's largest integrated system. The entire generating and transmission systems of these six companies were operated as a single unit irrespective of state lines. To control load dispatching and coordinate planning among the companies, Martin created a central production and transmission department in Birmingham under the direction of G. H. Middlemiss, his former superintendent of operations. Also located in Birmingham was the southern office of the service organization—the name of which was one thing Cobb and Martin failed to simplify. It was called Commonwealth & Southern (New York), the parenthetical clarification needed to distinguish it from the parent company by the same name incorporated in Delaware. In addition to Birmingham, the service company had offices and staffs in New York City and Jackson, Michigan.

After the merger, the Southern Group continued expanding its service territory, at least initially. One property purchased by C&S in late 1929 was the Public Light & Power Company, serving communities in northern Alabama and south central Tennessee, which C&S merged into the operations of Alabama Power and Tennessee Electric Power. Some new acquisitions also were added to Gulf Power, South Carolina Power, and Georgia Power, the largest being the Columbus Electric and Power Company, which served nearly seventy towns in Georgia.

But the acquisitions and construction programs faded as investment funds dried up and the economic outlook kept getting bleaker. Everyone looked for signs of an upturn; economists initially viewed the Depression as part of a normal business cycle. By the time C&S completed its merger, Hoover had proclaimed that "we have passed the worst." And even the American Economic Association predicted a recovery by summer 1930. When it became clear there would be no quick rebound and excess generating capacity started piling up, power plants on the drawing boards were scrapped. Allied Engineers closed shop and was dissolved by the end of 1931. Yates and a reduced staff of engineers merged into the service company and finished projects still under construction, including the Lower Tallassee hydro

operations and management of the companies, but as the Depression persisted and projections showed C&S earnings dipping into the red, pressures from the board to shore up the books pushed operational considerations to the backseat.

The board first cut dividends on common stock in 1931 and eliminated them altogether after the first quarter of 1932. The day was approaching when C&S preferred-stock dividends also would be reduced or eliminated, and that was getting close to jeopardizing operating company securities. Martin had sold thousands of Alabama Power preferred shares to customers who now depended on the quarterly dividends to survive hard times. Employees would suffer, too. Other companies were beginning to follow U.S. Steel's lead in cutting wages across the board, and it was not a matter of *if*, but *when*, C&S would cut salaries and make dramatic layoffs, as well.

Martin also was greatly bothered by utilities that fell at the Depression's onset and those that were still falling. Most notable was the widely publicized collapse of the Insull empire. The industry considered Samuel Insull a terrific operations manager who initially built his organization—239 utilities operating in nearly forty states—the old-fashioned way and established affordable power prices for small consumers. Insull had defied and remained independent of Wall Street bankers for decades, but his downfall occurred when he eventually had to turn to them to help finance some of his holdings. When stock prices took another plunge in 1931, Insull was forced to put up more and more of his securities as collateral on those loans while the Wall Street bankers moved in for revenge, calling for an audit of his books and declaring his largest utility group insolvent. Panic selling and rumors of fraud, improper bookkeeping, and embezzlement wiped Insull out, along with his stockholders. After he resigned, his empire went into receivership, and he fled the country in disgrace. Suddenly, Insull's very name became a symbol for everything wrong with the holding company system.

The Insull collapse, which preceded Martin's resignation by several months, was particularly troublesome because Insull had been Martin's friend and strong supporter during a long fight over private versus public ownership of the power resources at Muscle Shoals, Alabama. Although investigations did not reveal until later the particularly vicious role the "House of Morgan" played in driving down the price of Insull's securities, those predatory moves would have been well known to Morgan's friends on the C&S board at the time. Any discussion of the events during board meetings—and New Yorkers were talking about little else when Insull fell—would have dismayed and disgusted Martin even further.

There was yet another compelling reason for Martin to escape New York and return to Birmingham. The Alabama Public Service Commission was bothered by rumors that Cobb and C&S were making all major decisions affecting Alabama Power and growing concerned that the utility's top officers resided out of state. The criticisms were hurting Alabama Power's effectiveness in dealing with a number of politically inspired challenges. Whatever the reasons, and there were probably many, Martin returned to Birmingham and plunged himself vigorously into business and civic activities, determined to help rebuild Alabama's economic health and advance his company and state in every way humanly possible.

WENDELL WILLKIE ENTERS THE PICTURE

For a while, Cobb wore hats of both chairman and president of C&S, but by 1933 he began suffering health problems, and the board decided it was time to fill the position Martin left behind. Cobb turned to someone he had been keeping an eye on since 1926, someone who looked capable of leading C&S through the worst of the Depression, someone by the name of Willkie.

He was born Lewis Wendell Willkie in the small town of Elwood, Indiana, on February 18, 1892. Both parents were lawyers, idealists, and intellectuals who raised their children to be voracious readers, a habit Willkie retained all his life, his luggage often crammed with as many books as suits, shirts, and socks.

After graduating from Indiana University, Willkie worked as a teacher and then as a chemist in a Puerto Rico sugar factory before returning to Bloomington to study law. During the First World War, he enlisted in the U.S. Army, married Edith Wilk, and had a son. The military transposed the order of his first and middle names, but he liked the change and decided to remain Wendell L. after service.

Attracted to politics, he toyed with the idea of running for public office but on the advice of his favorite professor decided to sign up with Firestone Tire and Rubber's legal staff. He next joined the Mather and Nesbitt law firm and, while in Akron, became the city's bar association president, Democratic Club leader, and a delegate to the 1924 Democratic National Convention, where he campaigned passionately for Woodrow Wilson's proposal for the League of Nations.

Among Mather and Nesbitt's clients was a utility in northern Ohio, which is how Willkie came to meet Cobb in 1926. "We should not let this young man get away from us," Cobb had written to one of his officers. "He's a comer and we should keep an eye on him."

Though mentally sharp and articulate, Willkie's big-boned dimensions gave him a clumsy and careless appearance. Even the way he read a newspaper was messy—peeling off each sheet as he read the front and back of each section and worked his way toward the middle, keeping stories that jumped in mind for when he came to them later. The floor about him was covered in dropped pages by the time he finished.

The sloppy habits must have driven the emperor of order to distraction at times. But Cobb somehow tolerated the Hoosier image and in August 1929 convinced Willkie to join his general counsel's law firm—John C. Weadock in New York—to handle legal matters for C&S and to assist its subsidiaries with major litigation.

When he became C&S president, Willkie was barely forty years old, but in fighting the company's legal battles he had received the best training possible for the challenges of the 1930s. The economy was still headed toward rock bottom, and populist politicians were determined to have the government take over the power industry and shut down companies like C&S.

"Gentlemen," he proclaimed during his introductory meeting with Consumers Power's management, "I am a Democrat. I'll take care of the politicians. I want you to know that our best defense of private enterprise, of our investor-owned company, is that we'll sell so much power at such low cost that those politicians won't want any part of our job."

The largely Republican assembly of "Cobb yes-men" might have been stunned at his directness and liberal politics, but they welcomed a change from Cobb's conservative formalities. Even the southern companies were charmed by Willkie's humor and interpreted his boastfulness as overabundant optimism instead of arrogance, since they never received from Willkie the condescending treatment suffered under Cobb.

Within a year, Willkie began transforming C&S into a different type of company. His approach and personable style dominated as Cobb, under faltering health, relinquished more and more duties. When Cobb retired in spring 1934, the board made Willkie CEO and president. A promoter and champion communicator, Willkie turned out to be the right man for the times, the right man to lead a company under siege.

SURVIVING A DEPRESSION THROUGH SALES

The Depression was entering its fourth year. National unemployment was approaching 25 percent. Millions lost their homes to foreclosures and their life savings to bank closings. The dispossessed became everyday fixtures, going from house to house seeking food and a job, huddling around campfires or in boxcars, hitching a ride to anywhere there might be work. Michigan and Mississippi—two states where C&S operated—were particularly hard-hit. As heavy industries closed and automobile production fell to one-third what it had been in 1929, Michigan's unemployment rose as high as 50 percent. More than 200 banks closed as mobs of shouting depositors shouldered up to teller windows to withdraw their savings. With only six banks standing in 1932, Michigan became the first state to declare a bank holiday, suspending all banking operations until the panic settled down.

In Mississippi, on a single spring day in 1932, one-fourth of all the land in the state passed under the auctioneer's gravel for tax default. The price of cotton sank below the cost of seed, fertilizer, and labor, and 40,000 farms passed into the hands of loan officers, insurance companies, or the state. With a per capita income already at $239 before the crash, Mississippi sank below the range of minimum subsistence when average income fell to $117 per capita in 1933. Municipalities behind on streetlight bills let their towns go dark, and electricity theft rose to an all-time high. In the Gulfport Division alone, Mississippi Power lost $50,000 a month to the "jumper" business—the dangerous practice of using a U-shaped wire to bypass the meter.

Other southern states were faring only marginally better, especially in the large cities. Birmingham was among the worst hit in the South. Men who could find work in the U.S. Steel mill labored for 10–15¢ an hour, payable in scrip redeemable only at the company store. The local government, virtually broke, attempted to sell city parks to raise money. In Atlanta, half the businesses on famed Peachtree Street closed shop, and local leaders concocted a "back-to-the-farm" movement, a hopeless cause since hundreds of cotton farmers, unable to sell their crops, already were flocking to the city looking for work.

When Willkie became C&S president in 1933, the company's earnings were already in the red, inadequate to cover preferred dividends, and sinking even lower. But Willkie was determined to "sell" his company out of these problems. "We've got to increase sales," he told management and marketing teams as he toured his companies. "We've got to increase the use of electricity. And the way we are going to do it is that we are going to reduce our rates to

joined the terminations list, which included two future CEOs. Lansing Smith, who lost his position as Gulf Power's assistant general manager, later returned to service in a job promoting new industries and eventually became Gulf Power's president in 1955. Ernest C. Gaston was laid off in the Birmingham engineering department, but he kept returning to his office, finding work to do without pay, believing that when things picked up, "those who know the most about current operations and problems will be the first ones back on the payroll." He became president of the service company in 1957.

All employees were affected by the pay reductions. Mississippi Power employee Red Howard remembered the day the Hattiesburg office handed out checks reflecting a 10 percent cut: "Everybody got the same . . . . Nobody quit. . . . They just kept working because a job was hard to keep." According to Jim Crist, management sometimes received a deeper cut. "My salary was $5,000," he said. "They cut it to $4,000." In 1935, however, as earnings began exceeding expenses again, Willkie saw that 5 percent was returned to employees making less than $125 per month.

Mississippi Power faced problems much greater than pay cuts and layoffs. In 1934, when its earnings fell below the ability to pay a dividend on preferred stock, the company's resale bureau was buried under an avalanche of requests to redeem shares. Investors weren't pleased to learn that, contrary to what they had been told by some overenthusiastic salesmen, the company was under no obligation to refund the full purchase price—a disclaimer that was printed on the stock certificates. Sixteen stockholders filed lawsuits to recover their original investments, and, when a circuit court jury ruled in favor of one investor, Mississippi Power faced possible foreclosure. President Barney Eaton hopped on a train to New York to seek relief from C&S, which already was financing the company's bonds. Willkie agreed to get the board to suspend a pending bond-interest payment, provide $150,000 needed for the overdue preferred dividends, and create a trust for future dividends should Mississippi Power's earnings prove insufficient.

"The offer hinges," Willkie told Eaton, "on your success in persuading your preferred stockholders not to sue the company. If you can get 95 percent to sign consent agreements, we'll be able to ride this out. Otherwise, the lawsuits will take the company down no matter what amount of money we throw at it." Eaton waged a campaign to get his stockholders to sign release forms while keeping bankruptcy papers tucked inside his desk, ready to execute on a moment's notice. Eaton's campaign worked, but he came within a few months of having to shut the company down, for the Mississippi Supreme Court upheld the lower court's ruling in 1935, saying promises made by employees were enforceable commitments. If Eaton had been unable to persuade investors to keep faith with the company, and if Willkie had not taken a risk in extending credit, Eaton would have been forced to file the papers concealed in his desk. Mississippi Power employees expressed their appreciation by selling more appliances than at any time in the company's history during December that year, which had been declared "Wendell L. Willkie Month" throughout the C&S system.

REFORMATIONS AND APPROACHING BATTLES

Willkie remained the most revered of all C&S leaders. In spite of the cutbacks and reduced wages, he gave employees hope in the face of a devastating economy. He never lost touch with his organization and spent much of his time on the road, traveling from one company to the next and visiting communities served by his utilities. He was not a technical man and, during detailed engineering discussions, would sometimes walk out of the office to explore the city, dropping in on newspaper editors or the community librarian. In between meetings, he also checked out company merchandise showrooms, approaching some unsuspecting sales clerk to see if he or she could demonstrate an appliance. If he was pleased with what he heard, he'd buy something on the spot for cash, often returning home with packages of toasters, percolators, broilers, or irons. He thought it was "just dandy" when an elevator operator at one of the companies tried to sell him a refrigerator.

"That's dandy" was his favorite expression, used anytime he was happy about something. "Right now" was his second favorite, used when asking for action. Once while waiting at a train station, he ordered two hamburgers and two cups of coffee. When the waiter gave him one cup with a promise to fill it up as soon as it was empty, Willkie blurted, "Hell no, I said I want two cups of coffee, and I want them right here and right now."

Willkie also never wore a watch, thus he was always asking those around him for the time. The world moved far too slowly for him, and he lost patience with nitpickers, people sluggish in making up their minds, or second-guessers once a decision was made. If he approved a proposal at a budget meeting, it was handled on the spot with, "That's dandy. I approve the item." No need for further discussion.

What endeared Willkie to the entire executive team, and even won Martin's respect, was his removal of the Wall Street bankers from the C&S board. No one knew exactly how he pulled it off, and the continued FTC investigations, no doubt, made the decision politically expedient. After Cobb retired, Willkie began working behind the scenes, and by 1934's end, the "money changers" were gone, replaced with six operating CEOs. Three new members were presidents from the Southern Group—Preston Arkwright from Georgia, E. L. Godshalk from South Carolina, and J. C. Guild Jr., from Tennessee. Later, when an FTC report suggested that C&S was controlled by United Corporation and the "House of Morgan," Willkie could deny the charges with a clear conscience and confirm that his directors and officers managed the company's affairs without any control of the financial houses.

"We take no direction from United Corporation, Electric Bond & Share, American Superpower, 'House of Morgan' or any other corporation, banker, or combination of bankers or financiers," he told Congress in 1935. "All we use bankers for is to get their money. They neither control us nor seek to control us, and if they did seek to control us, they would not do it, not as long as I am president of the organization."

Willkie's leadership and broadminded policies were good for his subsidiaries and their operations. "He was extremely liberal with this company, extremely liberal," Arkwright told a group of employees in Georgia. "We had no difficulty with Mr. Willkie in getting money that our own earnings didn't justify for the purpose of improving, expanding, and bettering this company. He was liberal enough to take a risk on it if, after investigation, it seemed a reasonable risk. He was very liberal in his attitude toward the treatment of customers, toward the treatment of employees, and, in general, toward the treatment of the public which this company serves." Employees saw Willkie as a champion of civil liberties and the rights of workers, as well as an effective defender of the company—saving it not only from the Depression but from attacks from populists throughout the 1930s and a New Deal president who had moved into the White House three months after Willkie had occupied his new office.

A Democrat who later switched parties, Willkie had been a Franklin D. Roosevelt supporter, even though as New York governor, FDR had become known in utility circles as a "dangerous man" for advocating state ownership of power projects and denouncing the "sins of wildcat public-utility operators" and the "Insull monstrosity" with insinuations that all utilities were guilty of betraying the public's trust. He also proclaimed the rights of any community unhappy with its service to take over private utility operations and develop their own power sites—a "birch rod in the cupboard" to be used when good service was not provided by private companies.

FDR had unveiled his plans for creating the Tennessee Valley Authority (TVA) on day thirty-two of what was termed Roosevelt's amazing "Hundred Days." TVA would take immediate possession of the Muscle Shoals properties and generate its first power from Wilson Dam, built on the land Alabama Power had donated sixteen years earlier to the government in a wartime gesture of patriotism.

Muscle Shoals had been Martin's quandary for nearly two decades, but the last battle had been Willkie's. Barely three months on the job as C&S president, Willkie had assembled a Southern Group contingent and marched into the chambers of Congress to make an eleventh-hour plea for cooperation. It was a final attempt to hold the line of defense at the switchboard, the critical point between power generation and the business of transmission and distribution. Willkie's team offered to exit the plant construction business, purchase power from TVA dams, and redistribute the electricity to customers at rates set by the government—radical concessions discussed with FDR in a White House meeting and then argued by Willkie and five of his executives for nearly ten hours before Congress.

The arguments were simple, reasonable, and solid—accept everything in the bill except building government-owned transmission and distribution lines. The strategy might have worked at an earlier time and under a previous administration. But political support for public power was too high and public support for private utilities too low. On May 18, 1933, the president signed the act into law, setting the stage for an unavoidable feud between FDR and Willkie so dramatic that it would transform Willkie into a national spokesman for his industry and free enterprise—and leave an enduring mark on Southern Company's future.

LESSONS LEARNED

For three generations, the hard knocks of the Wall Street crash and Great Depression would remain firmly etched across the nation's psyche. But flights of fancy would eventually return to the markets from time to time. Decades later, in an era of LBOs, IPOs, and dot.coms, when the brave and reckless were once again racking up unbelievable paper fortunes in their portfolios, utility executives would have to pump up their quarterly earnings and stock prices, frantically pursue mergers and acquisitions, and protect themselves from stalking corporate raiders.

Once the 1987 and 2002 corrections brought investors back to earth, these same utility executives could look back on the delirium of the 1920s with a better understanding of why things got so far out of hand in an age before there was a Securities and Exchange Commission, before there was a Banking Act and Federal Deposit Insurance Corporation, before there were a hundred other regulations and tools in place to educate, protect, and warn investors and corporations alike. They could look back on 1929 and appreciate how Martin had lost control of his own creation during a time when no substantial laws regulated the actions of holding companies.

The protective measures Martin put in place in 1924 didn't work by 1929. He and his company learned that to be big and successful was not enough to forestall invaders. Even giant, overvalued properties were being gobbled up. Most important, in a time of rapid change with new deals coming together monthly, Martin was terribly deficient in the critical ingredient of market intelligence. If he had maintained close relationships with Wall Street insiders, he might have been warned that someone was trying to gain control of his company. Working against him were his distrust of investment bankers and his bias for conducting business, where possible, within his service territory—in the South, to which he was totally devoted.

Utility leaders like Martin also learned how quickly prudent business judgment and ethical standards could be compromised—or cast aside altogether—by a market driven by greed. As the financial manipulations of certain utilities grew more outrageous, some executives protested loudly. Arkwright called on the holding companies to adopt a strict code of ethics and business integrity. "If anything is wrong, we should not wait for others to correct it, but should do it ourselves and do it right," he told industry leaders. But there were no effective mechanisms in place for the industry to police itself; its trade associations at the time were focused on generating sales, publicity, and political influence. And the idea of self-restraint was almost a laughing matter to financial houses that were issuing new utility securities to a clamoring crowd of fevered investors.

Some politicians accused the holding companies of causing the crash almost single-handedly. While that kind of blame is unwarranted—all stocks were booming and investment trusts weren't limited to the utility field—the holding companies certainly earned a share of guilt. Because prices of utility stocks were increasing faster than other industrials, they were a leading contributor to what economists called a financial bubble in the great bull market leading up to the 1929 correction. The shakeout exposed the financial shakiness of those holding companies that had manipulated their structures and systems in shady ways, but the financial crises that followed punished the guilty and innocent alike. More than fifty utility giants representing $1.7 billion of securities came tumbling down. Nationwide, utility stocks lost $16 billion in value between 1929 and 1933. The big bet of C&S's creation could not have come at a worse time.

"Too late, the investor discovered the difference between the regulated operating companies and unregulated holding companies," FDR's National Power Policy Committee observed several years later. Too late, the investor "learned how much of his money had been wasted in feeding the hopes and greed out of which vast utility empires were conjured." The suffering of many small shareholders added thousands of voices to the great public outcry against the "power trust." Utilities were a natural monopoly, a quasi-government business necessary to avoid duplicating expensive power delivery facilities at the local level. But after the crash, fewer and fewer people were willing to extend that grace to large utility systems scattered over multiple states with no connected operations. As the Depression stretched out, the public began to trust big government more than it did big business. The opportunity for self-policing passed. The struggle for self-preservation was at hand.

Another lesson utilities learned during the Great Depression was the critical role that sales and marketing could play in "saving the company." Willkie made a big bet that cutting prices could help him aggressively increase sales, proving that electricity price and demand were far more elastic than utility founders and operators had ever imagined. Willkie's sales strategy also taught the company its earliest lessons in how to gain efficiencies through economies of scale and spreading fixed costs over greater and greater volumes of sales. That development, combined with technology advancements, would produce a declining-cost business that eventually would fuel utility growth for more than two decades. Although Willkie's bet could not offset all revenues lost during the setbacks of the 1930s, it played an essential role in helping to sustain C&S—just as Roosevelt's New Deal programs helped sustain the nation—through the Depression's darkest days.

Creation of the Tennessee Valley Authority on May 18, 1933: President Franklin D. Roosevelt signs the "Muscle Shoals bill" into law and hands the pen to chief sponsor Senator George Norris. After five embattled years over service territories in the Tennessee Valley, Commonwealth & Southern president Wendell Willkie (at right) finally has his say before a joint congressional committee investigating TVA activities in 1938. *Bettmann/CORBIS*

FIGHTING A FEDERAL INVASION

IN THE DEPRESSION SOUTH, STRUGGLING townships anticipated Saturday afternoons when farmers and factory workers would come into town for light shopping and a soda, if they had a spare coin for a drugstore treat. On November 11, 1933, it seemed that all 6,000 people living in Lee County, Mississippi, showed up in downtown Tupelo, filling the streets with merchants and mill hands, cotton pickers and gin operators, and flocks of chirpy children. Lanky, leathery-necked farmers left their fields early and piled the wife and kids into dusty pickup trucks, stopping along the road to give a lift to friends or strangers walking to Tupelo. Politicians in sporty suits and fine felt hats also were there to press the hands of voters and rub shoulders with big boys rumored to be coming down from Knoxville and all the way from Washington, D.C.

"Everybody was talking about getting electricity; only people downtown had lights," recalled Frankie Kirpatrick, thirteen years old at the time. The Kirpatricks lived on a farm in the nearby Saltillo community. "My parents drove my brother, sister, and me to town in the old Chevrolet. We went to the Jeff Davis Hotel, a perfect spot to view the parade."

The procession started at Spring Street with the sheriff and police chief in front astride spirited stallions, leading a string of government officials, floats, bands, and representatives from civic clubs, the Boy Scouts, the Civilian Conservation Corps, and two dozen school groups waving banners, singing songs, and shouting school cheers. The line stretched a mile long, spilling out past the Civil War monument at Legion Casino, where a giant grandstand had been erected, lavishly decorated with red, white, and blue bunting.

Armistice Day was a fitting occasion for the "New Power Era Celebration," proclaimed Mississippi congressman John E. Rankin, an avid supporter of the bill establishing the Tennessee Valley Authority. "Tupelo's contract with the TVA means an armistice—an end—in the war of the people against private power interests," he told the cheering crowd, proud that his hometown would become the nation's first to get TVA power—Muscle Shoals power, cheap electricity imported by wire from Wilson Dam in Alabama.

"TVA was going to make a big change," said Frankie Kirpatrick "and we knew it was going to put Tupelo on the map." Even Movietone News was there to record the event. "Tupelo is going to be in the public eye from this time forward," predicted TVA director of power development David Lilienthal, who presented a contract to the mayor. TVA chairman Arthur E. Morgan spoke at length about his vision of a balanced rural-industrial society and the "ultimate complete electrification of every farm home in Lee County." Expecting a simple contract signing with the city fathers, Morgan was stunned to see the crowd and wrote fondly about one country school group carrying a banner reading, "When the moon shines over the cowshed there will be a light inside."

Described as the "greatest one-day celebration ever staged in north Mississippi," the event was a jubilee for Tupelo, a coup for a New Deal president, and a glorious victory for TVA and public power proponents.

The day was a dark, disastrous one for Commonwealth & Southern. In New York, C&S president Wendell Willkie was stewing and scheming. He had been negotiating for peaceful coexistence with TVA since its creation earlier that year. But no easy détente was in the picture. The invasion of his Southern Group subsidiaries already had begun. In Gulfport, Mississippi Power president Barney Eaton was grieving the loss of a wholesale customer, knowing Tupelo was only the beginning. Municipal votes were coming in from other customers in Corinth, Iuka, and Tishomingo.

Joe Conn Guild was brooding in Chattanooga. His entire Tennessee Electric Power operation was threatened. The TVA staff had set up encampments in Knoxville and already had taken over Guild's proposed dam site on Cove Creek, a Tennessee River tributary.

In Atlanta, Preston Arkwright was uneasy. If TVA gained Chattanooga, it would easily invade Georgia Power's northwest territory. En route to Tupelo, Lilienthal had stopped through Atlanta to tell lunch and dinner gatherings that TVA needed load diversity and a territory comparable to a private operation, "including some cities of substantial size." Arkwright knew Atlanta was on the potential target list.

None of the Southern Group presidents were more agitated than Tom Martin in Birmingham. Ten Alabama towns already had voted for TVA power, with more referendums scheduled. Martin had fought longer and harder than anyone to keep the Muscle Shoals properties from public power advocates. Now, right in his Northern Division, TVA was selling its first energy from a dam that should have belonged to Alabama Power.

Tupelo would receive wholesale power at seven mills a kilowatt-hour, Willkie read the following week in the *New York Times*. Described as the "standard for all contracts for towns of corresponding size," the rate was ten mills below Mississippi Power's rates. The city of Tupelo would pay $12,370 for wholesale power the coming year, compared with $31,144 the town had paid in 1933. Even more upsetting were the retail prices dictated by TVA. Tupelo Cotton Mills would get a 45 percent rate cut. The power bill for homeowners would fall by two-thirds. It was Willkie's first confirmation of the much-anticipated, much-lauded, much-ballyhooed TVA rates, the "yardstick" by which his companies and other utilities across the country would be measured and browbeaten. Low TVA rates set regardless of cost—that was how the approaching war would be fought.

Willkie contemplated his next move. TVA had fewer than three months to string a transmission line seventy-five miles from Wilson Dam to Tupelo to service the contract by February 7, 1934, the day Mississippi Power's franchise expired. By that time, he intended to have a treaty negotiated and signed. While arming his legal team for an eventual fight in the courts, Willkie hammered out a list of concessions from Eaton, Martin, and Guild— minimum properties that could be forfeited during his next session with TVA negotiators, sacrifices to achieve a cease-fire. He had to stop the invasion and halt the destruction of his stockholders' investments. The bright, sanguine C&S chief had not expected it to come down to this.

EARLY SKIRMISHES AND THE FIRST TREATY

Things had started out more amiably. Hoping to avoid a hostile relationship with TVA, Willkie had extended an olive branch as soon as Roosevelt named Arthur E. Morgan chairman of the new agency. A man of integrity, high ideals, and moral values, Morgan appeared to be the type of person who would deal fairly with private utilities operating in the Tennessee Valley. As a hydraulic engineer, he had conducted pioneering work on dams and reservoirs to control flooding rivers. As an educator and administrator, he had saved Antioch College in Ohio from extinction by introducing new "character building" work-study programs. "Only as men can trust each other are they free to achieve life purpose," he had written in a 1926 issue of *Antioch News*. He sounded like someone with whom Willkie could work.

"Your new undertaking presents to both of us problems of mutual interest, the proper solution of which, for the good of all concerned, will require our early and continued cooperative efforts," Willkie wrote Morgan, requesting a meeting as soon as TVA was incorporated in June 1933. The TVA chief was receptive and promised to take action on Willkie's invitation at his first board meeting. Selected a full month before his other two directors were named, Morgan immediately took up the task of planning, the activity he loved most dearly and a passion also shared by the president. When they first met, Morgan and Roosevelt spoke a common philosophical language "chiefly about a designed and planned social and economic order." They hardly mentioned power or TVA's other programs.

"The president wanted somewhere . . . a deliberate social planning for the future," Morgan said of that first meeting, when he told Roosevelt that his new job was "the kind of thing I have been wanting to do all my life." A student of the early social and economic successes of the Soviet experience, Morgan prepared himself for the new assignment by touring the valley, talking to the people, and spending a night in a humble shack with a farm family. The poorest part of the poorest region in the nation, the hills were home to people subsisting on a dismal diet and income of less than $100 per year. When mills in the area closed during the Depression, workers returned to farming marginal lands made worthless and severely eroded after a couple of crops.

The valley was a planner's paradise, an open field where Morgan could, as he put it, "pick up the wreckage of rugged individualism and the chaos of lack of planning" and—through TVA—eliminate waste, tap potential wealth, and transform the "relative aimlessness and hopelessness of young people into effective economic production and prosperity." While building dams, he would attack problems of land management, soil erosion, reforestation, education, nutrition, town planning, highway planning, and every other aspect of planning required to carry out what Roosevelt had called "the greatest social and economic experiment in modern times."

A noble vision. But Morgan quickly learned that not everyone shared his views on how to bring about that dream. At TVA's first board meeting, held June 16, 1933, at the Willard Hotel in Washington, D.C., Morgan asked for comments on actions he already had initiated. Right away, different opinions surfaced about policies, strategies, duties, and the workings of the board itself. His fellow directors eventually pressed him to allocate areas of responsibility among the team. Problems and programs related to agriculture went to Harcourt A. Morgan; those specific to power production were delegated to David E. Lilienthal—a division of duties that the TVA chairman later called his "worst mistake."

Harcourt Morgan—or Dr. H. A., as he would come to be known on the inside to distinguish him from Dr. A. E. Morgan—was an entomologist and president of the University of Tennessee. Disarmingly humble, his true love was the land; he had headed Knoxville's agricultural experimental stations and the Tennessee Food Administration. He preached his own philosophy, which boiled down to the importance of maintaining balance in nature and was well suited for becoming the driving force behind TVA's farm program.

A Harvard graduate, Lilienthal was an ambitious, determined, and snappy lawyer, largely credited with rewriting Wisconsin's utility laws and transforming its public service commission into a tough and effective regulatory agency. At thirty-three, Lilienthal was half the age of Harcourt Morgan and twenty-two years junior to Arthur Morgan. Wanting to reform the nation's holding companies, Lilienthal attacked everything he did with intensity and a sense of "cosmic importance." While at Harvard, he caught the eye of law professor Felix Frankfurter, who became an influential member of the New Deal administration's "brain trust." Frankfurter recommended Lilienthal's appointment, as did "TVA father" Senator George W. Norris, who wanted a keen mind and compelling voice to fight the inevitable battles facing TVA.

The three-member board "had powers that kings might have envied," wrote Donald Davidson, poet and Tennessee historian. "They were in the position . . . of playing God to the Tennessee Valley." A clash of these titans was inevitable, however, given their appointed powers but peculiar personalities. From the start, they argued over Willkie's letter and how to deal with utilities in the valley. Arthur Morgan favored cooperation—in "an open and frank manner, with the understanding that they will deal with us in the same spirit." Lilienthal considered private utilities to be far from trustworthy and talks with them premature. With Harcourt Morgan playing the mediator, the three finally consented to the chairman's meeting with Willkie as long as he promised to make no premature commitments.

On June 28, Willkie and Arthur Morgan enjoyed a cordial dinner at New York's University Club. They agreed to communicate with each other openly and honestly, but they accomplished little else, since they held few views in common on the TVA Act. Neither did the TVA board members. Conflicts between Morgan and Lilienthal emerged as they hammered out a power policy for the agency. According to historian Thomas McGraw, Morgan wanted to peacefully acquire a representative rural-urban area to set up a "yardstick" experiment to be structured like scientific research for comparing public and private power rates. Electricity was merely a "by-product" of their work, he argued, and should not distract from the greater goals of "regional reconstruction" and "reawakening the American spirit." These high ideals would guide them even in the housing plans for the Cove Creek construction site. Morgan designed a permanent rural-urban community with its own post office and schools, stores and restaurants, garden plots, and picturesque green spaces—a utopian model of a planned community. Morgan also planned libraries, adult education programs, and a score of cooperatives from furniture and poultry to pottery and country crafts. This important work of regional planning, Morgan feared, might be undermined by political squabbles over power issues. And Roosevelt had promised him TVA would be "entirely free of politics."

For Lilienthal, electricity was far more than a by-product. It was the means to finance the authority's work and an opportunity to create multiple small yardstick areas. The "yardstick" wasn't a scientific proving ground, he argued. It was to serve as a political spur to private utilities, a creative and potent form of regulation. As for politics and propaganda, they created clamor for service—some 165 municipalities already were making inquiries— and TVA could capitalize on that excitement. Negotiations with utilities should wait, he said, refusing to meet personally with Willkie until the board had finalized its power policies. That plan, issued late in the summer of 1933, defined TVA's territory in the short term as being the northeastern section of Mississippi, the area around Muscle Shoals in Alabama, and a strip "immediately proximate" to the transmission line TVA intended to build between Wilson Dam and the Tennessee Cove Creek project, now called Norris Dam in honor of the senator who had made it all possible. In the long term, however, the power policy described the TVA "yardstick" as encompassing roughly the entire state of Tennessee, the watershed in small parts of several other states, and at least one city of significant size, such as Birmingham, Memphis, Louisville, or Atlanta.

The press release announcing TVA's eleven-point power policy essentially served notice to C&S and other utilities in the region that TVA intended to run them all out of the valley. That news didn't make for a smooth first encounter between Willkie and Lilienthal. They met over an awkward lunch at the Cosmos Club in Washington on October 4, 1933. After initial cagey and carefully guarded pleasantries, Willkie boldly offered to buy the entire electricity output of TVA dams. "You fellows have $50 million, and that is all you are likely to get," he warned, emphasizing that Congress could reverse its generosity at any time and boasting, "I will take all your power off your hands, and that will . . . make you independent of Congress."

C&S still was TVA's only customer through interconnections with Alabama Power and an agreement Martin had made with the War Department—a contract that would expire within three months, a contract Lilienthal needed to renew. "I was pretty badly scared," Lilienthal wrote in his journal upon leaving the meeting, feeling "somewhat overwhelmed" by Willkie's "cocksureness."

By the time they met again, however, Lilienthal had the upper hand, having secured the Tupelo contract and received results of referendums from other cities voting for public power. He also had the means to serve those municipalities whether Willkie cooperated or not. Funds were being unleashed through the Public Works Administration (PWA), another New Deal program that, in addition to funding roads and public buildings, could issue grants and loans to towns and cities wanting to construct their own electric systems. Relishing his turn at playing bully, Lilienthal gave Willkie an ultimatum to sell out or TVA would build duplicate transmission lines to reach his customers and help towns build duplicate distribution lines, as well. Corinth, served by Mississippi Power, had just received one of the first PWA grants issued, and other requests in the region were being approved. Initially, PWA wrote checks for 30 percent of the cost of municipal systems and provided the balance as a low-interest loan but soon became more generous, for his agreement with C&S to expire before he could officially sign a contract with Chattanooga. But that was little consolation for Willkie. The loss of Tennessee Electric Power's headquarters city was a psychological blow for C&S, and the voting gap—three-to-one in favor of public power—was convincing.

Relations between Willkie and Lilienthal became more splintered. Oddly, they shared similar backgrounds—both born of German-speaking parents, raised in Indiana, inspired with liberal ideals, and schooled in law. But their personalities and views were as divergent as their accents and appearances. Lilienthal, having lost his midwestern tenor and style at Harvard, was the epitome of primness and polish. Willkie, still pronouncing power as "pa'ar," looked the part of a rumpled Hoosier even in a fresh-pressed suit. Like two men on opposite shores of the same river, they had ended up in separate worlds, taking different sides of the same passionate issue. The great divide between them began to grow ever wider.

THE WAR OF WORDS

While TVA and C&S were trying to checkmate each other in courtrooms and the marketplace, both parties were engaged in a war of ideas. *Tupelo* became a synonym for *yardstick*, as New Dealers treated the town as a trophy to the wisdom and virtue of TVA's low rates. Tupelo residents more than doubled their electricity use during the contract's first year, a success served up as "proof of the mismanagement and wrongdoing of private utilities."

Commemorating the contract's first anniversary, Roosevelt visited Tupelo in November 1934, praising the "yardstick" rates and the new hope and determination he saw in the faces of the people who had "not come by the thousands" to see him but "literally by the acres"—100,000, according to some reports. "There were people lined everywhere," recalled Frankie Kirpatrick. "You couldn't walk. You couldn't move. But we got to see him up close as his car passed at the hotel."

"People's eyes are upon you," FDR told multitudes filling the stands, outfield, and hillside of the city stadium. "You are going to give to the nation an example which will be a benefit not only to yourself but to the whole 130 million of Americans in every part of the land." And in a rash statement that threatened utility executives across the land, Roosevelt announced, "What you are doing here is going to be copied in every state of the union before we get through."

Regional lawmakers such as John Rankin continued to repeat old claims that Alabama Power had purchased Wilson Dam kilowatts for two mills and sold them for 5¢ to 10¢. "My God, what a racket!" Rankin told the National Conference of the Public Ownership League of America in February 1935. To the point that private utilities had expenses that TVA doesn't, he responded, "That is true. Here are some of them: dividends on watered stock . . . tributes to holding company . . . enormous salaries, which grafting officials and directors pay themselves . . . bonuses and other rake-offs . . . high-priced lawyers . . . expenses of propaganda . . . money spent to buy up newspapers and magazines . . . expensive lobbyists."

Willkie and other utility leaders responded with indignation. TVA's conservation program was only a masquerade, they argued, and the "yard-stick" was a flawed, meaningless concept with TVA rates based more on achieving results wanted than on the true cost of electricity, since the authority was free to allocate its expenses among multiple programs. At a time when the Federal Trade Commission was crucifying utilities for inflating investment values, TVA was playing a similar game of deflating investments by allocating the larger portion of dam construction to navigation and flood control, by not properly accounting for depreciation, and by "writing down" assets, booking only $21 million of Wilson Dam's $60 million cost.

"Thus we see that in both private and in public operation, the temp-tation to arrive at conclusions by bookkeeping rather than by actual method is somewhat alluring," Willkie told a joint meeting of the New York Economic Club and Harvard Business School Club. "Only it appears that the government outdoes the private industry."

The "yardstick" rates were an unfair comparison for other reasons, as well. TVA paid little or no taxes, interest, and return on capital invest-ments—expenses that ate up more than half of a utility's revenues. And being a government agency, TVA received a bundle of other subsidies.

"If TVA was to be an honest yardstick, it should observe the same requirements as those imposed upon the private utilities," said Willkie, claiming his companies could reduce residential rates 25 to 30 percent below TVA's and still earn the same income if given similar subsidies, gifts, and loans. By selling its power at less than cost, TVA operated at a deficit, and Willkie made sure every audience he addressed understood that those short-falls landed on the shoulders of taxpayers. "Whenever a householder in Tupelo, Mississippi, switches on a light, everybody in the United States helps

In Alabama, TVA sent representatives to community meetings to urge people to form co-ops instead of signing up for Alabama Power service, sometimes suggesting that government employees would lose their jobs if they didn't vote correctly. Alabama Power retaliated with a few scare tactics of its own, issuing a brochure with twenty-seven questions to ask before taking TVA power, including: "If some of the members of the association fail to pay their bills on time or don't pay them at all, won't you have to help make up the amount they fail to pay? If there is an accident to someone, who will be liable?" Although Alabama Power competed vigorously for the farmers, TVA was able to win more than half of the state's cooperative business.

Between the PWA, REA, and TVA, Willkie was feeling the big squeeze. Norris Dam was going up more rapidly than anyone had expected, and the C&S agreement with TVA would be ending a couple of years early. Then in February 1936, the Supreme Court ruled against the stockholders in the Ashwander case and reaffirmed the government's rights to dispose of Wilson Dam power any way it chose. Following the order, Alabama Power turned over the Wheeler Dam site and transmission facilities in northwest Alabama and began selling distribution systems to municipalities in the area. The company settled with Florence on July 15 and with Tuscumbia the following February. However, Martin was unable to reach an agreement with Sheffield, which had built a duplicate distribution system, forcing Alabama Power to take down and salvage its facilities there. Willkie began preparing for another lawsuit. In ruling on the Ashwander case, the Supreme Court had limited its judgment to Wilson Dam, leaving open the door for contesting the legality of TVA's other dams. It was time for C&S and other private utilities to band together in placing a big bet on their survival by stopping TVA through another legal contest.

"The present status is practically one of open warfare," Willkie wrote to Roosevelt on May 21, providing notice of the challenge he was about to launch. "As long as that status continues, the utilities in that district naturally feel that they are fighting for their lives and are obliged to defend themselves by every legitimate means." The lawsuit was filed eight days later in federal court in Tennessee. Some nineteen utilities united in the case, seeking to stop TVA from further raids on their markets. "They have seen their customers taken away from them, the value of their property seriously impaired, and the interests of their stockholders unfairly injured," explained Willkie. "Against this, they had only one immediate weapon—and that was the law." Known as the TEPCO case—Tennessee Electric Power Company being the first complainant listed—it would become the most important legal test of TVA's power program.

In fall 1936, as the lawsuit made its initial advance in the courts, Lilienthal notified Willkie that their "no-compete" agreement would end November 1. Great blocks of TVA power were about to become available. Chattanooga was at the top of Lilienthal's list of markets to take, the paperwork already prepared. Some 1,300 miles of transmission lines were almost complete, ready to carry Norris Dam power from Knoxville to Memphis, to communities in between, and to surrounding states where several municipalities were already building distribution systems. The Joe Wheeler Dam was almost complete, as well, and construction on four other dams was under way. In all, eleven TVA projects were planned for the next six years—eleven dams capable of producing 5.8 billion kilowatt-hours annually, about half the total capacity of all utilities in the seven states touched by the Tennessee Valley.

The final battle was about to begin.

Apprehension was high on all fronts. Lilienthal prepared for all-out war, blocking possible interference from Morgan by pushing through a board resolution "prohibiting any future agreement by TVA to stay out of Willkie's territory." Outvoted and outraged, Morgan appealed the decision directly to Roosevelt. The president put Morgan off, even though some of his advisors expressed fears the Tennessee Valley was about to explode—a situation far too volatile for the upcoming presidential campaign, they said. In his May letter to the president, Willkie also asked Roosevelt to intervene to help end the hostilities, saying, "You, and you alone, are the one person who has the power to bring such a settlement about." At the time, it had not been a priority, but now the animosities inside and outside TVA threatened to cost FDR valuable votes. Just as things were headed toward a catastrophic collision, the president held out an olive branch.

THE POWER POOL PEACE PIPE

The peace offering was developed by Alexander Sachs, an economic planner for FDR's National Recovery Administration and head of an investment firm interested in utility finance. He urged Roosevelt to have public and private producers pool their resources instead of competing with each other. TVA and C&S would each sell power into the pool, and electricity would be distributed to all users at uniform wholesale prices. The concept was similar recalled Louis Wehle, an expert on public corporation law who was one of only two neutral parties present. The six delegates from public power and six from private power—Willkie and Arkwright among them—sat strung in a single row facing the president. Viewpoints on how the pool would work were all over the board—ranging from a simple agreement to interchange surplus power only to an elaborate restructuring of the utility system under a joint corporation requiring congressional approval. The discussion soon degenerated into a Lilienthal and Willkie argument over fairness of the "yard-stick" and TVA's theft of C&S customers.

FDR ended the first session by calling for more engineering studies and an extension of the TVA-C&S agreement. Wehle was assigned the impossible task of mediating between Lilienthal and Willkie. Wehle was disgusted by the petty quarrels by the time Lilienthal and Willkie finally signed an extension October 7.

Following Roosevelt's landslide re-election in November, the power pool idea cooled considerably. Many of FDR's advisors saw no reason to continue cooperating with the utilities, particularly since most had supported Republican candidate Alfred Landon. "For God's sake, do not give our laurels of victory to those whom we have defeated," Norris urged the president, claiming Willkie's companies had resorted to "everything, which in their madness, they thought might injure either one of us." Rankin worked the House to generate several resolutions condemning the pool, and both Congress and the president were inundated with grassroots protests from Chattanooga, rumored to be stirred up by Lilienthal.

Roosevelt perhaps was looking for an opportunity to cancel the truce, when a good excuse arrived in the form of a federal district court ruling in the TEPCO lawsuit. On December 14, 1936, an order to stop TVA takeover activities while the case awaited trial was signed by Judge John J. Gore—grandfather of future vice president Al Gore. The injunction even prohibited TVA from extending its transmission facilities, and FDR soon sent word to the power pool participants that future talks were canceled. "The securing of an injunction of this broad character, under the circumstances, precludes a joint transmission facility arrangement and makes it advisable to discontinue these conferences," the president said.

Willkie responded that all parties knew the injunction application had been filed before the first power pool session was even scheduled. "I am unable to understand how the temporary injunction precludes either the pooling of transmission, the studying of the various problems arising out of the TVA operations, or the working out of a permanent solution," he replied to Roosevelt. Because TVA had declined to discontinue its attacks, he added, dismissing either the lawsuit or the injunction "would place our property at the mercy of the uncontrolled discretion of the TVA."

If the power pool idea had been introduced before the situation overheated, it might have solved problems for both TVA and C&S. It was the "right idea at the wrong time."

FIGHT TO THE FINISH

The Gore injunction shifted the balance of power suddenly to Willkie. Even after the "no-compete" agreement expired February 3, 1937, TVA's hands were tied while lawyers appealed Gore's injunction order. TVA and utility officials began living in courtrooms. Some fifty lawsuits were filed against the authority during the early operating years, but the TEPCO case, because of its constitutional challenge, commanded center stage. After his success at the polls, Roosevelt designed a "fix" for the lawsuit with a controversial proposal to reorganize the judicial system, a thinly disguised plan to force retirements and pack the Supreme Court with up to six new appointments. The high court had declared several New Deal programs unconstitutional, and the president feared TVA and other initiatives would be thrown out as well. Seen as a blatant effort to subvert the Constitution, many of FDR's longtime supporters deserted him on this issue, passing instead a measure giving retirement benefits to justices but making their retirements optional. TVA supporters, however, squeezed through a provision in the Judiciary Act that "fixed" the lower court by requiring a three-judge panel to rule in constitutional cases. That requirement proved helpful to TVA once the Gore injunction was overturned in May 1937 and the case remanded to a district court.

The district court trial proceeded with all the elements of a modern television courtroom drama. Trains pulling into Chattanooga were loaded with lawyers, many of the nineteen utilities sending representatives to observe or offer sideline strategies in smoky restaurants and hotel meeting rooms. Willkie, Martin, and other utility executives often observed from the galleries and, in the trial's early stages, were horrified to see their lead attorney, Newton D. Baker, fall stricken to the courtroom floor.

"The trial came to an abrupt halt," said Harllee Branch Jr., recalling Baker's sudden illness. Branch was a young attorney working as an assistant to the legal contingent representing Georgia Power. "We had to have him carried to the railroad station on a stretcher in an ambulance. He was loaded in a Pullman car and transmitted back for hospitalization in Cleveland, Ohio." Days later, Judge Walter Colquitt, head of Georgia Power's legal firm, traveled to Cleveland to confer with Baker. "He too became ill and never fully recovered," said Branch. "So in addition to all of the legal casualties from that trial, it also claimed the lives of Baker and Colquitt."

When the trial resumed, Raymond T. Jackson, new lead attorney for the utilities, laid out a case showing how TVA's growing electric power developments were overshadowing its major mission of navigation and flood control. He argued that selling electricity was a primary TVA goal, a plan that fraudulently replaced local and state regulation with federal and, because of the subsidies, represented unfair competition, resulting in a loss in value of utility business and property.

TVA principal lawyers James L. Fly and John Lord O'Brian contended that TVA's dams inevitably created hydroelectric power as a "by-product" of navigation and flood control goals, and they objected to virtually every offer of proof otherwise. With few exceptions, the objections were sustained by the court. At one point, an exasperated Jackson declared, "I didn't know that it is the rule that only the government can offer testimony" and resorted to prefacing each question with, "Let the record show that if the witness had been permitted to testify, he would have stated. . . ." When witnesses tried to prove TVA was selling power for millions of dollars less than cost, Judge Florence Allen declared that "rates of utilities and TVA are not material to this case—this is not a rate hearing." When Mississippi Power's Lonnie Sweatt explained his company's role in bringing electricity to towns that previously had none and recruiting new industries, the panel of judges deemed his testimony "remote" and refused to allow it.

Sensing the tide was turning against him that November, Willkie proposed a new formula for peace: have the Federal Power Commission set public and private power rates and set up an objective tribunal to determine the value of properties being sold to TVA. "What has the government to lose by making peace?" asked the *New York Times*. "Its only loss, on such terms as these, would be to surrender 'the utilities' as a political issue." The *New York Herald-Tribune* praised Willkie's proposal as "too honest . . . too straightforward and . . . too easy to understand to be dismissed with a gesture."

But dismissed it was. Lilienthal wouldn't accept arbitration, and the administration was not yet willing to make peace with an old, but still politically useful, enemy. FDR and Lilienthal also could sense the balance of power shifting back to TVA. They waited, and two important victories were soon delivered. On January 3, 1938, the Supreme Court ruled on *Alabama Power v. Ickes*, saying the company had no right to question the PWA's actions, successfully sidestepping the constitutional issues of the gifts and loans. Then on January 21, the federal district court at Chattanooga declared the TVA Act valid, ruling that the TVA program did not infringe on utilities' rights, that unlawful competition had not been proved, and that the complainants had no legal right to be protected from such competition even if it destroyed their business. It was a crippling defeat for the utilities, enabled in large part by the three-judge provision of the Judiciary Act. Gore dissented, but the rest of the panel ruled in TVA's favor.

The situation looked grim for Willkie. C&S stock was selling below $2 a share, and the bonds and preferred stocks of the southern subsidiaries were trading more than $88 million below par value. While the TEPCO case was being appealed, Willkie made a dramatic proposal—to sell "lock, stock, and barrel" all his operations in the valley at a price fixed by three arbitrators, to define respective market areas for public and private utilities, and to settle future disputes under the Federal Power Commission. Tennessee Governor Gordon Browning helped push Lilienthal back to the negotiating table by announcing his state would "join hands with TVA" in acquiring Willkie's operations.

Lilienthal had no incentive to speed up the process. With each passing month, TVA's position was improving. Alabama Power was losing battles in several cities, including Decatur, Russellville, Hartselle, and Guntersville, where some communities were already building duplicate distribution lines. Other north Alabama towns also voted for TVA power in 1938, including Martin's hometown of Scottsboro. In Mississippi, Sweatt was losing battles in Aberdeen and Columbus and struggling to keep those towns from building duplicate systems. And while Willkie and Lilienthal were negotiating, half a dozen other northeast Mississippi towns voted for public power. TVA was taking the territory "just like chicken taking corn off the ground," recalled Arno Mills, local manager of Mississippi Power's Forest office.

Although TVA didn't invade Georgia directly, it was instrumental in the formation of the North Georgia Electric Membership Cooperative (NGEMC), which built power lines in seven northwest Georgia counties, most of them parallel to Georgia Power lines. NGEMC agreed to confine its operations to rural areas, and Georgia Power withdrew from most rural areas but retained rights to serve municipalities and industries. Before the settlement, it wasn't unusual for lines built during the day to be torn down that night by the other party.

The situation was even worse in Tennessee. Two months after the ruling on the Ickes case, Chattanooga secured $4.33 million in PWA funds and an additional grant of $3.3 million later in the year. When TEPCO rebuffed offers for its distribution facilities, the city began drawing blueprints for duplicate lines. Parallel lines also were under construction in Memphis and Knoxville, turning the whole state into something of a war zone. TVA crews pirated customers by connecting them to the new lines, cutting off service from the private utilities, and sometimes setting their poles afire. Construction men on both sides carried guns stuck in their belts, and threats occasionally escalated into shootouts.

Meanwhile, Lilienthal was having his own shootout with Morgan, with TVA board meetings becoming a powder keg. Often with a prearranged agenda, Lilienthal and Harcourt Morgan presented and voted on decisions over the objections of Arthur Morgan, who grew more isolated and bitter, occasionally making disparaging statements about the integrity of his fellow board members and their "conspiracy, secretiveness, and bureaucratic manipulations." In turn, they accused him of refusing to carry out board decisions and "collaborating with private power companies."

Roosevelt finally called the three directors to his office for a series of "hearings" in March 1938. Appearing to be near a breakdown, Arthur Morgan grew more rigid with each question, called for a congressional investigation, and challenged the president's "right and the power to remove or to suspend me." Realizing Morgan would never yield, Roosevelt finally fired him.

Morgan lost his job but got the congressional investigation, during which he testified nearly six hours about "deceptive publicity regarding the yardstick" and "misleading accounting and reporting." Lilienthal bore the brunt of the barrage. Morgan accused him of "hypocrisy, arbitrariness, and misrepresentations" and called him "a scheming individual" who made a persistent attempt "to build up in the public mind a false understanding of the attitude of Commonwealth & Southern." The following day, Harcourt Morgan responded with a forty-four-page chronicle of the former chairman's campaign of "dissent and obstruction," and Lilienthal played the martyr, proclaiming, "I doubt, if in all the records of American public life, there can be found another instance of such an unfair attack upon the personal integrity of a colleague."

The hearings produced 101 witnesses, 15,470 pages of testimony, and 588 exhibits. Although the final report concluded that Arthur Morgan's charges were without foundation, the trial helped dispel the "yardstick" myth and raised considerable doubts about TVA policies and Lilienthal's questionable practice of changing TVA board minutes, particularly those related to his negotiations with Willkie.

When Willkie testified, he offered another dramatic idea for setting a price for facilities being sold to TVA, this time using valuations made by another New Deal agency. "If you can persuade the TVA to [accept this proposal]," he told Congress, "I publicly agree to abide by the valuation which the Securities and Exchange Commission may finally set upon our properties." Responses to the proposal were enthusiastic. "For a man on the spot, Mr. Willkie behaved in a manner that should draw the favorable attention of the public to the situation," reported the *New York Times.* "It is a pleasure to see Wendell L. Willkie . . . in action," said *Newsweek.* "His greatest offense is that he is articulate," said the *New York Herald-Tribune.*

Although Willkie's offer wasn't accepted by TVA, his appearance in Congress helped get negotiations back on track, and a settlement was being finalized when the ruling came on the TEPCO case. On January 30, 1939, the Supreme Court upheld the lower court's judgment, stating that in spite of damages claimed by the complainants, they nevertheless had no right to bring suit and had suffered no legal injuries since the franchises under which they operated were nonexclusive and did not protect them from competition. The utilities were bitterly disappointed that the Supreme Court refused to rule on the constitutional question in either the Ashwander or TEPCO case. "In short," said Willkie, "these two cases mean that a privately owned corporation has no standing to challenge either the direct business competition of the federal government or indirect competition made possible by federal gifts to state agencies, however unconstitutional the competition may be."

Two days after the ruling, Willkie signed an agreement to sell Tennessee Electric Power facilities for $78.6 million, close—ironically—to the offer Lilienthal had refused five years earlier. Willkie pressed for guaranteed protection from future invasion but received only an indirectly worded agreement from Julius Krug, TVA's chief power planning engineer, who helped draw up territorial lines in Willkie's office. Krug assured C&S that TVA was not interested in further expansion. "We have offered to purchase facilities in an area which will absorb our entire output," he wrote.

.Electric power battles propelled Wendell Willkie to political power. In Chicago, thousands cheered him as the Republican Party's nominee during the 1940 presidential campaign. Despite Willkie's robust, nationwide tour, victory belonged to Franklin D. Roosevelt (at right). *Bettmann/CORBIS*

FACING A DEATH SENTENCE

A BITTER WIND SWEPT ACROSS the frozen Potomac, whipping its way up the National Mall corridor all day January 24, 1935. Brave, fur-laden pedestrians darted around snowdrifts and scurried to shelter inside offices and hotels along the icy streets of Massachusetts and Maryland, Virginia and Vermont. At 1600 Pennsylvania Avenue, three utility executives stepped out of a car, grabbed fluttering papers, and rushed through the northwest gate entrance. The tall, clumsy one confronted the chill completely cloakless and hatless.

Wendell Willkie seldom bundled up, but he might have packed an overcoat this trip had he known what type of winter storm was approaching. The afternoon before, his train departed New York City just ahead of the heaviest blizzard to hit the East Coast since 1888. After blasting northern states with subzero temperatures, the storm dumped eleven inches of snow on Washington, D.C., keeping fifty-five plows and graders working through the night to clear downtown roads.

The tough-skinned Willkie brushed back a shock of unruly, dark brown hair and untangled his tie but gave no further thought to his disheveled appearance. His mind was on saving his company—saving Commonwealth & Southern from a bill being marked up that week by a congressional committee, a bill that would soon make its way to the floors of the House and Senate, a bill designed to bust up the holding companies that ruled over most of the nation's investor-owned utilities. Break them up or maybe kill them off altogether.

The harsh weather outside was but a prelude to the cool climate Willkie faced inside the White House. Considering the chiefs of private power to be robber barons, President Franklin D. Roosevelt had doled out special punishments to them during his first two years in office. He had invaded their markets with the creation of the Tennessee Valley Authority and the Public Works Administration, hit them with three types of federal taxes, and sent federal agents to search the high seas to capture utility magnate Samuel Insull for a politically charged trial designed to depict the collapse of his Commonwealth Edison empire as investor fraud. By 1935, Roosevelt was ready to crush the utility holding structure itself, calling for the "abolition of the evil of holding companies" in his State of the Union message. At a follow-up press conference, the president had corrected himself, admitting he meant to say the "*evils* of holding companies," since he didn't want to imply that all holding companies constituted an evil.

A fine point. Willkie took no offense to that, for he considered his own company to be innocent of the evils FDR referenced. In fact, Willkie was an outspoken critic of some of his industry peers, who loaded their books with arbitrary asset values, pyramided their corporate structures, and reported bogus paper profits by overcharging for services between self-dealing subsidiaries. Willkie called these practices "grotesque, wholly without reason," supported efforts to clean them up, and had been one of the few utility executives to cooperate with Benjamin Cohen, whom Roosevelt had borrowed from the PWA staff to draft a comprehensive bill for dealing with holding companies. Regulation was the answer, Willkie told Cohen, not abolition. Now Willkie had an eleventh-hour opportunity to talk directly to Roosevelt about his proposal to incorporate multistate holding companies and regulate them at the federal level.

Joining Willkie at the White House conference were C. E. Groesbeck, Electric Bond & Share chairman, and Harvey Couch, Arkansas Power & Light president. All three had operations under siege in the Tennessee Valley, so expecting that sore subject to come up, Roosevelt had invited David E. Lilienthal to the session. As director of TVA's power program, Lilienthal was well acquainted with all three utility executives.

Prior to congregating at the White House, the group met with Frank McNinch and Basil Manly, chairman and vice chairman of the Federal Power Commission. "Our discussions got no place," wrote Lilienthal. "Willkie looked tired and very low. Couch was suave and soothing but had nothing specific to offer. . . . Groesbeck kept saying in his best manner that of course nobody wanted to really abolish holding companies but only remedy their evils. . . . The bill did provide for abolishing holding companies, so his premise had something wrong with it."

Given the trio's inability to present a consensus view, the White House conference was ill-fated. Once inside the executive office, everyone gathered in a semicircle around the president's desk. Closest to FDR's left, Couch led the initial discussion on behalf of the utilities. The friendly banter soon gave way to grim faces once Roosevelt showed no signs of backing down from imposing a "death sentence" for holding companies. He personally had insisted Cohen include that clause in the bill. Willkie seemed off balance throughout the meeting and frustrated by his inability to work his usual persuasive magic. Getting "hotter and hotter," Willkie began arguing without using the proper "Mr. President" courtesy. "If you will give us a federal incorporation law, we can get rid of holding companies," he said, suddenly pulling his glasses from his coat pocket and using them as a pointer.

"Couch and Groesbeck recoiled as if Willkie had suddenly produced a gun and started shooting," wrote Lilienthal, who was delighted to see the conference flare into an open argument. "There had been a good deal of talk going around Washington that the reason why I hadn't worked out an agreement [for purchasing Tennessee Electric Power] with this very 'reasonable fellow' was that I was a pretty arbitrary person. And, at the time, I was glad to have the president see the way Willkie can perform on occasion."

FDR glared at Willkie, jutted out his chin, and grew less and less conciliatory as the talk got louder and louder. "Do I understand then," Willkie finally blurted, "that any further efforts to avoid the breaking up of utility holding companies are futile?"

"It is futile!" The president's curt pronouncement echoed through the room.

"After that," recalled Lilienthal, "we got out as quickly as could be done decently." In the antechamber, Couch and Groesbeck attempted to retrieve the situation by planning a follow-up meeting. Still "sulking and mad as hell," Willkie stood apart from the others and probably took a long walk to cool off in the winter wind before returning to his hotel room.

The idea of another meeting was soon dropped. It was futile.

SINS OF THE FATHERS

Fraud, deceit, misrepresentation, dishonesty, breach of trust, and *oppression* were terms used in press releases to describe the evils the parents supposedly procreated. The Federal Trade Commission (FTC) published a summary of these "crimes" it claimed had "taken sums beyond calculation from the rate-paying and investing public" at the conclusion of a seven-year investigation. The government's probe had been undertaken with a bias firmly in mind, a clear agenda to seek proof that holding companies were taking profits from the people's pockets. The investigation was "only to find out the evils of holding companies," complained Georgia Power president Preston Arkwright, "not a single solitary word in their report about the benefits." After spending several weeks in C&S offices in New York, one federal agent had congratulated Willkie on the way his organization conducted its business. When Willkie thanked him and asked, "Why don't you put that in your report?" the agent replied, "Mr. Willkie, I should be severely criticized if I put anything favorable to a utility holding company in my report."

Since 1928, proponents of "public power" had been using these FTC reports to attack the credibility of "private power." The findings helped Senator George Norris keep Muscle Shoals in government hands until the New Dealers could come to power and create TVA. Now Roosevelt would use the findings, together with a study conducted by the House Interstate and Foreign Commerce Committee, to reform the industry he most distrusted.

On February 6, 1935, the president's "final solution" was introduced in the House by Representative Sam Rayburn of Texas. Burton K. Wheeler of Montana sponsored the companion bill in the Senate. It was first called the Wheeler-Rayburn Act, then the Public Utilities Act, and later the Public Utility Holding Company Act of 1935. It would become known as PUHCA—a bill to dismantle the entire holding company edifice within the power industry. After introducing the measure, Wheeler told Willkie that if all the utilities had been as clean as C&S, the industry would not be in trouble with the administration. Economist and utility regulation pioneer James Bonbright also praised C&S as a corporate model that functioned as a holding company should. Therefore, Willkie believed there would be some differentiation made between responsible and irresponsible firms.

"Its sponsors say it is designed to put the utility holding companies out of business by 1940," Georgia Power's *Snap Shots* reported in its February 1935 issue. "More likely, the purpose of the bill is to terrify—to break the back of any and all opposition to the plan to substitute government ownership for private ownership in the electric business." At the time, constitutional challenges to both TVA and PWA still were undecided, and early court rulings had favored private utilities.

"Before we become alarmed," a *Snap Shots* editorial cautioned readers to wait for details: "We seriously doubt that the administration actually intends to bring about the widespread destruction and damage which would result from a wholesale slaughtering of each and every holding company, regardless of guilt or innocence."

The following month, *Snap Shots* carried a screaming headline, "DANGER!" and warned that the bill was even worse than first proclaimed, "causing an overturning and an upheaval throughout the company, from top to bottom, of such magnitude that the Georgia Power Company, as we know it, would cease to exist. . . . Quick death for the holding companies by execution is proposed. And slow death for the operating companies."

It was hardly an exaggeration. Initially, Title I of the act contained a "death sentence" clause that would have left few, if any, holding companies standing. The only exception to "execution" was for the Federal Power Commission to certify there was no economical way to split them up. FDR's National Power Policy Committee had already concluded in its report to Congress that there was no justification for "common control by a few powerful interests of utility plants scattered over many states and totally unconnected in operation."

Title II of the act was even more disturbing, intending to replace state regulation of operating companies with federal regulation. Local and state utilities would be grouped within regional districts so the government could oversee their joint planning and resource sharing. In addition to setting wholesale electricity's interstate price, the FPC could divide service territories to achieve more economic regroupings and direct the construction of new facilities or interconnections, transforming all transmission systems into common carriers managed through regional and national power grids.

"This, in effect, is government ownership without the necessity of paying to the owners of the property any compensation," said Willkie. Throughout as well, although the Federal Power Commission retained jurisdiction over wholesale interstate rates. Title I eventually was softened to permit holding company existence in cases justified by an integrated operation.

More compromises might have been won had it not been for an uproar over utility lobbying efforts to amend or stop the bill. More than 800,000 notes and telegrams flooded Congress during June's last two weeks as the bill was making its way through final markup in the House, and the lobbying grew so intense it became the subject of a special investigation. Congress already viewed the utility lobby as heinous, thanks to a series of Hearst newspaper reports that gave special attention to utility influence over newspapers and educational, religious, and political bodies. Several months before PUHCA was introduced, the FTC released two reports documenting more than a thousand pages of utility "propaganda and publicity" activities. Most findings were harmless—chambers of commerce dues, support of Rotary and Kiwanis clubs, fundraising for youth camps, and even a $60 donation to Piedmont Institute in Waycross, Georgia. Unfortunately, there also were enough examples of political gifts and vote-buying to give the impression that the books were loaded with those types of abuses. "The power trust is the greatest monopolistic corporation that has been organized for private greed," said Senator Norris, accusing utilities of "buying legislators, clergymen, and even Boy Scouts."

The Senate passed PUHCA on June 11 with the "death sentence" intact. The House, however, approved a watered-down version July 1, which allowed holding companies to continue indefinitely as long as the SEC found them to be in the public interest. The *New York Times* called the House vote "the most decided legislative defeat dealt to President Roosevelt since he assumed office." Enraged New Dealers blamed the "power trust," and FDR threatened to veto the final bill if it didn't retain the death clause. Rayburn labeled utilities "the richest and most ruthless lobby Congress has ever known," and in retaliation Alabama senator Hugo Black led one of the most ruthless investigations utilities would ever know.

A native of Clay County, Alabama, Black had been a successful trial lawyer, a captain in the army during World War I, and a prosecutor for Jefferson County before being elected to the Senate in 1926. A fiery populist, he was a staunch supporter of civil liberties, despite former ties to the Ku Klux Klan. Upon FDR's 1932 election, Black became one of the president's most fervent, some say "evangelistic," New Deal supporters. Black's probe uncovered unethical lobbying activities—bribing and strong-arming politicians, fake names on letters and telegrams, and job threats to utility employees who failed to write letters. Claiming the industry lobbyists had spent $1.5 million to generate a flood of mail, Black squeezed confessions from utility executives and Western Union employees to reveal an estimated 250,000 telegrams were signed with forged names—some from the city telephone directories, some from messenger boys paid 3¢ a signature, some from entire employee payroll lists and their next of kin, and some deceased or just made up. Also uncovered were ad placements used to buy favorable newspaper editorials, speech drafts provided to congressmen, and a box wrapped in newspapers delivered to one Texas representative, whose nephew boasted, "Hell no, that wasn't cigars!"

With bulldog tenacity, Black badgered every utility in the country, asking each to complete forms to document its lobbying sins. Georgia Power's Arkwright copied state newspapers on his response, showing that his company's lobbying expenses amounted to $7,567.83 and had involved "no fake letter and no fake telegrams." Willkie and his companies were not implicated directly in unethically opposing the PUHCA bill. The entire industry, however, was damaged by the bad behaviors Black uncovered during his hearings and by the outrage that followed, as utilities were called "creatures, wicked, cheats" on the floors of the House and Senate.

Most disturbing was Black's blistering cross-examination of Howard C. Hopson, who took pyramiding to new heights at his Associated Gas & Electric Company, which operated primarily in New York, Ohio, and Pennsylvania. He stacked up holding companies on top of subholding companies, on top of intermediate subsidiaries and other paper companies— more than 260 of them in a $1 billion pyramid controlled with only $50,000 of his investments at the top. He also used more than thirty-five kinds of securities to make it impossible for holders to sort out their rights and risks. Hopson had long evaded FTC and congressional committees, but Black threatened a nationwide manhunt before Hopson's attorney finally arranged for his surrender and appearance before Black's committee, where he was accused of spending at least $875,000 in the lobbying campaign even though his company had no money to pay dividends. Revelations about his fantastic financings showcased holding company manipulations at their worst and were partially responsible for retaining the "death sentence" within the compromise conference bill.

"Its size, its power, its capacity for evil, its greed, its trickery, deception, and fraud condemn it to the death it deserves," proclaimed Black when the held public office before. He was a Washington outsider. He was a recent party-switcher. In spite of all that, he proved to be a formidable campaigner, zigzagging across the country and whipping up more support than either of FDR's two former challengers. A gifted writer, Willkie also penned magazine articles critical of New Deal policies. In a speech to 200,000 in his hometown of Elwood, Indiana, he called for business growth as the solution to the nation's troubles: "I say that we must substitute for the philosophy of distributed scarcity the philosophy of unlimited productivity. I stand for the restoration of full production and re-employment by private enterprise in America." Even though Willkie captured 22 million popular votes—only 5 million fewer than FDR—he carried only 10 states and 82 electoral votes. Roosevelt took 38 states with 449 electoral votes.

Willkie never returned to C&S or big business, although he was flooded with offers from blue-chip corporations. He rejoined the legal profession briefly but could not remain apart from political life. He decided to visit war-torn England as a private citizen, but before his departure, Roosevelt summoned Willkie to the White House and gave him a package to hand-deliver to Prime Minister Winston Churchill. After key government officials and the royal family received him in a warm reception, his presence in the streets created a sensation. Several thousand people gathered outside his hotel room and cheered until he made an appearance on the balcony. When police tried to break up a crowd chasing him in the heavily bombed South Side district, Willkie waved the cops aside, hopped on a bicycle, and yelled, "Everything's dandy." When he made his way into a shelter during an air attack, an old man with a harmonica began playing "The Star-Spangled Banner," and brave Londoners spontaneously joined in singing America's national anthem. Slapping him on the back, a woman said, "Go home and tell them we can take it."

Upon his return, Willkie reported on the courage and struggles he witnessed and England's dire need for armaments. He debated leading isolationists, including Charles Lindbergh, and was successful in delivering critical Republican votes for the Lend-Lease Act. Roosevelt expressed his gratitude by naming Willkie one of his special envoys, sending him to China, the Soviet Union, and a dozen Middle Eastern countries, Eastern Europe, and North Africa. The goodwill tour helped demonstrate U.S. unity to Allied leaders. Willkie met with heads of state, but what moved him most were encounters with ordinary people in the streets, shops, and public places. In Moscow, at the end of a Bolshoi Ballet performance, the crowd roared, "Willkie! Willkie!

Willkie!" when he presented a bouquet to a prima ballerina. His account of that journey and vision for a better future became a best-selling book, *One World,* in 1943 and helped influence U.S. foreign policy and a generation's support of the United Nations.

Returning to law, he successfully argued a landmark civil liberties case before the Supreme Court in 1943 and became a passionate critic of racism and religious intolerance—"the only man in America," a labor leader proclaimed, "who has proved that he would rather be right than be president." Willkie was not yet finished with politics, however. He tried again in 1944 to win the Republican presidential nomination but withdrew from the race after an early defeat in the Wisconsin primary. Later that year, in a shock to the nation, he was hospitalized with a streptococcal infection, suffered a series of heart attacks, and suddenly died. At age fifty-two, he was laid to rest back home in Indiana.

"This corporation's personnel was fortunate," concluded a C&S board resolution, "in having years of close contact with a professional and business leader whose counsel and ability in managing the system's operations and protecting its property rights, whose generous good fellowship with all his associates, and whose consideration of the rights of employees and his especial personal regard for them, endeared him to all."

WHITING: A PONTIFF FOR LINGERING LAST RITES

Compared with Willkie's magnetic personality and showmanship, Justin R. Whiting was as dry as an undoctored Idaho spud. His wife once said she never knew whether he had one suit or thirty. They were all the same color, same material, and same cut. He was the perpetual introvert: shy, self-conscious, stuffy, and formal. He was perfect—perfect for the job of leading Commonwealth & Southern during the 1940s, a decade dominated by interminable hearings and legal proceedings that took many paths but eventually led to the inevitable dissolution of the company.

A native of St. Clair, Michigan, Whiting received his law degree in 1907 from the University of Michigan and practiced in Port Huron, Jackson, and Detroit before returning in 1921 to Jackson, where he began his association with C&S by handling legal matters for Consumers Power. In 1933, when Willkie moved into the C&S executive offices, Whiting moved into Willkie's spot on the legal team and began handling cases for all the subsidiaries. Again following Willkie, Whiting became C&S president July 17, 1940.

Whiting shared more traits with Tom Martin than he did with Willkie. A stickler for details, Whiting was completely dedicated to his work. Like Martin, he was fussy, methodical, and responsible to the extreme. He also was short in stature. A special long-legged chair was moved into the boardroom so Whiting would appear taller during board meetings. During the SEC hearings, Whiting's calm and pontifical manner reminded some people of an Episcopal bishop. Others credited him with handling a difficult job with dignity and skill, picking up the pieces and wrangling through proposals and counterproposals to unscramble C&S in a way that would protect stockholders.

Whiting initially shared Willkie's optimism that C&S might be able to justify retaining most of its empire. The Southern Group was an established model for integrated operations, even though its northern territories were isolated islands of electric service. To strengthen interconnections among the Northern Group, Whiting acquired Michigan-based Citizens Light & Power, strategically situated between his two largest subsidiaries in that region. And in responding to innumerable SEC notices and questions, he presented a convincing case for keeping his company together. On March 19, 1941, however, the commission delivered a surprising answer to the problem of what to do with C&S—a 317-page report that gave Whiting three choices: keep Consumers Power and dispose of all other properties; keep Alabama Power and possibly the Mississippi and Gulf companies and dispose of the others; or keep Georgia Power and possibly South Carolina Power and dispose of the others. The report warned that the choices were tentative, since the SEC reserved the right to mandate further divestment if it later decided the company or any group was still too large.

Whiting was unprepared for the hard-line verdict. The market didn't expect that type of news either. C&S stock fell below $1 a share and would be trading for less than a dime within a year. "It must come as a shock to the stockholders of Commonwealth, as it did to its management," Whiting wrote to investors, "that the commission should find even tentatively that the economic and efficient operation of the southern companies under the Commonwealth's ownership should be broken up." The verdict was even more extraordinary considering the building program C&S had initiated in support of national defense, an effort Roosevelt had stepped up dramatically since the outbreak of war in Europe.

"The territory we serve is critical to the armament program and includes military establishments from Camp Custer at Battle Creek, Michigan, to the naval defense area at Pensacola, Florida," Whiting explained. "The times are critical. No one can afford to do anything which might make the electric industry less efficient than it now is. Everyone recognizes that the future power supply of this country is vital to our national interest."

Whiting asked the commission to appoint a committee of government and industry representatives, independent engineers, and economists to set reasonable standards for enforcing PUHCA, but the suggestion was ignored. Some SEC leaders used national defense as a reason for speeding up proceedings and believed that splitting up the holding companies would bring about better and cheaper service. "The present scattered systems have 'Balkanized' the utility assets of this country," said SEC chairman Edward C. Eicher. "The resultant hodgepodge utility operations require the surgery of Section 11 [PUHCA's 'death sentence' clause] in order that integrated utility properties may be developed in accordance with the power needs of the area served."

During the months leading up to America's entry into World War II, the commission worked out key legal issues and guidelines for enforcing PUHCA, and, with little hope of retaining the Northern Group, Whiting prepared his first plan for splitting off those utilities and continuing C&S operations as the parent of its five southern subsidiaries. The new plan, submitted July 2, 1941, acknowledged that the bid for retaining the C&S empire was lost; Whiting and his southern CEOs threw everything behind a big bet to keep the Southern Group together.

When the attack on Pearl Harbor focused the nation's energies on converting industries into wartime production, utility executives complained loudly that the SEC hearings were a distraction. Many sent pleas to Roosevelt. "Is it not reasonable and proper that such proceedings be halted until the war has been won?" wrote Jim Crist, South Carolina Power vice president. "We've got a bear by the tail. By the grace of God, we will handle the bear, but let us give him our undivided attention until he's handled." Although the hearings continued unabated, executives admitted later the government didn't press as hard to dissolve the companies as it would have.

Throughout that period, Whiting responded to SEC mandates for whittling down capital structures and organizations. By forcing holding companies to go to one classification of securities, the SEC believed the assets could be more easily and fairly dismantled. As the war in the Atlantic and Pacific raged, Whiting eliminated C&S preferred stock, filed plans for distributing the company's common stock, sold seven transportation properties, and merged two northern subsidiaries. As for his plans to continue C&S operations in the South, Whiting received no encouraging words from the commission. By the end of 1942, the SEC had already generated 5,000 pages of testimony on the southern subsidiaries, and the mountain of paper continued to grow throughout the war years.

ENERGIZING THE WAR ENGINES

While Whiting was shepherding C&S through these legal battles, Eugene Yates was overseeing the company's response to a more important battle, World War II. Considered an engineering genius and a master of details, Yates commanded the respect of all C&S's operating units. He had played a critical role in the company's success throughout its history, standing tall behind all his bosses as chief engineer for James Mitchell, as architect of the southeast integration plan and general manager for Tom Martin, as executive engineer for B. C. Cobb, and as southern operations coordinator under Wendell Willkie. For Whiting, Yates would continue to manage the Southern Group while returning to the business of building steam plants and dams.

The excess capacity C&S had available throughout the Depression quickly disappeared as global aggressions reignited the engines of industry. As early as 1937, the Northern Group was adding capacity, but the Southern Group couldn't finance construction until after the battles with TVA were resolved in 1939. The need for additional power in the South was growing more urgent. In December 1939, Yates participated in a planning session directed by the newly established National Power Policy Committee, which expressed concerns about inadequate power reserves in the Southeast, especially in the Tennessee Valley, where a giant aluminum company was located that would be critical to the production of military aircraft. For that reason, C&S's Southern Group, TVA, and the aluminum company were treated as a common "power region," which the policy committee said would be short of capacity by 1941. As soon as he returned from that session, Yates increased his construction program. Six months later, following a similar meeting held by the Federal Power Commission in Atlanta, Yates again moved up his schedules and added 100,000 kilowatts of capacity to his construction plans. The government's concerns were well-founded. Power shortages arrived early, during a prolonged drought stretching through the 1940 and 1941 "rainy" seasons.

To keep power flowing to defense manufacturers, voluntary curtailments from nondefense customers started in May 1940. Dependent almost entirely on hydroelectricity, TVA was so short of reserves that the U.S. Office of Production Management (OPM) and the U.S. Army ordered mandatory curtailments and power pooling of forty utilities throughout the surrounding thirteen-state region. Air-conditioning and outside lighting were shut down. Even restaurants, hotels, gas stations, and movie houses were prohibited from lighting signs and marquees. Yates poured everything available into the Tennessee Valley and moved George Middlemiss into the OPM temporary offices in Atlanta to help direct the emergency effort. Donald M. Nelson, OPM's director of priorities, sent a special note to Yates praising the "operation of the Southeastern Power Pool . . . as well as the results of the conservation program." During his testimony before the SEC, Yates used the experience as an example of why the Southern Group should not be split up, and Whiting told stockholders: "We believe that the principles of unified operation, which have been developed and applied by our southern companies for many years, have been demonstrated in a most graphic manner to be economical and in the public interest."

Although the mandatory pooling order was extended into January, the emergency power curtailment order was canceled December 5, 1941, two days before the attack that brought the United States directly into the war. Demand for power rapidly accelerated beyond anyone's greatest expectation. Existing industries stepped up operations to three shifts, and new war factories, army camps, flying fields, and other military loads sprang up almost overnight. Hattiesburg doubled its population in six months with the opening of Camp Shelby; counting the troops, it became Mississippi's second-largest city. Along the Atlantic and Gulf coasts, new shipbuilding plants were constructed and others expanded. Mobile's population nearly doubled, and military towns boomed from Biloxi to Pensacola, from Anniston to Montgomery, from Savannah to Columbus. Metropolitan regions such as Atlanta and Birmingham also benefited economically from nearby armaments, aircraft manufacturing, assembly plants, and iron and steel industries.

Yates hustled to meet the energy needs fueled by this growth. At one point during the height of the building period, his team was designing or constructing twenty-six different units for C&S subsidiaries. From 1940 to 1947, the Southern Group added 450,000 kilowatts of capacity, including two units at Plant Atkinson, three at Plant Arkwright, and one at Plant

Mitchell in Georgia; two at Mobile, two at Gorgas, and an expansion of Mitchell Dam in Alabama; one at Plant Eaton in Mississippi; and one in Florida. In 1942, shortages of materials caused the government to mandate delays on the construction of the Mississippi and Florida units. To fill the energy gap, Gulf Power secured a surplus Navy floating power plant, barged it through the Intracoastal Waterway, and kept the electricity flowing to the military bases in Pensacola until Yates was able to work out a new contract with TVA to purchase surplus power near the war's end.

World War II affected the company in many ways beyond construction and engineering. Sales programs, for example, were canceled as appliances became scarce. The company and the War Production Board began running aggressive conservation campaigns, urging the public to limit electricity or gas consumption to bare essentials, thereby releasing additional fuel and manpower for more vital defense needs. Electricity demand was growing 15 percent a year but would have been much higher without the conservation programs.

Like most companies, C&S utilities constantly marketed war savings bonds through employee payroll deduction plans and promoted recycling, victory gardens, and sensitivity in handling customer relations. "These are the days when a feller needs a friend," proclaimed Mississippi Power's handbook on customer service. Arkwright told his employees, "The stress of war does things to the emotions of people" and asked employees to demonstrate "kindness, consideration, a spirit of helpfulness" to customers. C&S lost 4,090 employees to the armed services, 20 percent of its work force. By the war's end, 72 employees had given their lives in service, 2,500 were still in uniform, and 1,223 had been re-employed, while others found work elsewhere. As part of its postwar planning to make positions available for returning employees, C&S developed a pension plan in 1944, its first formal program for releasing employees who had reached the normal retirement age, providing an annual compensation based on age and years of service.

In spring 1945, as the Allies were pushing Germans across the Rhine and wartime pressures began to ease, the SEC sent a signal that C&S would not be permitted to survive even as the parent of the five southern subsidiaries. Whiting met with George Roberts and Hayden N. Smith, partners in the New York law firm of Winthrop, Stimson, Putnam & Roberts. After spearheading the battle to preserve C&S and retain as much of the corporate structure as possible, Whiting, Roberts, and Smith came to terms with the fact that no plan short of disbanding the corporation would satisfy the SEC.

They began work on what was their sixth plan, the one that called for dissolving C&S and releasing the northern subsidiaries as independent entities—and creating a new holding company in the South.

But the SEC withheld its verdict on the plans for creating Southern Company until January 1947, when it agreed to support the new parent company under two conditions—that the operating companies dispose of all transportation and gas properties and that C&S sell South Carolina Power Company.

Almost immediately after getting the order, Alabama Power sold its gas properties in Phenix City and bus transportation in Tuscaloosa; Gulf Power signed contracts to sell its Pensacola gas companies; and Georgia Power negotiated the sale of gas properties in Columbus and Americus. Other sales followed, but it would take several years to find buyers for some of the transportation units and overcome local and state opposition to separating the services.

The mandate to sell South Carolina Power was disappointing. It was as integrated into the system as the other Southern Group utilities, Whiting argued. But the SEC just said "no." South Carolina was one more state removed from the coordinating center in Birmingham, an arbitrary decision driven largely by the SEC's determination to control the size of holding companies it let out of the PUHCA gates. Whiting had no choice but to place South Carolina Power on the auction block, and the most determined bidder emerging was state-owned South Carolina Public Service Authority, referred to as Santee Cooper.

"I was determined to prevent this if I could," said Crist, who had fought a bitter war with Santee Cooper ten years earlier when it had used PWA money to build a hydro plant and steal away some of South Carolina Power's customers. Crist pleaded for a last chance to find another buyer, and largely through his efforts the utility was eventually sold to investor-owned South Carolina Electric & Gas. Although PUHCA legal proceedings would drag on for two more years, the concept of creating Southern Company had been approved. Except for South Carolina Power, the utilities that Tom Martin had assembled in the 1920s would remain together.

C&S would be dissolved, and no one was happier about that than Martin. "It was one of his greatest hours," wrote Martin's biographers. After having lived under the shadow of C&S for twenty years, he was able to see the light of liberation approaching and probably felt he had been personally redeemed for his moral stand against C&S. "Condemned," Martin wrote in his book a few years later. "The company of scattered enterprises . . . was condemned by the act of Congress. The company of sister, interconnected companies in adjoining states of the South is an economic and physical natural."

Commonwealth & Southern had been condemned. Southern Company had been blessed. The big bet James Mitchell had made on creating a south-eastern energy market, the dream that Martin had advanced by first bringing together the southern utilities, the dream that Yates had engineered and helped build—that vision was again shining brightly.

LESSONS LEARNED

The same forces that spawned the TVA, PWA, and REA progeny also gave birth to PUHCA. The loss of confidence in business leadership and the hatred of privileged monopolies allowed Roosevelt to break up groups like banking and utility holding companies at the same time he was trying to pump up the nation's economic engines. Some political analysts criticized Roosevelt for policies that went in two directions at the same time. But following contradictory paths also helped him retain political power since it reflected the nation's mixed emotions during the chaos of the Depression years, when all manner of populists, socialists, communists, utopians, agrarians, and demagogues were demanding action and offering solutions from "redistributing the wealth" to completely dismantling capitalism. In that environment, utility holding companies became a natural target. Attacking them provided a convenient pressure-release valve, an outlet for the nation's disenchantment and distrust of big business.

Martin believed Commonwealth & Southern had played its part in building up these hostilities. Its merger, he claimed, had been unwise and uneconomic. Certainly, C&S was uneconomic from the standpoint of those investors who bought its stock immediately after its creation in 1929, just before the stock market crash. And by leading the industry fight against TVA and "government takeover," C&S drew more political fire than many holding companies. Otherwise, its guilt is debatable given the prominent role that it played throughout the 1930s. C&S helped sustain its subsidiaries during financial famines induced by the Depression and federal invasions, a decade during which southern subsidiaries could not raise a nickel of new investment. The holding company also provided the leadership and legal support essential to containing TVA and producing a less punitive PUHCA.

It supplied engineering and management support to build critical generation needed during America's greatest military buildup. It fostered industrial development, expanded rural electric service, helped its subsidiaries reduce costs to customers, and introduced benefits such as the pension plan and other personnel policies. In short, C&S demonstrated the advantages of a holding company structure, advantages that were critical to convincing the SEC the southern operations should remain together.

Commonwealth & Southern may have been among the best of the holding companies, but it was still condemned by association. The fate of C&S had been decided two decades earlier, when it was damned by the very institution that created it. The company was, after all, the product of mergers manipulated by investment bankers, the child of the corrupt system that brought about PUHCA. It didn't matter that C&S grew up to be a responsible adult. It would suffer the same fate as the most abusive of holding companies. The lesson was clear: An entire industry can be tainted and brought down by the actions of a few wrongdoers. In 1938, there had been 214 registered holding companies controlling 922 electric and gas subsidiaries and 1,054 nonutility companies. By 1949, 72 holding companies remained under SEC review. By 1958, only 18 were left. Giants like Electric Bond & Share and the Insull holdings were splintered into dozens of pieces. One of the large integrated groups evolved into American Electric Power, another one became Middle South Utilities, later called Entergy. Some units became independent operating companies, like Florida Power & Light and Commonwealth Edison of Chicago. One of Electric Bond & Share's subsidiaries, Birmingham Electric Company, became part of Alabama Power, enabling Martin to finally serve directly the customers in his headquarters city. One of the Insull properties—Georgia Power & Light, serving the southern section of Georgia from Valdosta to Waycross—became part of Georgia Power.

A few people, like Howard Hopson, were sentenced to jail for mail fraud, which at the time was virtually the only federal crime that could be used to convict those engaged in securities fraud. After a prison term, Hopson died in a sanitarium, shattered mentally and physically. His unethical dealings contributed a great deal to the perception that the nation's electric utilities were being run by crooks.

After highly publicized trials, Samuel Insull was eventually found not guilty. Even a jury of "little people" decided in his favor when his questionable methods could not be proven illegal after his attorneys showed that his accounting systems were used by the government itself. Some jurors may have felt Insull already had been punished enough since his personal fortunes had been wiped away with his empire's collapse. Three years after his last trial, Insull fell dead awaiting a subway train in Paris. The man who once reigned over an eighth of America's electric utilities was found with the equivalent of 8¢ in French currency on his body. Although vindicated by the legal system, he forever remained guilty in the court of public opinion. His positive contributions to the industry were forgotten, and his very name became a symbol for wrongdoing and the excesses of the old holding company system that made its destruction necessary.

The lessons from these excesses and the narrow SEC doorways through which each newborn had to squeeze helped shape a new type of holding company for the future—rigid in its accounting systems, simplified in its organization and financial structure, highly ethical and prescriptive in its business practices, attentive to regulatory and legal implications of its decisions, restricted in its ability to diversify, and conservative in its management, strategy, and operations. No holding company would reflect these characteristics more than Southern Company, the first to be approved by the commission.

A half-century later, some lessons from the age of holding company abuses would have to be relearned when a new breed of high-flying marketers would enter and conquer a changing and competitive energy landscape. This new millennium breed would dredge up the same questionable practices of the old holding companies—pyramiding, off-balance-sheet partnerships, fictional earnings and write-ups, unethical affiliate transactions, insider trading, and stock price manipulations. The abuses of giants such as Enron would bring crashing down a whole new segment of the energy field and inflame once again the ire of government, investors, and the public. At the height of this New Age feeding frenzy, many utilities would be tempted to join the competitive and speculative games Enron was playing. And they would suffer dearly. The more traditional energy companies like Southern Company would take a cautious approach, venturing only on the margins of the impetuous playing fields but also escaping burial under the collapse— ironically saved in part by the conservative constraints of the 1935 act their predecessors had fought so hard to kill.

More than any other piece of legislation, PUHCA shaped the industry by placing federal restrictions on the scope, structure, and ownership of electric utilities, and by creating legal parameters within which the industry was allowed to develop in the twentieth century. In addition to owing its creation to PUHCA, Southern Company would function for seven decades under its purview with every aspect of its operations, financings, disclosures, accounting, affiliate transactions, and political activities being scrutinized by the SEC. Over the years, attempts would be made to reform or repeal the act—during the 1970s when utilities would need to diversify in attempts to prop up profits and during the 1980s when they would seek to participate in a growing independent power production business, a right eventually granted in 1992. Though slightly modified, PUHCA would stand for seventy years—long after its main goals had been achieved and long after the act was considered obsolete, given numerous other laws, industry reforms, disclosure requirements, and the increasing number of other utility regulations.

The 1935 act would eventually be abolished by the Energy Policy Act of 2005, bringing an end to SEC oversight and onerous restrictions brought on by mistakes of a bygone era. PUHCA's repeal also would reopen doorways to new utility mergers and diversification. But by then, the energy marketplace would be dramatically transformed, and utilities would be operating in a world very different from the one Arkwright, Martin, Willkie, and Whiting had known.

Shortly after its formation, Southern Company placed its first ads (above top) in national business publications. First president Eugene Yates (seated) with his executive team (L-R): Tom Martin, Harllee Branch Jr., Lonnie Sweatt, Herbert Scholz, James Barry, C. B. McManus, and Jim Crist. At right, an initial share issued when Southern Company split off from Commonwealth & Southern. *GPC Archives*

YOU COULD CALL IT A WAR-BOOM BABY. SOUTHERN COMPANY
was conceived two months after Japan surrendered aboard the
USS *Missouri.* Although November 9, 1945, was meticulously
typed on its certificate of incorporation, the newborn
company remained little more than a paper organization long
after most soldiers returned home to father America's boomer
generation. For nearly two more years, Alabama Power,
Georgia Power, Gulf Power, and Mississippi Power remained
Commonwealth & Southern subsidiaries while waiting for the
Securities and Exchange Commission to decide their fate. In
breaking apart utility giants like C&S, as mandated by the
Public Utility Holding Company Act (PUHCA) passed ten
years earlier, the SEC was reluctant to approve utility groups
of any substantial size.

Hayden Smith's sharp legal wits and Eugene A. Yates's
engineering mind chipped away at that hard-line position,
trying to convince commissioners of sound reasons for the

four utilities to remain together under a holding company arrangement. Lead counsel for C&S, Smith was a Yale graduate who had worked for Chief Justice William Howard Taft in Washington, D.C., before joining Winthrop, Stimson, Putnam & Roberts, at which he had become a senior partner. In masterminding the strategy to gain SEC approval for Southern Company's formation, Smith brought before the commission credible witnesses to prove the southern utilities of C&S achieved substantial economies by working together. Time and again, he called on Yates to deliver those messages in rational, analytical terms. Vice president over the Southern Group utilities since 1932, Yates presented data proving how integrated operations saved at least $3.4 million annually and how separating the group would cost $24 million in new capital to build 220,000 kilowatts of additional capacity needed if the utilities no longer shared reserves.

The commissioners, however, did not understand the extent of integrated planning and operations taking place among the Southern Group. They asked each witness why the same savings could not be achieved through interconnections, cooperation, and contracts among independent companies. The savings "required more than cooperation," explained Yates. "Common ownership would be needed to centralize planning, location of plants and lines, and operations in the interest of the entire group."

"It is a very difficult thing to take those companies and chop them off from the thing that makes them run," said Georgia Power vice president Charles Collier. "It would decrease the efficiency if the C&S group in the South were broken up," added E. W. Robinson, Alabama Power's vice president of operations. "We would lose certain benefits that we now gain and that run to all of the companies in the group."

"I think the effect would be disastrous. The savings would disappear and the economies would disappear," said Lonnie Sweatt, Mississippi Power's general manager. "It would increase cost," added L. C. Parks, Gulf Power's general manager. "I would have to put in generating plants to protect myself."

"I don't think you could develop a contractual relation to obtain the benefits that are obtained under single ownership," said C. B. McManus, Georgia Power's director of operations. Having managed operations at both Alabama Power and Georgia Power, McManus showed how the two companies were geographically and economically compatible and how, if separated, they could not coordinate their plants and operations "as efficiently as companies which are under common ownership." Over the course of several months, McManus was called back to address SEC questions, and his testimony marked a turning point in the hearings.

The commissioners were at last persuaded. On August 1, 1947, the SEC formally blessed the creation of Southern Company and authorized it to own and operate the properties of Alabama Power, Georgia Power, Gulf Power, and Mississippi Power as a single, integrated and coordinated system. Language in the order reflected the impact of sermons preached by Smith, Yates, McManus, and other operating company witnesses: "According to the record, there are substantial savings in operating costs and fixed charges resulting from coordinated planning and operations. Power supply economies are achieved through sharing of reserve capacity and through joint planning of generating facilities so as to stagger construction and cause facilities to be erected at the sites of cheapest operation, irrespective of corporate limits. Further power supply economies result from central load dispatching whereby, by the control of reservoirs, run of river, and fuel-electric plants, substantial amounts of water which might otherwise be wasted are conserved, and thereby the need for additional generating facilities with accompanying fixed charges is averted or delayed."

The company's official birthday was celebrated September 1, 1947, when C&S transferred an initial equity investment of 10 million shares of common stock to the new firm, and the four operating companies became subsidiaries of The Southern Company—"The" remaining part of the legal name until the unnecessary article was officially dropped in 1996. Although it began operating as a separate entity with its own board and officers, Southern Company was not yet completely free of the old parent. Before C&S could be dissolved, the rest of its assets had to be separated and distributed among all the subsidiaries being spun off. Obtaining regulatory and shareholder approvals would take more time. In the interim, Southern Company took up the challenges of building a new organization, putting management talent in place, financing a growing construction program, and promoting the economy of its defined territory. Coordinating much of those efforts fell on the broad shoulders of Yates, selected by the board to head the new utility group.

For forty-five years, Yates had been a man in the background, enabling the success of five leaders of predecessor companies. The supporting role suited his style. He was extraordinarily brilliant but painfully shy. He was a towering giant of a man, about 250 pounds, with big feet and long arms, requiring his clothes to be tailor-made. In college, he once "imprisoned" fraternity mates in the dining hall simply by stationing himself at the exit and stretching his arms across the double-doorway opening. On observing his wide strides in crossing the street with his team, one of his executives once quipped he looked like "Mother Goose Yates," with a covey of "baby goslings" trotting along behind, trying to keep pace.

He was approaching age sixty-seven when the board asked him to be president. "We cannot afford to lose him as long as he is willing to stay with us," said Tom Martin, CEO of Alabama Power. Leading the company would mean stepping out of the background and into the spotlight, but it was not Yates's nature to walk away from a job unfinished. So it wasn't surprising that Yates postponed his retirement and agreed to see the company through its rebirth.

MAKING SOUTHERN COMPANY SOUTHERN

At the time of its formation, Southern Company was serving 730,000 customers in a 94,000-square-mile territory in the Southeast with nearly 1.4 million kilowatts of generating capacity, almost half of which was hydro. On March 29, 1948, Southern Company declared its first dividend—15¢ a share. All proceeds went to the old parent, since C&S continued to hold all Southern Company's common stock while awaiting SEC approval of plans for splitting up the assets. Separating the new company from the old—and establishing an independent structure and identity for Southern Company— became a two-year challenge for Yates, as well as Justin Whiting, who as CEO of C&S was still commander in charge of the restructuring plan.

Not the least of Yates's challenges through the transitional years was mediating between the divergent views of Whiting and Martin, two strong-willed directors on his board. A Michigan native, Whiting was planning to remain in the north after the split-up to head Consumers Power—the largest of C&S's northern utilities—but he wanted to keep together as much of the existing C&S organization and services as the law would allow. Martin wanted to re-create the success of the former Southeastern Power & Light, the system of companies he had put together two decades earlier before it was taken over by northern aggression. The incompatible philosophies of the two men began colliding during the first strategy sessions at Atlanta's Henry Grady Hotel in spring 1946. Yates had been named chairman, but Whiting pushed to have a separate position of president established so it could go to Granville H. Bourne, controller of Consumers Power and a financial officer with the C&S service organization. Whiting's first draft of the bylaws and organizational plans also called for keeping Southern Company headquartered in New York at existing C&S offices at 20 Pine Street. Its board of directors and officers also would continue to be dominated by northern representatives, and all budgeting, financing, and engineering functions would be performed under contract with the existing New York-based C&S service organization. That was a model being promoted by several other utility giants such as Electric Bond & Share, which divested its utilities while reinventing itself as EBASCO Services to continue performing many management services for the individual parts of its former empire—under highly profitable contracts.

That was not the model of a "southern" company that Martin had in mind. Although Southern Company had been incorporated in Delaware and would keep a New York office, those were the only things northern about it. All the new company's operations were in the South; therefore, its board should be dominated by southerners and its service organization based in the South, argued Martin, who had the wits and legal background to do battle with Whiting. The tug-of-war erupted into an ugly public argument aboard a train bound for Wilmington, Delaware, for the February 1947 board meeting. Martin's temper boiled when he discovered that his suggested changes had not been incorporated into Whiting's draft of the bylaws.

"I have decided, and this is what it is going to be," said Whiting.

"We will not accept anything that takes away our freedom," Martin shot back. "This company is going to be a true southern company, and I will never yield on that."

Aboard a return train to Birmingham the following day, Martin dashed off a more reasoned, though still impassioned, letter to Whiting that emphasized the advantages of creating a separate service organization and making Yates both chairman and president. Neither Whiting nor his predecessors found it necessary to have two top officers, Martin argued and, furthermore, Bourne was ill-suited for the job as president. "He is highly competent in the field of accounting," Martin wrote, "but has had no experience, so far as I know, in the complex problems of public relations and the innumerable things that are involved in the development of goodwill of our business so essential to our enterprises. No one knows these things better than you do." If the company was to have both chairman and president, said Martin, then the president should be someone "well known in the South" who would "live in Atlanta all of his time."

Yates kept peace with Whiting while advancing Martin's views in logical, unemotional terms. By the time the SEC had approved Southern Company's creation, Whiting had agreed to have Yates named president and eliminate the title of chairman. Bourne was bumped to the position of vice president. Also elected as vice president at the August 1947 board meeting was Jim Crist, a southerner who previously served as a South Carolina Power officer and who had early career ties to Alabama Power. Those were significant concessions, but over the next two years Yates and Martin brought about many other changes that helped put a southern stamp on the company—a mission aided by the counsel of Eugene W. Stetson, a native Georgian and retired chairman of New York's Guaranty Trust Company, who was instrumental in getting influential investment bankers and large stockholders behind the "southern rule" plan. Stetson also rallied support from his key allies in the South, including Atlanta magnate Robert Woodruff and Trust Company of Georgia president John A. Sibley.

Meanwhile, Yates was lobbying the SEC for faster approval of the C&S plan for disbanding so Southern Company could raise its own capital and equity needed to finance new construction. "We have done nothing but struggle to put in generating plants," he told the SEC in explaining the difficulty of meeting an energy load that grew by 15 percent in 1948 alone. Whiting also pressed the SEC for action since neither Consumers Power nor any other C&S subsidiary could operate independently until the old parent was dissolved. The SEC, however, couldn't keep up with the PUHCA workload. By the time it ruled on one plan, circumstances had changed, and a revised plan had to be considered. Because Southern Company was growing faster than the Northern Group, Whiting had to keep reworking the formula for splitting up C&S assets, while stockholder opposition to each filing resulted in legal challenges and still more hearings.

In summer 1949, when a U.S. district court judge approved one of the final SEC proposals for dissolving C&S, it appeared that the painful proceedings might soon end. Investors began anticipating the different stocks they would receive under the break-up plan, and large volumes of C&S stock began moving for a fraction of a point's gain in the $4 to $4½ range. On July 19, nearly 800,000 shares changed hands and accounted for half the day's business on the New York Stock Exchange (NYSE).

Also on July 19, brokers began trading Southern Company's common stock for the first time. Because no shares were physically in investor hands, early trades were made on a "when distributed" basis in the "over-the-counter" market. The "bid" price of $8 and "asked" price of $9 gave Yates and his team a good indication of investors' appetite for the new stock and what market price the shares might trade for when eventually listed on the NYSE. That valuation was below the stock's book value of $10 a share, and Yates had limited time to influence that range. As he submitted an application for listing Southern Company's common stock on the exchange, he dispatched Crist to organize a "security analysts' inspection trip," a summer tour designed to introduce Southern Company to the financial community. "It was a new name," Crist wrote in his memoirs, "its track record virtually nonexistent. We were, of course, strangers to the security investment fraternity."

To help educate Wall Street about the new enterprise and the Southeast economic boom, Yates and Crist called on securities dealers, met with consultants, and hosted financial information meetings throughout 1949. But the 1,500-mile system tour hosted by Crist proved to be their most effective strategy for marketing the new brand.

Fifteen security analysts representing large investment houses in New York, Chicago, Boston, and Nashville joined the eight-day tour July 17. Beginning with an inspection of the north Georgia hydro projects, the group traveled south, stopping in Atlanta, Macon, and Albany. They saw the entire coastal region from Panama City to Gulfport and then headed northeast to Hattiesburg, Montgomery, and Birmingham. They toured 14 power plants and dams, as well as some of the region's progressive industrial, military, and research facilities. At every break and meal, they met competent operating company managers; business, government, and community leaders; and the top officers on Yates's team—among them, Martin and his Alabama Power general manager James Barry; McManus, president of Georgia Power; L. C. Park, general manager of Gulf Power; and Sweatt, president of Mississippi Power.

In a follow-up meeting July 28 with other New York security analysts, the investment specialists reported on what they saw—a South on the march and rapidly growing; new industries and robust economic development; diversified agricultural crops, forestry, dairies, and livestock; military bases, scenic beaches, and progressive port facilities; and a political climate conducive to business. Most important, they saw modern, efficient power plants and a strong network of utilities.

"We in the East have read a whole lot about the development of this section. It has sounded almost too good to be true. But we've had convincing proof on this trip," said an officer with Irving Trust Company. "I returned to New York with a most optimistic feeling concerning the Southern Company system and the territory it serves," added a Lehman Brothers representative. "Management is top-notch, ranking with the best in the utility industry," said a Kidder Peabody analyst. Another added, "This type of management . . . assures the future success of this enterprise and is the best indication that the securities of the companies are, and will continue to be, sound investments."

Even the *New York Times* took note of the tour and follow-up New York meeting, calling it "the first of its kind in Wall Street . . . highlighted by the analysts' reports that reflected favorably on the utility." The positive feedback helped boost Southern Company's confidence and its stock price. By September 26, the week of the spin-off, the bid price on Southern Company's "when distributed" stock inched above $10 a share.

On September 30, 1949, the SEC approved the proposal that finally dissolved C&S and distributed its assets the following day in the form of new common stock—4,035,491 shares of Consumers Power; 792,686 of Central Illinois Light; 2,020,400 of Ohio Edison; and 11,785,665 of Southern Company. (Disbursement of a few remaining C&S shares was delayed by lawsuits until finally awarded to Southern Company in the form of 234,335 common shares in 1952.) Also on September 30, Southern Company made its NYSE debut, although the stock had to continue trading on a "when distributed" basis for three more days until enough stock reached investors' hands that actual shares could begin trading.

October 1, 1949, was "independence day," when the new company became legally free of C&S—and free of its northern influence, a victory again aided by Eugene Stetson, who served as proxy for a large number of stockholders voting for southern control of the company's policies as well as its operations. At the October 1949 board meeting, Southern Company directors approved a plan for domesticating the parent company in Georgia and accepted the resignations of Whiting and Bourne. Together with other changes and new appointments made earlier that year, Southern Company's board was finally dominated by southerners—among them Atlanta attorney and golf hero Bobby Jones. The following month, Yates terminated his agreement with the old C&S service company and signed a contract with Southern Services, Incorporated—a newly created organization headquartered in Birmingham, designed to provide engineering, financial, and other specialized services for the operating companies.

"All the investments of The Southern Company are in the South. Its interests all are in the South," proclaimed Yates, acknowledging that the new enterprise had effectively been transformed into a southern company, not only in name and location but also in its structure and corporate soul. Yates and his team had little time to celebrate, however, because their fledgling firm faced yet another crucial test: Could it stand on its own financially by selling 1.5 million new shares, its first public offering of new common stock? The new equity was desperately needed to help fund a construction budget of $168 million to install 600,000 kilowatts of new capacity the next two years, more capacity than had been added during the previous seven years combined.

"We approached the offering with considerable trepidation," confessed Crist. A year earlier, he and Yates had abandoned their first attempt to sell stock when none of twelve investment groups consulted offered even book value. They knew what was at stake. If they now couldn't attract bids above $10 a share, the new offering would deplete values of the current shares—disastrous for a stock that had been on the street less than two months and purchased largely by small and medium-size investors, whose confidence in the company could be rattled by one misstep this early.

On December 6, Yates and his team opened the bids from Wall Street banks. Their fears were dispelled in a collective sigh of relief. Lehman Brothers was the high bidder at $11.5825, a nice premium above book value.

Southern Company had passed all the critical tests. Everything had come together within the final quarter of 1949—becoming independent of C&S, creating a new service company, trading stock on the NYSE for the first time, issuing the first public offer of new stock, and successfully transforming the company into a truly southern enterprise. These were all victories to celebrate as the founders said good-bye to an old decade and welcomed the 1950s.

SELLING SOUTHERN COMPANY AND THE SOUTH

The 1950s brought almost uninterrupted prosperity as America's factories produced half the goods and services for the entire world. In spite of the Korean War, the H-bomb scare, McCarthy "witch hunts," segregation, and other contentious social issues, many people remember the 1950s as the happy days of Hula Hoops and poodle skirts, drive-in movies and carhop restaurants, Elvis Presley and rock and roll. The nation built the interstate highway system, and 50 million cars took to the roads. *Ozzie and Harriet* moved from radio to television, and *Roy Rogers* turned every boy in the neighborhood into a shoot-'em-up cowboy. "I Like Ike" campaign buttons helped usher in the first Republican president in two decades, and the "atoms for peace" program ushered in the nuclear age. Personal income doubled, and Americans went on a spending spree—new homes, new appliances, and the luxury of air-conditioning and refrigeration.

For Southern Company, "the good old days" meant uninterrupted growth. Demand for electricity grew rapidly, consistently, and predictably. Engineers could plan just by plotting a line on a graph, rising upward at a forty-five-degree angle. Growth trends were depicted that way year after year in stockholder reports. Throughout most of the decade, Southern Company's power sales grew more than 10 percent a year, about 25 percent higher than the national average. Electricity prices, on the other hand, were some 25 percent below the national average. Residential rates, which had been above 3¢ a kilowatt-hour two decades earlier, dropped to 2.29¢ in 1950 and were below 2¢ by 1960—decreases afforded by better technology and larger, more efficient power plants.

During the first three years of the 1950s, Southern Company undertook an ambitious construction program: twelve new steam and hydro units at ten locations, including the first 100-megawatt units at Alabama Power and Georgia Power. No one expected that type of growth to continue. But it did. By 1957, the tenth full year of Southern Company's operations, Yates had built more than 2 million kilowatts of new capacity, more than doubling the company's size. Annual electricity sales during that period had increased from 7 billion kilowatt-hours to 18 billion, a boom fueled by growth in number of customers, appliance sales, and industrial development the company itself was largely responsible for creating.

Financing became a constant challenge as annual construction budgets went from $57 million to $125 million by the decade's end. In all but one of the ten years he headed the company, Yates would have to go back to Wall Street to sell more common stock. He pounded the doors of New York's investment bankers and got to know dozens of security analysts. To maintain those connections and coordinate an endless stream of financings, Yates retained his office in New York, along with corporate secretary Carl James, treasurer Leonard Jaeger, and two assistants. Almost as soon as the C&S influence was gone from the board, Yates regained his chairman title and named McManus president. Both McManus and vice president Crist were stationed in an Atlanta office, located in the William-Oliver Building on

Peachtree Street. The corporate staff was so small everyone did a little of everything—financial reporting, stockholder communications, government relations, public speaking, even stuffing brochures into envelopes prior to the start of information meetings. To introduce potential stockholders to the new company, Yates and Crist traveled to regional financial centers—Boston, Philadelphia, Chicago, Los Angeles, San Francisco, Houston, and New York. And to boost stock ownership inside the service territory, they held meetings in Atlanta and Birmingham. Wherever they went, they introduced people to their new company and the New South.

"The Southern Company's service area is a land of industrial and agricultural promise," read the first brochure distributed to thousands of new investors. Generously crammed with dozens of large photographs, the brochure showcased the region's metropolitan centers and factories, minerals and natural resources, agriculture and forestry, and educational and transportation facilities. The pictures came to life with audiences treated to a motion picture entitled "Power of the South"—in color and with sound, the company proudly noted in its 1950 annual report. Then, in 1951, Southern Company launched its first national advertising program, with headlines reading, "Better Service for a Better South" and "Business is up in Southern City USA." Placed in national magazines and newspapers, the economic development ads sold the region to business leaders at the same time Southern Company was selling itself to investors. The South had finally been touched by modern industrialization during World War II, when new factories produced war goods. Company leaders worked hard after the war to transform war factories into producers of consumer goods and attract new business. Industry needed electricity, and electricity needed industry. And good jobs were needed for hundreds of thousands of returning soldiers.

How can you keep them on the farm once they've seen Paris? "Let's make rural Georgia a decent, attractive place in which to live," suggested Georgia Power executive Charles A. Collier. "Our small towns need everything: better agriculture, small industries, better service establishments. But most of all, they need to be cleaned up, painted up, spruced up and, if necessary, rebuilt entirely." To help the state retain bright young talent, Collier developed a "Better Home Towns" program that inspired more than a hundred Georgia towns to organize garden clubs, Boy Scout troops, school groups, and merchants in an effort to plant and paint, remodel and repair, and clean and compete for annual Champion Home Town awards. The campaign was so successful it was featured in the *Saturday Evening Post, Newsweek, Reader's Digest,* and dozens of other national publications.

In Mississippi, Sweatt, who embodied his name with the belief that hard work would make a company or a people great, penned a series of "open letters" to Mississippians, which called on "the businessman, the farmer, the housewife, the student and public servant, and the entire community" to join in helping solve the state's economic, political, and social problems. At Alabama Power, every service truck carried on its doors the slogan "Helping Develop Alabama," and Martin used his influence to help establish Birmingham as the South's research center. The Southern Research Institute attracted a staff of scientists and academic leaders and, by the early 1950s, had projects under way to develop new industrial, agricultural, and manufacturing processes.

"Research Turns Resources into Profits in Southern City USA," proclaimed the headline of a 1952 Southern Company ad. Campaign themes changed yearly, but the promotion of the region remained constant—"Move Forward, Move South." By acting as the unofficial chamber of commerce for an entire region, Southern Company was betting on the investments eventually paying off. And they did. During its first ten years of operation, the company helped recruit nearly a thousand new industries, and the opening of thousands of commercial businesses followed, creating an explosion of new job opportunities.

The region's economy also was stimulated by the Korean War during the 1950s, since half of the nation's military bases were located in the South. However, nothing transformed the company's market more vividly than the quick spread of air-conditioning. The phenomenon seemed to seep in through the back door while the company was opening the front door to industrialization. The South was a sweatbox environment primed for the new technology. Office workers contended with gritty dust sucked in by window fans and with loose papers gone with the wind. First, movie houses and commercial establishments began inviting people to come inside and cool off. Then businesses began including air-conditioning as a new construction prerequisite. By 1951, the company's annual report was citing "greater use of air-conditioning equipment" among the reasons for its sales and revenue increases.

Homebuilders began adding the luxury of central air-conditioning as a standard feature, and owners of older homes started buying window units, which kept company engineers busy upgrading electrical equipment. The load jumped overnight. Harry Bell, a Mississippi Power engineer assigned to the Biloxi area, was responsible for service to nearby Keesler Air Force Base. "The officers started buying window air-conditioning units and plugging them in," he recalled. "We were up all night for weeks on end replacing transformers that couldn't carry the extra load." After air-conditioning made the region a more hospitable place, businesses became more willing to move south, bringing more jobs and people.

While population and electric load were growing, the size of Southern Company's territory also was expanding—from 94,000 square miles to 120,000. In 1950, Birmingham Electric Company, a wholesale customer of Alabama Power, was acquired, adding 114,000 retail customers to the system. Then, in 1957, Georgia Power bought Georgia Power & Light Company from Florida Power Corporation, adding 38,000 customers in a twenty-county area in south Georgia. Between the acquisitions and population growth, Southern Company's customer base more than doubled in its first ten years. It was beyond Yates's wildest expectations.

LEGACY OF YATES AND HIS TEAM

Each year, the board extended his retirement date in order to keep Eugene Yates. Even though the board could not entice him to move his office and family to Atlanta or Birmingham, he stayed in close touch with his companies by traveling often to the Southeast to review operations. "He watched them like an osprey," said Crist. "A deviation from expected performance standards brought a worried inquiry, often a rebuke."

What numbers Yates didn't have planted in his brain, he recorded in a "black book" stuffed in his coat pocket and filled with corporate data, budgets, and performance measures. "When he pulled out his notebook, even the boldest subordinate was inclined to cringe," recalled executive Harllee Branch Jr. "It was as if he was pulling a revolver, and you knew he wouldn't miss his target. He tolerated no glossing over of figures, no puffery, no exaggerations, no excuses."

"Hotel clerks, Pullman conductors, and other public servants, including utility executives, quailed at his approach," said Crist. If a hotel did not have his room ready, he would listen to the cowering clerk and then simply say, "I know. But I want my room." Then he would refuse to budge from the waiting line and repeat the same response to every excuse offered until the frantic staff came up with a room. If an investment newsletter published an overly optimistic outlook, he would call the editor, point out the errors, and insist he publish a correction right away. He intimidated almost everyone, not only because of his size and bulldog face but also because of his terse talking style and solemn, distinguished demeanor. As a result, many thought him to be severe, cold, and gruff—a bear.

Actually, he was a "warm and affectionate person, deeply devoted to his family, his associates, and his friends," said Branch. "He was a very private sort of person, but deep down, a man of great sympathy and affection." Yates displayed this softer side in small-group meetings, private dinners, or occasions where he felt comfortable bringing out his family photographs and telling stories about his playful granddaughter. Board members praised him as having "a beautiful mind . . . a blend of intelligence, scholarship, and wisdom." Because of his analytical bent, he seldom became distracted and could see clearly through the clutter and flutter of difficult decisions to determine what needed to be done. Some of his most important work was putting into place the right structures and people to meet the challenges of a rapidly growing company.

In 1952, Yates created the position of executive committee chairman, endowed it with some of his own responsibilities, and named Alabama Power president James M. Barry to the post. Barry was put in charge of system expansion and financial planning, overseeing all Birmingham-based operations and any number of "other powers and duties" that Yates or the board might assign. The job was rated on par with the title of president, which McManus continued to hold in overseeing system operations from Atlanta. Yates, Barry, and McManus made a formidable team. Engineers who saw eye-to-eye, they all had first signed on with the company under visionary James Mitchell, whose early investments in engineering talent were still paying dividends. Now, they were running the company some forty years later.

Barry had the gift of gab that Yates and McManus didn't. He became an effective spokesman for the company, was a key negotiator in acquiring Georgia Power & Light and Birmingham Electric, and aided Yates on sensitive matters of governmental affairs. A California native, Barry was a University of California honor graduate who had worked for several California and Oregon utilities before becoming Alabama Power's local manager at Anniston in 1918. His outgoing, big-hearted nature quickly won him loyal friends, and his engineering and leadership skills moved him quickly through the ranks. He held so many positions that future leaders counted him "among the men who literally built Alabama Power."

McManus had the talent of knowing operations inside out, a technical wizard responsible for many innovations. Electricity was in his blood. As a boy, he helped his grandfather operate a grist mill that supplied electricity to his hometown of Smithville, Georgia. McManus took Westinghouse's engineering course at Pittsburgh and advanced power engineering at GE's Schenectady, New York, facilities and was Alabama Power's Northern Division manager by 1925. In 1927, he transferred to Georgia Power, became a vice president and director in 1945 and its president in 1947, before also being named Southern Company president in 1950.

Yates selected yet another engineer as the first president of Southern Services: Herbert J. Scholz, who was serving as vice president of the C&S service organization at the time of the split-up. Scholz also was a Californian who, after graduating from Stanford University and working for Pacific Gas & Electric and GE, found his way to Alabama in 1920. He became an electric engineering star and was placed in charge of designing plants toward the end of the Depression. For Yates, Scholz put together much of the organizational structure for Southern Services and assembled a staff of superior talent, including two former C&S engineers who would follow him as future presidents of the service organization—Ernest C. Gaston and William R. Brownlee.

Scholz also helped Yates put Southern Company in the forefront of technology and innovation by placing Donald Early in charge of the power pool. A graduate of Massachusetts Institute of Technology, Early developed a contraption called the "world's first Incremental Cost Computer for Delivered Power." The invention brought power coordination and dispatch to a new level by continuously calculating the most economic generation to use in meeting a load anywhere on the system, taking into consideration a score of factors, from fuel costs to transmission losses. Early and his two assistants, Grady Smith and Bob Usry, worked calculators for months to come up with a design for coordinating the system's fifty-four steam units and eighteen hydro units. Nicknamed the "Early Bird," the computer produced $400,000 in savings the first year and won the admiration of engineers from around the world, many coming to Birmingham to see the small, mustachioed inventor quietly demonstrate how it worked.

Scholz was also responsible for involving Southern Company in the growing field of nuclear technology. After following the early studies of nuclear fission for power generation, he secured Yates's support in joining a consortium of twenty-one utilities and manufacturers in 1954 to develop one

STEPPING INTO A POLITICAL TRAP

It all started innocently enough. In January 1954, the U.S. government called on private enterprise to help meet the increasing electric load in the Tennessee Valley. Yates didn't regard it as a big bet at all, just a simple and solid business opportunity. Expecting a shortfall in capacity, the Tennessee Valley Authority submitted a plan to build a new steam plant in Fulton, Tennessee, thirty miles north of Memphis. But President Dwight Eisenhower had other plans. Viewing TVA as an example of "creeping socialism," he told his staff to find alternatives to building the generation at taxpayer expense. The staff came up with the idea that free enterprise could help supply power to TVA's largest customer, the Atomic Energy Commission (AEC), with a portion of the load needed to enrich uranium at its facilities near Paducah, Kentucky.

The government's solicitation of proposals brought Yates together with Edgar H. Dixon, president of neighboring Middle South Utilities, which operated utilities in Mississippi, Louisiana, and Arkansas. Dixon wanted to build a power plant large enough to meet the entire 600-megawatt load the government was seeking and invited Yates to join the venture. They began talking in earnest and held a strategy session in New York in February. Yates brought along Barry, and Dixon invited Adolphe Wenzell, vice president of First Boston Corporation, which planned to finance the deal.

Dixon's proposal involved building a plant on land owned by his Arkansas subsidiary and delivering the capacity over a transmission line to be constructed across the Mississippi River connecting "private power" with "public power"—West Memphis, Arkansas, with Memphis, Tennessee. Paducah was nearly 200 miles away, but Dixon knew that displacing part of the AEC load was just a technicality since there was plenty of generating capacity available in the Paducah area. From an engineering and economics standpoint, Yates had to agree it made sense to locate the plant near Memphis, the market short on capacity. The location, however, complicated matters because the power would not flow directly to AEC, the agency holding the contract for the plant's output. TVA rightfully opposed the idea, but Eisenhower's budget department forced a three-way secondary contract that placed TVA in the middle position of accepting the free-enterprise kilowatts as "replacement energy" from AEC. Both Yates and Dixon thought that was an awkward arrangement, but when Dixon complained, he was told not to worry, that the administration would work out agreements between TVA and AEC. Dixon told Yates that their job was to put together a solid proposal and to stay out of the politics. That suited Yates fine. A few days later, after taking the proposal to his executive team and board, Yates called Dixon to say Southern Company would accept the invitation.

Yates would admit later that he believed he "had no choice." For years, Southern Company had joined utilities opposing TVA's entrée into the steam generation business, saying it was outside the agency's original charter of developing dams. Because it needed backup power to hydro, TVA had prevailed in that debate and built its first major steam plant in 1948—and then quickly built six more to meet defense needs during the Korean War. During peacetime, utilities tried to stop TVA's new steam plants, and Southern Company was one of the voices complaining most loudly. By calling on private enterprise to provide the solution, Eisenhower was handing the utilities a rare opportunity to check TVA's growth, but he was also calling their hand. For Southern Company, it was time to put up or shut up. "It seemed expedient that we join in a minor way in making an offer to AEC," said Yates.

Southern Company took a minority interest of 21 percent in the $107 million joint venture. In addition to feeling a "moral obligation" to support the plant, Yates was concerned about the frightful size of TVA's defense contracts—3 million kilowatts, almost as much capacity as the entire Southern Company system. If defense needs decreased, TVA would have to dispose of a vast supply of surplus power. And if TVA built the Fulton plant it would have even more surplus capacity to market. "From bitter experience," said Crist, "we knew where that market would be found."

On February 25, Dixon and Yates made their initial proposal to provide AEC the power at $9.6 million annually, and during the next two months they reconvened several times to revise financial assumptions. In many of those sessions, banker Adolphe Wenzell provided estimates on bond sales and advised setting up a separate corporation to treat the financing program outside the holding company structure. As a result, Dixon and Yates formed Mississippi Valley Generating Company, which could be financed with 95 percent debt. The higher-than-normal debt allowed them to reduce the bid to $8.8 million. Because a slight miscalculation could gobble up projected profits, Dixon and Yates considered Wenzell's input strategically vital. What they didn't know was that Wenzell was a weasel whose involvement would pull them hopelessly into a political quagmire.

SCANDALIZING THE DIXON-YATES PROPOSAL

Already, opposition to the contract was building. Neither AEC nor TVA cared for the way Eisenhower's budget bureau was forcing them into an artificial pact, and both bickered over which would get stuck with the related tax and transmission costs. Meanwhile, TVA feared an invasion of its markets as much as private utilities feared assaults from public power—"those bastards" having become a common term used by each to describe the other. TVA chairman Gordon Clapp grew ever more hostile once he learned the plant would be built near his Memphis market and worked to undermine what he called "an opening step in a program deliberately planned to destroy the TVA."

Friends of TVA rushed to the defense, led by Alabama senator Lister Hill and his Tennessee counterparts, Albert Gore Sr. and Estes Kefauver, who successfully delayed the contract while putting together a game plan to kill the deal. Labeling Dixon and Yates as hired "hatchet men," Hill organized twenty hard-core Senate supporters to meet weekly and work under his direction throughout the campaign. Tennessee governor Frank Clement rallied the support of power brokers in the valley. And five national public power groups coordinated lobbying efforts through the Electric Consumers Information Committee. Among their chief complaints was the lack of competitive bidding. But the Eisenhower administration justified its negotiated approach by pointing out that the only other serious proposal came from a financial consultant who had no experience building power plants, required profit guarantees, and shifted all cost-related risks to the government.

By contrast, the Dixon and Yates offer seemed a much better deal. AEC's Kenneth Nichols called it "a fair and reasonable contract." Although most commissioners voted to endorse the proposal, several said they would sign only if instructed to do so by a higher authority—meaning the president. On June 14, Budget Director Rowland Hughes secured Eisenhower's approval to go forward with the contract, not bothering to tell the president about the brewing discord. When Stephen A. Mitchell, Democratic National Committee chairman, first saw the newspaper account of Eisenhower's order to execute the contract, he said it struck him "like a hammer over the head." For the first year and a half in office, the president had given the opposing party no explosive political ammunition to use against him, but a government contract negotiated with private business without being competitively bid looked like it could be repackaged into political dynamite.

"The president will rue the day he ever signed that order," vowed Mitchell, joining forces with Tennessee Valley groups to elevate the regional matter to a national level. For the remainder of 1954, the conflict became the Democrats' most important political issue and was mentioned in the press so often that "Dixon-Yates" became shorthand for both the proposed contract and the controversy. Resolutions condemned the deal, and amendments to stop it were attached to completely unrelated bills; the Senate Judiciary Committee conducted hearings to see if Dixon-Yates had violated antitrust laws; and numbers showing how much it would cost the government were suddenly pulled out of the air, some claiming Dixon and Yates would make a profit as high as 20 percent. Accusations bounced around the headlines like a ping-pong ball hitting all the hot buttons—corruption, bribery, political payoffs, government giveaway, secret dealings, anticompetitive actions, and other denunciations summarized by Kefauver's cry of "bad business, bad government, and bad morals."

On August 16, Mitchell fired a broadside directly at Eisenhower by claiming the contract was motivated by the president's friendship with golf champion Bobby Jones, a director on Southern Company's board, whose cottage was next door to the president's at Augusta National Golf Club. The following day at a press conference, Eisenhower said he was astonished Mitchell would impugn the integrity of Jones and offered to throw open the White House books, inviting the press to "get the complete record from the inception of the idea to this very minute." From Atlanta, Jones confirmed he had never discussed the issue or any Southern Company matter with the president, adding, "It would come as a surprise to me if he had ever known I was one of its directors."

Some Democrats even split with their colleagues to chastise their party leader for the attack. Kefauver said Mitchell was "carrying guilt by association too far," and Georgia senator Walter F. George added, "I have known Bobby Jones and his family back to his grandfather, and he is not the kind of man who would undertake to influence the president."

Throughout the hullabaloo, Dixon and Yates remained curiously silent. "Who is Dixon, and who Yates?" asked *Time*. "A few months ago they were simply able businessmen," said *Barron's*. "Today, they have become probably the most notorious utility executives since Samuel Insull."

With their names "bobbing up from one end of the country to the other," Dixon and Yates decided it was time to speak up and tell their side of the story. Their silence had hardly kept them out of the politics and was doing considerable damage to their reputations. In fall 1954, they hired a public relations firm and soon were being quoted in interviews appearing in the *New York Times, U.S. News & World Report, Time*, and *Life*. They also appeared on NBC's "Meet the Press," with Dixon doing most of the talking. The experience must have been painful for Yates, camera-shy and short on words. Yet he managed to smile, explain how he became involved in the project, and respond to skeptical questions about whether the project would benefit taxpayers: "Well, certainly if the private funds build the plant instead of the taxpayer's money, there is a savings." One reporter described him as "looking somewhat like a kindly Saint Bernard" and said he "comported himself almost as impressively as his partner in front of the hyphen."

To help tell its side of the story, Southern Company placed advertisements in fifty daily newspapers throughout its territory. Under the banner of "Straight Talk About the Dixon-Yates Proposal," Yates responded to allegations and emphasized the contract would save taxpayers $100 million, offer no profit guarantees, and could be canceled by the government at any time.

"The whole thing is a pain in the neck," Yates told the *New York Times*. While many newspapers gave them fair treatment, Dixon and Yates were too late to curtail campaign rhetoric leading into the congressional elections that fall. Even former President Harry Truman weighed in, saying, "The trail of double-dealing and deceit in that affair leads straight into the White House and straight up to that desk in the West Wing where I used to sit."

The issue was credited, in part, with returning both houses to Democratic control in November 1954. "The Dixon-Yates thing can be given a quiet burial," boasted Senate Majority Leader Lyndon Johnson. Proclaiming they had a popular mandate to kill the proposal, victorious party members returned in January 1955 to launch investigations under three separate committees.

Speaker of the House Sam Rayburn called on the electric utility industry to press Dixon and Yates "to withdraw from the whole controversy." The industry's trade association instead threw its support behind the two CEOs. "We cannot withdraw," said Yates, claiming that to retreat because of harassment "would establish a dangerous precedent for our country."

But in February 1955, the critics would find a hammer to use in driving nails into the coffin of Dixon-Yates.

THE END OF THE "AFFAIR"

The death knell started when someone turned up an innocuous memo containing an obscure reference to a meeting Adolphe Wenzell had at the budget bureau.

"Who is this Mr. Wenzell?" asked Senator Hill, not finding Wenzell's name on any of the documents released by Eisenhower's people after the books had supposedly been "thrown open" in defense of Bobby Jones. It soon was discovered that, prior to his work on the Dixon-Yates proposal, Wenzell had conducted a study for the budget department on options for funding future power needs in the TVA market. When questioned, Rowland Hughes claimed Wenzell had discontinued his consulting services before he began working on financing plans for Dixon-Yates.

Hill challenged that point and told the Senate, "This man participated in conferences and meetings on the Dixon-Yates matter which were held in the budget bureau at the very time when the First Boston Company was making arrangements for financing the Dixon-Yates plant." Investigations proved Hill to be correct. Although Dixon and Yates had known about Wenzell's study, they hadn't suspected him of doing double duty. Early in the planning process, Dixon had advised Wenzell to make a clean break with the administration to avoid even the appearance of conflict. But Wenzell kept showing up for White House meetings a month after Dixon and Yates submitted the first proposal.

All hell broke loose.

Senator Hill tried to stop TVA's appropriations so it would be unable to build the transmission line needed to receive Dixon-Yates power. Tennessee senator Kefauver started antitrust and monopoly committee investigations of the contract and Wenzell's double role. The Tennessee legislature hastily passed a law to allow cities to build their own plants, and defiant Memphis leaders announced they would do just that rather than purchase power from a private utility. TVA claimed it no longer needed the Dixon-Yates capacity. A congressional joint committee rescinded its earlier approval and asked the AEC to cancel the contract. The White House press secretary had to correct a statement defending Wenzell made by an ill-informed and embarrassed Eisenhower. So many political cartoons lampooned the scandal that, when later collected, they filled a 110-page book. The decision by Memphis to build its own plant gave Eisenhower a way out while still limiting the increasing involvement of the federal government in the power business. Following a

Wilsonville—a project so big he created a new subsidiary to own and operate it. The Southern Electric Generating Company, or SEGCO, was to become the first jointly owned plant in the system. Co-owners Alabama Power and Georgia Power would split the power output of four units totaling 1 million kilowatts of capacity. That was nearly three times the capacity of all the dams in Martin's plans. More important, it would be year-round firm power, not subject to seasonal shifts in generation that Mother Nature dictated.

Yates and Martin quarreled. Martin did not want to compromise his hydro plans, and he did not want to share ownership of a facility with Georgia Power. The SEGCO plant would be built in Alabama and would burn Alabama coal. He argued that it also should be owned and operated by Alabama Power and that its construction could wait until his company could take on the full financial challenges. The disagreement became more heated as the price tag kept increasing for the Coosa and Warrior developments because of changes in scope, political obstacles, litigation, and cantankerous landowners who saw opportunities to "make a killing" on their farms or idle property. The cost overruns worried Yates and interfered not only with his SEGCO plans but also with his capital budgets, requiring more bonds, more preferred stock, and more Southern Company equity. Yates also was smarting from the Dixon-Yates firestorm, and the Coosa was looking like another political pain in the neck. Public power proponents were calling it a government giveaway and blasting Eisenhower for "turning it over to . . . the company which spearheaded the fight against TVA." Yates grew so wary at one point that he proposed abandoning the Coosa project.

"That very, very much infuriated Mr. Martin," recalled Joe Farley, a lawyer with the company's legal firm at the time. "Lots of jawing about that went on."

Yates and Martin were at odds again when a fourteen-foot addition to Lay Dam required a relicense. Because the original project had been built before the FPC's creation, a statutory permit granted by Congress would have to be surrendered for a limited, fifty-year license. Martin was willing to make that sacrifice. To Yates, filing for a new license represented more money, more delays, and more political battles.

"If you keep trying to cancel the project," Martin finally threatened, "I'll go to the Securities and Exchange Commission and force a separation of Alabama Power from Southern Company." Yates did not consider that to be an idle threat. He had worked with Martin for four decades and knew how fanatical he could become when he set out to accomplish what might have been the impossible for others. The ultimatum presented Yates with a dangerous dilemma during what were still Southern Company's fledgling years. The SEC was largely done with splitting up the holding companies, but the PUHCA hearings were still fresh, and some of the SEC rules were still being tweaked. Yates knew the commissioners would have lent a listening ear to any company that wanted to reopen its case.

"The flap ended when Mr. Yates backed down and the company went ahead with the project," said Farley. Yates extended Martin a little more patience and, in the end, also won Martin's cooperation on SEGCO. Each got his pet project, and the two pioneers patched up their disagreements before construction on either development got under way. The SEGCO venture was launched in May 1956; the first Coosa groundbreaking came in 1958.

Yates's retirement was long overdue. In preparing for his departure and the anticipated retirement of Barry, Yates moved Harllee Branch over to Southern Company as president and named McManus vice chairman in January 1957. That spring, he oversaw the successful sale of 1.5 million new common stock shares and the company's largest financing program yet. He also oversaw the first bond sale to help finance the giant SEGCO development. He lived to see construction begin on his brainchild but not his own retirement. On October 5, 1957, Yates died of a heart attack at his New York City home. He was a month shy of seventy-seven. His funeral was held at Manhattan's St. James Episcopal Church on October 8, and graveside services followed two days later at Atlanta's Westview Cemetery.

"It was appropriate that a transplanted northerner should have found his final repose in the Southland which he loved and which he had helped so greatly to develop," said Branch, who led an honorary escort of officers and directors to the funeral. Joining them were many community, government, and business leaders from throughout the Southeast, all of whom had come to appreciate what Yates had done to help build up the economy of their states.

LESSONS LEARNED

During Southern Company's formative years, a design was imprinted and the die cast. What took shape were the structures, strategies, and standards that not only ensured the company's success in the 1950s but also endured into the twenty-first century. In the Yates decade, the company register" of the two company owners. Accounting and legal complexities and differences in tax treatments between the two states caused so much grief that Alabama Power later would be given a contract to operate the plant, the separate management staff would be eliminated, and SEGCO would be transformed into a paper entity. When the next joint project came along, the dual-tenant structure was avoided. Alabama Power took a majority 60 percent interest in the Greene County steam plant, and Mississippi Power owned 40 percent.

The Dixon-Yates proposal to build a plant that would feed into TVA territory was a big bet lost to the political pull of public power. The scandal also exposed the company's political naïveté and reminded Southern Company that it was forever in a political business. Utilities were an easy target for lawmakers looking to boost their careers by beating up on power symbols. And even though the TVA wars had taken place two decades earlier, the wounds of the public versus private power fights had not healed. The Dixon-Yates affair reopened them, exposing raw nerves and bitter resentments on both sides. In the controversy's final resolution, the company learned that judicial proceedings also could be politicized. Although the U.S. Court of Claims upheld the contract and assessed the government $1.9 million in cancellation costs, that victory was reversed in a 1961 U.S. Supreme Court ruling that Mississippi Valley Generating Company was "not entitled to damages even though it was guilty of no wrongdoing." Southern Company had to write off more than $500,000 for its portion of the loss.

Despite the scandal attached to his name, Yates would be remembered for his dignity, honor, and many achievements. By shepherding the company through its critical formative years, he also became the father of modern-day Southern Company. He put together its organizational structure, developed a solid stockholder base of some 125,000 investors across the nation, and put in place a leadership team that would help shape the company's future success.

Those leaders soon discovered that Southern Company was far from finished with the public power debates. Foreshadowing battles to come, James Barry presented a disturbing report to the board just three months before Yates's death. Congress was undertaking new bills that would give TVA the freedom to finance its own steam plants and possibly expand without traditional congressional controls. Cooperatives were posing another threat by expanding beyond their chartered rural areas and competing for service to towns and cities. And utilities were facing yet another worry exposed by the Dixon-Yates controversy. If Memphis could build its own power plant, so could other local and state public power groups. These problems would have to be confronted head on because they presented direct challenges to Southern Company's territory and financial future. They were troubles that would define the big bets for the next group of leaders.

Tennessee Valley. If TVA could self-finance, it would bypass controls that Congress exerted through appropriation hearings and explode beyond its boundaries. That would mean another range war with neighboring utilities. More than anyone else in the industry, Branch was determined to prevent that from happening.

Although still new in his Southern Company role, Branch was not new to the fight and was already considered the nation's strongest voice for private power. In praising his promotion a year earlier, *Fortune* had called Branch "a tense, talkative man" who was "a devoted worrier about the encroachment of government on the utility industry." Now Branch had plenty of new worries, none idle or imaginary. The revenue bond bill would allow TVA to extend its territory 25,000 square miles, threatening Southern Company's markets in Rome, Georgia, and Meridian, Mississippi, and more than 40 percent of the Alabama load, including the cities of Birmingham, Anniston, and Gadsden.

"This new area includes some of the largest and most important communities served by our companies," said Branch in pleading for the House Public Works Committee to place territorial restrictions on TVA. "If it [TVA] is to continue, please, in the name of fair play, limit in clear and unambiguous terms its area of operations to that now served." In other words, put a "fence" around TVA. A fence was needed, Branch argued, not only to protect his market but also to attract new capital—$500 million over the next three years to finance Southern Company's largest construction program yet. Investors wanted reassurance the service area would not be invaded as it had been during the 1930s. Branch was getting anxious calls from some of his large stockholders; a defined boundary would put those fears to rest.

Throughout the hearings, friends of TVA assured private utilities a legislated border was unnecessary, that the authority had no sinister expansionist plans. After TVA had acquired its existing 80,000-square-mile territory in the 1930s, the agency made peace with its neighbors and had honored a commitment to stay within its boundaries, a reassurance that had allowed utilities to attract capital and grow. However, that "gentlemen's agreement" was not a legal contract, and under a different political administration and different economic circumstances, TVA might be tempted to expand. It already was growing at a phenomenal rate. What had started as a river development program in 1933 had become an energy empire by 1958. TVA had more than $1.7 billion invested in power facilities, and 75 percent of its generation was coming from new steam plants, not hydro dams.

Southern Company had another reason to be paranoid. Recently, it had been party to the Dixon-Yates contract—a failed joint venture with Middle South Utilities to build an investor-owned plant that would feed into TVA's Memphis market. The controversy had ended with Memphis building its own plant, a decision that, together with President Dwight Eisenhower's opposition to new TVA appropriations, had ironically created the need for the agency to find another way to finance its projects. The bill authorizing it to self-finance passed the U.S. Senate in August 1957, but a House committee deliberated various amendments for nearly two years. Relations between public and private power were still raw from overheated rhetoric during the Dixon-Yates debates, and some TVA supporters wanted further revenge. Under its new leader, would Southern Company stumble once more in this tempestuous political field?

Aware that he was making another big bet in the same arena that challenged his predecessor, Eugene Yates, Branch pored over the bill to spot every loophole that might allow TVA to expand. Unlike Yates, who shunned the spotlight, Branch was a natural in front of the microphone. He loved debate and was good at it. Both an effective communicator and a public relations strategist, he wrote to his stockholders, briefed newspaper editors, composed and delivered highly compelling talks, wrote letters and articles, and tapped into his vast network of friends in business and civic circles—a crusade that helped delay the bill until lawmakers arrived at an acceptable solution. By the time Branch returned to the House committee hearings May 11, 1959, that solution was presented by highly regarded Georgia representative Carl Vinson, whose amendment limited TVA's territory to the area served on July 1, 1957, the year the revenue bond act was introduced. Vinson said he strongly supported giving TVA self-financing powers but asked, "Why tack onto it a provision extending TVA territory 25,000 square miles? Let's not use a steamroller when a simple sledgehammer will do the job. My amendment converts the gentlemen's agreement to law. That's all the proposed amendment does."

Taking the stage next, Branch embraced the Vinson solution and recounted statements and conversations he held with TVA directors, managers, and engineers who claimed they wanted to maintain the status quo. "If this is a true statement of TVA's desires—and I have every reason to believe it is—then I see no reason why anyone should object to placing a clear-cut limitation to that effect in the bill," he said. "May I make it clear that we seek nothing that TVA now serves, that we have no desire to hobble or interfere in its operations? All I am saying to you is, please don't give us a bill tending to support them in their legitimate operations which destroys us in ours."

To reinforce the argument, Branch called forth his entourage of operating company chiefs—Walter Bouldin, Jack McDonough, Lansing Smith, and Jack Watson, presidents of Alabama Power, Georgia Power, Gulf Power, and Mississippi Power, respectively, each taking a turn in front of the microphone. McDonough recalled his early days with Georgia Power when he worked in northwest Georgia. "There was chaos in that part of the state," he said in describing scuffles with TVA that frightened investors and made it impossible to raise new capital.

"We have lived in peace with TVA for twenty years," said Bouldin, who also warned that the peace was threatened by language in the bill inviting TVA into seven counties served by Alabama Power, representing 4,239 square miles and 255,621 customers. Ambiguities also would "specifically and unquestionably" encourage TVA's expansion into five counties served by Mississippi Power, added Watson. Another loophole, Smith pointed out, would permit a line connection into Gulf Power's territory. "We hope and urge . . . an amendment," he pleaded, "and then we can still say we are not worried about the TVA in northwest Florida."

Two months later, the House of Representatives approved the act with the Vinson amendment included, but the job was only half done. The Senate version did not include the territorial restrictions and, by some estimates, allowed TVA to more than double in size. So in June 1959, Branch and his management team returned to Washington to plead their case before a Senate subcommittee. On the first day of hearings, Alabama Power's aging chairman, Tom Martin, explained the origin of the "gentlemen's agreement." He recounted negotiations held with former TVA director David Lilienthal and provided copies of correspondence containing commitments TVA had made twenty years earlier when it signed contracts to take over service to thirteen north Alabama counties. "We were willing to execute this contract, for it had the effect of creating a boundary," he said. "Had that not been so, our company would not have sold its properties voluntarily." To recognize TVA threats to Alabama Power, Martin needed only to gaze out his office window in Birmingham toward the nearby cities of Tarrant and Bessemer, both with municipal systems served by TVA.

The Senate version of the bill was eventually amended, and on August 6, 1959, President Eisenhower signed the landmark act setting TVA free of

Congress. In giving the agency the freedom to issue its own bonds, the new law required TVA to repay the U.S. Treasury $1 billion over the next fifty-four years, as well as interest on a large portion of the money it had received from taxpayer funds. The act limited TVA's expansion to a five-mile-wide strip around the perimeter of its existing territory.

The territorial limitation was perhaps Branch's most important political victory. The "fence," as it came to be known, would remain in place through the rest of the century and into the next millennium. Despite the company's political naïveté exposed by the Dixon-Yates affair three years earlier, it appeared that Southern Company would fare quite well under its new chief executive's leadership. In fact, Branch looked and acted as if he had been recruited from central casting for the big bets ahead.

BECOMING HARLLEE BRANCH JR.

In some ways, Branch had been in training for the role all his life. In the seventh grade, he won a school medal for writing and delivering his first speech. Born in Atlanta in 1906, he was educated in the city's public schools and grew up in a "country" neighborhood close enough to Atlanta's exclusive Druid Hills district to be exposed to the refined and privileged class. Branch's father, city editor for the *Atlanta Journal,* gave future *Gone with the Wind* author Margaret Mitchell her first job as a cub reporter and trained other journalists who later became renowned writers—Erskine Caldwell, Ward Morehouse, and Grantland Rice.

Throughout his school years, Branch Jr. held any part-time job he could talk his way into—newspaper carrier, grocery clerk, elevator boy, department store bundle wrapper. His association with Georgia Power began at age fourteen when he worked as office boy in the advertising department, a favor no doubt returned to his father by advertising manager John Marsh, spouse of Margaret Mitchell. At Boys High School, Branch was the senior-class orator, and his academic and speaking skills earned him a scholarship to Davidson College in North Carolina, where the college yearbook praised him as "a man possessed of genial culture and blessed with a clear, aggressive intellect." Upon graduation, he went to Emory University Law School and worked nights at the *Atlanta Journal* and WSB radio station, all the while leading school debate teams that made shambles of opponents wherever they went.

After completing law school with honors in 1931, Branch pounded the pavement for six months, looking for work like everyone else during the Depression. Through persistence, he landed a position at Georgia Power's law firm, Colquitt, Parker, Troutman, and Arkwright. "I'll give you a desk and the use of the library if you just stop those letters of recommendation," said partner Bob Troutman. "We'll give you a place to practice, but we can't afford to pay you." So Branch worked free for three months until he received a portion of the legal fee at the close of his first case.

Within a couple of years, he was working on Georgia Power legal matters and spent several months in Ringgold, accumulating affidavits to document TVA's intrusion into northwest Georgia—his first confrontation with public power. The next came in 1936, when he helped represent Georgia Power in a lawsuit with nineteen utilities contesting the constitutionality of TVA. "My function was to read the transcript of the trial every night and to mark any corrections," he said. "We knew we would likely lose the case in the circuit court, and we were already thinking about a possible appeal to the Supreme Court."

Branch remained with the law firm for eighteen years, interrupted by two years of service in the U.S. Navy. While handling cases for Georgia Power, he worked closely with longtime president Preston Arkwright, whose performance on the witness stand became a role model for Branch's own developing style. Georgia Power leaders began watching Branch and, in 1949, invited him to join the company as vice president and general manager. Two years later, the onetime office boy was named Georgia Power president and emerged as a key industry leader as well, becoming Southeastern Electric Exchange president in 1954 and Edison Electric Institute (EEI) president the following year. In those roles, he acted as private power's chief spokesman.

"You've got to fight," he told his industry counterparts. "If you don't, government power zealots will invade your territory, demoralize your employees, mislead your customers, and disturb your investors." Most of his career, it seemed, had become dominated by this issue. While Yates was struggling to free himself from the Dixon-Yates political tar baby during the mid-1950s, Branch was embroiled in a very public power quagmire of his own. The dispute was over a hydroelectric dam on the Savannah River at a point above Augusta, Georgia, called Clark Hill—previously called Clark's Hill until a Corps of Engineering clerical error forever changed the spelling. The struggle—and the national attention it commanded—helped prepare Branch for the role he would assume at Southern Company.

THE BATTLE OF CLARK HILL

Southern Company's connection to Clark Hill was through a little-known subsidiary called the Savannah River Electric Company, which owned nearly 40,000 acres at the site and held a permit to build a dam there. During the Depression, the permit expired with little hope of reactivating the project until after World War II. By then, groups were lobbying for Clark Hill to become a federal development, claiming public power provided a catalyst for reducing private power rates. "For the past twenty years, you have seen the rates of the Georgia Power Company reduced by 66⅔ percent. Do you think they would have voluntarily reduced the rates in Georgia?" argued Walter Harrison, Georgia Electric Membership Cooperative (GEMC) president. In a victory for co-ops, the Corps of Engineers undertook construction of the dam. The government acquired the company's land at a loss to Southern Company stockholders of $653,000, and the Savannah River Electric subsidiary passed out of existence.

Because it owned the only transmission lines into the area, Georgia Power offered to buy Clark Hill's electricity from the government and resell it to the state's forty-four municipalities and thirty-seven rural electric cooperatives. This "tri-contract" continued a long-established arrangement with public power groups, treating them as wholesale customers and forestalling their need to build their own transmission and generating facilities. In some areas of the country, municipal and co-operative customers built their own transmission lines to shut investor-owned utilities out of the transaction, and GEMC wanted that type of arrangement at Clark Hill. The Flood Control Act of 1944, however, emphasized "wheeling" arrangements between private and public utilities to avoid building duplicate lines at taxpayer expense, so the Interior Department endorsed the tri-contract concept for Clark Hill as the dam was being built.

That agreement was unraveled by opposition to Eisenhower's power policies during the 1950s. Viewing tri-contracts as shotgun weddings between public and private power, Democrats campaigned to roll back the contracts and conducted hearings to investigate any influence private utilities might have with Douglas McKay, Eisenhower's secretary of the interior. Among the more publicized hearings were those staged in six states by Earl Chudoff, a Pennsylvania Democrat and chairman of the House Public Works and Resources Subcommittee.

On Friday, August 31, 1955, the Chudoff road show stopped in Atlanta, setting off what the *Atlanta Journal* called "a machine-gun burst of accusations." Secretary McKay was accused of showing bad faith and conspiring with Georgia Power to shortchange "preference customers" at Clark Hill, and Branch was accused of "propagandizing and trying to build a private power empire." Branch himself was shut out of the meeting and told that the committee was interested only in obtaining testimony from public power groups. Actually, Branch may have received better press as a result of Chudoff's cold-shoulder treatment, since reporters readily gave space to his responses outside of the hearings.

As EEI president that year, Branch embarked on a national speaking tour and was frequently quoted in newspapers using vivid prose to depict public power groups as "a privileged class . . . nurtured on government subsidies and tax exemptions and growing lustily on preferences and special dispensations." He told an industry group in Wyoming, "The irony is that those who are taxed in their electric bills to help pay for the government power projects . . . must also pay, as part of their electric bills, the cost of transporting this power to the tax-exempt." Branch's "A Privileged Class for America" speech quickly became a theme repeated by EEI members across the country.

By the time Chudoff opened a final round of hearings in Washington, D.C., that fall, Branch had already handed the co-ops the most important concession they had asked for—allowing GEMC to contract directly with the government for Clark Hill power, with Georgia Power simply providing wheeling services. Apparently unaware of the new contract, Chudoff opened his October 11 session by accusing Assistant Interior Secretary Fred G. Aandahl of "fraud, bad faith, and blackjack methods" in his attempts to dismiss a controversial legal opinion on the old Clark Hill contract. The legal matter was "moot," Aandahl responded, because the tri-contract had already been replaced with the new agreement. Unfazed, Chudoff referred to Georgia Power as a "Dixon-Yates affiliate" and attempted to portray a meeting Branch had at the White House as proof the Eisenhower administration was giving preferential treatment to private utilities.

"Actually, we are the ones who have been blackjacked," Branch told the press, "and apparently an effort is still being made to bludgeon us into further unsound and unwarranted compromises." Branch released records showing he had been permitted only a brief, "inadequate" session with a White House staff assistant, while GEMC officials had been granted an audience with President Eisenhower.

Once again, Branch was denied the opportunity to testify, and Chudoff overrode all attempts to allow Georgia Power to present its side of the controversy, saying, "maybe next year if more hearings are scheduled." Because of the shutout, the *New York Times* and the *Washington Post* gave space to Branch, who was quoted as saying he believed "fair-minded Americans will condemn this high-handed and un-American treatment." In an editorial, the *Post* wrote, "If the subcommittee is going to air one side of a controversy, it has a solemn obligation to air the other side while the issue is hot." In a lengthy letter to the editor, Chudoff defended his decision to exclude Branch from the hearings because "no evidence has been adduced . . . which demonstrates any illegal or improper action or influence on the part of the Georgia Power Company."

"We are gratified of that admission at long last," replied Branch. "We feel that our company has suffered irreparable damage on account of careless and baseless insinuations made at the hearings." Editorials across the country began appearing under headlines of "Unfair Tactics," "Witch Hunting," and "Biased Hearing." In the end, Branch won both the political skirmish and the war of words. By waging a strong defense, he prevailed in getting wheeling rights and stopping construction of duplicate transmission lines at Clark Hill. As the debate turned in his favor, the co-ops grew more conciliatory. At midnight May 20, 1956, Clark Hill power began flowing over Georgia Power lines, and the company worked out an arrangement for using surplus power from the dam during the high-water season and providing public power groups with replacement power during the low-water season.

Branch's victory at Clark Hill did not go unnoticed. One Saturday afternoon later that year, Southern Company chairman Eugene Yates rang up Branch at home and asked him to meet the following morning at Atlanta's old Ansley Hotel on Forsyth Street.

"Would it be all right if I come after church?" Branch asked.

"No," replied Yates. "Hayden Smith is with me, and we need to get back to New York. The Southern Company board of directors is meeting on Monday morning."

SOUTHERN COMPANY MOVES SOUTH

"Harllee, we've got to have somebody who is at home in the courtrooms, in the committee rooms, in the congressional chambers," said Yates, who at age seventy-six was eager to line up his successors by naming C. B. McManus vice chairman and Branch president. After voicing a self-effacing, "Am I the right one?" objection, Branch got down to negotiating an important condition, saying he could not move his wife and four school-age children to New York.

Yates let Branch ramble for a few minutes before cutting him off with a simple answer, "Well, why don't you move the company to Georgia?"

"Would that be possible?" Branch stuttered, expecting Hayden Smith, the company's New York legal counsel, to oppose the idea. But Smith assured him that was no problem. During its formation, the board had gone through the legal motions of domesticating the company in Georgia, but Yates had kept his corporate office in New York to build relationships with security analysts, rating agencies, and investment bankers. With Southern Company's financial credibility now well established, the New York base was more a matter of preference than a prerequisite.

"Well, if I can move the company to Atlanta," Branch conceded, "I'll be delighted to try to be president of Southern Company." Getting that concili-ation was far more coy and calculated than Branch ever let on. It would mean relocating the New York-based financial staff to Georgia and eventually replacing Southern Company's legal counsel, allowing Branch to toss the business to his old law firm, present-day Troutman Sanders. It also would successfully checkmate any attempt by Tom Martin to move the headquarters to Birmingham after Yates's anticipated retirement. During the past decade, Martin had made numerous attempts to attract Yates to the Magic City, including instigating a board resolution offering housing and other incentives for the move. With Yates's backing, Branch knew the board would support locating the corporate office in Atlanta, and he could escape having to nego-tiate that decision later with Martin, a battle he wasn't sure he could win. Patriarch of both Alabama Power and Southern Company, Martin had a larger-than-life persona, having been the recipient of every honor and award bestowed by the utility industry, the state of Alabama, and major business organizations throughout the South.

"Martin was very jealous as an Alabamian," said Branch. "He wanted to move it [Southern Company] back to where Southeastern Power & Light had been headquartered as the holding company in Birmingham." Technically, Branch had it wrong. Southeastern had been based in New York, even though Martin had directed most of its operations from Birmingham. Still a powerful influence on Southern Company's board, Martin had favored other candidates over Branch's nomination. Among those considered by the selection committee was Jim Crist, who had been led to believe he would get the job. Having coordinated investor communications and headed Gulf

Power, Crist was president of Birmingham-based Southern Electric Generating Company. Furthermore, he had gotten his start with the company working for Martin at Alabama Power. Both of Southern Company's previous leaders—Yates and McManus—had been "Martin men." But Yates prevailed in selling Branch to the board. Having suffered through the Dixon-Yates scandal, Yates was convinced Southern Company needed an articulate national spokesman, someone well-schooled in battling government regulation and competition. The board agreed and named Branch president January 1, 1957.

After learning some of the inside politics behind his selection, Branch realized his statesmanship would be tested as much internally as externally. In his new role, he would work hard to keep the Alabama contingency in his corner, consulting often with Martin and accommodating the Alabama Power chairman's wishes whenever possible. "Although he never formally was listed as an executive of Southern Company, no officer of the company ever thought of making a significant corporate decision without first discussing it with Mr. Martin," said Branch. "And only rarely were his views overruled."

Eventually, Martin became "reconciled" to Branch's election and Southern Company's move to Atlanta. The corporate secretary's office and a few plant accounting and statistical employees joined Branch and McManus in a suite of offices at 1330 West Peachtree Street. Following Yates's death later that year, the financial vice president and most of the New York-based staff made the move south. Under Branch, the corporate staff in Atlanta, as well as the service company staff in Birmingham, would grow exponentially. That expansion would be just one of the outcomes of Branch's efforts to reshape the company to better meet the growing challenges of the 1960s.

THE ECONOMIC MIRACLE OF THE SOUTH

Branch's term as CEO turned out to be a tipping point for both Southern Company and the region it served. The southeastern economy shifted from an agricultural base to an industrial base and then rapidly accelerated. What had been accomplished since World War II was a marvel. What was still happening was an even greater marvel. The region blossomed in nearly every field of commerce and industry, fueled by the company's marketing and economic development efforts to recruit a wide variety of businesses to provide a diversity of jobs so the region would have the financial strength to weather a downturn in any one field. The textile mills of King Cotton no

Martin had died December 8, 1964. No other Southern Company leader served as many years—fifty-three—or left a more permanent mark on the system of companies he helped create. Although he did not live to see his prized project finished, he survived long enough to see construction on the last dam in the series get under way—and to receive the industry's Edison Award for initiating what was cited as the "most comprehensive waterway development program ever undertaken by an investor-owned electric utility."

NEED FOR ANOTHER "FENCE"

Long after TVA was "fenced" in 1959, Branch continued to earn his reputation as "the country's most articulate and best-known advocate of the private power viewpoint." His war with public power was by no means over. Throughout the 1960s, Southern Company faced challenges from cooperatives in Georgia, Alabama, and Mississippi. In northwest Georgia, Ringgold and Chickamauga were exceptions to TVA's territorial restrictions, and the towns could vote on their power supplier. In heated referendum campaigns, Georgia Power was able to retain service in Ringgold, but in what was termed the "second battle of Chickamauga," the company was opposed by that town's major employer and "lost handsomely."

But these battles paled in comparison to those in Alabama and Mississippi, where resentment was still high from TVA takeovers during the 1930s. Co-ops in those states commanded enormous political power and were often favored in regulatory and court rulings and state legislative battles. Competition for customers and territory grew fierce, sometimes becoming a race to see who could build lines first to a new load and occasionally boiling into a public fight with both sides arguing their positions in paid newspaper ads. The war became even tougher after President John F. Kennedy named Norman Clapp to head the Rural Electrification Administration in 1961. Clapp was brother of the former TVA chairman who had bucked President Eisenhower over the Dixon-Yates contract. "When he came along, he came up with the idea that 'we needed a more competitive source of power . . . more federal power [to] give these utilities more competition,'" said Alabama attorney Eason Balch. "And so they started making loans all across the country."

By the mid-1960s, co-ops were borrowing $365 million annually and using many of the loans to build plants and transmission lines that displaced those of investor-owned utilities. Cooperative groups received $38 million in such loans in Mississippi and $20.4 million in Alabama, provoking passionate public debates and decade-long legal maneuvers to stop their projects.

"There is no economic justification for either the Alabama or the Mississippi loans," said Branch, calling the co-op plans "a wasteful and uneconomic duplication of facilities." REA had been created to bring electric service to unserved rural areas, and its sponsors in 1936 had loudly disavowed any intention of competing with private industry. With rural electrification 98 percent complete by 1960, co-ops started claiming rights to serve entire areas, including businesses, industries, and suburban communities. Branch called it "power by stealth!"

Branch made a serious tactical error by intervening in contract negotiations over wholesale rates that offered the only hope for saving the co-op business in Mississippi. Fearful that too many concessions would set a bad precedent for other subsidiary contracts, he refused to allow Mississippi Power to cut costs beyond a certain point. The "Branch proposal," as it came to be labeled, so infuriated the co-ops that they closed the door to future discussions and became more determined to build their own generation and become independent of "the horrible Mississippi Power Company and the Southern Company."

In challenging the Mississippi and Alabama co-op projects, Branch took appeals all the way to the U.S. Supreme Court. The high court refused to hear either case, and the company lost a large portion of its wholesale business in those two states. Construction of a Mississippi cooperative power plant supplanted most of the load Mississippi Power provided to four co-ops. A similar plant in Alabama supplied power to three co-ops Alabama Power had been serving.

Those losses were painful because they represented lost energy loads inside Southern Company's territory, causing some executives to bemoan that REA impacted their companies more than any other form of government competition.

PREPARING FOR A DIFFERENT FUTURE

Branch spent a lot of time contemplating the future. He was the quintessential planner, a forward thinker, an avid reader. He consumed volumes of information, from the most obscure research and economic reports to the national newspapers and journals. His office was filled with books, magazines, papers, reports, and hundreds of clipped articles. The collection spilled smart, modern look that seemed to encapsulate Branch's vision. He had, in fact, inserted himself into many decisions on floor layouts, furniture selections, and even the design of the mirror-glass tower.

Branch managed to maintain a sparkling optimism about the future even in the face of growing social issues in the 1960s. The civil rights movement would eventually have a dramatic impact on the company's work force. Although Branch reportedly advised Dr. Martin Luther King Jr. and made speeches in support of equal rights and better race relations, he rejected King's call for a corporate boycott of Alabama in 1965, saying that suspending Southern Company's $93 million construction program in that state was "unthinkable" and "unwise." "It would damage the innocent as well as the guilty," he wrote to Ralph David Abernathy, chairman of the Alabama Boycott Committee. "It will alienate thoughtful and well-intentioned persons whose support is essential for any enduring improvement of race relations and any real advancement of true civil rights."

Preferring to work behind the scenes with progressive community leaders to help address the troubling issues, company executives sometimes appeared to sit mum as painful chapters in American history played out in the streets within blocks of company facilities. The civil rights movement heralded the first of several waves of public protest. The social revolution ushered in the environmental, antiwar, and women's rights movements and reshuffled the nation's political, social, and economic priorities. It would be only a matter of time and money before utilities would find themselves in the crosshairs of protesters opposing the rising cost of electricity.

Branch sounded warnings about the potential destructive force of inflation during the mid-1960s and limits to the company's ability to offset price increases through the economies of scale. He also saw that labor costs were outstripping gains in productivity. In 1966, when Alabama Power and its union could not agree on a new contract, Branch drew a hard line beyond which he told Alabama Power not to cross in pay negotiations. Neither side would budge when it got to that point. The union walked out over two-tenths of 1 percent, and a debilitating strike followed. A few years later, new contract negotiations were settled without incident, but at a higher cost. In 1970, labor expenses increased by nearly 10 percent.

Other costs were increasing as well. A nationwide coal supply crisis in 1969 resulted in Southern Company's fuel expenses climbing 20 percent in 1970 and another 27 percent the following year. When one of the operating companies sold bonds at 7.14 percent in 1967, Branch complained loudly about "the highest cost of money in forty years." Within three years, the going rate was above 9 percent. By 1970, total operating expenses were increasing in the range of 20 percent, nearly double the rate of sales and revenues. Net income's upward climb slowed to a crawl and then turned painfully downward.

Alabama Power was the first operating company to ask for a general rate increase, something that hadn't happened in decades. The Alabama Public Service Commission (PSC) denied the request in 1968, but the ruling was reversed by the state courts. Later the same year, the Georgia PSC approved a 2 percent rate increase for Georgia Power. In 1969, Mississippi Power filed its first general rate increase following the devastating Hurricane Camille. Gulf Power filed its first request in 1971, and by that time all the other companies were back in begging for more relief at both the retail and wholesale levels. Southern Company and its affiliates found themselves trying to explain to customers that rates were not increasing nearly as much as they imagined, that the dramatic hikes in power bills were mostly caused by the simple fact customers were using more electricity than they had "in the good old days." Even Southern Company's forward-looking advertising theme of "working toward tomorrow, today" added a postscript: "costs more than yesterday."

The good old days, it seemed, were gone for good.

LESSONS LEARNED

"There probably has not been, nor will there ever be, another CEO like Harllee Branch," claimed Southern Company's former public relations executive Dwayne Summar. "Every time I took anything in to him, the first thing he did was pick up his red pen. You finally learned that no matter how much red ink bled on that piece of paper before it was over, you couldn't be too upset about it because it was that much better than before you took it in. He wrote beautifully, he was an eloquent speaker, a lawyer, a talented sketch and watercolor artist. We used to say he was a Renaissance man, and he truly was."

Branch's effectiveness as a communicator is what most distinguished him among the leaders in Southern Company's history. He emulated Preston Arkwright in laying out an eloquent, invincible business case or legal argument. But when he faced federal challenges, he was more like Wendell Willkie—passionate and compelling in his convictions. By helping establish the "fence," Branch was able to leave an enduring legacy and finish one of the jobs Willkie had started. After Commonwealth & Southern sold portions of its southern properties to TVA in 1939, Willkie had tried to obtain a legislated boundary but was only able to obtain an informal promise from TVA directors, a "gentlemen's agreement." The fence included in the TVA Revenue Bond Act eased tensions between the investor-owned and federal power groups, stabilized Southern Company's markets, and led to future cooperative dealings. Good fences do indeed make good neighbors.

From the success of that big bet, Southern Company learned its top executives must be involved in public policy. By the 1960s, industry executives had begun taking an objective look at the growth in public power—from 5 percent of the nation's electricity sales in 1932 to 23 percent by 1959. The answer, some concluded, was not always that their business had been stolen by subsidized competitors, but that the industry shared the blame by "missing opportunities and not fully living up to its responsibilities," American Electric Power president Philip Sporn told EEI members in 1961, citing the timidity of industry leaders in telling their own story. "I do not believe it is possible to have any effective influence in Washington if one stays away from Washington," he warned the utility chiefs.

Branch sent copies of the speech to all his CEOs, labeling it "must reading" and asking them to think "what you can do, individually and as a group, to assure our company's leadership in the exciting but difficult years that lie ahead." As a precursor to establishing a full-time office in Washington, Branch assigned a corporate officer the responsibility of monitoring and responding to federal legislative issues. Southern Company didn't oppose government power, Branch told a reporter, unless it posed a competitive threat. Branch would find it impossible, however, to stop the raids of co-ops and municipalities. To contain the encroachments, the next group of leaders would have to hammer out solutions state by state, either through territorial legislation, legal action, or joint-ownership arrangements.

The "Branch years" would become known for rapid advancements in technology and industrialization. A 250-megawatt unit in 1957 was considered gigantic, the typical units at the time having a capacity of between 60 and 125 megawatts. By 1971, the company was building 800-megawatt units. In 1965, when the system installed 230-kilovolt transmission lines with four times the capacity of 115-kilovolt circuits, company experts announced it would be the "optimum top transmission voltage for at least the next fifteen years." Five years later, the company was installing its first 500-kilovolt lines. Other advancements would come from decisions to create a research department, build a centralized Data Center, design a new digital power coordination system, and enter the nuclear power field.

Lessons learned from the previous decade about the inseparability of electricity and the economy were only reinforced by the company's growth during the 1960s. The company continued to build and sell and build, its success being driven by regional industrialization. By helping recruit those industries and create more than half a million new jobs, Southern Company was ensuring its own good fortune. Customers more than doubled, and revenues and earnings almost tripled during the company's first two decades of operation. Southern Company's ability to deal successfully with that type of growth helped reaffirm the advantages of keeping operating companies under a holding company structure. The financial umbrella made possible some of the system's boldest and most extensive undertakings. The Coosa-Warrior projects were made easier because Alabama Power was part of a unified system with common financial resources, and the benefits of the megadevelopment became available to the entire system. One study showed the integrated operations saved more than $30 million each year over what it would cost the companies to operate separately.

From the Branch era, Southern Company learned the value of business planning. "Project Look Ahead" prepared the company for changes in technology and regulation and many of the social, political, and economic forces that would impact its operations. The studies left an imprint on the company for decades to come. "As a collection of studies, no single exercise ever did more to change all the operating companies and to prepare Southern Company to have the prominent role that it has today," said Summar in 2005. "That change happened in every single function."

One of the study's outcomes was the emergence of the "system concept," allowing Southern Company to remain strongly decentralized in its structure while achieving essential centralized decisions. Before the study, Branch held regular meetings of his top executives to address common problems, but after a full exchange of views, he would mandate systemwide policies if a consensus couldn't be reached.

"We make a fetish of decentralization, except on matters of systemwide importance," Branch told *Business Week*. "We don't make committee decisions; the head of the holding company bears the ultimate responsibility." After "Project Look Ahead," system committees at all levels of management were institutionalized and consensus decision making became the norm in approaching many issues.

Another outcome of "Project Look Ahead," however, created tensions by increasing and expanding the role of the service company. Prior to the study, only engineering and a few technical functions were centralized at Southern Services. After the project, departments were created in a dozen other areas, including the nontechnical functions of human resources, public relations, marketing, and governmental affairs. The service company's growing influence sometimes created conflict with the operating companies and inter-group rivalries over who should do what and which efforts were being duplicated. Despite this friction, the divergent trends of centralization of responsibilities and consensus decision making would continue, bubbling up issues for each succession of leaders to grapple with—sometimes successfully, sometimes not.

One of the Branch era's great paradoxes was the emergence of both the service and parent company identities inside the territory. Branch strongly believed they should maintain a low profile and that operating companies be given credit for any donations, sponsorships, or community involvement. Ironically, he was largely responsible for bringing both "invisible" companies out of the shadows. His decisions to create a data processing center and build a new corporate headquarters gave Southern Company its first public profile—a bold sign on I-285 in Atlanta where thousands of commuters passed daily. The service company's growth in Birmingham similarly resulted in a new building and sign on Highway 280.

Additionally, one of the "Look Ahead" outcomes was a corporate identity program that resulted in the system companies all adopting a common trian-gular symbol a few years after Branch's retirement—the first time all the companies began to look like they belonged to the same parent. Out of that initiative, the name "Southern Services" was changed to "Southern Company Services," a decision which further elevated the presence of Southern Company and began to blur the identities and roles of the parent and service organizations.

As he prepared to retire, Branch saw the company moving toward a different kind of future and tried to prepare his successors for it. The next leaders would have to make bigger bets than he ever had to deal with, so he warned them to "analyze not where your companies were twenty years ago, but where they and you are today. The world changes, and you either keep up with those changes, capitalize on them, accommodate them, or you're in deep trouble."

The winds of change were blowing in troubles from every direction— fuel shortages, new environmental expenses, inflation, and the ever-increasing cost of money. For a capital-intensive company committed to an overly ambitious construction program, it would become a recipe for disaster. Branch could look back with pride on what had been accomplished. But in looking ahead to the 1970s, he could see only a gathering storm.

tering hours, tourists sought refuge in air-conditioned hotels and vacation cottages. Up and down the coast, thousands of electric meters were spinning faster and faster, counting the kilowatts as the heat index approached the afternoon peak.

Harry Bell, Mississippi Power's vice president of engineering and operations, made a daily stop by the control room, a one-story brick building on Seventeenth Street in downtown Gulfport. Except for one unit, the turbines were running at capacity at plants Watson in Gulfport, Eaton in Hattiesburg, and Sweatt near Meridian, each named for a Mississippi Power president. Watson unit 4 had been taken off-line in late July for a boiler leak. "We were all concerned about having enough generation," recalled Bell, "and monitoring the transmission system to make sure we didn't have an overload."

In Pass Christian, Elizabeth Dambrink chatted freely with customers who dropped by to pay their bills. Having worked in the local office for twenty-two years, she was the face of Mississippi Power in the quaint, sleepy community. Everyone called her "Sis," even the customers. Pass was a friendly town, known for its giant magnolias, stately summer homes, and tranquility. Buck Ladner, the other half of the Pass customer service team, was out reading meters and checking on problem accounts. He had joined Mississippi Power the very day a hurricane named Betsy came whisking through the coast in 1965. He tried not to view that as a bad omen.

In the coastal Biloxi office, Winona Latimer, director of the home service department, was wrapping things up before leaving for vacation to visit relatives in Washington, D.C. Latimer's team of home economists conducted educational programs for customers, a role that fit nicely with her community service work. She loved Biloxi's white colonial-style homes and ancient oak trees dripping with Spanish moss.

Back in Gulfport, accountants Norman Yandell and Wallace Majors were trying to get out payroll checks and issue bills for industrial and commercial customers. Both Yandell and Majors ran their programs on a new IBM computer located in the new general office building. Moving into the modern, total-electric headquarters earlier that year had been a morale boost for employees, who previously had been scattered in four downtown locations. At seven stories, the stone-and-glass structure was the tallest and newest building in town. From his office window on the top floor, Mississippi Power president Jack Watson Jr. could see large cargo ships unloading and loading at the deepwater port a half mile to his right and crusty fishing boats and polished yachts lining up at a thriving marina directly across the street. Ten weeks earlier, he had proudly hosted Southern Company's annual meeting at his new building and told stockholders about the great things happening in his territory. Energy sales had more than doubled in the past five years, business was expanding, air corps and naval training bases were bustling, and orders for aircraft parts and shipbuilding were pouring into industries located in Meridian and Pascagoula.

Mississippi Power's new office tower was a testament to this economic growth. Earlier in the year, Watson had dedicated his building "to the fortunes of Mississippi and Mississippians" and promised more than 2,300 residents attending the open house that his company would "continue to keep the faith as, together, we face the challenges of the future."

Watson did not realize just how quickly and severely that promise would be tested. On that beautiful summer day in 1969, neither he nor Bell knew that their operations were about to be threatened by a little rainstorm moving farther out to sea and picking up moisture and speed. On that humid August morning, neither Dambrink nor Latimer, Yandell nor Majors—nor any of Mississippi Power's 850 employees—had any way of knowing their lives, their company, and their communities were about to be changed in a permanent way.

LESSONS IN A SERIES OF UNFORTUNATE EVENTS

Throughout its history, Southern Company has had to deal with natural disasters that wreak havoc on electric operations. Serving communities along the Atlantic and Gulf coastlines makes the operating companies susceptible to the ravages of tropical storms and hurricanes. Even more prevalent are thunderstorms, tornadoes, heat waves, and ice storms that plague the otherwise temperate and pleasant Southeast.

In February 1923—little more than eleven years after James Mitchell created Alabama Traction, Light & Power—a sleet storm descended on northern Alabama. Ice accumulated on conductors, snapping the wires and cutting off electricity from Gadsden to Huntsville. Construction crews went without sleep for up to sixty hours to restore service. "A glowing tribute is due these boys," wrote George Middlemiss, superintendent of maintenance, "for their splendid work in the interest of service and in maintaining the ideals for which our company stands." That dedication to reliable service became a trademark of the new utility system.

In September 1926—exactly two years after Tom Martin had created Southeastern Power & Light—a major storm demolished Pensacola's wharves. The bay front was flooded by a twelve-foot tidal wave, and the entire distribution system in Pensacola was wiped out. Although limited temporary service was returned after two weeks, 600 workers from three states would need two months to rebuild the system and restore power to all customers.

In spring 1936—six years after the southeastern utilities had been absorbed into Commonwealth & Southern—a tornado demolished the city of Gainesville, Georgia, killing 200 people, including Georgia Power district engineer Paul Cox, who was thrown against the substation building. Another 1,200 were injured as the downtown area was reduced to heaps of stone, wood, and steel. Crews responded from throughout the state.

From these and other disasters, operating companies learned how to respond to Mother Nature's fury. As Southern Company evolved and expanded, its utilities got better at planning for emergencies and began sharing lessons learned from their experiences. In the first half of the twentieth century, before hurricanes were given names, several major hurricanes made landfall along the Mississippi coast. The worst arrived September 19, 1947—the month the four operating companies became subsidiaries of newly formed Southern Company. That storm wrecked harbors and piers and damaged the bridge across the Bay of St. Louis. "That bridge had on it our 23-kilovolt line that fed Bay St. Louis," said Watson, who was a transmission supervisor at the time. Charged with coordinating restoration, Watson used one of the company's first two-way radios to tell operators when to energize or de-energize the lines, critical communications during the bridge repairs.

"We didn't know much about how to handle one of these storms," said Watson. "We learned that we needed to have a lot of preparation work in the planning of manpower . . . and to have written procedures that could be used for spreading that information." After the 1947 hurricane, Mississippi Power put together its first formal plan for dealing with disasters. In 1965, when Hurricane Betsy slammed Louisiana with 150-mph winds, Watson surveyed the damages. Seeing giant hardwoods on the ground in the Crescent City, he returned to Gulfport to further tweak the plan.

In January 1965, the winter before Betsy's arrival, the U.S. Army Corps of Engineers had released a study of storms on the Mississippi coast that called on local authorities to establish better building codes and zoning regulations for developments subject to flooding. The Corps also asked communities to put together their own emergency plans but otherwise recommended that "no improvements for hurricane protection along the Mississippi coast be undertaken by the United States at this time."

That was four years and eight months before the arrival of the most intense storm to strike the American mainland during the twentieth century.

PREPARING FOR CAMILLE

Each tropical wave has a kink in its winds, a band of clouds spiraling in semi-circles toward a center, until it picks up enough speed to form a complete circle, at which point it is a tropical depression. After showering the Leeward Islands with rain August 10, this tropical depression began to strengthen, its low-pressure center pulling in warm, humid air from a vast body of water that had been absorbing solar energy all summer. It kept expanding until its winds exceeded thirty-nine miles per hour, the point it officially became a tropical storm and commanded the attention of Robert H. Simpson, director of the National Hurricane Center in Miami. Satellite pictures were primitive in 1969, so Simpson called on the U.S. Navy to secure a plane to fly into the storm to gather enough readings to "put up the warnings for this thing." On August 14 at 1 p.m. EDT, he issued Advisory No. 1: "The new storm, to be known as Camille, was located about 60 miles west of Grand Cayman or 480 miles south of Miami. Camille is moving west northwestward 12 to 14 mph with strongest winds about 60 mph over a very small area near the center." Later that afternoon, Simpson predicted Camille would head toward the western tip of Cuba, placing it along a path to enter the Gulf of Mexico.

When Watson heard the news, he consulted with Bell, who advised his operations team to review staffing charts and make sure their plans were current. At 9 a.m. Friday, August 15, the weather service issued a bulletin proclaiming Camille a "full-fledged hurricane" with winds at ninety miles per hour. Watson was watching closely. Camille had not yet officially entered Gulf waters, the trigger point for activating Mississippi Power's emergency plans. But with the weekend approaching, Watson decided to set his plans in motion ahead of schedule.

Vice president Bell was in charge of the company's response, his command post being the Seventeenth Street control center, where his operators could quickly spot trouble, close switches remotely, isolate faults, and reroute power on the transmission grid. "We had a plan, and people knew what their assignments were," said Bell. By Friday afternoon, trucks were filled with fuel, supplies were packed, and emergency materials were sent to local offices along the coast and a few miles inland. Employees not scheduled to work over the weekend knew to stay tuned to weather forecasts and be available to report on a moment's notice.

That night, Camille battered Cuba with 115-mph winds and ten inches of rain, killing three people and flooding the island's sugar and tobacco crops. "Headed for the open Gulf," Advisory No. 7 warned at midnight. "Camille, a dangerous hurricane, entering the east portion of the Gulf of Mexico, poses a great threat to the United States mainland." A watch was issued for almost the entire coast—from Biloxi, Mississippi, east to St. Mark's, Florida. But after passing over Cuba, Camille weakened and inched forward at less than ten miles per hour. At times, it seemed to stop and sit in one spot, appearing to lose its intensity. In Miami, Simpson was "sure the storm was getting stronger." From satellite pictures, he could see changes in the eye structure, but he needed readings on Camille's central pressure and wind strength. He made an appeal to the Air Force, and that evening a C-130 penetrated Camille's eye.

"The thing was solid," said Captain Frederick J. Foss. "I've never seen it rain harder before or since. . . . The eye was about eight miles in diameter and clean inside. I could see sky above and the sea below. It was a classically formed hurricane." The data Foss brought back gave chills to forecasters—a central pressure of 26.72 inches. The lower the air pressure, the stronger the storm. Only one previous hurricane had recorded a lower barometric reading. "This shook everybody up," said Simpson.

All day Saturday, a handful of Mississippi Power workers came into the office to handle storm preparations. The weather outside could not have been more perfect—crystal clear skies and bright sunshine. No one could believe a killer was approaching. Between weather advisories, Watson placed calls to New Orleans meteorologist Nash Roberts, clinging to the hope that Mississippi would be spared.

"HERE COMES CAMILLE!"

Sunday morning, August 17, Watson and Bell received the bad news. With Camille's slight shift in wind direction, Mississippi Power's territory was now clearly in its path. "Estimated at one hundred and sixty miles per hour," reported Advisory No. 13 at 5 a.m. CDT Sunday. Bell skipped church, returned to the control room, and began placing calls, dispatching workers to their assigned locations. During an early morning service in Hattiesburg, an usher came down the aisle to deliver a message to George East, an engineer in the local office: "Call in. The storm is coming this way." East left immediately and called his supervisor. "The rest of the day, we prepared our own division, looking at the list of materials we needed, getting them together—special wire sizes, connectors, clamps, and splices."

Wallace Majors, who had taken his family to Meridian for the weekend, was putting on his tie for church when he heard someone on the television say, "Here comes Camille! It's going to hit Gulf Coast Mississippi tonight." His first thought was that he had to get back to take up his assigned storm post in Pass Christian. He telephoned the local office and learned a truck was leaving for the coast in a half-hour. "I rode down with the line crew," he said, "leaving my wife and three children in Meridian."

Under drizzling rain along the coast, Mississippi Power workers moved to their assigned posts. Crews went to Ocean Springs and Bay St. Louis so they could operate independently if those towns became isolated by rising waters and bridge damage. Some twenty distribution workers from Alabama Power traveled to Hattiesburg so they could more quickly reach the coast the following day.

More than 200,000 tourists and residents evacuated, the procession of cars stretching ninety miles north. Those who stayed behind boarded up windows, filled bathtubs, buckets, and pots and pans with water, rounded up batteries, and stocked up on food, candles, and other supplies.

Most store shelves had been cleaned out by the time Winona Latimer arrived in Biloxi late Sunday evening. She heard about the approaching storm Saturday night from her nephew in Washington, D.C., who was serving in the military. "When he came home that night, he told us we were going to have the worst storm ever," she said. Latimer drove straight through to the coast. Knowing she would need to help feed work crews at the service center, she went shopping. The owner of a small grocery told her to take what was left.

As night approached, news of Camille's intensity grew more frightful—pressure at 26.62 inches, winds at 190 mph. "No one had seen the wind whip the sea like that before," said copilot Robert Lee Clark, who helped fly the second plane inside the eye. "The sea surface was in deep furrows running along the wind direction. . . . The velocity was beyond the descriptions used in our training." Simpson warned that the storm surge might reach fifteen to twenty feet.

None of the restaurants she had counted on could open, and because the emergency generator was diverted each time she used the kitchen, she would have to take the canned goods home, heat them on a gas grill, and bring lunch back in large pots. "I didn't know pork and beans could be that good!" one hungry worker told her. To prepare supper, Latimer had to retrieve provisions from the Gulfport supply center. Navigating the perilous path along the scenic drive, she was shocked by the damage. The yacht club was washed away. Baricev's restaurant, gone. Even the Magnolia Hotel that had stood undamaged for a hundred years was gutted.

For the team at Pass Christian, it was a morning of miracles and tragedies. Majors, Yandell, Ladner, and Benvenuti gazed in shock at what once had been the town. Every building was damaged, if not demolished. Pass's historic Trinity Episcopal Church was leveled; sixteen members of one family having sought shelter there were dead or missing. Only foundation slabs remained of the Richelieu Manor apartment complex, where at least eight residents lost their lives. The bank, post office, and dozens of businesses were simply gone. In their place were vacant lots or masses of wood, furniture, trees, concrete blocks, appliances, pipes, and plumbing.

Suddenly, out of that war zone stepped the linemen they had given up for dead. During the storm surge, the crew had scrambled up the hotel fire escape to a section of the top floor that held together long enough for them to survive. Mississippi Power's local manager, Tom McDonald, also emerged from the rubble. No one remembers how he got there. McDonald and Sis Dambrink had been scheduled to come on duty at 6:30 a.m. But Sis never arrived. Her brother, Joey, came by later to say, "We lost Sis, Mom, and Dad last night."

"That just about floored us," said Ladner.

"That boy had the most faraway look of horror in his eyes I've ever seen," added Majors. Joey Dambrink had been found that morning clinging to a pine tree. The bodies of Sis and the elder Dambrinks wouldn't be found until later in the week. Nothing remained of their house.

Yandell's truck was found on the beach almost buried in sand. It couldn't be dug out for another month. He rode back to Gulfport with Majors, whose car amazingly started up even though it had been under water a short while. The normal ten-minute drive took an hour and a half. Yandell perched himself on the roof, helping Majors navigate around tree limbs, debris, and missing highway sections. They both wept at the sight of dazed survivors sifting through collapsed buildings and rescue workers struggling to recover bodies. In Gulfport, they found only more destruction and had to maneuver around a large diesel barge deposited in the middle of the highway. After checking the condition of his home, Yandell went to work in the storeroom, issuing materials to line crews. Majors would return to Pass the next day to help shovel mud out of the office before going to Pascagoula to handle trouble calls and set up a soup line.

By noon Monday, 85 percent of all Mississippi Power employees expected to be at work were at their assigned posts. Others who were not scheduled to work that day showed up anyway to help. By noon, two units were up and running at Plant Watson and two at Plant Eaton. The first substations in Gulfport and Hattiesburg were re-energized. By day's end, service had been restored to two hospitals, and substations were re-energized at Pascagoula, Ocean Springs, and ten upstate communities.

Winona Latimer made it back to Biloxi in time to prepare sandwiches for the crew. The round trip to Gulfport had taken four hours. It would be two more days before any restaurants were up and running, so she recruited three cashiers, and they became short-order cooks. "It's unbelievable what you can do with a fry pan and a griddle," Latimer said, "and the number of people you can serve and what you can serve."

In addition to feeding the crews, housing them became a Herculean task. The navy base offered a warehouse converted into a refugee center, and that's where a Georgia Power team led by Rome district engineer Roy Cagle Jr. was housed along with about 600 men, women, and children. "I slept on a cot with a straw mattress and a lot of mosquitoes," he recalled.

By midnight, 115-kilovolt service was restored to Camp Shelby south of Hattiesburg, and early the following day substations were re-energized at Keesler Field near Biloxi. All three Plant Eaton units and Plant Watson's four units were back on-line. The company had accomplished a great deal in the first twenty-four hours. In spite of the frustrations, confusion, and bleakness of the first day, restoration had begun. It was only a small step on the long journey Mississippi Power employees were undertaking.

HARSH REALITIES AND RUDE AWAKENINGS

If Monday had been a day of shock and bewilderment, Tuesday and Wednesday were days of rude awakenings. As reality sank in about the degree of damage and destitution, Mississippi governor John Bell Williams declared martial law and stationed National Guardsmen in every community along

LESSONS LEARNED

Hurricane Camille was more than a natural disaster. It was a watershed event that left a mark on the people it left behind. Those who survived it, those who saw its devastation, those who worked to restore the broken homes, economy, and electric systems would ever after view time in terms of B.C. and A.C.—life before Camille and life after.

Camille taught many lessons on personal, corporate, and national levels. "It taught us that we had to think differently about what was going on around us, that nothing was permanent—anything could be jerked out from under you in a minute," said Mississippi Power vice president Kerry Ezell. "It caused us to sit down and ask, 'When the next hurricane comes along, what are we going to do different?'" Watson encouraged input from everyone, and employees throughout Mississippi Power came up with hundreds of things they should do differently next time. Bell put together a management team to sort through and assess the lessons and adopt the best ones.

Before Camille, the company's response plan had considered all hurricanes the same and assumed damage would be limited primarily to coastline areas. After Camille, the company would have more comprehensive and flexible plans to respond to various levels of storm intensity. Staffing would increase depending on anticipated damage. Plants would follow orderly shutdown procedures based on predicted wind strength. Crews maneuvering in advance of the storm would be housed inland, away from the immediate impact but strategically positioned for quick access to damaged areas after the storm. Employees not directly involved with critical operations would remain home with their families and not report to their stations until after the danger passed.

Before Camille, the company approached restoration the same way it approached heavy-line construction: with a large number of crew members working in units using a wide range of heavy equipment. After Camille, small "storm crews" were organized, with bucket truck, derrick, and pickup crews and other operations split into separate units. Employees had seen the effectiveness of helpers sent from Mississippi Power & Light, who were structured into three-member teams. The company would copy that approach in the future.

Many other practices and tools used by sister companies and outsiders caused Mississippi Power to change preparations in a wide variety of ways: using mobile storerooms and trailers for supplies; adding extra gasoline tanks to provide trucks fuel for several days; renting extra bucket trucks and equipment prior to hurricane season; prepackaging kits for all crews with area maps, specification sheets, fuse and switching diagrams, and connector tables; developing lists of emergency radio and telephone numbers; purchasing newer and better equipment, hydraulic derricks, diggers, and hand tools powered by motor-generated electricity.

The lessons led to improvements of all types—quicker damage assessments, more effective reporting methods, better training and annual drills, an up-and-ready backup control center, better tree-trimming practices, backup food and housing options, more comprehensive staffing assignments, effective use of administrative personnel, and better communications.

A recommendation to improve weather intelligence resulted in Southern Company placing meteorologists on retainer for future hurricane seasons and eventually led to the company establishing its own weather-tracking technology and in-house expertise. Another recommendation—that system crews use a common radio frequency so they could communicate in an emergency—sparked the creation of SouthernLINC Wireless. By 1995, crews traveling from one state to another were able to talk seamlessly while responding to two hurricanes that season.

On Camille's thirtieth anniversary, a study commissioned by the National Science Foundation examined lessons learned and lost since Camille and concluded with this warning: "Another storm of Camille's intensity *will* strike the United States. . . . When this future storm strikes, it will make landfall over conditions drastically different from those in 1969."

POSTSCRIPT: LESSONS IMPLEMENTED

Each stormy season, Southern Company lives under the threat of being hit with another Camille-sized disaster. Although none has yet reached that intensity, many storms have inflicted damages equal to and exceeding those of the 1969 tragedy.

In 1979, on Camille's tenth anniversary, Hurricane Frederic came ashore in the Mobile Bay area. Packing 145-mph winds, it essentially tore apart the electric system in Alabama Power's Mobile Division, leaving behind a tangled mass of distribution lines, thousands of broken or leaning poles, and 240,000 customers in the dark. An electrical system that had required years to build was reconstructed within twenty-one days with the help of 2,000 outside crew members. Gulf Power's territory in Escambia County also was hit hard

Prior to the storm, 2,400 workers from system companies and neighboring utilities were positioned in nearby locations, ready to move in. By the time Katrina hit, more help was already on the way. Worst-case-scenario planning had anticipated the need for up to 5,000 outside workers, but Katrina was worse than worst-case. Ultimately, 11,000 workers from twenty-three states and Canada joined in the restoration, which progressed at record speed because teams were empowered to make decisions close to every trouble spot. Instead of directing repairs from the top down, Mississippi Power's plan relied on a flexible and decentralized response. Crews reporting to team leaders had broad authority to accomplish the mission of getting the power back at the substation level, each serving five thousand people on average.

Visiting workers were housed in air-conditioned circus tents that held up to 1,800 workers each. A well-organized Southern Company team kept them fed and their trucks stocked. The challenges involved serving 30,000 meals a day, delivering 140,000 gallons of fuel to 5,000 trucks every night, ordering supplies from across the country, and shipping materials to twenty-four remote staging areas. In a single day, sixty semitrailers of material were unloaded and distributed.

Throughout the effort, critical communications were facilitated by SouthernLINC Wireless. Like all communication networks in the area, LINC was severely damaged, but it was the first to restore service. LINC's radio features provided the only communications available for Mississippi Power operations during the initial days. LINC's cell phone functions were restored within three days. And to increase communication with the outside world, Southern Company workers hastily installed microwave dishes to bypass the disabled telephone switches of other providers.

Service restoration was originally estimated to take at least a month, but after the first week, Topazi scrawled across the storm center board the numbers "9-11-05," the anniversary of the 2001 terrorist attacks on the World Trade Center and Pentagon. Topazi challenged his team to "associate that date with a positive memory for people of south Mississippi." The goal was met. In an amazing twelve days, service was returned to all Mississippi Power customers who could safely take power. Only 27,000 remained off-line, all because of repairs needed in order to receive electricity. As in Camille's aftermath, some customer losses would become permanent, and as was the case in 1969, repairs to the company's operations and the state's economy would take years of more hard work. Even as Mississippi Power continued its own reconstruction, the company became a key member of a "Recovery, Rebuilding, and Renewal" commission that Governor Haley Barbour formed to develop a strategy for rebounding from $30 billion in damages to the state's economy and making the coastal region stronger than before.

Although the hurricane unleashed its worst fury on the Mississippi coast, Katrina would be remembered for the suffering it caused in New Orleans, where levees failed to hold back Lake Pontchartrain, which flooded 80 percent of the city, leaving thousands stranded and exposing glaring deficiencies in emergency responses from all levels of government. Once human error in New Orleans transformed the national disaster into a "national disgrace," the accomplishments in Mississippi looked all the more miraculous. Southern Company president David Ratcliffe was summoned to Washington, D.C., to share lessons learned with a Senate committee investigating the government's preparations and response.

Every disaster teaches new lessons. After recovery, Southern Company subsidiaries are careful to critique their response and improve preparations for the next challenge. Southern Company's quick, effective response to Katrina in 2005 was a tribute to advances that operating companies made over the years to planning and coordination efforts. In many ways, the successful responses to Ivan, Frederic, the "storm of the century," and dozens of other natural disasters were credits earned against a debt paid—and hard lessons learned—when Camille visited the Mississippi coast back in 1969.

PSC chairman Ben Wiggins returned to the second-floor hearing room of the state office building across from the Capitol in Atlanta to make an announcement: The five-member commission had voted to uphold a motion by the PSC staff to postpone hearings until January 20 because Georgia Power's application had been based on the need for more earnings "coverage," so it could issue more securities for the financing of construction. "Coverage is not a test under state law for adequacy of rate relief," said deputy assistant attorney general Robert Castellani.

Scherer and Georgia Power's other leaders were furious, believing the PSC was dodging its responsibility. "Ben Wiggins [PSC chairman] was not a man of great backbone, but it was still surprising that he would run away in the face of the seriousness of our situation," Scherer said. Meetings began immediately at corporate headquarters at Peachtree and Baker streets. The company's first move was to file a motion to reopen the hearing, which the PSC denied the following day. Georgia Power then filed for $305 million in permanent relief, including $86 million in emergency relief and $49.9 million in fuel-cost recovery. The move was bold but also strategic. Fuel-cost recovery gave the PSC an out, as increased fuel costs could be passed on to customers through a fuel adjustment rider. "So it was easy for them [the PSC]," Scherer said, "because . . . they could say, 'We don't have any control over that.'"

By Thursday, December 19, Georgia Power's miserable financial condition was laid out for all to see in the testimony of Allen Wilson, financial vice president. He said the company's cash position had deteriorated drastically during five months of declining income and rising costs and that the next day Georgia Power would have approximately $400 million in bills due, primarily delinquent property taxes in nearly every county in Georgia.

What should have been the best of times for an "engineering company" had devolved into the worst of times. Georgia Power had placed four new generating units in operation in 1974, installing more megawatts in one year than it had in its first thirty-five, but inflation had sent the cost of virtually everything an electric utility needed to operate soaring. Even the price of power poles had nearly doubled during the year. As a result, the cost of electricity was rising across the United States. New York City's rates were up 37 percent from 1973, Boston's 32 percent, and Cleveland's 29 percent. Georgia Power's rates had jumped 22 percent. "It was a bad, bad time," said John Hemby, then division manager in Macon. "People did not understand, even when you talked about our rates being lower than they had been in 1930. They were nearly 6¢ a kilowatt-hour in 1930, and we were just 2½¢ then. You could tell people that, but they didn't want to listen. 'I don't care, I don't want my electric rates going up, and you ought to do something about it! Georgia Power has been a good company in the past, but you are no longer a good company.'"

By the end of 1974, Georgia Power's financial condition was, in Scherer's words, "a real bad pot of stew. . . . We were unable to pay our taxes. We didn't have enough coming in to adequately cover what we had going out. We didn't have the cash. Under the law, we probably would have been considered insolvent."

THE MAKING OF A PERFECT STORM

Georgia Power's financial crisis came at the ebb tide of an unparalleled period in electric utility history. Between 1940 and 1970, the real price of electricity in America dropped 70 percent; Georgia Power's decreased 71 percent. The price decline was driven by increasing demand and a decreasing cost system. "We had all of the benefits of building larger-scale plants, and the efficiencies incurred by that—the better efficiencies of burning fuel and everything else," Scherer explained. "We were spreading our base cost, our fixed cost, over many more units." The cost curve, however, had changed dramatically and quickly in the late 1960s. "All of a sudden, we struck a wall and determined that, yes, this might be the end of the economies of scale and that we had to go to the PSC," said Scherer.

Prior to 1970, Georgia Power had sought only two rate increases—and ten rate reductions—during the previous thirty-seven years, creating a culture that made Hatch reluctant to go before the PSC. "He did not want to be known as the president who asked for a rate increase after Jack McDonough and others served without having to do this," Baker said.

Hatch was a CEO in a difficult place at a difficult time. It did not help that he followed the popular McDonough, a natural leader who had been class president and quarterback of the football team at Georgia Tech. Unlike McDonough, Hatch neither came from Georgia nor came up through the ranks. He grew up in Uniontown, Alabama, and was a three-sport letterman at the University of the South before moving on to the University of Alabama School of Law. He came of age in the law firm of Martin, Turner, and McWhorter, the legal counsel for Alabama Power started by Judge Logan Martin, the brother of longtime Alabama Power president Tom Martin. Hatch left the firm in 1955 to become an Alabama Power vice president. He was named executive vice president in 1958 and was moved to Georgia Power in 1962 to be in place to succeed McDonough in less than a year. He was one of the three former partners of the law firm who would make up the Southern Company triumvirate of the 1970s, along with Alabama Power CEO Joe Farley and Southern Company CEO Alvin Vogtle. All three were elected to their positions under Southern Company CEO Harllee Branch, who also had started as a legal counsel.

Hatch made a good impression. He had a deep, resounding voice, the speaking ease of an attorney, and a miniature red rose on his lapel. If an employee did him a favor, he would unfailingly send a note of thanks. "I don't know of anybody who didn't like Mr. Hatch. He was easygoing and a very likable guy. He was a charmer," Hemby said. Hatch's leadership, however, would be compromised by illness. In 1968, he contracted hepatitis and would eventually go to Yale University for treatment and use a retreat on the Georgia coast for his lengthy recuperation. "When the chief person is not available, you seem to have a loss of command lines," Scherer said. "It sort of diffused the operations."

Bill Bowen, a senior vice president, essentially ran the company during Hatch's nearly two-year absence. When Bowen retired in 1971, the mantle of second-in-charge passed to Scherer as executive vice president, but he soon found himself functioning as a quasi-chief operating officer even after Hatch returned to work. "I think Hatch felt that his presence in the community and within the business community was adequate," Scherer said. "He felt the nuts and bolts could be done by someone else. That was his perception of the [president's] job."

But with costs and load continuing to climb in tandem, Hatch was finally forced to go back to the PSC. And once he went back, he had to keep going back, filing three rate cases in the thirty months starting in May 1971. With each trip, public hearings were more hostile, rate increases were harder to win, and opposition was more organized. The first foe was the Georgia Power Project, with the stated goals of socializing U.S. business and blocking Georgia Power's rate request. Then, after the PSC shamelessly played to the voting public and gave a break to residential customers when granting emergency rate relief, the Georgia Industrial Group became a heavyweight opponent. One rate case dragged on for eighteen months before the Georgia Supreme Court finally turned down Georgia Power's appeal in November 1973, while warning the PSC that it should examine its future rate-making structure, especially related to "construction work in progress."

By then, though, the perfect storm of energy crisis and financial peril had already struck—a worldwide storm that would sweep out of the Middle East and crush the great southeastern economic boom. It began October 6, 1973, when Egypt and Syria attacked Israel, and the United States responded by rushing military aid to Israel. The other shoe dropped October 17, when angry Arab nations, all members of the Organization of Petroleum Exporting Countries (OPEC), imposed a total ban on oil sales to the United States. Within weeks, the Dow Jones Industrial Average dropped 200 points—more than 20 percent—and a massive recession set in, with annual inflation rates of more than 6 percent and prime rates in double digits. Within a year, the Dow had dropped another 200 points.

Georgia Power was not hurt by the embargo as directly as utilities reliant on oil, but the cost of all fuels increased, and about half the company's costs were related to fuel. "Fuel prices went up, inflation went up, the cost of borrowing went up. And all those things happened at the same time. Every cost we had was going up," Dahlberg said. By April 1974, inflation had driven the company's expenses up 33 percent from the previous year, and interest charges were up 37 percent.

Georgia Power's troubles were not occurring in isolation. Alabama Power and Mississippi Power were also ensnarled in repeated battles with state regulators, and the overall effect was crippling Southern Company financially. The parent company had been reeling since 1971, so when Georgia Power was unable to sell bonds in mid-1974, Southern Company CEO Alvin Vogtle knew he had to act. As chairman of the Edison Electric Institute in 1973–74, he was helping lead the industry through the mounting turbulence and thought no company would survive the 1970s unless it could cope with the changes engulfing society and business. He believed the issues mandated creative, active leadership and a willingness to meet them head on. He realized Harllee Branch's utility company would not be his utility company. Branch told him as much after retiring as chairman in 1971. "I said, 'Alvin, I don't have many things I can lay claim to, but I knew exactly when to get the hell out of that company,'" said Branch, who believed Vogtle's emotional and mental maturity were perfectly suited for the turmoil ahead.

THE FEARLESS ONE

Alvin Vogtle had always seemed older than his age. When he ran away from home at age ten, his mother and sister found him in downtown Birmingham, wearing one of his father's suits and looking for a job, his pants cuffs dragging the ground. That was about the same time his school administered IQ tests to every student; his score was reportedly the highest ever recorded in Birmingham public schools. He was promoted from the fourth to the seventh grade.

Vogtle grew up quickly, the oldest child of a mother who was a former schoolteacher and a father who was a coal company vice president. He was the quarterback of the Ramsay High School football team and worked summers for the railroad, even doing a hitch in the coal yard. By fifteen, he had entered Auburn University. Within two years of graduating from Auburn, he had completed law school at the University of Alabama. He immediately sought a position at the Martin, Blakey, and McWhorter law firm, as his father was a friend of Tom Martin and Judge Logan Martin. When Judge Martin told Vogtle he had no openings, Vogtle said he would not have to pay him, he just needed the experience. When Judge Martin told him he had no extra chairs, Vogtle replied, "I'll just stand."

Within a year, Vogtle was off to World War II as a fighter pilot. When he returned to Birmingham and the law firm, he began impressing most everyone he worked with, particularly the Martins. Judge Martin, a taskmaster with a red pen, became Vogtle's mentor. Tom Martin, meanwhile, would tap Vogtle to be his personal lawyer. "Few people, I suspect, had Mr. Martin's confidence in the way that Alvin did. The way that he operated was very impressive to all who worked with him," said Joe Farley.

Like Judge Martin, Vogtle was a man of few words, but he could make a good impression on strangers. One of them was Branch, who met Vogtle at a system meeting in the early 1950s. After Branch became Southern Company CEO in 1957 and began considering a successor, he thought of Vogtle, who was handling a lot of his firm's work for Southern Company and Alabama Power.

One day in 1959 when Branch was in Birmingham, he walked into Vogtle's office without warning. By this time, the sign on the door read "Martin, Vogtle, Balch, and Bingham." Branch offered Vogtle an opportunity to join Southern Company. Making no promises, Branch said the move would involve some risk but it could lead to Vogtle having "a great shot" at becoming Southern Company's next CEO. "Alvin said he would like to think about it," Branch said. "After he did, he said he would be willing to take the risk."

While still with the law firm, Vogtle was made president of Southern Electric Generating Company, jointly owned by Alabama Power and Georgia Power. In 1962, he was named executive vice president of Alabama Power, and three years later, Branch brought him to Atlanta as Southern Company vice president, promoting him to executive vice president nine months later. He was elected president of Southern Company in 1969, CEO in 1970, and chairman in 1971. "Alvin was one of the best disciplined, most self-reliant, and efficient executives I ever knew," Branch said. "Alvin rarely gave the impression that he was confused or bewildered. He was a straight thinker. You never saw his desk cluttered with papers, never found his mind cluttered with a lot of things."

Vogtle was the antithesis of Branch, whose desk was piled high with stacks of paper. Vogtle never lost himself in details, delegating them instead. His conversations were short and to the point, with minimal chitchat. He believed strongly that a piece of paper should be touched only once. Rarely did a visitor to his office see paper in the in-box. "He was quicker than the rest of us," said Tom Nunnelly, one of his vice presidents.

Vogtle's daily *New York Times* crossword puzzle was always done in ink and always finished. His memory was photographic. Before the annual stockholders meeting, he would retreat to a small room, drink hot tea, and look over his speech text. Then he would go on stage, deliver the address almost word for word, and handle stockholder questions calmly, using humor spontaneously. "One of the amazing things about Alvin was his ability to absorb a vast amount of information and then use it to make prompt decisions," said Vic Daniel, Mississippi Power president, who reported to Vogtle for a decade.

Partially because he had not grown up in the company, Vogtle was more of a portfolio manager than a business manager, allowing operating company CEOs to run their own show. "Anytime I needed Alvin, he was right there," said Daniel, "but he wasn't going to bother you if he thought you were making a good return on equity. He told me once that I wouldn't see him around very often, but that if he came down here, he was going to look around and see if I was running the company right. If I wasn't, he was going to get somebody else to run it."

Despite being only five-foot-seven, Vogtle was incredibly comfortable with himself. He was a man of action, believing that worrying interfered with "the proper thinking process." He did not like meetings, committees, or people getting too close to him. "He was the most private man I ever knew," Branch said. "He never told anyone where he was going or what he was doing and neither asked for nor tolerated outside advice. He liked people individually but disliked them in crowds."

Yet, Vogtle could be absolutely charming—a good listener, courteous, appreciative of any kindness or effort by a subordinate, and overwhelmingly modest, often referring to Plant Vogtle as "the so-called Vogtle nuclear plant." He used humor to make others feel comfortable around him. Someone would walk into his office, and he would say, "Sit down, I want to tell you this joke." He loved to laugh out loud. He also loved Auburn football, flying his Beechcraft airplane, and playing golf at Augusta National Golf Club, where he was a member. And he loved his family. A widower, Vogtle and his second wife and their four children lived on a seventeen-acre horse farm in Cherokee County. Rising at 4:15 a.m., he would exercise, take the kids to school, and be at Southern Company's headquarters at Perimeter Center by 8:00, ready for whatever challenge the day might bring.

On a late-summer morning in 1974, Vogtle made the tough decision that company engineers could not force themselves to make. He announced September 12 that Southern Company would cut its construction budget for the next three years by one-third—a whopping $1.7 billion. He said his decision was the result of low earnings by the operating companies and the "unsettled state of securities markets." He warned, however, "The reliability of electric service in the years ahead may be affected."

Vogtle knew his company was staying alive on a half-billion dollars of short-term debt but was also drowning in it. What Southern Company needed was cash, and he knew the way to get it was to sell stock. Southern Company could use the net proceeds from a stock sale to buy common stock in the operating companies, each of which could then take the proceeds and retire debt used to finance construction. But the message Vogtle kept hearing was that issuing new shares would be folly for any electric utility in 1974. Financial experts told him repeatedly: You don't sell stock until the conditions are just right, until your earnings are such that people are encouraged enough to invest in your company.

Conditions were anything but ideal. The industry was in the midst of its most serious crisis since the 1920s holding company scandal, and Southern Company's shares, which had traded at more than $17 in early 1974, were now selling below $10. Because new shares would have to sell at about half of their book value of $18.36, Vogtle's advisors warned that a stock sale would dilute the value of the existing 81 million shares. Vogtle not only wanted to issue new shares, he wanted to issue 17.5 million of them—potentially the largest equity sale ever by a utility in terms of the number of shares. He knew it was a gamble. No one was sure the shares could be sold, and even if they were, the proposition would be costly, with underwriters taking 8 percent of the proceeds. Vogtle's back was to the wall, but he had been in a few tight spots before. He was a man who refused to be fenced in.

Army Air Force Lieutenant Alvin Vogtle had been captured in January 1943 after being forced to crash-land in North Africa on his thirty-fifth mission of the war, his Spitfire fighter coming in wheels-down at eighty miles an hour, hitting a drainage ditch, and splitting in half but leaving Vogtle uninjured. He was quickly captured by German soldiers, but they would never make a model prisoner out of him. Five times during the next twenty-six months, he would attempt to escape from their prisoner-of-war camps. Imprisonment was intolerable to Vogtle because he was so intensely private and independent. It made him feel like a caged animal, and he constantly searched for ways to escape. Once, he sneaked out by burying himself in a trash wagon and made it all the way into Czechoslovakia before civilians, fearing the Gestapo, turned him in. Another time he leaped from a train transporting him to another POW camp and made it seventy-five miles through the German woods before being captured while hiding in a barn. Then, in the winter of 1945, Vogtle—dressed like the British orderlies who delivered water to the camp every day—slipped away yet again. He hiked through snow drifts, biked down country roads, disguised himself as a Frenchman, and, in the predawn of a cold March morning, rowed across the icy Rhine River into Switzerland. Mission accomplished; singular focus still intact.

Needing to get out of another tight spot, Vogtle took Southern Company to market Wednesday, September 18, 1974, looking for buyers of 17.5 million new shares of stock. It was an incredibly bold move. It was also a sellout. All the shares sold the first day, mostly to small investors coaxed into buying a 14.7 percent dividend yield. At $9.50 per share, Southern Company generated $152.9 million. The *Atlanta Constitution* called the stock sale "ice-breaking." It was a watershed moment, indirectly mobilizing the entire securities industry. Vogtle had won for Southern Company "the respect of investment analysts, bankers, stockholders, and regulators," according to Branch. "He did it not only with brains but with guts."

"When he [Vogtle] went forward with the sale of the diluted stock," Scherer said, "he had the resolve to say, 'We are going to do whatever we have to do.' He could have let the operating companies flounder about if he had wanted to run. But he stood up there, cinched up his belt, and sold the stock. I think it was the same determination he had as a POW."

WOLVES AT THE DOOR

Vogtle's bold stock sale did not rescue Georgia Power from its financial precipice; it just bought the company a little more time. Within three months, with Christmas fast approaching, the wolves were back at the door. Friday, December 20, 1974, was the due date for property taxes all over the state, and Georgia Power had property in virtually every county. "I can remember trying to figure out how much money we had, trying to figure out on a Friday, 'Do we pay our employees or do we pay bond interest?' We didn't have enough money to pay both," Dahlberg said. "We were broke."

The company never missed a payroll during those final weeks of 1974, but paying $21 million in ad valorem taxes had to wait. For rural Putnam County in middle Georgia, for example, that meant waiting on two-thirds of the county's 1974 tax income. For Georgia Power, it meant paying $262 in interest to Putnam County every day, and a lot of legwork. "We dispatched people around the state to the various counties and municipalities to request they hold off on any action against us," Scherer recalled.

The three bank presidents on the Georgia Power board of directors—First Atlanta's Tom Williams, Citizens & Southern's Bennett Brown, and Trust Company of Georgia's Bob Strickland—also helped make contacts. The personal communication blitz worked, for the counties and municipalities were patient. "I think they all realized their future depended on our future, so they didn't buck it," said Scherer.

Relief came two days before Christmas, when the PSC granted $35 million of the $49.9 million the company had requested six days earlier for fuel-cost recovery. It was not enough. Two days after Christmas, the company announced 1,500 job cuts, including 1,200 contract workers who were building plants. "They didn't give us what we asked for, but they gave us enough to clear the hurdle and to make the checks good and to give us reasonable viability," said Scherer, who was overseeing the finishing touches on a major agreement he had brokered nearly two years earlier—the state's Territorial Electric Service Act, which attempted to settle forever who would serve the thousands of new electricity customers moving into the state weekly.

Georgia Power, electric membership cooperatives (EMC), and municipal utilities had previously abided by what was known as a "closer-to" agreement. "If your line was closer to the customer than my line, then you would serve that customer. If my line was closer, I would serve that customer," said Scherer. "We also had a stated exception that Georgia Power would serve any load in excess of a certain level [initially 100 kilowatts], which was basically industrial or commercial customers." Some forty co-ops blanketed the state, and although Georgia Power had more customers, the co-ops controlled more land, partially because Georgia Power had been historically hesitant to move into the state's less developed areas.

Scherer was increasingly hearing of conflict. "You had an aggressive EMC manager wanting to serve a particular new load or an aggressive Georgia Power manager wanting to serve a new load," said Scherer, who was also hearing from his lawyers. Based on what was happening in other states, they said that, without legislation, the "closer-to" agreement might be in violation of antitrust laws. Congress had recently passed a law making it more difficult for co-ops to borrow money through the Rural Electrification Administration. "This meant they would have to go to private sources to borrow money, and their financial people felt it was going to be difficult to borrow money while sitting in the shadow of this huge electric utility they believed could take over their territory at almost any time," said Grady Baker.

Scherer had two options—negotiate a settlement or wait for the courts to dictate one. Legal counsel for both sides agreed a correction was necessary. "We had to come up with an intelligent piece of legislation that would serve the interests of Georgia Power as well as the co-ops," he said. "They were strong enough politically to keep anything from happening that wasn't an acceptable compromise."

Georgia Power invited all the state's co-ops to join the negotiations. However, the state's municipal utilities, which, under the "closer-to" gentlemen's agreement, served customers inside city limits, had declined an invitation to negotiate and helped defeat the bill in the 1972 legislature. A study committee was then formed to redraft the bill to include the municipals.

"The one thing that I really felt strongly about," Scherer said, "was the opportunity to serve loads in excess of a certain level. We finally settled on 900 kilowatts connected. If that customer wanted to choose a supplier, then the customer would have that opportunity. I felt it was important to the state that Georgia Power be able to serve these larger loads, because it was superior in its ability to deliver, service, and maintain the customer's requirements and, as a result, would help the state win these loads from other states."

After the Territorial Act passed easily in 1973, the real work began. "To make sure everything was completely defined, we had to develop a series of maps to present to the PSC for ultimate approval," Scherer said. "We wanted to define clearly every area in Georgia, and that was going to be a Herculean job."

Scherer chose Baker, his assistant, to lead Georgia Power's efforts in drawing the maps because "Grady was very imaginative, very creative. If you wanted something done, you asked Grady to do it."

Baker's eight-person territorial affairs team leased the top floor of a bank building at Peachtree Street and North Avenue and began negotiating with thirty-nine co-ops and fifty municipals. "We set up a conference room as a negotiating center," he said. "We also traveled around the state negotiating." The negotiator assigned to work with a specific co-op or municipal would obtain as many maps showing distribution and transmission facilities as possible and then drive around the territory for a day or two, adding to the maps. That was the process for 159 maps, one for each county. It was a tedious chore, one made more difficult by the fact that the negotiating parties had been—and would continue to be—competitors. "Historically, we had not liked each other very much," Baker said. But traditional animosity never colored Scherer's view. He believed a solution could be found that satisfied all parties. Conceived in that optimism, a cooperative relationship with a competitor was born.

Scherer had never been one to bemoan his fate anyway. When he had been given the chore of leading a company in crisis without an appropriate title, he was unfazed by the extra responsibility. "I learned early on that I should not worry about someone else having greater benefits or being rewarded at a higher level," he said. "The most important thing to me was not to be goaded by who got the credit for what, because that is an awfully consuming kind of passion and makes you ineffective."

Scherer had grown up in the Dutch section of St. Louis wearing cardboard in his shoes. His grandfather was a German immigrant, his father a tailor who struggled through the Depression, his mother a keypunch operator. His parents taught him obedience, thrift, the value of hard work, and more thrift. They also instilled in him a compelling desire to better his station in life. He was a drugstore delivery boy in high school and landed in Georgia because he took the Marines' V-12 officers test and his scores had been high enough to be sent to Georgia Tech. But when World War II ended and the V-12 program was terminated at Tech, Scherer transferred to Yale, earned a mechanical engineering degree, and then took a job with Westinghouse in Pittsburgh.

Married to an Atlantan, he soon returned to the city, taking a draftsman job at Georgia Power for $200 a month and moving into an apartment in Little Five Points. Life was good. Then, one day, he received a card from the Veterans Administration saying he was eligible to go to college under the GI Bill. Believing he needed "further development," he started taking night classes at Emory University's law school. "I started law school with the idea that whenever I got tired, I could quit. But because it was so fascinating, I never got tired," he said.

Scherer was dispatched to Rome in 1959, eventually becoming division vice president before returning to Atlanta in 1969 as a senior vice president at forty-three. In little more than two decades, he had gone from a Midwest-born outsider to heir apparent at Georgia Power, a ladder rarely climbed at Southern Company by nonsoutherners. His grasp of the business was that exceptional, his attitude that extraordinary. A small plaque in his office read: "Promise yourself to think only of the best, to work only for the best, and to expect only the best."

THE DEAL THAT WALKED IN THE DOOR

The solution to Georgia Power's financial crisis walked through Scherer's office door one day. Even the optimist in him couldn't believe it. "They said, 'We want to buy your plants. We want to buy in,'" he recalled. "I sat there rather stunned. I didn't say 'yes,' I didn't say 'no.' I said, 'We will have to study that.'"

Scherer's visitors that fall day in 1974 represented Oglethorpe Electric Membership Corporation, the new bulk power cooperative formed in August by the Georgia Electric Membership Corporation to own generation and transmission assets for thirty-nine co-ops. The first thing Scherer did when they left was ask himself and every other officer he could find, "Why do they want to do this?" He decided it was at least partially ego. "It [generation] would finally put the crown on. 'Not only do we have transmission lines under the Territorial Act, but now we also have generation. We are one integrated company,'" Scherer said.

Oglethorpe's leadership believed generation ownership would reduce its cost because it could acquire money more cheaply than Georgia Power through federal loans guaranteed by the Rural Electrification Administration. The proposal followed months of conversation between Scherer and the co-ops. "We were in constant contact because I was concerned that their growth was greater than our growth, and they were a full-requirements customer, meaning we had to provide all their [generation] needs," he said. Georgia Power was the largest investor-owned wholesaler of electricity in the United States, serving not only thirty-nine co-ops but also fifty municipalities.

Regardless of its basis, the proposal seemed too good to be true. "They wanted to buy into existing plants but mostly into plants under construction," Scherer said. "That would put our lower-cost plants, which had been devoted to serving them, into our customer base and put our higher-cost plants into their customer base. So it was a great thing for us in two ways. We were relieved of raising capital for new construction, and they were, in essence, providing for their own generation needs."

The proposal promised to spare Southern Company a possible future write-off. "We already had about $200 million invested in generating facilities that we would have had to cancel," Baker said, "so it would have been just written off as a loss. And bonds would have been impossible to sell, the price of Southern Company stock would have gone zip, and we would have been in bad, bad financial trouble. We were trying to avoid a write-off, and the only way that we could avoid it was to build these plants. And the only way we could build these plants was to get somebody else to pay for them. These guys wanted to help pay for it—and they just wanted to own a little. We certainly thought that was fair."

But the sale of generation to federally backed cooperatives flew in the face of Southern Company tradition. It was certainly not a deal that Harllee Branch, the former Georgia Power and Southern Company CEO, would have done. "Mr. Branch said, 'If they get into the generation business, the next thing you know, we are going to be the tail wagging the dog,'" recalled Hemby. Scherer had heard similar "company tradition" arguments while negotiating the Territorial Act but was even less inclined to listen to them when the company's future was on the line. "Tradition had very little currency as far as I was concerned. It's not that I didn't think tradition was important, but if you weigh it against survival, it comes up a little light," he said.

Still, Scherer knew he was making a big bet, that the decision resting on his shoulders could make or break the company. "I had the responsibility, no one was contesting that. I guess no one else wanted it," he said. Hatch seemed disconnected, deferring with utmost confidence to his executive vice president. "I didn't ask permission, and he didn't resist," Scherer said. "Even when we were negotiating the Territorial Bill, he never came into the room. We'd deal with a paragraph in the contract, and out of obligation I would go say, 'We are going to do so and so,' but it was not a matter of great consequence as far as he was concerned."

After conferring with Georgia Power's lawyers and other leaders, Scherer reached his decision. "If we could relieve ourselves of the burden that was not profitable in the first place," he said, "I was not wed to the concept that we were somehow ordained to run all the electric business in the state. That wasn't reality anyway because we had co-ops all over the state. We had followed what [Preston] Arkwright had said, 'Where we cannot build, we will help others to build.' So, if we had created this situation, why was it almost a sin to bring them into the fold, as long as they came in as full partners with both the benefits and responsibilities of partners?"

Most of those within Southern Company who opposed the sale could recall losing large chunks of territory in Alabama and Mississippi to the federal government under the guise of the Tennessee Valley Authority. "We had a lot of people out of Alabama who said, 'You cannot do that,'" said Scherer. "It was their contention that these people [co-ops] should not be in the generation or transmission business, that we are an integrated system and should maintain total integration, that they [co-ops] are customers, not partners. Their view was that we were courting disaster because you just don't let the camel in under the tent. In a lot of ways, I think they viewed the co-ops as enemies. I didn't view them as such; I viewed them as deep pockets."

Scherer understood Alabama Power executives were "conditioned by their previous experience" with TVA. "The only thing I could do was exercise my prerogative that 'I run my own show. We are separate companies and have to deal with our circumstances as we see them,'" he said.

The next step was to take the deal to Alvin Vogtle at Southern Company's headquarters at Perimeter Center. "We had an elaborate presentation," Baker said. "We started putting up charts and making speeches." Within five minutes, the short, quiet man at the end of the table spoke up. "You guys can go ahead with the presentation if you want to," Vogtle said, "but I think you are going to have to do this." Like Nunnelly had said, Vogtle was "quicker than the rest of us."

"So we adjourned the meeting," recalled Baker, "and immediately started negotiating with the co-ops and the municipals."

"The co-ops wanted to know how much they could buy," Hemby recalled. "Mr. Scherer said, 'How much do you want?'"

"We negotiated it all in about three nights," said Baker, a member of the joint committee that finalized the agreement. "We had a set of contracts about six inches high. The closing occurred at Troutman Sanders's law office. The guy from the REA came down and brought us checks totaling $205 million. He brought three checks because the REA could not write a check for more that $99 million. We closed the deal, signed the contracts, walked across the street, and put the money in the bank."

The sale of 30 percent of Plant Hatch was completed January 16, 1975, and reported in the press as the first phase of an agreement that potentially could include portions of two other plants and eight units in all. The immediate impact for Georgia Power was an injection of inexpensive construction funds and a $332 million reduction in external cash requirements, as the REA money enabled the company to reduce its short-term debt by paying off construction loans.

Four days later, hearings began on the rate case filed the final week of 1974. Three Atlanta police officers were there to control the turnout of some 200 people, who packed themselves along the walls, sat on the floor, and spilled into the hall outside the PSC hearing room. By lunchtime, the session had been moved across Washington Street to Central Presbyterian Church to accommodate all the onlookers. Among them was Bill Dahlberg, who was not scheduled to testify and was sitting with the other spectators. As Allen Wilson was testifying, the woman next to Dahlberg leaned over and asked him: "Do you know that guy?"

"Yeah, I do," Dahlberg replied.

"I hate that gray-headed [expletive]," she said. "I'd like to grind that little pissant up and spit him out."

Dahlberg was shocked. "A lot of people thought that way then," he recalled. "It was a tough environment. You were asking elected officials to increase the price of the product we sold. It was hard on them, too. They'd never been in that situation before."

Wilson, Georgia Power's financial vice president, blamed "worldwide runaway inflation" for raising operating expenses "36 percent in one year."

His testimony was alarmingly blunt—"this company is on the brink of insolvency." Dahlberg recoiled again. "That was great for telling regulators we needed a rate increase," he said, "but it also told financial analysts that we didn't have any money." Before the day was out, following a sudden influx of sell orders, the New York Stock Exchange halted trading on Southern Company stock for the second time in five weeks. The stock closed at $9.50, down $1.

On February 6, the PSC granted Georgia Power only $25 million in emergency rate relief. The decision spawned outrage from company employees, who began a letter-writing campaign to the PSC at Hatch's urging and took out newspaper ads in protest. Less than two weeks later, Georgia Power was back before the PSC, this time to begin hearings on its requested $305 million increase. A week after that, February 25, Scherer and Wilson went to the Georgia Capitol at the request of Tom Murphy, the new Speaker of the House, and made a two-hour presentation on the state of the company. "He [Murphy] wanted to make sure nothing was going to hit us in the face while we were trying to stay afloat. I think he felt we were important to the state and needed to get our story across to the important people in the state," said Scherer, who welcomed the opportunity to educate because "no one knows your circumstances unless you tell them."

Noticeably absent from the Capitol appearance was Hatch. Ironically, Hatch had worked in his law firm's Montgomery office, dealing very successfully with state agencies and the legislature for Alabama Power. "Ed was a master at governmental relations. He was as good as anybody I have ever seen," said Farley, his former law partner. "He was absolutely outstanding. He was the best, most effective lobbyist, year in and year out, at the Alabama legislature and was good in Washington, as well."

Hatch, however, had been unable to develop effective relationships with Georgia's regulators. Although two previous Georgia Power presidents started their careers at Alabama Power—William Mitchell and Clifford McManus—both were engineers and had worked for Georgia Power approximately two decades before taking over. By contrast, Hatch arrived from Alabama as executive vice president and was elevated to president within six months. "It was tough. He came into the maw of an unrelenting, tradition-bound company," Scherer said.

The Georgia PSC never warmed to Hatch. "He would arrive down at the hearings in a chauffeur-driven car with a boutonniere in his lapel, looking like a million dollars and crying, 'We're going broke.' The visual communi-

that it was created to build generating plants," he said. "I felt we needed to bring all these people together to help them understand that this enterprise wasn't just for one specific purpose, that the overall purpose was to serve customers, derive a reasonable profit for stockholders, and treat employees properly." Scherer summoned all senior management to a series of two-day and three-day meetings for a no-holds-barred examination of the corporate conscience, with rank and insignia checked at the door. "I wanted us to develop a view of what the company should be and how we were going to get to where we had to go. The way to do that was to get people talking to each other about their own specialty and about how it related to the company's well-being and growth," he said.

Scherer received some grace time to implement his programs in April when the PSC granted Georgia Power an increase of $116 million, short of the requested $305 million but sufficient to permit the selling of bonds in July. Throughout the spring and summer, Scherer delivered a message of hope to employees, who were bearing the brunt of the company's surging unpopularity, repeating over and over that Georgia Power was not "a candidate for a funeral." "Bob kept us going with his optimism," Dahlberg said. "If I had ever come into his office and said, 'Bob, the world's going to come to an end tomorrow,' he'd have said, 'Well, the next world will probably be better.'"

"It never dawned on me that our task was impossible," said Scherer, "because I could never conceive of this company, as important as it was to the state and its citizens, not meeting its obligations. I knew what we had to do would not be easy, but I had no doubt that we could do it." At employee dinner meetings across the state, Scherer was as candid as he was optimistic. "I felt it was absolutely essential that we level with employees to the fullest extent possible, that they understand where the company was, where it was endeavoring to go, and how it was going to get there," he said.

Despite his engineering degree from Yale and law degree from Emory, Scherer was still the same guy who grew up on the south side of St. Louis. When he told managers to tighten budgets, he first eliminated the CEO's chauffer-driven car. "I wasn't the crown prince. I didn't own the company. I never thought my job came to me by virtue of being endowed," he said. "I was an employee of the company. I was operating in a function that was assigned to me. I had a responsibility, a job description." He thought his greatest possible contribution was integrity—"the most important thing that a person has is his reputation, and if you sell that, you don't have anything else that's worth selling."

Scherer chose to be a stand-up guy for not only employees but also the public, going to consumers face-to-face. His photograph appeared in a series of newspaper ads informing readers that Georgia Power was committed to the state and asking customers to write if they had questions or complaints—every letter was answered. "We must make the facts about our business known," he told employees. "Misimpressions can only be dispelled by openness and a willingness to communicate and respond to every question."

Whether he was talking to PSC members or employees, Scherer never mentioned a return to the good old days. He was creating a different kind of company, and he had another change agent working at his side—Jim Miller Jr., who had been sent from Alabama Power to shape up Georgia Power's generation operations. Miller became executive vice president at the same time Scherer was promoted to president. Unlike Hatch, Miller was able to gain quick support from the Georgia Power executive team, partially because he had been given a mission and worried little about his popularity, but mostly because of his technical competence. "He was one of the greatest operating men that I've ever seen—direct, no frills, demanding," Scherer said. "Jim liked to say, 'In this company, you can't have too much cash or too much coal.' That was Jim Miller."

By the end of 1975, interest rates had dropped slightly, the stock market had stabilized, and the economy was starting to turn around. During that year, Georgia Power and its sister companies had attracted more capital in stock and bond markets than any other U.S. electric utility system. "Twelve months ago, we were desperately requesting emergency rate relief, enduring the lowest earnings in the company's history, and facing the imminent loss of our bond rating," Scherer told employees at year-end. "Today, we see a leaner and stronger operation as a result of a continuing austerity program and a management team whose objective is to keep this company running right for both customers and employees."

Then, in 1976, building on the relationships Scherer and the company had formed over the previous four years, Georgia Power entered an agreement to sell parts of Plant Vogtle units 1 and 2, enabling construction to be restarted after a nearly two-year hiatus. Oglethorpe bought 30 percent, the Municipal Electric Authority of Georgia (MEAG) 17.7 percent, and the city of Dalton 1.6 percent, leaving Georgia Power with 50.7 percent ownership and the role of construction and operation agent. MEAG also agreed to buy 17.7 percent of both Hatch units and 10 percent of Plant Wansley's two units and Plant Scherer's four units. In all, Georgia Power reached agreements for its wholesale customers to invest $1.1 billion of the $3.3 billion needed to build new facilities between 1977 and 1980. The financial challenges were not over, but Scherer's bold bets had saved the company from bankruptcy and eventually restored stability. Earnings finally increased in 1978, the same year Scherer moved up to CEO at last. By that time, however, the financial crisis within Southern Company had migrated west.

AN ADVERSARY IN ALABAMA

Following the "winter of our discontent" in 1978, when the entire industry was rocked by a 110-day coal-miners strike, Alvin Vogtle went to Mobile, Alabama, and related the utility story of the 1970s and the saga of one utility in particular, Alabama Power. He told Southern Company's annual meeting of stockholders: "The climate of the nation seems to be best described by the word 'adversary'—an adversary climate of 'me against them, us against the world.' It is a dangerous climate, one that polarizes and divides. . . . It is within the framework of this adversary climate that utilities are all too often being viewed and portrayed as enemies of the people."

Nowhere was that more true than in Alabama, where utilities were being attacked as the enemy of the state and its people. Following nearly a decade of vilification, rejected rate increases, and political bully pulpits, Alabama Power was running in crisis mode. Eight months after filing an official complaint against the utility, Governor George Wallace was still proclaiming loudly that Alabama Power's rates were just too high. PSC hearings were such theater they were staged in a coliseum to accommodate all the spectators and hecklers. Employees rarely admitted publicly where they worked and lived in the long shadow of layoffs that most assuredly lurked behind the next unfavorable PSC or court decision.

Alabama Power had sought its first rate increase ever a decade earlier, in 1968, when the PSC chairman was Eugene "Bull" Connor, the infamous Birmingham public safety commissioner quoted so often on national television during the civil rights struggle. The increase was denied outright, although later granted in part by the courts. The company was in deeper financial trouble when it returned to the PSC in 1971, but this time it would face a different name out of Alabama's past—Wallace. Prevented by law from seeking a second term in 1966, he returned to the governor's office in 1971 a different politician. "Governor Wallace had been very much involved with [opposing] civil rights in the 1960s, but that was something that was no longer credible to talk about politically," said Joe Farley, Alabama Power president from 1969 to 1989. "He had, as a new issue, us arriving on the scene with utility rate increases. He was a populist and could become a fierce spokesman for what he perceived that the public wanted, and the public did not want rate increases." While other utilities in the state also faced rising costs, "we were the big one because we served more customers and were obviously much more important to people's pocketbooks," said Farley.

"He picked up a new whipping boy, the electric utilities," explained Eason Balch, longtime Alabama Power counsel. "He jumped on Alabama Power Company while he was running for governor in 1970, and one of the first things he did when he took office in 1971 was hire a special lawyer [Maurice Bishop], who he thought would fight tooth and toenail against the utilities." After Wallace was elected but before he took office, Balch and Farley went to see him, knowing another rate case would soon be necessary. "He was polite, cordial, and friendly but said that the public did not want these increases, that we needed to do something to avoid having them," Farley said.

The battle was on. During the next eight years, it would repeatedly revolve around two combatants—Wallace, the scrappy populist from Clio, Alabama, and Farley, the youthful utility prodigy and product of a prominent Birmingham family, the downtown Farley Building carrying its name. Educated in Birmingham's private schools, Farley had struggled only in deciding what he wanted to be. "Joe was just a bright young guy who started out at Birmingham-Southern before he went to Princeton [after World War II] and got a mechanical engineering degree and made Phi Beta Kappa," Balch said. "Then he went down to the University of Alabama and did some graduate work in economics and finance." After a year in graduate school, Farley realized that the course he had most enjoyed was business law, so he applied to Harvard Law School and was accepted. A better education for an electric utility executive could not have been scripted in a boardroom— engineering degree, law degree, and graduate school in business.

In 1952, Farley went to work for Alabama Power's law firm; his cousin, Hobart McWhorter, was a managing partner. Farley's quick mind impressed his superiors, and he became the protégé of Tom Martin himself, Alabama Power's president. For the next thirteen years, his primary legal work would be done for Alabama Power. In 1965, while still in his thirties, he was elected executive vice president of the company. Four years later, he became president at forty-one. Within just two years, he would enter the ring for a war of words with Wallace, one of America's formidable political forces, having finished third in the 1968 U.S. presidential election. And if Wallace made Alabama Power public enemy number one, then Farley's was the face he put on the poster.

"I think Governor Wallace, if you could have gotten the truth out of him, would have said he sort of personified his demagoguery on Joe," said Balch. But if the boyish-looking Farley was intimidated, he never blinked. He was, in many ways, the quintessential match for Wallace. "I think Joe must have felt like he was in a life-and-death struggle to wring out sufficient recognition of the need for rate relief," Balch recalled. "Joe knew what the responsibility of the company was. The whole culture and society of the state would break down without electric power."

"At one time," Farley said, "we took out a five-minute information commercial on several television stations for me to explain why we were doing what we were doing. We tried talking to all the political and media leadership, going to public meetings, taking every civic club role we could get, and sending stuffers with our bills." Usually, though, the opposing view just had too much clout. "You do not have the ability to get through to the public that the governor has. He was fussing at us on statewide television and in front of the legislature," Farley explained.

Despite being paralyzed from an assassination attempt during his presidential campaign of 1972, Wallace sought re-election in 1974 and won, the state constitution having been amended to permit two successive terms. His assault on Alabama Power intensified. After he appointed Kenneth Hammond as PSC chairman to fill Connor's unexpired term, the commission rejected outright Alabama Power's $106.8 million rate case in 1976—in Farley's words, "a zero award." The PSC, according to Farley, "by and large tried its best to do a good job, and they took a lot of flak for that. They were severely attacked, and some of them lost their office for granting us some increases."

"George Wallace not only influenced the commission," said Balch, "he also influenced the courts, and he influenced the legislature." Annoyed that Alabama Power had received a $61 million rate increase in April 1977, Wallace filed a "complaint case" against the company in late August, alleging its rates were too high and forcing the PSC to call a hearing to set whatever rate it deemed appropriate. However, the complaint case dragged on for fourteen months, a critical period in which the company's tattered public image received repeated pounding. During that span, Alabama Power was forced to cancel its Barton nuclear plant under construction on the Coosa River north of Montgomery, writing off its $25 million investment over five years. Only two years earlier, the company had canceled units 3 and 4 of the plant and stopped work on units 1 and 2.

Although some editorial pages had actually started the decade sympathetic toward Alabama Power, that support "wears thin after seven or eight years of rate increases," said Farley. "We had to go back to the well again and again, and this left the public with the impression that there was just something wrong. There seemed to be no way to explain it that really worked."

Because rate cases were so publicized, customers thought "we were asking for a new rate increase every week," said Bruce Hutchins, Alabama Power's financial planning manager. Customers often vented their frustrations on Alabama Power's work force. "Our employees and their families would be insulted at the grocery store or on the streets, and people would get snide remarks made to them at church," said Farley, who had to have a security guard at his house. "We had a lot of attrition of employees, and people had to work harder than usual."

"You did not go out in public and bring up the subject that you worked for the power company," said Bill Whitt, vice president of division operations. "We had a lot of people that would not pay their bills, and the people on the collection end of the business were in pure hell."

The animosity eventually forced the PSC hearings in Montgomery to move to the state highway department's auditorium and then to Garrett Coliseum. The PSC decided it could not limit attendance at a public meeting, so on hearing days buses would stream into Montgomery. "We did our share of that as simply a matter of self-preservation," Farley confessed. "We had to get our friends and allies there. The union was part of our team and recognized the problems that we had and helped recruit people to show up at these meetings, just as the consumer advocates would solicit people to come."

The atmosphere at the coliseum was "surreal," according to Farley. "The chairman, Mr. Hammond, thought it was great entertainment. You wouldn't think a legal proceeding could go on in front of several thousand people cheering and booing. . . . It was somewhat unnerving, coming and going through a mass of people when you are trying to be a witness or a participant in a hearing like that. . . . It didn't help the image of the state of Alabama one little bit."

After more than a year of hearings and headlines, the complaint case finally ended the day before Thanksgiving in 1978, when the PSC announced approval of a 25 percent surcharge, equivalent to $210 million annually. Within six days, however, Wallace's allies in the Montgomery circuit court had halted the increase. "The governor was absolutely incensed because he had filed the complaint, and we wound up with an increase instead of a decrease," Farley said. Alabama Power appealed to the Alabama Supreme Court. "With a divided vote, they rejected the increase because, they said, the public did not have notice that the complaint might involve an increase instead of a decrease, although there was nothing in the statute to back that up. I'm convinced that it was Governor Wallace's power and threats directed toward the court, which is politically elected," Farley said.

Employees were disheartened; their company had been granted a desperately needed increase only to see it yanked away by a court that never examined the need for additional revenue. Economic destitution set in. Alabama Power drastically reduced spending, limiting expenditures to only those necessary for continued emergency operation, and halted almost all construction work, laying off 2,700 construction craft workers, 550 contract personnel, and 520 employees. Strapped for cash and prohibited from selling long-term securities, the company resorted to short-term bank loans at credit card interest rates. The year ended with an average rate of return on common equity of only 4.46 percent, the worst since the Depression. "That was our worst financial situation up to that point. We sold office buildings and leased them back to get money for payroll," said Farley, who met every Friday with financial executive vice president Walter Johnsey to decide which invoices to pay.

In Farley, Alabama Power employees had a trusted leader who they knew was doing all he could to keep their company afloat. Farley had a brilliant mind yet was a modest man who ate in the employee cafeteria and listed his number in the phone book. He was a straight arrow, a leader with no hidden agendas; his only frailty was a temper forged by his hatred of losing and his absolute commitment to Alabama Power. "I am so deeply committed that it gets personal sometimes. I'm almost obsessed with it," he once said. His leadership ability was founded on his credibility and the indelible impression that he wanted only to do what was right for his company.

Farley led Alabama Power through the worst of times while simultaneously persevering through the most trying and tragic times in his own life. His wife, Sheila, died in July 1978, in the midst of the complaint case, leaving him a widower with three young children. "Sheila came down with kidney failure and died from it," Balch said. "She was on dialysis for a long time, and Joe was forced to give her a lot of attention just for her livelihood. He had to, in effect, become mama and daddy to the three children because Sheila was not able to do it." One of the first calls Farley received when his wife died was from Governor Wallace. "I feel that he was very sincere and that he was genuinely sorry," Farley said. "I think he had the ability to keep things from being a personal vendetta. They were political, and he could compartmentalize his own approach to things in a very different way than maybe the rest of us do."

Although Alabama Power limped through the first half of 1979, with return on equity dipping all the way to 3.7 percent by July, there was hope. Wallace had left office in January, and shortly thereafter his successor, Fob James, called an unpublicized meeting with Farley and the three PSC members. He told them future PSC decisions should be based on the case's merits and, whatever the decisions might be, the governor's office would not interfere. In July, ruling on a $288 million rate request, the PSC granted a three-phase increase totaling $208 million. Ironically, more relief arrived in September on the winds of the worst hurricane ever to hit the company at that time—Hurricane Frederic, which struck Mobile and left Alabama Power with $25 million worth of damage.

"We didn't have $25 million to spend on storm restoration, but Frederic actually got us a lot of very good PR because our people worked really hard," Farley said. "It was obvious to Governor James that the company was doing a Herculean task of restoration, and we got, for once, some very good comments from the governor's office about what we were doing. You could almost feel the tides turning with the public."

By the end of 1979, ROE had climbed to 5.8 percent. Inflation began to ease off, interest rates started downward, and the company was able to sell bonds in June 1980 for the first time in two years. Then in July, a record-breaking heat wave enveloped the South, increasing energy sales and improving Alabama Power's financial condition slightly. The worst was over. At last.

"The period of 1978 and 1979 was very difficult for the company and all of us," Farley said. "You put one foot ahead of the other and keep going. You are thinking the whole time, 'One day we are going to get through this mess, and we are not going to see interest rates continue at 17 percent or 18 percent and inflation at 10 percent or 12 percent. One day we will be out of this mess.'"

Farley was strengthened by his familiarity with company history, which he had learned as Tom Martin's protégé. "When I think what our company people were going through when TVA was taking over the northern 20 percent of the territory and had eyes on the Birmingham market and as far south as Mobile, that wasn't a very easy time either," Farley said. "There have been a number of times that life has not been easy. Many people have seen their businesses collapse and go into bankruptcy. Things get bad and they can get worse, but they can get better. So you just keep doing what you have to do."

MONEY WOES IN MISSISSIPPI

Although regulators in Alabama and Georgia had the greatest effect on Southern Company's financial health in the 1970s, Mississippi Power also encountered regulatory impasses, as did Gulf Power with the Florida PSC. But because of Mississippi politics, Mississippi Power's difficulties were far greater.

"The PSC hearings were generally hostile," said Vic Daniel, Mississippi Power president from 1972 to 1982. "The general conclusion then was the commission was supposed to be just for the customer. So we were not very welcome up at that place [Jackson] at that time." After receiving 100 percent of its first-ever general rate increase request in 1970, Mississippi Power returned for additional increases four times in less than six years. The first three times, the PSC denied the request outright.

The three commissioners were committed to protecting consumers and, thereby, their elected offices—at the PSC's urging, Mississippi Power delayed its 1975 request until one day after elections. "They knew what the ratepayers wanted. They wanted lower rates—no rates at all, if possible," said Harry Bell, who was vice president of operations. "They would use every trick in the book to see that the rates were kept as low as possible and, politically, to see that we got nothing at all, if possible. They would badger witnesses, give them trick questions to try and trip them up." All three commissioners were from rural areas, giving the PSC a "small-town" agenda. "This was a rural state at that time, and everybody was trying to help the farmers," Daniel said. "The REAs were helping the farmers, and they were better politicians than we were. We had not really developed that part of our business, the political part."

Mississippi Power eventually came to expect the PSC to deny its requests without considering testimony. But company officials still gave full testimony so it could be entered into the record that would go to the courts upon appeal. Denied rate increases could be collected under bond in Mississippi, subject to refund if the increase was later denied or reduced by the courts. However, the appeal process could be expensive and lengthy, putting Mississippi Power in the precarious position of never really knowing its exact financial situation.

"Kerry Ezell was financial vice president at the time we were building plants and not getting rate increases," Daniel said. "He came into my office one morning and said, 'Listen, we have enough money to operate on until about May [1979], and after that, we're going to be out of money if we don't get some rate increases.' That was in the winter sometime, but we were able to make ends meet."

While budget cutting was taking place inside, a group calling itself "Citizens for More Power and Less Change" picketed outside the general office building in Gulfport, and employees reported to work never knowing if they would get another good cussing-out from a customer. "The meter-readers were just about crucified," said Hollis Brown, who was Hattiesburg Division vice president. "I was being called at home at night, and my children were actually being threatened in school because their daddy was 'a thief.' I had been called such in the newspaper."

"It was very stressful. When you don't have the money, you wake up at night screaming in kind of a quick way," said Daniel, who underwent heart bypass surgery in 1977.

The three Mississippi Power rate increase requests denied outright by the PSC were all overturned in chancery court or the state supreme court, with the company eventually receiving its total request. The 1975 filing was not settled until September 1979. Two months later, Mississippi Power filed for another increase, and this time the PSC granted 70 percent of the requested $23.9 million. On its lawyers' advice, the company did not appeal the decision.

The decade was finally over, except for the shouting. In 1983, former state attorney general Bill Allain—who had repeatedly intervened on consumers' behalf in rate cases by both Mississippi Power and Mississippi Power & Light, fanning the passions of the public and the PSC—rode his populism into the governor's office. The spoils of war were still being doled out.

The 1979 accident at Three Mile Island revolutionized nuclear regulations and played havoc with the physical and fiscal challenges of completing Plant Vogtle in Georgia—job one for Southern Company CEO Ed Addison (at right). *Owen Franken/CORBIS, GPC Archives*

SOUTHERN COMPANY TAKES CENTER STAGE

JOE FARLEY WAS IN PARIS WHEN HE GOT the word. As an insurance company board member, he had joined the firm's officers on a European business trip, a welcome break from his usual hot seat as Alabama Power president. For nearly a decade, Farley had battled the governor's office, regulators, and court judges over the company's rate cases and mounting financial woes. All of Alabama Power's credit lines were exhausted.

So was Farley. He was looking forward to getting away for a few days. But as soon as he arrived at the hotel March 28, 1979, he heard the news—something about an accident at a nuclear plant in the United States. He checked into his room and immediately placed a call to Pat McDonald, his vice president of power supply and nuclear operations, to find out what was happening.

Georgia Power president Bob Scherer was at the Hyatt Regency Hotel in downtown Atlanta, playing host to the Edison Electric Institute's annual meeting. He was chatting with a number of utility leaders when someone made an announcement that suspended all conversation.

"Everybody's mouth dropped," said Scherer. "There was a great shudder through the crowd—'What is this going to be?'"

The announcement was about developments still taking place a thousand miles away. In the early morning hours March 28, a water pump had gone on the blink at a nuclear power plant in Middletown, Pennsylvania. The plant's backup pump failed to start. What first seemed a "weird kink in the system" turned into a disastrous series of equipment failures and human errors. The turbine tripped off-line, a valve failed to re-close properly, hot water spilled into the basement of the containment building, and a plant operator shut the cooling system down too soon. Inside the containment vessel, part of the nuclear fuel overheated and melted. Radioactive gases escaped to the outside world.

The unthinkable was happening. And happening in a chaotic way. Plant officials and the Nuclear Regulatory Commission (NRC) were overwhelmed by conflicting reports about the problem and a barrage of questions. By the end of the day, they still had not determined the accident's cause or the extent of danger. Overnight, Three Mile Island, and the acronym "TMI," entered the nation's vernacular. With its nightlights glowing eerily on the evening news, unit 2's cooling tower became forever identified as a fearful symbol for nuclear power.

Between paled proceedings in Atlanta, utility executives kept tabs on the unfolding nightmare—more radiation leaking, a large hydrogen bubble forming inside the core vessel, operators struggling to stabilize the reactor, congressmen calling for more government action, and news media descending on the scene like a swarm of locusts. As the EEI meeting broke up that Friday, families living near TMI were dashing to buses, automobiles, and train depots. Panic evacuations started as soon as Pennsylvania governor Dick Thornburgh suggested that all pregnant women and small children within a five-mile area should leave. Youngsters were pulled from classrooms. Hospital and nursing home patients were moved to facilities in nearby counties. Cars jammed every gasoline station in the area.

Throughout the following week, TMI dominated news. A parade of tractor-trailer rigs carted off contaminated water inside concrete, lead, and steel tanks. In a San Francisco rally, Ralph Nader led 30,000 protestors trying to halt the start-up of a nuclear plant in California. Marchers in New York City chanted, "Two, four, six, eight, we don't want to radiate." President Jimmy Carter—a trained nuclear physicist who, as Georgia governor in 1974, had dedicated Georgia Power's nuclear Plant Hatch—visited TMI and sent in

NRC official Harold Denton as his representative on the scene. Denton dispelled rumors with a friendly, jowly grin and such confidence that he quickly became a credible voice of reason, providing reassurance to returning evacuees after the plant cooled down.

Farley kept checking in long-distance from Paris and following developments through articles in the *International Herald-Tribune*. The news spelled nothing but trouble for the nuclear industry. General Public Utilities halted construction of a nuclear unit in New Jersey. The New York State Power Authority dropped plans for one in upstate New York. Hearings were indefinitely suspended on Long Island Lighting Company's proposal for two others.

"I knew it was a significant problem for the industry," Farley recalled, "though not nearly as hazardous as the media would have everyone believe." Farley would know. Having enmeshed himself in the details of building his namesake plant near Dothan, Alabama, he knew more about the operations and safety features of nuclear plants than any other utility CEO in the industry. He also understood the politics and wondered what implications the accident would have for his company's nuclear plant. Having operated successfully for eighteen months, unit 1 was down for refueling, and construction on unit 2 was 75 percent completed. "It was hard to know what the consequences would be," he said, "but we knew there would be a serious aftermath."

Scherer was even more fearful of the troubles ahead for Georgia Power's nuclear program. The second unit of Plant Hatch, near Baxley, Georgia, was preparing to start up, but construction had barely begun on Plant Vogtle, near Augusta. "The first concrete had been poured," he said. "The question is, 'Do we go forward?' This is a time of uncertainty. What do you do?"

Scherer and Farley knew the nuclear power industry was about to undergo sweeping change. So did Alvin Vogtle, Southern Company president. He quickly assembled a top-level task force of nuclear experts on April 3. Vice president Ruble Thomas, the company's most experienced nuclear engineer, led the group in re-examining every safety system in place at the company's nuclear plants. While findings confirmed that designs and procedures were sound, the team made twenty recommendations to further enhance safety and improve operating procedures, training, controls, plant designs, emergency planning, and communication.

The industry responded rapidly, as well. EEI set up an ad hoc committee to help with communication. The Electric Power Research Institute created a capacity had to be finished and financed. That challenge would fall on the shoulders of Ed Addison, named president of Southern Company in April 1983 and CEO upon Vogtle's retirement in November that year.

"It was frightening," said Addison, who faced his board of directors January 16, 1984, with one of the most ambitious construction budgets in the industry's history—$2.3 billion for the year and nearly $8 billion during the next five. "It was like you had your hands on something big that you couldn't control. You couldn't stop because . . . too much was already invested in it." To keep going, Southern Company and its subsidiaries needed to raise $1 billion in 1984 alone and billions more in the years that followed, all from a financial market growing more and more terrified of touching anything nuclear.

Other frightening challenges faced utility leaders in 1984. Federal agencies were busy drafting far-reaching new controls for an environmental problem called "acid rain" and rattling the industry's foundation with threats of deregulation and competition. To protect stockholders' investments, Addison would have to devote as much energy to these issues as financing construction.

Acid rain was an environmental enigma hardly known at the time of the TMI accident. By 1984, eleven bills to control it were fighting for center stage in Congress. One legislative proposal, Addison warned, could cost Southern Company $8 billion in additional capital, a challenge looming as large as Plant Vogtle.

The push for competition was coming from an independent agency within the Department of Energy—the Federal Energy Regulatory Commission (FERC), formed in 1977 from what previously had been the Federal Power Commission. Aside from being the new watchdog over interstate and wholesale energy matters, FERC was looking for ways to promote the growth of cogenerators and independent power producers (IPPs). Cogenerators were large industrial customers that generated their own power and used the waste heat in their factories. A 1978 law required utilities to buy excess electricity from these facilities at high prices on the premise it helped avoid costly new plant construction. IPPs were builders of small power plants that sold energy wholesale to cooperatives, municipalities, or utilities. Needing a competitive environment in which to thrive, IPPs asked FERC to open access to transmission grids, force utilities to bid projects to them, and allow market-based pricing of their energy sales. In short, deregulate the electric industry.

Deregulation, a buzzword of the 1980s, had already occurred in the airline, trucking, banking, and telecommunications industries. "It naturally follows that some people would turn their thoughts to another great big sector of the economy, the electric utility industry," said Addison. At the time, he didn't realize that deregulation for utilities would require the Orwellian concept of *doublethink*, meaning utilities would not actually be set free of regulation, just strapped with a new set of rules for deregulated segments of its business. Addison did understand, however, that his company's destiny was increasingly being reshaped by Big Brother.

"We need to strengthen the Washington office," Addison told his executive team. "Not just strengthen it, but put a heavy presence there." Although the operating companies routinely sent representatives to the nation's capital to communicate with state constituents, Southern Company's D.C. office was still a two-person operation. Creating an influential national voice would entail more than beefing up staff. Addison knew the far greater challenge was creating a stronger, united front among his own team. "It was a loose confederation of companies," he said of the system of utilities he inherited. "There was very little effort made between the operating companies to work together on day-to-day problems. . . . We would have one major company in Washington on one side of an issue and another major company on the other side of the issue."

"I knew a lot of things had to change," he reflected years later. "And if they were going to change, I had to be the driving force that was going to change them." Transforming the loose confederation into a stronger union, preparing Southern Company for competition, building a national voice in Washington, dealing with deregulation and acid rain, completing the construction program, and managing the cost of Plant Vogtle were the challenges and big bets facing Addison in 1984. And they would dominate his decade at Southern Company's helm.

Another issue emerging in 1984 would also stalk Addison. The problem was brewing in Pensacola, resulting in the dismissal of an employee, the first unpleasant task Doug McCrary faced as Gulf Power president. McCrary previously had headed Southern Company Services's engineering organization during six challenging years of plant postponements and design changes, so he thought he had been handed a dream job when he moved his family to the Sunshine State. Political and business leaders had warmly welcomed him to the community. Public support was high, Gulf Power's operations were solid, and employees were enthusiastic and dedicated.

But the honeymoon ended once McCrary started hearing the rumors and then received an anonymous letter warning that something was amiss inside his company. He called his friend Alan Barton, president of Mississippi Power, and asked if he could borrow his security manager for a short investigation. By the end of January 1984, McCrary had a report on his desk about employee theft, vendor kickbacks, and abuses of employee and executive perquisites. Among the first resignations was his manager of general services operations—commonly known as "the warehouse," from which several hundred thousand dollars of company equipment allegedly had been diverted to a construction company in which the manager owned an interest. Initially fired, the warehouse manager was allowed to resign after a follow-up special meeting with Jake Horton, a senior vice president.

To deal with perk abuses, McCrary set up an amnesty program, allowing employees to pay the company back for any goods or questionable services received. He thought the issue would end there, but before the year was out McCrary had to fix another matter—this time with his senior officer, Horton, who attempted to have the company reimburse a vendor for a $1,000 political contribution. McCrary insisted Horton reimburse the vendor from his own pocket. The incident was a forewarning that Gulf Power's problems were a bit deeper than McCrary originally suspected and would keep resurfacing to plague the rest of his career—and that of Ed Addison, as well.

ADDISON: THE MAN WITH THE GOLDEN CHARM

Handsome, tan, and engaging, Addison had been compared to the "Marlboro Man" and Robert Redford. "You just can't help but like him," claimed one Gulf Power employee. "Somehow he makes the rest of us feel important, too." He was "younger and less tested" than the two leading candidates for Alvin Vogtle's job—Farley and Scherer—acknowledged a *Business Atlanta* article contemplating Vogtle's successor in 1982. But noting Addison's charisma, the writer speculated that "Southern's directors are likely to award plenty of points to a good image." Few could deny that Ed Addison was adept at projecting a "professional and personable public persona."

Born on a farm near Cottageville, South Carolina, Addison grew up with his parents' Depression-era values of working hard and making your own way. "Daddy used to talk about always paying your debts," he recalled. "It was kind of bad news if you had to borrow money." After class and during the summer months, Addison and his brother—both still schoolboys during World War II—were given chores on the farm and forbidden to participate in frivolous entertainment, even the community's Fourth of July picnic. "There's a war on," their father told them, "and there are boys dying in the battlefield. We need to be working every minute."

After earning an electrical engineering degree from the University of South Carolina in 1950 and serving two years in the army, Addison signed on with Gulf Power as a junior engineer. He applied his work ethic to a number of engineering and marketing positions, made the transition into management, and worked a second job to help cover the financial needs of his expanding family, two sons and a daughter. He spent almost his entire career in Pensacola, working under five presidents—Jim Crist, Lansing Smith, Bob Pulley, Clyde Lilly, and Bob Ellis. From each of them, Addison learned something about leadership, but he learned most from the contrasting styles of Lilly and Ellis. A transplant from General Electric, Lilly brought modern management methods to Gulf Power before moving on to head the service company in 1969. Lilly's philosophy was that work ought to be fun—"a little bright spot," Addison called it—before the arrival of a "dark era" under Ellis's heavy thumb. A product of the old school, Ellis lacked Lilly's finesse and people skills; he ruled by command and control. As one of the company's officers, Addison often found himself trying to cushion employees from what he called Ellis's "brutal management" methods.

When the opportunity to leave that environment came along in 1977, Addison didn't hesitate to accept an executive position with Southern Company Services. Sadly, the opening had been created by a tragic company plane accident that claimed the lives of two SCS executives, CEO Lilly and executive vice president Bill Lalor.

At SCS, Addison gained a broader view and hands-on experience with coordinating planning and operating services. "It gave me an opportunity to . . . look at the entire Southern system," he said. He took that system perspective back to Gulf Power when he was named president and CEO, replacing Ellis in 1978. He also returned to Pensacola more confident and savvy, his easy speaking style more polished and persuasive. A reporter trying to prep him for his first television interview dropped the coaching lessons after seeing that Addison was a natural in front of the camera. He had the right voice, the right profile, the right smile. Over the next four years, he built positive relationships with customers, the media, and political and business leaders. He performed so well as Pensacola Chamber of Commerce president that he was asked to head the state chamber and did so. He also reinstated a progressive spirit at Gulf Power, boosting employee morale to new heights.

The positive image building did not go unnoticed by Southern Company's board. "His style of leadership, his administrative performance, and his ability as a communicator were major factors in his selection by the board," proclaimed Vogtle in announcing Addison's election April 18, 1983. What the release did not mention was that Addison's candidacy also had been aided by internal rivalry between the Alabama and Georgia factions on the board. Almost since the parent company's creation in 1947, healthy competition had existed between the two largest subsidiaries, occasionally turning contentious, though seldom vicious and never public—until the 1983 horse race, when the internal campaigns overheated.

According to insiders, Farley initially had been Vogtle's choice, but theatrics from the state house in Montgomery and Alabama Power's financial fall from grace had worked against him. "Farley has faced conditions so trying," observed one of his supporters, "that merely keeping Alabama Power alive represents a considerable achievement." Scherer, whose star began to shine brightly after he supervised a dramatic financial turnaround at Georgia Power in the mid-1970s, had been hurt by ambitious subordinates running an aggressive campaign without his knowledge. Some of the tactics and schemes—presumptuous personnel moves planned after the victory— escaped from behind the curtain. That was not the acceptable Southern Company way. "Everything is done in a southern manner, behind very tightly closed doors and in the most relaxed of tense atmospheres," *Business Atlanta*'s Jeffrey Lauterbach had written in 1982. "A step out-of-bounds of these longstanding ground rules could very quickly rule a contender out of consideration."

When the moment came for the critical vote, Vogtle excused the system CEOs from the room while he briefed the outside directors. Then in a surprise move, Vogtle also left the board meeting, leaving the decision in the hands of outside board members. Well before the meeting, Vogtle had made his preferences known in one-on-one discussions, his preferred communication method. Famed for his escapes from war prison camps, he successfully evaded internment in one of the most difficult boardroom sessions in Southern Company's history. "The debate went on for at least an hour and a half, maybe two hours," recalled Addison. "The rest of us were standing out there in the reception area, shuffling our feet, and looking at each other. . . . It was so very awkward."

When the candidates finally were called back into the room and the choice announced, the meeting reconvened with a full agenda of business items. The way the situation had been handled took the wind out of Addison's moment of joy. His rapport with Vogtle also cooled considerably during the transition that followed. "I went to him with lots of ideas and thoughts, and it became obvious to me right away that he wanted me to take charge and start running the company," said Addison. "I think he had decided in advance that I could make some decisions, that he was going to be there for six months, and that if I screwed something up, he could step in and fix it."

Vogtle's "aloofness" reflected his "portfolio management" approach. He approved budgets and financial plans but stayed clear of directing operations, letting each utility manage its own issues and problems, intervening only when necessary. Addison preferred a collaborative approach, brainstorming sessions, a full discussion of issues, and involvement in the details of each subsidiary's operations. He considered the parent company's role to be far greater than a fiduciary one and believed it his responsibility to bring about greater coordination among the companies. One of the first steps he took was to create the CEO Roundtable, monthly meetings of the system CEOs, which he used as a forum for addressing problems and gaining consensus on decisions. He also pushed the CEOs for system solutions to common problems, insisting that the subsidiaries be not only well managed but also headed in the same direction.

"These people wanted to be left alone," Addison said, "just as I did when I ran an operating company." Simple suggestions for common efforts often turned into endless debates among a dysfunctional family. At one meeting, the CEOs could not agree on a proposal to produce a single commercial that all their companies would use to promote heat pumps, even though it could save more than $1 million over creating four separate ads. When it came down to the last officer holding out a veto, arguing it would mean less business for his local ad agency, Addison asked, "Are you telling me that you would deny savings to the stockholders of over $1 million so you can protect some little guy in your bailiwick?" Reluctantly, the system ad campaign was approved, the first of many steps needed to tear down independent silos erected around each company.

To assure his board that everything possible was being done to manage the company's number one financial risk, Addison began sitting in on Plant Vogtle's project management meetings. Called the nuclear overview committee, the group was organized by Jim Miller Jr. in 1983 to speed problem solving and get "everyone in the same room at the same time talking about the same things." A former Alabama Power executive, Miller transferred to Georgia Power in 1975 to whip into shape poor-performing Georgia coal plants. Named Georgia Power president in 1982, he now was applying his "initiative and intensity" to the nuclear program, scrutinizing every detail with a rigorous review that earned NRC's blessing as the nation's best in quality of nuclear construction.

Financing the growing construction budget, however, would remain a top worry as Addison watched Southern Company's stock price stay depressed by a cloud hanging over the entire nuclear industry during a time when money had more exciting things to chase. Addison began traveling to financial centers across the country, paying personal visits to security analysts, speaking to investor groups, and talking to the financial press. He also brought a group of analysts to Atlanta to meet with his CEOs in a seminar featuring a tour of Plant Vogtle, where they could view construction progress and Miller's "readiness review process"—an intensive assessment and documentation of every aspect of the work as it was being performed. The efforts helped Southern Company sell more than 20 million new shares of common stock in 1984 and 75 million more during the next five years.

Addison's approach to the threat of punitive acid rain legislation was to get personally involved in leading the effort to modify or postpone action until more research could be completed. By the time Addison had moved to Southern Company, the industry already had been browbeaten to the point that some CEOs were ready to make concessions. In joining an EEI committee just prior to a session with Environmental Protection Agency administrator Donald Ruckleshaus, Addison pleaded, "Go talk to him. But for God's sake, don't go in there and give the game away."

As it turned out, Ruckleshaus had his own doubts about the causes of acid rain and methods for controlling it. The EPA chief later told Senate and House committees that "before launching the country on an expensive and potentially divisive control program, we feel we need more scientific information." Addison was appointed head of EEI's environmental steering committee, a role that would help position Southern Company as the industry's leader on acid rain issues and other policy battles brewing in D.C.

To help prepare his company for an era of competition, Addison began a long-term effort to reduce costs and improve productivity, warning that "companies that found a way to contain and lower their costs were the ones that survived in a competitive era." Southern Company did not compare well on productivity measures, and one consultant told Addison he had 10,000 too many employees. Projections also showed Southern Company's cost of service would rise from the low-cost quartile to the top of the third quartile in less than a decade.

Addison flattened organization charts, eliminated excessive middle-management layers, expanded each manager's responsibilities, and downsized staffs. "We need to develop a lean system where responsibility and decision-making authority rest as close as possible to the people who deal with our customers," Addison told a group of system managers who suddenly found themselves in 1985 with twice the responsibility but no increase in pay. Many of the seminar attendees had participated in grueling "roles and missions" studies to define activities to be handled on a systemwide basis and those that would remain decentralized. To questions about why all the upheaval was necessary, Addison pointed to changes ahead for the business requiring "the most significant transformation in our system since Southern Company was formed in 1947." Many managers thought Addison was overreacting to threats that few of them could see in the mid-1980s. Little did they realize, the transformation was only just beginning.

MORE NAIL-BITING YEARS

Important construction was under way on hydro plants Barletts Ferry, Mitchell Dam, Goat Rock, and Rocky Mountain. Workers were scrambling to meet critical schedules at coal plants Miller and Scherer. But it was the work at Plant Vogtle that continued to command the spotlight throughout the 1980s. On August 5, 1985, the unwelcome news came that Plant Vogtle's cost would increase once again—this time, to $8.4 billion. Even more disturbing was a schedule delay, which Scherer described as "the worst thing that can happen," given the high cost of money, materials, and labor. At the site, up to 12,000 workers toiled twenty-four hours a day, seven days a week on the "biggest construction project in Georgia history." Housed in a village of trailers, some came in from the Carolinas, Tennessee, and Alabama to work three twelve-hour shifts, then go home for four days while other crews replaced them. Despite the determined effort, unit 1's schedule had to be extended three months to June 1987, and the completion date for unit 2 was pushed out nine months to June 1989.

Regulatory changes had driven up forecasts for six years, but now the drivers were labor, interest charges, and time. "Each day we're late, it could cost us $1 million,"Addison said. The revised estimate set off alarms at the Georgia Capitol, where legislators already were concerned enough to pass a law requiring a phase-in of the approaching tidal wave of costs as a way of cushioning customers from rate shock. With antinuclear groups calling for a construction shutdown, the PSC grew nervous, tabled hearings on the phase-in plans, and ordered independent audits. One audit claimed that more construction delays were coming and the final cost would be nearly $1 billion above Georgia Power's latest estimate. Within twenty-four hours of that news, Scherer received a note saying things could not move forward until the commissioners were assured "there will be no further increases in the cost of Plant Vogtle."

It was time for Scherer to place a big bet. He responded by promising the PSC that Georgia Power would live or die by the 1985 estimate, essentially placing a cap above which he vowed the company would not attempt to recoup its portion of Plant Vogtle's costs. To cover that bet, Scherer had CFO Mike Harreld find a $1 billion line of credit. "The Swiss (banks) and others had commitments to us," said Scherer, "so that we were able to at least go to bed at night and say, 'Well, if the commission plays funny, we can still finish this plant.'"

More bad news arrived in spring 1986 when off-system sales dropped 40 percent, amounting to nearly 11 billion kilowatt-hours of lost sales. Texas-based Gulf States Utilities (GSU) stopped making payments on energy purchases and tried to void its long-term contract altogether—an action that jolted Georgia Power's Plant Scherer, where construction of the fourth unit had continued only with the backing of the GSU contract. Fearing forced write-offs, auditors qualified their opinion on Southern Company's financial statements for the first time. Even worse, that spring more troubles rained down on nuclear power, its safety once again called into question.

Seven years had passed since the accident at TMI. In late April 1986, nuclear workers in Sweden began detecting high radiation levels in the air. The Soviet Union later came forward with the announcement that an accident had occurred at a nuclear plant near Chernobyl, sixty miles north of Kiev in the Ukraine. The unthinkable had happened again, and the details were far more bleak than TMI's—at least twenty-six people killed, more than

200 injured, and thousands of evacuees dangerously exposed. No longer could the industry say "no deaths have been attributed to the use of civilian nuclear energy."

Only one plant in the United States had remotely similar technology to that used at Chernobyl, but the accident was so severe that the industry trembled in the aftershocks. Engineers, scientists, and nuclear experts grappled with questions of how it happened and whether it could happen here. A coalition of nearly twenty consumer, environmental, and scientific groups called for the phaseout of all U.S. nuclear power plants. Spooked by the bad news and shoved over the edge by computer trading, the stock market on April 30 suffered its worst single-day point loss, and utility stocks were hardest hit.

The price tag for Plant Vogtle eventually reached $8.87 billion. The final estimate came in summer 1987, soon after the first unit made its commercial debut June 1. Immediately off the table came $229 million, the amount exceeding Scherer's self-imposed cap. Stockholders took that hit. In April that year, Georgia Power filed "the rate case to end all rate cases," requesting $805 million, later reduced to $735 million—an 81 percent increase phased in over eleven years. Next came a dreaded "prudence audit," which recommended penalties as high as $1.8 billion. The commission eventually decreed $951 million as imprudent when it awarded Georgia Power phased-in rate increases totaling $464 million on September 30. Scherer appealed the order but eventually lost in court. Southern Company's earnings fell below the level needed to pay dividends.

Still ahead were the challenges of completing Vogtle unit 2, obtaining its operating license, and clearing hurdles of another rate case and prudence review. Also ahead was a long battle over GSU's contracts, hotly contested in FERC hearings and the courts. With financial risks topping tolerance levels, Georgia Power sold majority ownership in its oft-delayed Rocky Mountain pumped hydro project and turned its management over to Oglethorpe Power in 1987. The company also began looking for a better way to manage the risks associated with its growing nuclear operations, having had to shut down Plant Hatch in 1988 to fix multiple problems uncovered in an operations audit.

"It ate me alive," said Georgia Power senior executive Grady Baker, who had inherited management of power supply after Miller retired in 1987. "The running of the nuclear plants was so overwhelming that it was obvious to me that we needed to do something different." Baker called on Bill Dahlberg,

of Georgia Power's phased-in rates for recovering Plant Vogtle costs, complicating further what already had been the largest rate case in the state's history.

To contain the damage, Georgia Power pleaded "no contest" in October to misdemeanor charges related to Rowan's campaign. After investigating the circumstances, Dahlberg determined his officers were innocent of coercing employees to make contributions, but because messages regarding the political campaign could have become distorted as they passed through the chain of command, he believed the "no contest" plea was the quickest way to get the issue behind the company.

"We had to put the pieces back together with the Public Service Commission," said an embarrassed Dahlberg. "We were about to start rate hearings when all of this came up . . . and we were sitting there bleeding to death financially." Later that December, the PSC released its hold on Georgia Power's phased-in rates and decided to address the spare parts accounting issues in rate case proceedings for the second unit of Plant Vogtle.

Unfortunately, the problems were only beginning for Southern Company. "We don't know the extent . . . of the investigation or where it might lead," Barr had admitted in his initial press conference. By the end of 1988, it was leading to Pensacola, where another grand jury was busy uncovering information about Gulf Power that would bring the two probes together.

The problems McCrary thought he had fixed back in 1984 simply did not stay fixed. In 1985, the IRS had started requesting records of Gulf Power's former warehouse manager, a sign that another investigation was getting under way. Then in 1986 with the IRS closing in, the former manager filed a lawsuit against Gulf Power, claiming he had been forced to resign while six past and present company executives got away with misusing corporate funds because he had provided them with personal automotive equipment, building materials, appliances, and landscaping services. Gulf Power denied any wrongdoing, and its senior vice president, Jake Horton, described the services as "normal company perquisites which were provided for the executives of Gulf Power as they are provided in many other large corporations."

McCrary thought the "amnesty program" had taken care of those types of problems back in 1984 by allowing employees to pay the company back for any perks considered a "purely personal nature." From Atlanta, Addison had refunded nearly $10,000 for appliances and other benefits he received during his years at Gulf Power.

"Before it was over, there was a story in the newspaper every day," said McCrary, who tried to shore up employee morale and reinforce the company's code of ethics while instigating a new internal review of purchasing procedures and billings from vendors being called into question. The audit committee of Gulf Power's board of directors also began looking into a list of issues raised by security officer Tom Baker, who wrote the board a thirty-seven-page memo October 12, 1988, complaining that he had been demoted and denied a pay increase as retaliation for cooperating with the grand jury. After the board committee investigated the matter, it determined Baker's personal circumstance to be related to a restructuring happening throughout the company, not retaliation. Yet the memo raised other disturbing issues the board would investigate.

By summer 1988, federal judges in Pensacola had begun handing out sentences to several Gulf Power vendors. One electrical supplier allegedly paid three former Gulf employees $43,000 in kickbacks. A landscaping company had processed twenty-eight fraudulent invoices. Other vendors had been paid for questionable services ranging from roofing and paving to construction and scrap metal. Gulf Power's former warehouse manager was sentenced to only four months because he had entered a guilty plea and cooperated with the investigation. Although his lawsuit against Gulf Power was dismissed as having no factual merit, his accusations had already generated two years of negative press. One of his allegations—"donations to politicians"—attracted Barr's attention. Thirty-two Florida politicians received subpoenas, and more than two dozen employees, ex-employees, and vendors of Gulf Power were summoned to Atlanta.

Among those called to testify was Ray Howell, owner of Design Associates. He had done work for Gulf Power for ten years, but McCrary's internal audit recently had turned up problems with some of his invoices— billings for work not performed, questionable pricing, and inadequate explanations for some line-item charges. A talented artist, Howell was described as "a hard worker, personable, likable, and giving" though somewhat of an enigma and a "recluse." On the evening of December 7, he placed a call from his Atlanta hotel room to Gulf Power's public relations director, who later reported that Howell sounded "upset, scared, and almost incoherent" and believed he was facing three choices: "testify before the grand jury, hide, or kill myself." Just hours before he was to appear the morning of December 8, Howell mysteriously disappeared, setting off a year-long manhunt.

It was only the first of many bizarre twists and turns the case would take.

THE WORST CONTINUES TO WORSEN

A light rain was falling Monday, April 10, 1989, when SCS corporate plane King Air 30PC—"30 Papa Charlie"—departed Pensacola at 12:57 p.m. on its way to Atlanta. Less than three minutes later, pilots from the twin-engine Beechcraft radioed the airport tower: "Got an emergency . . . got an emergency!" Eyewitnesses reported seeing smoke pouring from the plane before it crashed into an apartment complex on the town's outskirts. One person on the ground was injured. All three aboard the aircraft perished—pilots Mike Holmes and John Major and passenger Jake Horton, Gulf Power's senior vice president.

Horton was a "workaholic" who came into the office early each day, worked into the evening, and talked work all weekend with his wife. His style was called a bit "unorthodox," but he managed top-performing organizations—marketing and economic development, government and community relations, communications, and human resources. His only avocations were collecting vintage cars, community projects, and country music. A "tireless community worker," he was described by Pensacola leaders as "an energetic, big-hearted man with an uncommon ability to get things done." He had fifteen to twenty projects going at the same time, claimed the local chamber of commerce president. "You dropped ideas in Jake's head," said the city manager, "and the next thing you knew, they were happening." The mayor delivered his eulogy; a state senator and former governor were among the pallbearers at his funeral. In short, Horton was "Mr. Pensacola," the man connected to everything and everybody in town.

"This tragic accident is a great loss for the company and for me personally," said Addison, who had known Horton most of his career. "Jake has been an enthusiastic leader of almost every major civic and charitable organization in the area."

Too enthusiastic, it seemed. Horton sometimes strong-armed company vendors into coughing up funds for good causes and, as it turned out, sometimes found creative ways to reimburse them through Gulf Power. Just before Horton left for Atlanta on April 10, he had been asked to leave the company. McCrary and Dr. Reed Bell, an outside director and chairman of Gulf Power's audit committee, met with Horton at 11:20 that morning to discuss his "possible circumvention of company policies and procedures" and to tell him the audit committee recommended that, after thirty-three years, he be "separated from active employment with the company."

Following security officer Tom Baker's thirty-seven-page memo in October, a six-month internal investigation uncovered a number of "invoicing discrepancies"—bogus bills or padded invoices from suppliers under Horton's purview. During an interview with the audit committee in February, Horton had been unable to specify the products or services obtained for some of the payments. He denied having ever defrauded the company, said he was unaware of any illegal action, but stated twice during the discussion, "I don't break the law; I just break the rules." In some instances, the phony bills turned out to be a tool for reimbursing vendors for contributions to charities and community events and, in other cases, for donations to political fundraising campaigns. The April 10 meeting with Horton concluded with McCrary allowing him time to consider the options—early retirement, a leave of absence, termination, or some other solution. McCrary didn't realize that Horton, having anticipated the nature of the meeting, had already ordered a corporate plane to Atlanta.

"This is certainly a sad and bleak time in our company's history," McCrary told employees the morning after Horton died. In coming days, things grew more bleak as the headlines reported "misconduct, misman- agement, and money laundering" and rumors that the plane crash could have been "suicide, sabotage, or murder." Among other revelations, the Escambia County sheriff's department disclosed it had received a telephone call three hours after the crash: "You can stop investigating Gulf Power now. We took care of that for them this afternoon." Horton's attorney, Fred Levin, who also had met with Horton the morning of the crash, told reporters the Gulf exec- utive feared he had become the target of the grand jury probe and wanted to "go to the U.S. attorney and take a lie-detector test." Later, when subpoenaed to Atlanta, Levin claimed his own life had been threatened and that a series of dead canaries were left at his homes and offices—a Mafia-style warning against "singing."

Although the FBI and the National Transportation Safety Board could not determine conclusively the accident's cause, one report stated agents found a "Mason jar top and broken bottle fragments" and "traces of hydrochloric and sulfuric acid" in the wreckage. The final cockpit transcript revealed that just before radioing in the emergency, one of the pilots had yelled, "What the hell was that?" And Horton had responded, "Fire!"

Amid the speculation, allegations, and leaks from grand jury pro- ceedings, McCrary appealed to customers in a videotaped message and newspaper ad, asking them to "allow accurate information and informed facts to be gathered" before forming opinions. Through a series of employee meetings, he tried to give hope and courage to a work force being called a "bunch of crooks" in the community. But McCrary himself was suffering from battle fatigue and frustration. His board was openly split on opinions about Horton, and his company was under financial strain after having withdrawn a rate request in light of the increasing controversy.

"I think it just about killed me," he confessed years later. He was not being metaphoric. Having already suffered one heart attack from the pressures of 1988, McCrary would soon find himself back in the hospital, stricken with a second heart attack.

Addison said it also "was the single most difficult period of my life." At Southern Company's board meeting January 16, 1989, Mississippi Power's Alan Barton had offered a resolution calling for a special committee of outside directors to investigate the issues. Catching Addison off guard, Barton's request set off an embarrassing exchange in the boardroom before being tabled by a quick vote. But before the year's end, the audit committee would find itself conducting just such a review.

In February 1989, several directors were subpoenaed to appear before the federal grand jury in Atlanta. In March, the Securities and Exchange Commission announced it also would conduct an investigation to see if Southern Company had violated federal securities laws. In April, the SEC staff began issuing subpoenas for information relating to political contributions prohibited under PUHCA. Then after the plane crash, disturbing articles under banners of "Mystery in Dixie," "Fatal Subtraction," and "Southerngate" began appearing in regional and national media, including *Time*, the *Wall Street Journal*, and the *New York Times*. Even *Sports Illustrated* mentioned the crash and dead canaries in a feature on a boxing champ whom Levin also represented.

On May 24, Addison had to stand before stockholders for the first time and explain the embarrassing "flood of rumor, allegation, innuendo, and speculation." He tried to reassure attendees of Southern Company's annual meeting that his companies did "not condone illegal political contributions or any other kind of illegal activity." He promised to "devote every ounce of my energy to leading our company through this time of turmoil, keeping our efforts focused on our basic business."

Distraction was unavoidable, however. In June and July, customer groups filed four separate lawsuits alleging the operating companies had obtained excessive rate increases by improperly accounting for spare parts. On July 21, federal agents armed with search warrants once again descended on Georgia Power headquarters to remove more records and a personal computer. Two months later, more than a dozen IRS agents closed off two floors of Southern Company's corporate offices and hauled out six boxes of files, memos, notebooks, letters, and tax records. In November, Horton's widow filed a wrongful death lawsuit against SCS, claiming the fire in the airplane's cabin was a result of negligent maintenance and operation of the aircraft and that the pilots failed to respond properly after the fire broke out. SCS filed a counterclaim against the Horton estate, asserting the plane was well maintained, the pilots acted properly, and actions taken by Horton himself were primarily or solely responsible for the plane crash. Also that month, four more Southern Company directors were subpoenaed by the grand jury.

"It was like it would just never end," said Addison, who grew anxious and frustrated by the "communication blackout" imposed by a circle of lawyers around his office. "I thought one of the things I could do best was explain myself," he said. "When I went to meetings, employees would want me to tell them something [in response to rumors], and I couldn't because the lawyers wouldn't let me talk."

The earliest step toward a resolution came Halloween Day 1989, when Gulf Power pleaded guilty to conspiring to violate the section of PUHCA prohibiting political contributions. "We consider this a very significant plea," said Barr, staging another press conference in Atlanta and releasing 123 examples of how Gulf Power had made hidden contributions to community organizations and politicians. Although Horton had been largely responsible for items on the list, a few other employees were soon dismissed by the company.

"We do not condone the abuses that we now know have occurred," said Addison and McCrary in a joint statement to employees and the public. "We cannot undo what has been done. But we can take positive and specific action to see—as far as humanly possible—that nothing like this will happen again at Gulf Power." Among the steps taken were stronger auditing practices, stricter vendor guidelines, a reorganization, an ethics code all employees had to sign, and a confidential program for employees to air any future concerns. For the federal offenses, Gulf Power was fined $500,000. For "mismanagement," the company was penalized an additional $4.8 million during the first two years of new rates the PSC approved the following year.

In January 1990, the U.S. Attorney's Office said it was ready to prosecute, the final step being a review by the Justice Department's criminal tax office in

Washington, during which the company's legal team was given a "last chance" to present arguments. A long, agonizing wait followed, but no word came—in February, in March, in April. No word. "When it gets quiet," said Dahlberg, "you worry that they're drawing up an indictment."

"Georgia Power Holds Its Breath" read a headline May 23, the day of Southern Company's annual meeting in Panama City, Florida, where Addison had to once again address the scandal with stockholders, warning them the probe could continue for months. Two days later, the U.S. Attorney's Office notified Southern Company and Georgia Power it would not seek criminal indictments against the companies or individuals on tax evasion. Dahlberg was at a chamber of commerce meeting when he got the good news. "Suddenly, this burden had been lifted," he recalled. "I was so happy." Later that day, he told employees, "At the outset, we said we had not violated any criminal law. We're very pleased that this matter is now resolved."

WAITING FOR REDEMPTION

Addison, too, was pleased and relieved, but he would have to wait two more years to celebrate his own liberation. In delivering news about the tax probe, the U.S. attorney had warned, "Other aspects of the federal probe remain unresolved."

Scandalous headlines continued through 1990 and 1991. Two more Gulf Power vendors pleaded guilty to tax charges and political contribution activities, one being Ray Howell, who after a year in hiding turned himself in to the Escambia County jail. In pretrial depositions for the Horton estate lawsuit, Levin said that Jake Horton's life had been threatened several hours before the plane crash, and the Escambia County sheriff's department announced it was beginning to study a possible organized crime connection in the case. Then April 8, 1991, under the banner of "Inside the Southern Company: Discord, Deception, Death," the *Atlanta Business Chronicle* published an investigative report rehashing all the old allegations, adding a few new ones, and portraying Addison as "a corrupt tyrant" who possibly obstructed justice. Dismissed by the company as an inaccurate "hatchet job," it nonetheless generated more bad press. And April 10, 1991, a stockholder derivative action lawsuit was filed, accusing current and former executive officers and directors of violating the federal Racketeer Influenced and Corrupt Organizations Act and breach of fiduciary duty.

"There just seemed to be no end to it, just no end to it," said Addison, who confessed years later there were many days he felt like picking up and leaving. "But there was nothing in my being that would allow me to do that. I couldn't have lived with myself. . . . The only way I knew to do it was to stay and fight."

The end of Addison's fight came May 4, 1992. As EEI president, he was attending a meeting between U.S. and European industry leaders in Pasadena, California, where he was to deliver a speech and paper on transmission access and pricing. He had almost canceled the trip after learning that his lawyers would be given an opportunity to make a final presentation to the U.S. attorney and staff that very day.

"It's your job to deliver the paper and mine to meet with the U.S. attorney," Stuart Baskin, Addison's personal lawyer, had advised. "You do yours well, and I'll do mine." Ten minutes into the question-and-answer period following his remarks, Addison was handed a piece of paper from the hotel bellhop: "Call your secretary immediately."

"My heart jumped in my throat because there was no indication whether it was good news or bad news," he recalled. "So I went to the pay phone around the corner and called. She said that the lawyers were still meeting downtown and she would patch me into them."

"The thing is over," Baskin announced. "The U.S. Attorney's Office will not be seeking a criminal indictment against you or the company. Forget about it. Enjoy your trip. And I will see you when you get back."

The first person Addison wanted to see was his wife, Bennie, a pillar of support he had leaned on during the long dark years of uncertainty. "I would go home at night, and she would be there," he said. "I could talk about my troubles, and she would listen. And the next day, I was ready to go again." On May 4, Bennie was waiting for him upstairs in the Ritz-Carlton Hotel. Addison took the elevator to his room and gave her the news.

Then they both broke down and cried.

The end of the SEC investigation came in March 1991, the case closed with no further action beyond a consent order Gulf Power signed the previous fall agreeing to make no political contributions.

The Horton estate lawsuit ended May 7, 1991, when the insurance firm providing coverage for SCS aircraft decided to settle for $1 million out of court, preferring to close the case quickly than endure an extensive and costly jury trial and negative publicity.

The dispute over spare parts accounting came to an end October 9, 1992, when Georgia Power settled with the IRS by paying $21 million in back taxes and interest that the government claimed the company owed after reviewing all tax accounting issues.

Customer lawsuits ended during a series of years as various federal and state courts dismissed the cases. The end of the derivative action lawsuit came in May 1996, when an appellate court upheld the 1995 dismissal of the case by a trial court.

The end of questions surrounding the plane crash and Horton's death never came. In preparing for a possible courtroom battle, the service company's insurance carrier hired a London audio expert who used sophisticated computer filters on the cockpit voice recorder to identify noises and words, suggesting there had been a struggle aboard the plane prior to the crash. The National Transportation Safety Board did not agree, saying it was unable to discern the conversation or struggle and rejecting a petition to cite Horton as the "probable cause" of the crash or that the fire was of a "suspicious nature." On July 21, 1992, the NTSB reconfirmed it was unable to determine the fire's origin or cause.

That was the final NTSB report, the final word on the crash. What really happened aboard "30 Papa Charlie" would remain a mystery.

THE SOUTHERN TRANSFORMATION

For Southern Company, 1990 through 1992 were pivotal years. Although Georgia Power had to record another $218 million loss that dropped Southern Company's earnings below the dividend level for the second time in four years, a turnaround was in sight because that ended the Plant Vogtle write-offs. After unit 2 went into service, Georgia Power received rate increases of $218 million in 1990 and $117 million in 1991. The settlement ended a decade of nail-biting over the company's nuclear risks. "It was like we got over this huge mountain," said Dahlberg. "The sense of satisfaction when the construction was completed was immense. The sense of satisfaction when we got the license was immense. And the sense of satisfaction when we got a workable plan completed at the PSC was immense."

Other pestilent issues came to resolution one by one. The Gulf States breakthrough came in 1990 when Addison arranged a meeting with the utility's chairman, Linn Draper. From their initial secret session came a series of trusting talks and eventually a settlement worth $300 million for Southern

Company. The related Plant Scherer dilemma ended with Georgia Power selling unit 4 to Florida Power & Light and the Jacksonville Electric Authority. The sale netted $810 million and an estimated profit of $67 million.

The revised Clean Air Act of 1990 ended uncertainties about the cost of acid rain controls. Under Phase I, eight Southern Company power plants would have to be retrofitted with low-NOx burners and switched to low-sulfur coal by 1995. Under Phase II, other system coal-fired plants would have to comply with the new standards by 2000. Phase I's expected cost was initially estimated at $3.4 billion, but actual costs turned out much less, thanks to emissions trading and research innovations that helped bring down the cost of pollution-control equipment.

In March 1991, unit 4 of Plant Miller began commercial operation, marking the finish line for Southern Company's frightening construction marathon. "For the first time in more than forty years—dating back almost to the end of World War II—we are not planning or building a large generating plant," Addison told stockholders. Earnings bounced back 45 percent in 1991, and the company's stock price rose more than 23 percent—three times the growth of the Dow Jones utility average.

Throughout the grand jury investigations, Addison had tried to keep moving the companies toward a common direction by creating Southern Company College to teach managers new leadership and competitive business skills and by hosting a series of forums to bring all leaders of the subsidiaries together to discuss challenges and learn firsthand from customers, competitors, and some of the nation's top business executives. Now Addison was anxious to regain the momentum lost during "a period that I was not at full strength."

"I think five years from now, you'll see this company working more like an entrepreneurial company in a competitive arena rather than a standard utility," he told officers at a November 1991 forum, just weeks after the management council had restructured fossil/hydro operations, the largest group within Southern Company. To oversee sixty-four plants in five companies without creating a separate subsidiary, the council decided to "functionalize" the generation group, keeping ownership of plants at the operating companies, while reporting the function to a central officer and treating it as a distinct business unit. That decision placed under common management more than 80 percent of the system's production expenses.

construction program. Even during the grand jury probes, the company's stock suffered only temporary setbacks. Plant Vogtle delays and cost overruns were punishing, the write-offs painful, and the bad press scandalous, but if investors had ever lost confidence, things would have turned out much worse. The value of building an open and credible relationship with the financial community was never more clear.

Misconduct and the grand jury investigations, however, inflicted considerable damage on employee morale and public opinion. The company's "circle the wagons" mentality and its failure to act quickly to uncover and correct bad behavior only led to greater troubles as the investigations and rumors continued. Repair to morale and reputation would take years of hard work and reforms.

Reviews by Southern Company's board led to a major overhaul of the security and audit systems and improvements in corporate governance. The board itself was restructured to reduce the number of inside directors and increase those bringing outside viewpoints. To increase its authority and independence, internal auditing was pulled out from under several management layers and reported to the top of the company. It also was functionalized to improve the coordination of reviews across company lines.

Southern Company learned the hard way that behavior is judged as much by perception as by the law. The company also learned that abuses occur when the tone of ethical conduct is not set high enough by its leaders. The board was particularly disturbed by Horton's attitude—"I don't break the law; I just break the rules"—which resulted in a culture of poor judgment within his organizations. Following the cleanup, Southern Company made sure all employees had access to credible, confidential avenues for raising concerns. Fundamental enhancements were made to codes of ethics, ethical training, and efforts to ensure compliance.

The potential impact of changes coming from the public policy arena taught Southern Company the value of creating a strong national voice. Achieving more reasonable regulations for acid rain controls and rules for transmission access saved the company billions of dollars and preserved its competitive position. As a result of building a permanent presence in the nation's capital, Southern Company was able to provide indispensable input on dozens of other issues vital to the company's interests. But assuming center stage also had its price. The company would become a constant target for competitors and advocacy groups during future public policy battles.

By taking on more clean coal research projects than any other utility, Southern Company would become a leader in one of the most successful government-industry partnerships ever. The research generated an estimated $100 billion in benefits to the U.S. economy by cutting the cost of nitrogen oxides controls in half and scrubbers by two-thirds. The work gave Southern Company experience that led to the development of the next generation of clean coal technologies.

To manage its nuclear risks, Southern Company learned it had to take a different approach during Plant Vogtle construction to avoid the nightmare other utilities experienced in obtaining a license once their plants were built. The Georgia Power team went to great lengths to apply to unit 2 more than 3,200 lessons from unit 1 and continuously communicate with the NRC. Southern Company also reaped the benefits of setting up a separate subsidiary to manage nuclear operations differently, which helped make its nuclear performance among the nation's best.

In preparing for competition, company leaders learned they could no longer do business as usual. Vast changes were required in the company's strategies, costs, and structure—and most especially its corporate culture. The struggle to create a "one-company mindset" was perhaps the most difficult. As far back as 1949, one investment fund manager returning from a tour of Alabama Power and Georgia Power had seen the potential challenge: "The question is whether or not two such strong individualistic groups can and will be willing to submerge certain individual considerations for the common good of the group." By constantly pushing for the "good of the group," Addison achieved efficiencies and cooperation that helped transform Southern Company into a more competitive corporation, one better prepared for a world unlike any the industry had ever known.

On the horizon were competitive threats on every front. FERC was opening transmission access to wholesale competition. Some New England states were preparing to join California in pushing competition down to the retail level. Some utilities were preparing to spin off their generation assets. Others were turning their transmission systems over to independent operators. And Enron was introducing energy marketers to the world of options, futures, hedges, indexes, tolling, and other creative trading-floor transactions that the electric power business had never seen before.

To make its next big bets, Southern Company would need creative new thinking and a different kind of CEO to navigate the company through what was becoming a strange and rapidly evolving brave new world of energy.

year shadow of scandal vanished, and Southern Company stood in the bright, shining sun of a new day of global expansion.

Bristol-based South Western Electricity—still known as SWEB from its regulated days as South Western Electricity Board—became a takeover target by happenstance. In investigating the possible purchase of generation capacity in England, Southern Company had gained a glimpse of the United Kingdom's twelve regional electric companies. The one that seemed the best purchase candidate was SWEB; it was relatively small and coastal, and Southern Company was experienced in storm restoration. "We thought we could make a difference in providing service there," Dahlberg said. After sending a team of six managers into southwestern England to clandestinely observe SWEB work practices, Dahlberg knew customer service could be improved. Following weeks of studying SWEB's books and operations, Southern Company made its move with stealth and decisiveness.

Southern Company's representatives—a cadre of investment bankers—quietly gathered just under 5 percent of the shares of South Western Electricity, as accumulating more than that amount would have forced them by law to reveal their intentions. The goal was to acquire another 6 to 7 percent of SWEB's shares to push the total shares owned over 11 percent, forcing South Western's management, by law, to sit down at a table and hear Southern Company's offer. First, though, in order to determine how much to offer for SWEB, Southern Company had to wait for UK regulator Stephen Littlechild to set the national electricity price for the next five years.

Littlechild made his announcement Thursday, July 6. Southern Company had expected the announcement on Friday, so its board meeting had been scheduled for that day. Having been already prepared individually by Dahlberg for this type of transaction, the directors signed off on the deal. "Once the regulator set the price, we thought there would be offers from other companies," Dahlberg explained, "so we wanted to be ready to go to market. If we waited for someone else to make the first move, someone else would have set the price. We had to go to the market first."

Southern Company's investment bankers, S. G. Warburg and Swiss Bank Corporation, knew whom they could buy the shares from, and as day broke Monday, they moved swiftly. "We went to big institutions that had holdings and offered them some premium they would consider. We bought the first 3 to 4 percent at market value and then had to pay a premium to get to 11 percent," Dahlberg said.

The takeover attempt attracted major coverage from the British press, with screaming tabloid headlines announcing a U.S. invasion. "Initially, the reaction of SWEB's executives was, 'Oh no, you can't do this.' We were saying, 'We have 11 percent of your company, and we would like to buy your company, would you like to discuss this?' We were offering to buy the shares of their company at a certain price—with or without their recommendation," Dahlberg said.

Next came the more difficult part—executing a hostile takeover. Sixty-five years earlier, Southern Company's forerunner, Southeastern Power & Light, had itself been the victim of a hostile raid that lived on bitterly in company lore. Now the shoe was on the other foot, and playing predator was not Southern Company's style. "Strategically, we knew we had to do it as a surprise," Dahlberg said, "but the board of directors of Southern Company had never made a hostile bid on anything. The term 'hostile bid' didn't seem southern and genteel. However, we believed that once we made the offer, it would not stay hostile, that we could convince management to sell."

After initially rebuffing the offer, SWEB's management began to listen, and "it very quickly turned into a friendly negotiation," according to Dahlberg. It took seven weeks, but the deal was finally done August 25, with South Western management accepting Southern Company's $1.7 billion offer, up $200 million from its initial bid. It was the largest acquisition ever of a foreign utility by a U.S. electric utility. With 1.3 million customers and 5,000 employees, SWEB immediately became Southern Company's third-largest subsidiary.

Back home, the purchase was celebrated. For nearly a decade, Southern Company employees had heard horror stories about the threat of competition. Suddenly, their fears turned to optimism—Southern Company could rule the new day. Unlike the prototypical utility CEO who played defense, their new leader was making it clear that Southern Company would become a global leader. Dahlberg brought an entrepreneurial zest that the company had not seen in its leaders since early days. "You have to grow by doing bold and measured things," Dahlberg told an employee group eight days after the dawn strike. "I think it [the SWEB proposal] demonstrates that we're going to set the pace of things and not just wait for things to happen to us."

Dahlberg was not like anyone before him. Before Dahlberg, every Southern Company CEO had been either a lawyer or an engineer—and so had every president of its two largest operating companies. Dahlberg broke all the molds. His degree was in management, and he didn't earn that until he was thirty years old. But more than anything else, Dahlberg was a visionary who sparked employees' imaginations and pushed the limits on everything he touched. His greatest frustration was not being able to do what he wanted when he wanted. He had little patience for naysayers telling him why something could not be done. His favorite question was: "Why can't we do that?"

Dahlberg needed only six months to transform Southern Company's self-image, but that had not been his primary goal. His consuming concern was not letting the company he loved fail on his watch. He had started his career on the bottom rung, at the absolute foundation of the enterprise, installing meters. Nothing else happens—engineering, finance, accounting—unless the meter is up and running.

Once he had reached the top of the ladder, Dahlberg could see the primary issue facing him would be competition. As Southern Company's president and leader-in-waiting, he had more than a year to reflect on the possible impact of competition as Ed Addison finished out his tenure as chairman and CEO. "We had been worried about where the industry was going for a long time. I used that year to develop my thinking about what we needed to do strategically. I didn't do it in isolation. We would bring groups of people together to help me," he said.

Debate about possible wholesale competition existed even before the National Energy Policy Act was passed in 1992. Having studied other industries that had been deregulated—telecommunications, natural gas, airlines, trucking, and banking—Southern Company's leadership knew that, as competition increased, costs would have to decrease. Dahlberg felt the number one question he and his strategists must answer was: "Is retail access inevitable?" The number two question was: "If it's not inevitable, what's wrong with planning as if it were?"

Then, in April 1994, in the midst of Dahlberg's year of planning, the California Public Utilities Commission sent shivers throughout the industry by announcing that retail competition would commence in that state in 1996 for large industrial customers and would be phased in all the way down to residential customers by 2002. The plan was labeled by the *New York Times* as a possible "national model," and soon twenty-two other states were exploring electricity competition. "To me, that was a clear step toward deregulation," said Dahlberg, who loved competition yet understood its consequences. "I knew some people were going to win and some people were going to lose. And I don't like losing."

Dahlberg would not let Southern Company's ship sink on his watch. His experience in financial services in the mid-1970s, when he had an up-close seat for Georgia Power's near collapse, had taught him what could happen when executive management assumed a caretaker role rather than a leadership one. "I knew you are much better to act ahead of the wave, than to get hit by the wave. You cannot just sit there and watch things happen. I believed that, as a group of managers and leaders, we had enough sense to figure out what to do. I had always thought we were very good at thinking ahead," he said. "I definitely felt the pressure of needing to be prepared for the future."

FEARLESSLY FACING THE FUTURE

When Addison retired March 1, 1995, Dahlberg was a racehorse stomping in the starting gate. Within three weeks, he held a two-day forum of his executives and unveiled his much-contemplated strategic plan—"Southern Beyond 2000"—designed to compensate for the possible revenue loss resulting from deregulation and the push for competition that was being driven by the global marketplace, technology, and the popular belief that competition, where possible, is better than monopoly. Southern Company, however, would be working from a position of strength, he said. His message to employees was: "We are good—and we will get better." To build a more competitive, entrepreneurial culture in a regulated company, he announced the company's productivity incentive plan would be expanded from only 200 executives to 2,500 managers and frontline leaders.

Global competition had already driven down electricity costs for major industrial and retail customers, as had excess generating capacity created by the previous era's plant construction boom and energy conservation movement. Industrial customers also now had the option of self-generation and the increasing ability to move their production to regions with lower energy costs. Southern Company's largest industrial customer was discussing an offer to leave the system; another customer had been offered electricity as cheap as 1.6¢ per kilowatt-hour. And the federal government was preparing to release proposed rules to give all competitors equal access to utility transmission systems in what would be called "the most extensive restructuring of the electric power industry since the New Deal."

Dahlberg explained that major industrial customers leaving a utility system could create a "death spiral," forcing costs to be spread over a smaller base, raising rates, and prompting even more customers to leave. He said the solution was to "drive costs down and customer satisfaction up."

To cut costs and compensate for a possible loss of revenue to competition, Dahlberg designed his "Southern Beyond 2000" strategy around four business units—the traditional, regulated business in the Southeast, a North American competitive energy business, an international competitive energy business, and a utility-related business that would be in industries such as water, gas, or even garbage. The resulting mix, Dahlberg said, would create "America's Best Diversified Utility."

The domestic and international business units already existed on a small scale within Southern Electric International, the subsidiary Southern Company formed in 1981 to generate consulting revenue from its underutilized engineering talent. Addison had given SEI an international presence with purchases the previous two years in Argentina, Chile, the Bahamas, and Trinidad and Tobago. But Dahlberg's plan called for a much greater role for SEI, transforming it into Southern Company's "growth engine." "I believed they could do a whole lot more if we let them," said Dahlberg, who had worked with SEI president Tom Boren at Georgia Power and was willing to bet his professional future on Boren's ability to make SEI a global energy force.

Expanding outside the Southeast flew in the face of the company's more than eighty-year history as a regional utility, but—like his mentor, former Georgia Power president Bob Scherer—Dahlberg believed the past should not be more important than the future, nor memories more important than dreams. To become a growth company, Southern Company had to move beyond its traditional service territory. The domestic electricity market was projected to grow only 2 percent annually, so staying in only the regulated business would be a slow-growth proposition. However, marvelous growth opportunities appeared to be waiting overseas. Privatization and the quest for foreign capital were creating opportunities with the lure of higher return on equity.

Dahlberg would develop intermediate goals to reach his "bold aggressive goal"—the BAG, or "big ass goal," as he liked to call it—of becoming "America's Best Diversified Utility." "The BAG was an aspirational goal. It was direction-setting, a target," he said. "I think the BIGs [big intermediate goals] are what helped provide direction." Among the targets were: generate 30 percent of net income from noncore business by 2003, while earning a higher ROE than the core business; rank among the top ten U.S. power marketers by 1997; and reduce overhead costs by 20 percent by 1998. "I didn't know if we could be in the top five in power marketing, or if 30 percent of our income could come from other sources," Dahlberg said, "but I thought we ought to shoot for it."

The goals were to be accomplished while living up to a new statement of values and behaviors called "Southern Style." Dahlberg wrote Southern Style during the same period he worked on his strategic plan because he believed companies with the highest principles earned the highest returns. Damaging headlines and innuendo from the previous era had caught Dahlberg in the crossfire. The IRS investigation, conducted while he was Georgia Power CEO, found no wrongdoing but had damaged morale and the company's image. He was ready for a cultural change. So were employees. They welcomed Southern Style. "We said, 'Here are our aspirations as a business, and here's how we conduct ourselves in achieving our goals.' In other words, you can't do it by cheating," Dahlberg explained. "Addressing both the 'whats' and the 'hows' at the same time was very important."

The tenets of Southern Style were straightforward: Tell the truth, keep your promises, and be fair; think like a customer and act like an owner; our focus must be more external than internal; turf issues are a waste of energy; create an environment that expects a diversity of viewpoints; set higher standards of performance.

Another principle of Southern Style was corporate citizenship, which Dahlberg had learned from Scherer at Georgia Power. Within two months of taking over Southern Company, Dahlberg demonstrated his commitment to the Atlanta community by announcing he was moving Southern Company's headquarters downtown. After more than a quarter-century at Perimeter Center in Dunwoody, Southern Company would reverse a trend of corporate flight to suburbia by becoming the first company in thirteen years to move its headquarters into the center city. "For the body to be healthy," Dahlberg said, referring to metro Atlanta, "the heart must be healthy. And the heart of Atlanta is downtown." Dahlberg was a downtown guy. He was intimately involved with the city's power brokers and even helped unite the state's disparate economic development forces. A Georgia business magazine named him "Man of the Year" in 1994 and "Georgia's Most Respected CEO" in 1996. The first person to simultaneously head both the state and Atlanta chambers of commerce, he championed state education initiatives and Atlanta's bids to stage the Super Bowl.

connecting to the rest of Europe, positioning Southern Company to take advantage of the impending deregulation of the European electricity marketplace.

"Bewag creates an immediate positive impact on our earnings, as well as the potential for further earnings growth in markets throughout Europe," Dahlberg told shareholders. "Berlin has a metro area of 6 million people. In two years, it will be the capital of the largest economy in Europe and the third-largest economy in the world. Germany is the largest user of electricity in Europe, and all of Europe will begin moving toward one electricity market in 1999. Bewag will give us access to markets in both western and central Europe."

Dahlberg described Southern Company's metamorphosis since the previous annual meeting: "A year ago when we met, Southern Company was a regional utility with a handful of international projects. Today, though, Southern can be defined as an international energy company, with regional utilities and operations around the world. We now conduct business on four continents and in nine countries."

That number grew to ten countries after the meeting, with the announcement that Southern Company was part of a consortium buying a minority stake in a utility serving Brazil's fastest-growing province. Companhia Energetica de Minas Gerais, known as CEMIG, was South America's largest electricity distributor and owned the world's fourth-largest distribution system. Its 15,000 employees served 4 million customers and a population of 16 million in southern Brazil. Its service area—the size of France—was surrounded by energy-poor states, strategically positioning CEMIG as a power marketer.

The deal allowed Southern Company to put up no money initially but to offer technical expertise and gain a glimpse of CEMIG's operations, before deciding by January 1998 whether to participate in the transaction by buying up to 3.6 percent of the company for $274 million. It also gave SEI a look into the Brazilian electricity sector, viewed as a hot market by U.S. companies lusting over the expected government privatization of utilities worth $25 billion to $30 billion.

A LIFE SPRINGING FROM HOPE

Bill Dahlberg grew up in the shadow of Georgia's Stone Mountain on a fifty-two-acre farm that was a dream of his father. The family moved there when

Dahlberg was five and lived the first year without electricity. Dahlberg helped his father find the stones for the rock house they were building. They called it Hope Springs Farm for the spring at the bottom of the hill and one of their favorite sayings, "hope springs eternal." Al Dahlberg worked as an accountant by day, so Ruth Dahlberg, a college graduate from Long Island, New York, figured out how to run the farm. "Mother was a tough lady who made things work," Dahlberg said. "At one time, we had a thousand chickens and laying hens, ten or twelve pigs, and about thirteen milk cows. She ran a produce route where she delivered buttermilk and butter and eggs from the farm, supplemented by produce she would buy from the farmers' market south of Atlanta." Riding along with her was Alfred William Dahlberg III, her oldest child and most dependable farmhand. The message was clear: All things are possible. An optimist and entrepreneur was in the making.

At nineteen, Dahlberg arrived at Georgia Power, a refugee from the huge Sears building in Atlanta. After a Christmas of sorting and moving packages in the basement for $1.37½ an hour, he was ready for another job. Georgia Power gave him one—washing meter covers. Officially, he was a meter department "helper," earning $1.69 an hour at the Forest Park Service Center south of Atlanta. He soon worked up to meter installer and then, in 1967, moved into district operations, where he repossessed appliances from customers three months past due on their account.

It was as a "repo man" that Dahlberg's boss, Walter Bartley, challenged him to finish his undergraduate degree. So, with the support of his wife, Jill, he started working days, taking classes at night, and trying to help her raise three kids in his free time. Finally in 1970, at age thirty, Dahlberg received his bachelor's degree from Georgia State University. Soon, he was moving from one job to the next at Georgia Power, from one function to the next, then from one subsidiary to the next. He once even took a demotion to broaden his experience base, confident that he would regain his position in time. By forty-five, he was president of Southern Company Services. In 1988, he was named Georgia Power president. Less than six years later, he was Southern Company president—he had not even known what Southern Company was when he was installing meters. The question, "Why can't we do that?" was hardly daunting after answering a much more difficult question, "Why can't a meter man become chairman?"

Dahlberg's popularity with employees was evident in the full-page advertisement that Georgia Power took out in Atlanta's newspapers to congratulate him on his promotion. He always seemed like one of them, and, in fact, he was. "Ego didn't create a problem for him," said Scherer, his mentor.

"I don't like pretentiousness," said Dahlberg, who viewed his background more as good fortune than liability. He believed few people had seen the company from as many perspectives as he had.

No job was more important to his development than his experience in financial services, where he went from junior financial analyst to vice president in three years in the mid-1970s, when Georgia Power was filing one rate case after another and fighting for its financial life. He was not even thirty-five when he began preparing testimony for company witnesses, sometimes working until nearly dawn running numbers. "Everyone was depending on you. It was a great experience," he said.

Dahlberg surrounded himself with "idea people" and did not hesitate to do things differently. As Georgia Power president, he offered a customer service guarantee. "If we misread your meter, we gave you credit on your bill. If we ran over your shrubbery and couldn't fix it, we'd pay a penalty. If we said we'd be there in three days to fix a blown-out security light and we weren't there, we'd pay a penalty," he said. "We were getting ready to go into a competitive environment, and we needed to discipline ourselves, and that gave us a great way to talk to our employees about the importance of customer service."

Dahlberg's ability to communicate creatively with employees was grounded in his authenticity. "I think it's important that I be myself. Having some sense of humor is being myself," said Dahlberg, who would don a costume in a heartbeat to get a point across to employees—a ninja, a sumo wrestler, Uncle Sam, General George Patton, he did them all.

While developing his management style as SCS president, Dahlberg was influenced by the writings of existentialist Viktor Frankl, an Auschwitz survivor and author of "Man's Search for Meaning." Frankl lost his wife, mother, father, and brother in concentration camps but wrote that, even when stripped of everything, individuals still have the freedom to choose their day-to-day attitude. "That helped me realize that if you could visualize doing something, you could do it. I was always optimistic, but I was even more optimistic after that. I saw how I could help cause something to happen if I could just believe it. If I made our goals important and talked about them, then other people would believe they were important and would achieve them."

As Georgia Power CEO, Dahlberg had gotten Plant Vogtle's second unit completed and both units in the rate base, demonstrating the ability to inspire a team effort to accomplish a huge project. "The Vogtle project became something of a litmus test for our system—a hurdle that some observers thought we could not surmount," said Dahlberg, who liked to remind employees, "Whatever we focus on, we can do."

Dahlberg's longest days as Georgia Power president were in Southern Company management council meetings, spending "too much time fiddling around with administrative stuff, instead of thinking about how we were going to drive down the price of our product." He believed the company was "too bureaucratic" and was determined to change that mindset.

One of his first actions was to restructure the goals of the management council—focused outward more than inward. He also immediately began positioning Southern Company in the marketplace, creating a Southern Company staff for the first time and bringing in Mississippi Power president David Ratcliffe as executive vice president of external affairs and strategic planning. "I made the decision to separate Southern Company from the service company, so Southern Company could look at external policies that made a difference and the service company could concentrate on internal issues," Dahlberg said. "People began to say they worked for Southern Company instead of working for Southern Company Services, and that was a really big step."

THE GORILLA YEARS

The newfound pride and confidence that Dahlberg had instilled in Southern Company and its employees became quite public with the publishing of the 1996 annual report, the cover of which included a picture of a huge, brooding gorilla and the question "What is Southern Company?" The answer inside read, "A 900-pound gorilla," with the explanation: "Others have referred to us as the 900-pound gorilla of our industry. We like that comparison. Like a 900-pound gorilla, we are a leader. We are successful. We are strong. When we want to, we move fast."

The gorilla fit well in Dahlberg's plan to build name recognition in advance of a national electricity marketplace. Under his leadership, Southern Company, the onetime regional utility, was coming to be seen as a business heavyweight in America.

In other parts of Southern Company's world, however, the future was not quite working out as planned. Bad news began arriving in mid-1997 with the Labor Party's landslide victory in England and then, two weeks later, with Queen Elizabeth's opening address to the newly elected Parliament. The queen said that high on the new government's agenda was a "windfall-profits tax" to be levied on the foreign investors who had swept in during a Conservative government on the recently privatized regional electricity companies and were now sending earnings back overseas. After Southern Company's purchase of SWEB, six more regional electric companies had been snapped up by U.S. utilities, inflaming a backlash against the invaders. Within seven weeks, the tax passed, with a total levy on the UK electricity sector of nearly $3.5 billion. Southern Company's share was $155 million and would have been greater if it had not sold 25 percent of SWEB in 1996 to PP&L Resources Incorporated, parent company of Pennsylvania Power & Light, for $189 million to generate cash for other expansions. Still, the tax was steep enough to wipe out two years of profits.

Just two weeks after the tax passed in early July, Southern Company announced that Gordon Wu was stepping down as CEPA chairman and selling his remaining 20 percent ownership to Southern Company. For Wu's 20 percent, Southern Company gave up $150 million in cash and the uncompleted Tanjung Jati B Power Station on the island of Java, as Wu's departure stemmed from a disagreement about whether to move forward with the plant.

The Java plant had been a concern from the start, as the initial acquisition called for Southern Company to withhold $138 million of the CEPA purchase price pending refinancing of the project. In the midst of an Asian financial crisis that summer, diverging views developed on the plant's future profitability. Wu, a micromanager who liked to jump in and fix problems, pressed SEI to make the $138 million contingency payment. Wu was willing to go forward without a power-purchase agreement from the Indonesian government, but Dahlberg—aware that Wu's projects did not always work out—was not willing to take that risk. "It turned out great for us because it made our numbers much better and improved our cash flow enormously," Dahlberg said. Within weeks, the deal releasing Southern Company from the Java plant seemed a godsend, as Indonesia's economy was sucked into a whirlpool that would squeeze three-quarters of the value out of its currency.

However, Wu walked out on CEPA with not only the Java plant and $150 million in cash, but also his *guanxi*—the Chinese term for deal-making connections—and all the regional expertise and influence that had prompted Southern Company to pay $2.1 billion for CEPA. Just one month earlier, Wu's top lieutenant, a well-connected, British-born dealmaker, had resigned as CEO of CEPA over a much-publicized philosophy difference with Southern Company, which wanted him to manage projects more tightly.

Although Southern Company had been praised by Wall Street for investing in one of the world's fastest-growing electricity markets, the deal's price was diluting its stock's value. Southern Energy did not expect CEPA to be profitable until 2000, but Wall Street kept screaming, "Show me the money!"

Despite its challenges internationally and on Wall Street, Southern Company was making significant progress in developing a competitive North American business unit by the end of the summer of 1997. SEI had begun opening regional business development offices—they would eventually stretch from New Hampshire to Oregon—but the big breakthrough came September 2 with the birth of Southern Company Energy Marketing (SCEM). The new company was a joint venture with Vastar Resources of Houston, a subsidiary of Atlantic Richfield Company and one of the nation's largest oil and natural gas exploration, production, and marketing companies. Based in Atlanta, SCEM was created to enable Southern Company to achieve its goal of becoming a top-five national marketer in both natural gas and electricity by 2003. A year earlier, the Securities and Exchange Commission had given Southern Company approval to market natural gas to wholesale and large industrial customers, and the company had gained initial experience in that business through a joint venture with Providence Energy, a natural gas provider and energy marketer in Rhode Island.

With half a dozen states scheduled to put some portion of their retail customer base up for competition in 1998, many marketers were preparing for nationwide retail wheeling, which would allow all customers to choose their suppliers and conceivably rely on power marketers rather than search for the best price themselves. Marketers of both electricity and natural gas would become total-energy providers who could offer customers both options, creating optimal energy pricing and the ability to arbitrage between power and gas. "Our competition—Enron, Duke—offer both commodities," said SCEM president Marce Fuller. "We believe that being in the gas business is the only way to succeed in this environment."

Duke Power had purchased natural gas giant Pan Energy ten months earlier in a $7.7 billion deal that stunned the industry and propelled the convergence of the two energy segments. Enron, however, was the pioneer and undisputed kingpin of energy marketing. The Houston-based gas pipeline company had been a big winner in gas marketing and was now aggressively dominating power marketing. Everywhere Southern Energy went in North America or around the world, Enron had usually already been there. The two companies became natural rivals, with Southern Company advocating deliberation and doing deregulation right and Enron pushing to revolutionize the industry and referring to Southern Company as a "dinosaur."

"If Thomas Alva Edison came back from the dead and called Southern Company to get some electricity, he'd find that nothing has changed," Enron president Jeff Skilling told the *Atlanta Constitution*. "These guys are living in an industry that was created a hundred years ago, and they want to keep it that way."

About the same time Southern Company kicked off its $10 million ad campaign, Enron unveiled a $25 million campaign. Enron had already found favor on Wall Street and, to a degree, in Washington, D.C. "I can remember an analyst telling me we should be more like Enron," said Georgia Power president Allen Franklin, who went head-to-head with Enron as Dahlberg's point man in the nation's capital.

Enron's message to regulators and politicians was, according to Franklin, "we have a better model coming out of our experience in competitive wholesale natural gas. There's a better way to run the electric power business, and we at Enron are a lot smarter." The message was well received in some regions because it used "the motherhood and apple pie appeal of every customer wants choice," said Franklin. "When we would have a debate in a Senate hearing or before a public service commission, the Enron proponents would say, 'You're against choice, and you're against competition in your market.'"

Franklin's message was "real-time power markets are different and don't move like natural gas or other commodity markets," but that was a difficult concept to explain in politically charged debates. "We were trying to accommodate competition in wholesale markets while maintaining a reliable and affordable electric power system," he explained.

Deep philosophical and cultural conflicts existed between the two companies. Franklin thought Enron was trying to "make a quick buck by blowing up the industry structure." "We did not believe Enron's message, and we did not like the way they did business," he said. "We were looking out for our shareholders, but we also felt a strong sense of responsibility to our customers. We knew that maintaining a reliable, low-cost electric system in a totally competitive market would be very difficult and ultimately that responsibility would fall to utilities like Southern Company, not the power marketers."

POWER PLANTS COAST TO COAST

Internationally, Southern Company announced its first major investment in Asia in nearly two years in 1998—a 9.9 percent stake in a $500 million joint venture to build a plant in China. "There are not the same development opportunities we saw at the time of our purchase of CEPA," said Dahlberg. Most of those opportunities had not worked out anyway. A $5.5 billion mega-plant in India that CEPA supposedly had in the pipeline fell apart. A $1.6 billion coal-fired plant in Pakistan had looked more promising but also hit one snarl after another and would never be built.

In the late spring of 1998, Southern Company sold another 26 percent of SWEB to PP&L Resources, reducing its role to minority stakeholder. Southern Company's management team—led first by Gale Klappa and then Paul Bowers—was left in place, having successfully reduced prices and power outages, cut staff, improved customer satisfaction, and learned all about competition. It had also learned much about the vagaries of politics in a foreign country. Regardless, financial analysts said Southern Company had gotten its money out of the deal. Nine American utilities had eventually bought into the British regional electric companies, and on a share-price basis, the last one sold for 35 percent more than SWEB.

The money Southern Company took out of England, as well as what it was not investing in Asia, was being used to develop a grid of power plants serving major metropolitan areas across America. With deregulation marching forward, the general consensus was that a half-dozen companies would emerge as national players, with everyone else taking a regional niche as a generation or distribution utility. To be one of the national players, Southern Company believed it would need strategically situated generation to support its energy marketing business.

The generation acquisitions began at the end of 1997 with the $68 million purchase from Commonwealth Edison of a 490-megawatt plant south of Chicago, in Hammond, Indiana. Then, in May 1998, came a $537 million purchase from Commonwealth Energy and Eastern Utilities Associates of 1,267 megawatts of New England capacity, spread across four sites in Massachusetts and Maine. In September, the company bought an 80-megawatt plant in Wichita Falls, Texas, and in October announced it would build a $100 million, 300-megawatt plant in Neenah, Wisconsin.

Two days before Thanksgiving, Southern Company announced two more deals, stretching its network of plants from coast to coast. It moved into California by buying 3,065 megawatts of generation surrounding San Francisco from PG&E Corporation, the parent of Pacific Gas and Electric Company. The cost was high—$801 million—but with it came the promise of experience gained in an electricity market set to be totally deregulated within three years. The other deal moved Southern Company into America's largest electricity market—New York City—with the $480 million purchase of 1,776 megawatts from Orange & Rockland Utilities and Consolidated Edison and the acquisition of gas, oil, coal, and hydropower generation at eight sites in New York state.

In roughly a year's time, Southern Company had struck six deals in seven states, accumulating approximately 7,000 megawatts of capacity at a cost of $2 billion. The march across North America was on.

But in the midst of its U.S. expansion, Dahlberg and his leadership team had started a strategy review in the summer of 1998 because Southern Company had not hit its long-term goal of being the best investment in its industry. "You can put together a strategy or a plan in an environment that is changing very rapidly, but you should not put that plan in concrete," he said. "The only thing that is permanent is that our strategic thinking continues to evolve."

In 1996, Southern Company's total shareholder return had been minus 3 percent. In 1997, it was 21 percent yet ranked in only the twentieth percentile of Goldman Sachs's group of eighty electric utilities. Although Southern Company was on track to meet the intermediate goals Dahlberg had set, it ranked only sixty-fourth of eighty-four utilities in total shareholder return from 1995 to 1997.

The key finding of the review was the need for a more aggressive growth strategy, so the company expanded its earnings-per-share growth goal to 6 to 8 percent annually, from a previous 5 to 6 percent a year. "We hit that goal every single year since we set it, but we still were not the best investment in the industry," explained Dahlberg. As a result, Southern Company would ask the Securities and Exchange Commission for approval to more than double—to almost $8 billion—its investment in unregulated business outside the southeastern United States.

As 1998 ended, Southern Company announced a $200 million write-off on its South American assets and its intention to sell its investments in Argentina and Chile, having significantly underestimated the amount of competition coming into those markets. Then, as 1999 began, came the announcement that the dividend would not be raised for the first time in seven years. Dahlberg explained the company could not grow sufficiently without reinvesting more of its earnings in the business. He also said the new dividend policy would reduce the payout ratio "over time" to retain cash for new investments. "Growing the company gives our shareholders a better total return," he said, pointing out that other utilities were taking a similar approach in the face of deregulation.

By the end of January, the media were reporting rumors that Southern Company was negotiating to buy a major gas company. One outcome of the strategy review was the need to obtain gas capacity. SCEM needed firm natural gas assets to be a full-service energy provider. Financial analysts were saying over and over, "If you're going to be competitive with Duke Energy and Houston Industries, you've got to have gas."

Since 1996, utilities had been seeking the synergies created by the convergence of gas and electricity. Positioning had been bought and won, and Southern Company had been left watching opportunities go by. One in particular still bothered Dahlberg.

"When Duke bought Pan Energy, it was because Paul Andersen [CEO of Pan Energy] saw the future changing and sold his company. He went out and started meeting with people," Dahlberg said. "He met with us. I spent an hour with him. He never said we ought to think about putting these companies together. It was just a sharing of thoughts, and the thoughts were consistent with what they did with Duke. Other people at Southern Company knew I was meeting with him, but no one said anything about it. I wasn't smart enough to figure out what we could have done together. Duke did. I don't know if the deal made business sense, but it certainly made a statement about Duke and their willingness to step out and do something big."

More than two years later, in early 1999, the most attractive remaining natural gas target was Houston-based El Paso Energy, a natural gas pipeline and marketing company with $9.5 billion in assets, market capitalization of almost $4 billion, and a transmission system stretching across the United States. Media reports in January had Southern Company holding merger talks with El Paso or preparing to launch a hostile takeover, sending El Paso's stock higher and higher and sending Southern Company's downward. It was reported that a Southern-El Paso merger would create a $17-billion-a-year international electric and gas provider. However, it was estimated the deal could cost Southern Company $4.8 billion—more than twice the amount of its CEPA acquisition.

The on-again, off-again negotiations finally broke down for good in early March over the insistence by El Paso CEO William Wise that he become Dahlberg's successor as chairman of the combined company. For tradition-laden Southern Company, turning the leadership over to outsiders was a deal-breaker. The company had historically been run by people who had grown up in the company, with outsiders rarely making it to the executive level. Dahlberg's rise from the company's lowest levels to CEO was just one example of its home-grown composition. The person considered Dahlberg's most likely successor, Georgia Power president Allen Franklin, had once worked under Alabama Power president Joe Farley, a protégé of Southern Company founder Thomas Martin.

With the deal dissipating, El Paso moved to block a possible hostile takeover by becoming too large for Southern Company to acquire, announcing it was paying $3.9 billion to acquire Birmingham-based Sonat Incorporated, forming the largest natural gas pipeline company in America. Southern Company's stock continued dropping. By April 6, the share price had hit a one-year low of $22.75—28 percent below its $31.56½ peak six months earlier. Southern Company's leaders felt the stock had also been hurt by the new dividend policy and the fact that thirty-year treasury bonds went up in January. Regardless, they knew something had to be done.

DAHLBERG'S DIFFICULT DECISION

On April 19, 1999, Southern Company announced the repurchase of 50 million shares during the next two years. "With our stock price at its current level and the confidence we have in our future prospects, a repurchase of our stock is a compelling investment," Dahlberg said. The stock price, already up to $24.62½ by then, jumped $3 the next two days.

In May, Dahlberg designated Franklin as his heir apparent by making him Southern Company president and the first chief operating officer in the company's history, giving him responsibility for the five southeastern companies, their plants, and their customers. Dahlberg said the move would strengthen the company's leadership as it continued to grow and that Franklin would be in charge of any pending regulation related to industry restructuring. SEI would continue to report to Dahlberg.

In July, two months after Dahlberg named Franklin COO, Boren retired as SEI president and as executive vice president of Southern Company. He was only fifty. Two weeks later, he was named president and CEO of PG&E National Energy Group, overseeing PG&E's four unregulated subsidiaries. To Boren, the selection of Franklin not only cut off his path to chairmanship of Southern Company but also indicated that in the widening split between Southern Company's two businesses—regulated and unregulated—Franklin's side had won. A vice president by thirty-two, the confident Boren had been ideally suited to lead SEI, transforming it in seven years from $39 million to nearly $14 billion in assets.

"Tom's aggressive guidance helped make Southern Company an international energy company," said Dahlberg, who moved quickly in naming Boren's successor, making Marce Fuller Southern Company's first female CEO the next day. Fuller had been president of SCEM since its creation and, prior to that, had been one of SEI's key players. An engineer who began her career at Alabama Power, she was a protégé of Franklin.

Fuller's first task was clear: complete the coal-fired Sual power plant 134 miles north of Manila. Sual was expected to be the lowest-cost independent power project in the Philippines and, with two 608-megawatt units, contribute 20¢ per share to Southern Company's net income in 2000. Fuller and her staff met the November deadline, and the income generated by the two units in the final two months of the year pumped up Southern Company's 1999 financial performance to record-setting levels.

When the year's final results were in, Dahlberg said, "We could not have had a better year." Southern Company posted its best year ever in net income at $1.28 billion, up more than 25 percent from 1998. Earnings per share jumped from $1.40 to $1.86, and the company hit its new target of 8 percent annual growth two years ahead of schedule. By contrast, growth had been only 2 to 3 percent annually as recently as 1994. The regulated business in the Southeast achieved levels of return on capital that ranked among the industry's leaders. And a decade of emphasis on customer satisfaction placed the five operating companies ahead of the entire industry for the second straight year in a survey of national key accounts. Southern Energy contributed $372 million in net income; before Dahlberg took over, its net income totaled less than $2 million. SCEM was now second only to Enron in power marketing, and 14 percent of SEI's earnings had come from Asia—a 150 percent increase from the previous year.

"Despite the economic turmoil in Asia, we're achieving better numbers than the business case that led us there," Dahlberg said. "We now operate more than 48,000 megawatts of generation worldwide. We own, control, or are building about 12,000 megawatts outside the Southeast. That's about halfway to our goal."

In many ways, the dawn of the twenty-first century could not have looked better for Southern Company. "We delivered," Dahlberg told the media. Everything was working according to plan except for one missing piece: Wall Street was not rewarding Southern Company for its growth.

In 1999, the last year of an extraordinary bull market, Southern Company's total shareholder return was minus 15 percent. The entire electric utility industry lost significant market value, with the Standard & Poor's electric utility index falling 19 percent. Dahlberg wrote shareholders: "The stock market did not reward our performance. You and I—as owners of our company—lost share value. That's amazing. How could that happen?" He then answered his own question: "I believe it's due, in part, to the ongoing dot.com investing frenzy. The stock market's interest in Internet and technology companies has lessened investor interest in backbone industries like ours. I believe it's also due to the ongoing change in our industry. Investors are sitting on the sidelines, waiting to see how it will shake out. They no longer have a single, predictable formula by which to judge performance."

Although Southern Company had accomplished what it set out to do, it was trying to be a growth company in an era when shareholders believed growth arrived only in double digits. "People have so many good alternatives now . . .," Dahlberg said. "They're beginning to say, 'Oh gosh, if I can get my stock to run up 50 percent, why do I want to put it in Southern Company and get a dividend and some small growth?'"

Not one to fear change, Dahlberg moved toward the problem rather than looking the other way, saying, "I'm patient, just not very patient. We just simply have to create value." He began considering options. "When you execute your strategy and perform well and the market doesn't reward you for it, what do you do?" he asked. "If you are committed to providing outstanding value to your shareholders, you re-evaluate your strategy."

Southern Company hired Goldman Sachs, the investment banker, to evaluate options that made the best sense for its shareholders. They included selling Southern Energy, spinning it off, breaking up the business and selling pieces that did not fit, and making an initial public offering (IPO) of SEI stock. The goal was to unlock the value that Southern Company had created but was unrealized in its stock price—to close the large gap between the company's market value and the value of the sum of its parts. That gap seemed to be widening weekly. By the end of February 2000, market value was down $5 billion over the previous twelve months. For the first quarter, earnings were up 9 percent from 1999, yet the stock had lost 14 percent since the start of 2000 and was trading at only two-thirds the value of its individual parts. Something had to be done.

The news came two weeks later—announced first at an executive forum and then to the rest of the world. "We have reached a difficult and different decision, not one we have taken lightly, not one we originally thought we would take," Dahlberg told his management team meeting in Savannah. "This is not the time to look back on history but to make history." Dahlberg then announced that Southern Company would spin off Southern Energy as a separate company. "We intend to hold an initial public offering of common stock in our Southern Energy subsidiary in the summer or early fall," he said. "Then, within twelve months after that, we intend to distribute the remaining shares in Southern Energy to our shareholders in a spin-off."

With stockholders to get two shares of the SEI spin-off stock for every five Southern Company shares they owned, Dahlberg estimated the spin-off could potentially create an additional $4 billion in value for company share-holders. Still, the decision was difficult. "From an emotional standpoint, it was very hard," Dahlberg later said, "but we are not in business to produce emotion. We are in business to produce value for shareholders . . . . Making these kinds of decisions is what leaders have to do."

At the annual meeting in Atlanta in May, Dahlberg talked of the strategy he laid out five years, to the day, earlier at his first annual meeting as chairman. "By executing our strategy well, we have built two very strong businesses within the same company . . . . However, I believe the financial markets have been telling us there is not a natural investor constituency for these two businesses living under the same roof. We believe that Southern Energy will be more appropriately valued as a stand-alone entity than as part of Southern Company. And we believe the remaining Southern Company will still be valued at a premium to other electric utilities."

Stronger growth had not changed the shareholder base; it was still income-oriented. "Traditional shareholders don't want excitement," Dahlberg told the *Atlanta Journal-Constitution*. "What our shareholders want is an attractive investment with growing dividends over time. That's what we're going to give them."

A critical factor in the decision was the future capital needs of both Southern Company and Southern Energy. Southern Energy's debt could potentially drag down the operating companies' credit rating and eventually cost them more to borrow money. Southern Energy, at the same time, needed to keep borrowing money to remain a growth company. Yet, it was reaching its borrowing limit by being attached to a regulated utility. The IPO in September raised needed capital for debt reduction at Southern Company and financed further growth for Southern Energy. It generated $1.46 billion in proceeds for Southern Energy, as more than 66 million shares sold at $22 per share, far better than the estimated price range of $15 to $17. By the end of 2000, the shares were selling at $28.31. Investors were also responding positively to Southern Company stock. On the last trading day before the IPO announcement, the stock closed at $23.62½. By the end of 2000, it was up 39 percent to $32.75.

In January 2001, Southern Energy, having to give up any ties to its Southern Company past, changed its name to Mirant. Developed by a New York ad agency as part of an $8 million rebranding campaign, the name came from the Latin root "mira," meaning to "see" or "envision." Expectations were high. Fuller, the forty-year-old CEO, said Mirant could be larger than Southern Company in five years. Dahlberg announced he would retire from Southern Company on April 1 and move to Mirant as chairman and take "an active but not full-time role," hoping his presence would boost the credibility of the new company as he transitioned into retirement.

The spin-off came April 2, 2001, with 272 million shares—80.3 percent of Mirant's stock—distributed to Southern Company shareholders. "This is the final step in unlocking the value we have created," Dahlberg said. "With the spin-off, we're delivering that value to our shareholders. We're also creating two great companies from one."

LESSONS LEARNED

The "gorilla years" felt good. The highly competitive world that utilities had feared for a decade had arrived by the mid-1990s, and Southern Company learned how to win in that environment. It diversified, transformed itself into a global energy company, and became the world's largest independent power producer. Domestically, it acquired generating assets in strategic regions across the country, developed natural gas partnerships, and positioned itself as a national energy supplier. It launched a national branding campaign, stamped itself as the largest U.S. generator of electricity, and grew into the nation's second-largest power marketer. Southern Company was doing all the right things to be a winner in the rapidly evolving world of energy.

The pace of change was unprecedented. It was a time when designs for the industry's future were being redrawn each year. A time when energy giants like Enron were trying to topple the traditional utility structure and replace it with a model saturated in competition. A time when federal agencies and many state regulators kept furiously rewriting the rules of the game. A time when the industry splintered into warring factions and many utilities, embracing the latest competitive scheme, rushed like lemmings toward change, change, change.

No one knew where it would stop. No one knew whether all the integrated parts of the business would eventually be pulled apart and tossed into the air. No one knew whether electricity markets would be deregulated all the way down to the retail level. But Bill Dahlberg knew he had to plan as if the unthinkable were inevitable. So he trimmed costs, enhanced customer service, and boosted a competitive mindset in the regulated core business. And he placed big bets in all the right places in the unregulated arena. He helped Southern Company stay ahead of the change curve by maintaining flexibility and exhibiting a remarkable sense of timing with his aggressive strategy and shifts in and out of changing markets. As a result, he repeatedly led the company into the winner's circle under almost all scenarios.

The company's culture was transformed. The work force became proud and more confident, no longer fearing competition, instead being energized by it even when a promising endeavor fell short of its goal. "Some of the things we tried worked out well, and some did not," Dahlberg admitted during a temporary setback in Asian markets. "I think it's healthy to dream, but you must have your feet firmly planted in reality also."

That firm footing enabled Southern Company to get increasingly better at risk assessments, protect its core business, and produce some of the best analysis on industry structure. Inevitably, that reality-grounded footing enabled Southern Company to make the hard decision to dismantle the empire it had just built. When Southern Company's stock dropped to two-thirds of its value in the face of record earnings, what needed to be done became obvious.

"This company had the excitement of growth, the excitement of opportunity, the excitement of being trailblazers, and it was all going up," said Dahlberg. "Then all of a sudden, we faced all the pressures that you can imagine. It was like hitting your head up against a wall." In the end, Southern Company learned that it had to listen to the signals sent by its stockholder base. The traditional utility investors the company had attracted since its initial offering in 1949 favored low-risk, conservative management, steady growth, and dividend yield. That source of support was still with the company and did not place much value in the type of new investments Southern Company was making.

The growth-oriented shareholders the company was trying to catch with its new strategy were off chasing higher-flying technology stocks. eBay, initially offered in 1998 at $18 a share, was up to $241 within three months. iVillage went public at $24 in 1999 and ended its first day of trading at $80. Priceline, with a stock price that jumped from $16 to $69 on the first day of its launch, was worth almost the entire infrastructure of the airline industry by the end of 1999, even though the company only resold airline tickets. A financial analyst once asked Dahlberg, "I am going to buy Enron and AES [another IPP]. Give me a good reason why I should buy you."

By the time Southern Company made its decision to spin off Southern Energy, a technology company was going public and doubling every other day. Internet fever had generated a market bubble—a stage at which people simply began imitating one another without regard to the underlying economics of hard assets, revenues, cash flow, and earnings potential. How could eToys, with revenue of only $25 million, possibly be worth three times more than Toys"R"Us, which had revenues of $11 billion? New Age investors scoffed at the suggestion that something was wrong with this picture. "The old rules are dead," they declared. "Toss out the yardsticks—a 'new economy' has arrived." It sounded eerily akin to notions being bandied about during the speculative passion preceding the 1929 crash.

The tragic lessons of 1929 had to be relearned by a new generation. The basic laws of investing had not changed. Markets go up and down. No matter how elastic and fantastic the bubble, there's always a downturn. The "new market" economy dwelled neither outside economic cycles nor outside history—just outside the sphere of reality. That lesson reinforced the importance of financial flexibility, keeping an equity-debt ratio that allows for managing through a serious downturn. "If you have a slowdown in sales, a slowdown in the economy, an increase in interest rates, you can get in trouble in a hurry," said Allen Franklin. "Every time we go through a long period of economic expansion, people forget that the economy can go in the other direction."

Southern Company learned it was in business to create stockholder value over the long haul and to not get sidetracked by short-term sentiments and hype. The market preoccupation with growth at levels beyond the industry's capacity to produce accelerated the "mindless march toward deregulation," pushing many utilities to take on too much risk. Southern Company's firm footing in reality ultimately saved the company and its shareholders from being badly burned during one of the worst downturns in utility history. Before the fall, Southern Company had already pulled back, saved in part by its conservative tendency and in part because it stayed focused on its long-term goals and listened to its stockholders.

And so after the spin-off, Southern Company returned to its roots. It had been a fantastic journey for a company that had staked its future to the Southeast from its formation. Within a few short years, it had hung its shingle out for business in the biggest metropolitan areas in America. It had traversed both the Atlantic and Pacific and raised its flag in international energy markets. But it was now time for the world traveler to go home. The party was over. The road home would be loaded with challenges and potential pitfalls, but the timing of the return trip seemed right. It would be back to the business Southern Company knew best in the market it knew best—the four-state regional economy it had helped build and served for nearly a century. The enterprise had come full circle, and Southern Company was once again a truly southern company.

Preparing for the future, company lineman B. J. Hall installs new transmission lines that will ensure reliability as the Southeast grows and "smart grid" technologies are deployed to meet greater demands for energy. CEOs Allen Franklin (top right) and David Ratcliffe secured Southern Company's success as a regional energy provider and a leader within the electric utility industry. *James Schnepf*

ALLEN FRANKLIN FACED TWO CHALLENGES when he became CEO and chairman of Southern Company in early 2001. First, he had to sell Wall Street on investing in the sans-Mirant Southern Company. Then he had to execute his strategy more consistently than the company had done in three decades. "Our financial flexibility was razor-thin," he said. "If we stumbled, we'd be in trouble."

Southern Company would be a very different kind of company without Mirant, its "growth engine" and headline-grabber for five years. The new strategy would be founded on a painful lesson learned during those exciting years: Southern Company's stockholders simply were not looking for the type of investment it was trying to become.

"Our thought, and the advice of our investment bankers, had been that, as we invested more and more in Mirant, our stockholder base would gradually evolve to a different stockholder base, a stockholder looking for higher growth and accepting of higher risk. That didn't happen," Franklin said.

"So when we spun Mirant, we intended to go back to an investment profile that matched what our shareholders wanted—a relatively low-risk investment with increasing and reliable dividends and as much earnings growth as we could produce, given those first two parameters."

Southern Company's formula for success would be: produce 5 percent earnings growth and a dividend yield of 5 percent for a total return of 10 percent. The primary questions were: Can that be accomplished with the high debt levels that followed the Mirant spin-off, and, then, will Wall Street value that type of company in a period when hyper-growth expectations were the norm?

"We went to Wall Street with a strategy that said, 'Look, there still should be a market for a company that can grow earnings 5 or 6 percent per year and, with dividends, produce a total return of about 10 percent with low risk. That still makes sense,'" Franklin said. To deliver on its promises, Southern Company would have to produce superior returns at all five operating companies for the next two to three years—a formidable task. "I knew the strategy was good and our people could execute it, I knew the territory was good, I knew the assets were good, and I knew the state regulatory situation was favorable in the Southeast," he said. "But our financial flexibility was not."

Lack of financial flexibility was a hangover from the spin-off of Mirant, when debt and equity were split in a way that would allow both Mirant and Southern Company a chance to be successful. "We gave Mirant everything they asked for and took all the debt they asked us to take, because the objective was for both companies to succeed post-spin," Franklin said. "As a result, Southern Company ended up with substantially more debt than would traditionally exist in an electric utility, so it was important for us to get the equity in the company back up and the debt down. In the interim, any misses on revenue or cost projections would create serious volatility in earnings, limiting our ability to pay down the debt."

The goal of 10 percent total return would be made even more challenging by the Southeast's projected growth in retail electricity usage of only 2 to 3 percent. To make up the difference between retail sales and earnings growth-rate goals, Southern Company would have to fire up a new "growth engine"—Southern Power, a recently created subsidiary that would sell bulk power under wholesale contract to other utilities. The competitive market in the Southeast was new, but the business was not new for Southern Company. In the late 1970s and early 1980s, when the demand for power slowed to a standstill as a result of the Arab oil embargo, economic recession, and energy conservation, Southern Company had avoided canceling plants already under construction by selling large, long-term blocks of power to utilities in Florida and Texas. They were called unit power sales then, and they launched the southeastern wholesale power market.

"Because it was still a largely undeveloped market in the Southeast, and a market that we understood better than anyone, we felt Southern Power could grow its earnings maybe 15 or 20 percent for a period of time without increasing our risk profile at all," Franklin said. "Combining the 2 or 3 percent retail market growth from the utilities with 15 or 20 percent wholesale market growth from Southern Power, it was clear that we could produce about 5 percent, maybe 6 percent, total earnings growth."

Southern Power offered the promise of much less risky growth than Mirant's wholesale business, which had entered unfamiliar domestic and international markets and took greater risks on fuel and electricity prices. Franklin constructed very different parameters around Southern Power. It would build plants only in the Southeast and only if it had a long-term contract for most of the plant's capacity with a creditworthy customer, usually a utility. The fixed portion of the electricity price would be established in the contract, and fuel-price fluctuations would be passed on to the customer. "We understood the markets in the Southeast extremely well. The better an entity understands the market, the less risky it is to participate in that market," Franklin said. "The way we constructed the business, our knowledge of the market, the critical mass of generation we owned in the Southeast, and the constraints we put around marketing and trading made the risk profile very similar to our regulated utility business. In effect, we were able to increase earnings growth without taking on additional risk. Our principal risk with Southern Power was building the plants on budget and operating them efficiently, and those were our core strengths." Southern Company's competitive wholesale power business in the Southeast had netted more than $100 million in 2000, but for Southern Company to achieve its goals, Southern Power would have to double its earnings in five years.

To execute his overall strategy, Franklin knew he would not only have to grow earnings but also take costs out of the regulated business. He planned to do that by increasing shared services and overcoming a corporate culture rooted in a legacy of independent-minded operating companies. "You'd be hard-pressed to find another company that has subsidiaries—in our case, operating companies—with outside boards of directors, because operating companies don't have any equity holders for the board to look out after," Franklin said. "Southern Company ultimately elects the board at the operating companies, but they're still separate boards, and that means that the management of an operating company is not only answering to Southern Company but also to its board." For years, Franklin had seen how the culture of strong operating companies undermined their opportunities to work together for Southern Company's benefit. "There was not much mechanism to get them to work together," he said.

While Franklin led an offensive in Atlanta to cut costs through increased cooperation among the operating companies, his team in Washington, D.C., would defend the existing utility infrastructure against a regulatory and legislative onslaught that threatened Southern Company with monumental costs, loss of its transmission system, and reduced reliability of the regional electricity grid. The formerly reactive Federal Energy Regulatory Commission had transformed itself during the previous decade into an activist change agent and was now pushing its ideas of industry structure on individual states. Franklin knew the battle would be a new rendition of an old war that his predecessors had waged—federal intervention versus the states and private enterprise. No one could have been more fit for the fight.

THE EDUCATION OF ALLEN FRANKLIN

The critical decision in Allen Franklin's young life came a month out of high school in an expansive Alabama peach orchard. It was June 1962, midday, and incredibly hot in Corner, Alabama. About two dozen teenagers had already worked all morning picking peaches when Franklin heard everyone start screaming. He turned to see hundreds of baskets of peaches crashing to the ground. The teenage boy driving the tractor had turned too sharply climbing a terrace and flipped the long trailer loaded with peaches. "So we'd been working all morning for nothing," said Franklin, who had been in charge of the work crew. That night Franklin talked to his father, who had just finished another day farming under the same Alabama sun and was about to head off to his midnight shift in a coal mine.

"Look, I want to go to college," Franklin said.

"Well, we'll figure how to make that work," his father replied. "You got to be thinking about where you want to go, and we'll talk about it between now and the fall."

"I don't mean this fall," Franklin said bluntly. "I want to go now."

Delton Franklin had begun coal mining at thirteen and completed only through the sixth grade. "So he didn't know what to say, like, 'Here's what you need to do,'" Franklin recalled. "But he said, 'All right, go do whatever you need to do.'" The next day, Franklin was in Tuscaloosa, Alabama—in the admissions office of the University of Alabama. Summer classes had started a few days earlier.

"Look, son, you can't enroll now because the semester has already started," the dean of admissions told him.

"If you'll let me in, I'll promise you I'll catch up," Franklin pleaded. He argued his case so well the dean let him start classes that week. "I had always thought about going to college, but I had never made any plans," explained Franklin, who was so naïve that he did not understand the dean when asked what college he wanted to enroll in.

"The University of Alabama," he responded. "Why else would I be here?"

"No," replied the dean. "What college within the university? Do you want to go into premed or education or engineering or finance?"

"Which one made the most money last year?" Franklin asked.

The space industry was cranking up, and the dean said engineers with a four-year degree had the highest starting salary.

"Sign me up," Franklin said.

The third of four children, Franklin was the product of a schoolteacher mother and a father with uncommon practical sense and analytical ability. Orphaned by age two and then bounced from one relative to another, Franklin's father eventually saved enough money mining coal to buy a forty-acre cotton farm. "He worked more hours than anybody I've ever known and could improvise ways to make things work," Franklin said. "He could think through what was a good idea or bad idea. He had a more conservative side, not seeing everything through rose-colored glasses"—attributes passed on to Franklin.

Upon graduation from Alabama, Franklin became a test engineer for Pratt & Whitney, first in Florida and then New England. He moved to Huntsville in 1967 with the Federal Electric Corporation, working on the Saturn V rocket and the moon shot. When the United States succeeded in its mission to put a man on the moon in 1969, he knew the industry would begin to dry up. "It was clear to me that, as much as that was fun, I had to get a real job in a more stable environment. In four years we'd lived in three different parts of the country," he said.

Just as aerospace was downsizing, the U.S. electric power industry was expanding, gobbling up engineers to build plants across America and supply the booming electricity demand coming out of the 1960s. When a Southern Company Services representative came to Huntsville for interviews, Franklin went to see him. He was offered an engineering position in system planning, accepted, and moved his family to Birmingham. Franklin figured it was a "step back [financially] to have a little bit more stable future." It would not be the last time he would be blessed by his conservative approach to life—"you work hard, you pay your bills, you don't go into debt, you do what you say you're going to do, and you treat your neighbor right"—for it was a life view that blended in well at Southern Company. Within five years, Franklin was a manager in load forecasting. By 1978, he was assistant to SCS senior vice president Bill Guthrie, a man after his own heart. "Bill was a very matter-of-fact kind of person, which is sort of the way I was, but he was even more so," Franklin said. Guthrie's approach was: "Get to the point. I just want to know the result and how you know it's right." "I'd never been around a boss that could really make that work as well as he did," Franklin said.

Guthrie had such confidence in the young Franklin that he asked him to conduct a secret study into the feasibility of forming a Southern Company generating company—hardly a popular idea at the time. "It was the most educational thing I ever did in the system because I got involved heavily on the financial side, the legal side, and the operating side and really had to think through some difficult, complicated issues. Having to present it to all the operating companies and their CEOs was a great experience, although it was not well received in some quarters," he said. The study found significant opportunity for savings, but the idea was scrapped for regulatory, financial, and internal political reasons. It was "sort of before its time," according to Franklin.

Working for Guthrie enabled Franklin to develop his strengths, and within eight months he was transferred to Alabama Power as assistant to the executive vice president of generation, working first for Alan Barton and then Bill Whitt. Impressing his superiors with his ability to dissect every detail of a decision and communicate his thoughts in a direct, unflappable manner, Franklin entered the executive ranks thirty months later at age thirty-seven, jumping in one swoop from an "assistant-to" to senior vice president of Alabama Power. Only nineteen months later, in mid-1983, he went back to SCS as executive vice president. With the promotion came responsibility for Southern Company's position on national policy issues, and rarely has there been a better match of man and role. It was a time when electricity deregulation was under study and regulatory agencies were starting to make decisions about the pricing of wholesale power and the use of transmission grids by new competitors.

"I think that role evolved, in part, just because my background in the company happened to fit what we needed at that time," said Franklin, who had done numerous transmission studies in system planning, looking at how much power could be moved reliably between companies and how much new transmission was needed. The flow of power over transmission lines was a central issue in industry structure debates in Congress. Also, Franklin's experience negotiating bulk power contracts and the marketing of power to other utilities gave him expertise in wholesale power discussions. When he was promoted to SCS president in 1988, his leadership position in policy debates grew, and he became so valuable as a system spokesperson on policy issues that he took the role with him when he was promoted to president of Georgia Power in 1994, when Bill Dahlberg became Southern Company president. Dahlberg once said, "Franklin probably knows more about the [restructuring] proposals than anyone in our industry." Thomas Kuhn—president of the Edison Electric Institute, the primary policy group for utilities—considered Franklin the industry's "principal leader" in formulating strategy as chairman of EEI's restructuring committee. Most other utility CEOs had financial or legal backgrounds, not transmission planning or bulk power backgrounds, so they easily deferred to Franklin on hard, technical issues. Franklin not only welcomed the hard stuff but was intellectually stimulated by it. "Trying to bring the engineering, operational piece together with the economic-market model, and deal with that in the political arena, was extremely interesting and educational," he said.

Dahlberg was happy to let Franklin handle Washington, D.C., their marriage being one of complementary strengths and interests. "We worked extremely well together, more as colleagues than anything else," Franklin said. "Bill tended to be much more emotional than I was about things and much more intuitive. I tended to be much more fact-based, by the numbers, without much emotion attached to it." The admiration was mutual. Dahlberg, the idea man, promoted the analytical Franklin to chief operating officer of Southern Company in 1999 and later publicly called him "one of the smartest people I've ever met." It was Franklin who had been successful in negotiating changes to the National Energy Policy Act of 1992 that kept FERC from ordering retail transmission access and left that issue for the states to decide. His voice of reason during negotiations also helped ensure a level playing field for utility subsidiaries like SEI in competing with independent power producers.

GROWING STRONGER BY GROWING SMALLER

Following the spin-off of Mirant, Franklin believed it would take four to five years to increase the equity in Southern Company and decrease debt to target levels. He was wrong. It did not take that long.

In 2001, Southern Company beat analysts' expectations with 6.6 percent growth in earnings per share and a 32 percent total return to shareholders. It was a powerful performance during a shaky year for financial markets; the Standard & Poor's Electric Index dropped 8 percent, and the S&P 500 dropped 11 percent. Instead of weakening the parent company, the spin-off of Mirant had actually seemed to energize Southern Company's leadership and employees. "It did simplify the management," Franklin said. "It focused the management on two things—this more conservative regulated business and Southern Power. Those two entities went together cleanly and smoothly."

Prior to the spin-off, two different cultures had been juxtaposed within Southern Company. Within Southern Energy, a culture developed that was quite different from that of the core business. It was competitive, which was necessary to survive in the fast-paced, growth-fixated environment being defined by market leaders such as Enron. Dahlberg as CEO and then Franklin as COO had been challenged by the need to preserve both cultures in making joint decisions, often emphasizing teamwork and minimizing the sibling-like rivalry. After the spin-off, though, the core business units no longer wondered if they were still an important part of Southern Company. "It was clear they were the only part of the company," Franklin said. "There was a higher level of energy and commitment."

Southern Company had returned to its southern roots. Its message to Wall Street was: "the business we know best, in the region we know best, with the customers we know best," and no one could have been better prepared to marshal that return than Allen Franklin. He had grown up in Southern Company's cradle of Alabama and then had matured in Southern Company under the tutelage of Alabama Power president Joe Farley, who had been mentored by Southern Company patriarch Thomas W. Martin. The three-generation leadership bloodline spanning ninety years—remarkable for a publicly held company—gave Franklin a direct transfusion of the company's heritage and strengths, including its multiveined ties to the South. "Joe Farley understood how the company was founded, and he understood what was important to Thomas Martin and what principles he was promoting," Franklin said. "I'd go to [Alabama Power] management council meetings and spend a good bit of time with him. And just his sense of history and what this company is about was pretty important at that time in my career."

It was from Farley that Franklin learned about Martin's view on building the region's economy. "It was a case of almost having to develop a demand for power before the company could get going. The whole concept in Georgia of being 'citizens wherever we serve' is essentially the same thing that Thomas Martin was doing in Alabama," Franklin said. "Some of my earlier impressions of the importance of being conservative financially—which doesn't mean you're not aggressive in your business, but you're conservative in your financing—came from Farley and talking about how Alabama Power was started and financed in the early part of its history."

Franklin's fiscal conservatism was right on time, as one corporate financial scandal followed another—Enron, WorldCom, Tyco, HealthSouth. Maintaining share price in an overvalued market had become a mandate at some companies, but ethical behavior, powered and promulgated by "Southern Style," was already a Southern Company standard. "Integrity and honesty in management are critical. That concept got lost among some companies and on some executives who got carried away with the potential increase in personal wealth and forgot they were really working for the shareholders," Franklin said. Still, Southern Company would be affected like all corporations by the collective greed, lax oversight, and the crisis of confidence in corporate America. In response, Congress passed the Sarbanes-Oxley Act of 2002, greatly toughening disclosure requirements. "In the end, we all suffered because of the regulations and laws and loss of confidence in business in general," Franklin said.

Southern Company's record of financial integrity and Franklin's straightforward communication style were what shell-shocked investors began seeking. In 2002, a year promises were being broken by former Wall Street darlings in all business lines, Southern Company was rewarded for delivering on its promises. The S&P Electric Index was down 15 percent and the economy was slumping, yet Southern Company's stock rose 12 percent, earnings per share shot up 8 percent, and total shareholder return was 17.6 percent. The strategy was working.

court, Ratcliffe had transformed his career's darkest days into a source of strength by building a foundation that would enable Southern Company to attract a diverse work force for the twenty-first century. "We have to change this culture," he had decided, "and we have to improve our whole ability to deal with and articulate issues around diversity and inclusion."

Franklin believed Ratcliffe could make the tough decisions looming ahead for Southern Company and keep the company on its strong, "post-spin" course. "David's been involved in planning and implementing the Southern Company strategy at every step," said Franklin in announcing his retirement. "He has exceptional business judgment and is a great team-builder. The company's strategic direction will not change under his leadership."

To Franklin, though, Ratcliffe's greatest gifts were character traits he had transformed into leadership skills. Even in a roomful of executives, Ratcliffe stood out simply by his confident yet unassuming bearing. Franklin thought Ratcliffe's credibility and stature would reinforce trusting relationships with the company's many constituents and that his willingness to stand strong on difficult issues would make him an industry leader, keeping Southern Company front and center in policy debates. And, Franklin believed, Ratcliffe's emphasis on ethical management would be welcome in the post-Enron era and help the industry repair its shaken image. Franklin considered him, in essence, "a model citizen, almost irritatingly so."

"You could trust your kids with Ratcliffe," he said. "You could trust your wife with Ratcliffe."

In the end, Franklin would trust his company with him.

RATCLIFFE'S CULTURAL AGENDA

Ratcliffe told the media that Southern Company would continue down the same path established by Franklin. His ego did not require a new agenda. "This company is not broken," he said. "People shouldn't expect some radical new vision, because we don't need one. I tend to think more about the people issues and cultural issues, while Allen thinks more about the hard business issues. We'd wind up with the same answer, though."

At his first forum with his executives, Ratcliffe made his interest in cultural issues clear. He made Alabama Power's safety slogan Southern Company's goal. It was straightforward and wrapped in two words—Target Zero. It was simple enough to remember and make universal throughout the company. "Southern Company is an industry leader in every category with the exception of safety," he said. "Our safety performance is historically in the third or fourth quartile of Southeastern Electric Exchange member companies. We can't be world-class unless our people are safe. Safety should take precedence over reliability, cost, customer service, and profits."

Believing safety was a state of mind, Ratcliffe would put it at the forefront of everyone's mind. All company meetings would begin with a safety briefing—even the annual meeting of stockholders. "We've evolved into a culture that accepts a certain number of accidents or injuries. We measure ourselves year to year and consider it a success to have fewer injuries than the year before," he told the forum. "What's our customer-service goal? We want every single customer to be satisfied, with no exceptions. This isn't any different."

At the same forum, Ratcliffe announced he was simplifying Southern Style, the company's "value proposition," as he called it, to make it easier for managers and employees to articulate. He took its seventeen values and behaviors and grouped them into three components—unquestionable trust, superior performance, and total commitment. The goal was to permeate the company with these values, as Ratcliffe had exemplified Southern Style before it was ever created by Dahlberg in 1995, so much so that Dahlberg enlisted his help in drafting it.

With his people priorities in place at Southern Company, Ratcliffe began assuming Franklin's role as an industry leader. Because of his willingness to listen and the absence of a personal agenda, he would be skilled at finding common ground to address challenges facing the industry, which was at risk of fragmenting from the array of opinions resulting from its increasing diversity—independent power producers, transmission-only companies, generation-only companies, distribution-only companies, and traditional vertically integrated companies.

Increasing environmental regulation and the threat of new laws to address growing concerns about climate change would become the major issues facing the industry. But unlike most CEOs, Ratcliffe had an advantage. For more than three decades, he had been thinking about the environmental consequences of producing energy. "I got a job with this company because we were concerned about the environmental impact around our power plants, so I understand that this is an evolutionary process and it takes time," he said.

His background and openness made Ratcliffe comfortable discussing issues with environmental groups pushing for increased regulation of the industry. "We will sit down and talk with anybody," he said. "We want to try to explain our views and the way we operate our business. We want to understand their views, and if there is some way to achieve their objectives without creating huge costs that are inappropriate in our judgment, then we are certainly willing to try to move in that direction."

Developed from experience, Ratcliffe's environmental philosophy was fairly simple—common sense, balance, and practical approaches. "Everybody is in favor of clean air. But there are huge technical questions about how clean we can make it and with what economic impact," he said.

Ratcliffe's consensus-building skills were critical to bringing the industry together on climate change, which was by his own admission the "most contentious environmental issue of my career." He repeatedly kept discussions focused on the economic impact on customers, with his peers eventually deciding that any Edison Electric Institute position on climate change must include what they dubbed the "Ratcliffe principle," which held that any discussion should involve the impact on customers. As a result of his leadership, Ratcliffe took over as EEI chairman in mid-2008, at the height of Congress's repeated attempts to pass a comprehensive energy bill—"as complex as any piece of legislation that Congress has ever tried to pass," according to Ratcliffe. He held the industry together despite the complexity and argued successfully for the need for new technologies and the time required to deploy them. "This is a serious global issue that requires a long-term, global approach," he said. "We strongly believe that technology and not more regulation is the best way for the United States to do its part in addressing carbon dioxide issues."

Simultaneously, Ratcliffe emerged as a leading spokesman for a balanced national energy policy. He believed the key to energy independence, or healthy interdependence, was a diversity of energy sources—from oil, coal, and gas to nuclear, hydro, and renewables. All options are needed, he said, but they must be balanced, again, with economic considerations and the availability of effective technology. His advocacy for diverse fuel sources was solidified by an Electric Power Research Institute study called the Prism Analysis, which projected what technologies would have to be deployed at what levels to achieve certain carbon dioxide reductions.

"When we looked at that diagram, one of the things that was clear to the industry was that there was not a single winner in the entire spectrum for meeting the needs of a growing industry and growing economy," Ratcliffe said. "What came through is you don't have the luxury of picking one technology; we really needed all of them."

A TIME TO PLAN, A TIME TO BUILD

For at least fifteen years, Ratcliffe had seen this time coming. In his early days at Mississippi Power, he had said the biggest challenge facing electric utilities was developing the next generation of base load capacity to meet America's demand for electricity because energy conservation would be insufficient. "The environmental effort seems to want to discard the use of coal. And the anti-nuclear movement does not want to see nuclear plants," he told a reporter, who even then described Ratcliffe as "all business, focused and circumspect."

For more than two decades, Southern Company had been able to postpone building base load capacity by investing in energy-efficiency programs and building gas-fired combustion turbines. But decision day had finally arrived. And Ratcliffe—who had never expected to be here, who had even been surprised when he was named Georgia Power president—was now CEO of one of America's largest utilities and staring at a forecast projecting electricity demand in the Southeast to jump 30 percent in the next fifteen years. He knew he had the ability to take nuclear power into the twenty-first century, to put both nuclear and coal back in play.

Six months into his new job—and a quarter-century after the accident at Three Mile Island threw nuclear power into a dark slump in the United States—Ratcliffe summoned Jim Miller III to his office. It was late 2004, and Miller, senior vice president and general counsel at Georgia Power, was already on Ratcliffe's radar as a potential next leader of Southern Nuclear, the subsidiary that operated the system's nuclear plants. He told Miller, "Jim, when you come back from the holidays, I want you to tell me how we would build Vogtle 3 and 4. I think we could do it, but we are going to have to put together a strategy."

America's approximately 100 reactors were providing about 20 percent of the nation's electricity and had a long-standing track record of very effective, efficient operations. With the climate-change debate threatening the long-term outlook for new coal generation, nuclear seemed the obvious alternative.

"Nuclear power is currently the only viable, zero-carbon option with the necessary scale to address our [base load] needs," Ratcliffe said. In the two to three years before he became CEO, Ratcliffe had watched the cost of new nuclear technology evolve until it was price-competitive with coal and natural gas. Ratcliffe also was encouraged by the Nuclear Regulatory Commission's new streamlined licensing process, which would enable utilities to get a combined construction and operating license and remove the risk of expensive changes later by regulators, as was the case in the 1980s. Southern Company had joined four other utilities and two reactor vendors in a consortium to test the new licensing process. With public support of nuclear power climbing higher and higher, Ratcliffe gradually realized there was more reason to build a nuclear plant than anytime in the past quarter-century. "If we could find a base load need," he thought, "it would be the right thing for us to do and the right thing for the nation to do."

Georgia Power was expected to need new base load capacity between 2014 and 2020, and Ratcliffe knew additional nuclear capacity could be constructed at Plant Vogtle, where four units had been planned in the 1970s but only two built after the energy crisis drastically cut projections for needed capacity and skyrocketing costs for nuclear construction removed new nuclear as an option. "This might be the opportunity," he thought.

Miller came back in January with a strategy to build the units. Ratcliffe told him, "I want you to put together some more definitive plans. I want you to assume that we want to start up this unit in 2015, and show me what we would have to do and when we would have to do it." Miller returned with what he had started calling Project 2015. "He had a big notebook and people that he got involved to help, and it began to come together as an idea," Ratcliffe said. "The more we talked about it, the more it made sense. But I knew we were going to have to do it differently than last time." This time, the Georgia Public Service Commission would need to be an ally, not an adversary, in meeting energy needs. Georgia Power's leadership soon began discussing new nuclear generation with the PSC.

To ensure other problems encountered with the first two Vogtle units would not be repeated, Ratcliffe summoned former company leaders Joe Farley, Jim Miller II, Bob Scherer, Bill Dahlberg, and Allen Franklin, and Southern Company director Zack Pate, chairman emeritus of both the Institute of Nuclear Power Operations and the World Association of Nuclear Operators. He asked them, "If we decide we want to do this, what lessons should we remember from the last time and how should we approach the project this time?" He then sent a team to meet with the managers who oversaw the actual construction of units 1 and 2 to learn "what got us in trouble."

Eventually, Ratcliffe had studied and researched the project enough. A decision had to be made if the power supply was to be ready when it was needed. Would the company move forward with regulatory filings and nego- tiations with a reactor vendor, or would it sit back and wait, putting the plan on hold, something to pull out if necessity mandated? Ratcliffe had already demonstrated he would attack difficult issues without hesitation simply on the strength of his commitment to doing the right thing. He would not leave the nuclear decision on someone else's desk. After much study by many people, Ratcliffe reached his conclusion. It was the right thing for Georgia Power, for Southern Company, and for America, he thought. If the world decided to curb carbon dioxide emissions, America would need nuclear power. Someone needed to do this, and not everyone could. Southern Company could. It had the financial stability, the regulatory relationships, and the operating experience.

Southern Nuclear filed an early site permit for construction with the Nuclear Regulatory Commission in 2006. Georgia Power, under CEO Mike Garrett's leadership, filed an application for certification of the units with the PSC in 2008. That same year Southern Nuclear filed with the NRC for a construction and operating license, and Miller became Southern Nuclear CEO and would get to implement the plan he had developed.

Throughout the process, Ratcliffe invited comment from groups that wanted input. "If anybody can point out something that we should be doing, we should fix it," he said, taking a direct, hands-on approach at every step. He created an oversight committee composed of six people—himself, Southern Company's chief financial officer and chief operating officer, Georgia Power's president, Southern Nuclear's president, and the lead project executive. Their role would be to meet regularly to go over the project's "status real-time and know what's working and what is not working," according to Ratcliffe, "and where we need to push and where we need to help."

Ratcliffe made sure there was ongoing communication with the boards of Georgia Power and Southern Company. "There were people on the Georgia Power board who lived through Vogtle 1 and 2 and had some uneasiness about starting a project again of this magnitude. Vogtle 1 and 2 was not a good experience. It was not a pleasant time for the Georgia Power leadership and the Georgia Power board. When you have a plan that is supposed to cost $900 million but ends up costing about $9 billion, that is awfully difficult to explain. We had a good explanation, but we still had to write off a billion dollars, and once you go through that, you don't want to do it again. But you can't be afraid to climb those hills again simply because they were hard to climb last time."

In February 2009, the Georgia legislature passed the Nuclear Energy Financing Act to allow Georgia Power to recover financing costs during construction, reducing the project's cost and saving customers $2 billion. A month later, the PSC granted a certificate to build the two units and approved recovery of $6.4 billion in construction and financing costs, with the remaining $7.6 billion in construction costs to be borne by the plant's joint owners. Then in August 2009, the NRC granted an early site permit to begin construction.

The two 1,100-megawatt Vogtle units, scheduled for start-up in 2016 and 2017, will be the first in the U.S. to use Westinghouse's AP1000, state-of-the-art technology that utilizes innovative, gravity-driven safety systems, 85 percent less cable, and 80 percent less piping than the average nuclear unit.

Ratcliffe also wanted to use new technology to retain coal as one of Southern Company's fuel options for new generation. With a 250-year supply of coal, America needed technologies for burning it more cleanly and capturing and storing its carbon dioxide emissions. "My view was if we could get a coal technology to the same environmental footprint as natural gas, then, by definition, it had to be acceptable because natural gas is the alternative to coal for all practical purposes," said Ratcliffe.

Southern Company had been researching ways to burn coal more cleanly for 30 years and during the previous decade had managed nearly $500 million in research and development to improve the generation, delivery, and use of electricity while reducing environmental impact. Its research facility in Wilsonville, Alabama, was chosen by the U.S. Department of Energy as its National Carbon Capture Center in 2009. One process developed there over two decades—integrated gasification combined cycle, which converts coal into a gas—showed particular promise for two reasons. It could burn coal more cleanly, removing 99 percent of sulfur dioxide and particulates, and when combined with carbon capture technology, also reduce carbon dioxide emissions by 65 percent. Most important, it could burn lignite and other lower-rank coal—traditional pulverized-coal units could not—and approximately half the world's coal reserves are lignite.

"Mississippi Power was in need of base load capacity," Ratcliffe said. "They have a huge lignite deposit that comes all the way down eastern Mississippi and into Alabama. All of that made this project make sense. Just like the Vogtle project, it needed state approval and regulatory approval. We brought a team of people together and, with the leadership of [Mississippi Power CEO] Anthony Topazi, ultimately got approval in Mississippi to move forward."

When the $2.4 billion, 582-megawatt plant is operational in 2014, it will be America's largest-scale commercialization of coal gasification on lower-rank or lignite fuel. It will feature carbon capture and be built on top of a lignite deposit in east-central Mississippi. "It is truly twenty-first-century technology, much like Vogtle 3 and 4," said Ratcliffe. "I think those two projects are demonstrations that Southern Company is committed to leading-edge technology and finding solutions to move forward in how we make and use energy."

The new Vogtle units were moving along on schedule in early 2010, continuing to receive regulatory approvals, when Southern Company received a huge and helping hand from the federal government, which selected the Vogtle units as recipient of its first clean-energy loan guarantee for new nuclear technology. As part of the Energy Policy Act of 2005 to help restart nuclear construction, the loan guarantee would lower the cost of construction for customers. "We wind up spending less money in interest costs and financing costs because the federal government is guaranteeing the loan. They are not giving us the money, they are just standing behind the loan so that we can get a lower interest rate," Ratcliffe said.

One month later, Southern Company made national news again with an announcement related to yet another fuel source—a joint agreement with Turner Renewable Energy to build one of the nation's largest solar installations in northeast New Mexico. Because of limited opportunity to develop significant solar energy resources in the Southeast, Ratcliffe had personally pursued discussions with media mogul Ted Turner for a working agreement that could develop solar resources nationally. Consisting of 500,000 photovoltaic modules using thin-film semiconductor technology, the Cimarron solar facility was operational by the end of 2010.

"We are using an entire spectrum of technologies," Ratcliffe said. "Our driver in all of these decisions is what is best for our customer. How do we get the maximum reliability and the lowest cost with less of an environmental footprint for our customers? We are trying to solve the equation for the benefit of our customer."

NATURAL DISASTER AND ECONOMIC RECESSION

Ratcliffe's dogged perseverance in developing energy sources that would ensure that Southern Company could meet its obligations years after his retirement was made more impressive by other major challenges that beset his tenure as CEO. In 2005, Hurricane Katrina devastated the Mississippi coast, creating, in his words, "the largest natural catastrophe we've ever had." Mississippi Power, again under Topazi's leadership, and Southern Company responded so quickly and valiantly that Ratcliffe was called to testify in Congress about how they did it, particularly at a time when so many other responders struggled.

A lawsuit against Southern Company by Mirant's creditors in bankruptcy hung over the company during the middle of Ratcliffe's tenure. It alleged that creditors were entitled to recover dividends paid and loans repaid to Southern Company prior to the spin-off. The suit was not settled until 2009, with Southern Company taking a $202 million charge against first-quarter earnings. By then, Ratcliffe and chief financial officer Paul Bowers were doing all they could to contend with the most challenging U.S. economic recession since World War II.

Beginning in December 2007, the recession was caused by a crisis in real estate markets and risky mortgage-backed securities that had been marketed around the world. When the real estate bubble burst, no financial institution was spared the growing nightmare, and the resulting recession rippled through all sectors of the economy, including the electric utility industry.

Southern Company would eventually see a decline in sales in all three retail sectors: industrial, commercial, and residential. The industrial sector would be the hardest hit, with some factories closing and others cutting back on production. The residential sector was hurt by the number of homes that sat vacant, either because of foreclosure or a sloth-like housing market. The commercial sector was the last affected, when unemployment rates started climbing and consumer buying began dropping. But declining revenues were only half the problem; customer rates were being driven upward by steep price increases for fuel and other commodities, installation of expensive environmental equipment, and expansion of the transmission grid. And the company would face much more capital investment to build nuclear and coal generation, complete environmental upgrades, and install smart-grid technology.

Ratcliffe responded to the recession in August 2008 by putting together companywide executive teams to identify cost containment opportunities in twelve areas. "As we continue to go to our regulators with requests for price increases . . . we should expect to be asked what we've done to lower costs across the entire business," Ratcliffe told his management team. The studies would become exercises in overcoming turf protection and identifying changes in operational practices or organizational structures. Ultimately, the teams would identify millions in cost savings for Southern Company.

Although energy sales dropped 2.3 percent in 2008, cost controls enabled Southern Company to maintain flat earnings in 2008, and its stock was down only 4.5 percent from the previous year. The financial crisis was far from over, however. "Our customers are facing a financial hurricane right now," Ratcliffe told employees in January 2009. "This will be one of the most economically challenging years in our history." As a result, he announced Southern Company would postpone 2009 salary increases, freeze hiring, and accelerate and expand cost containment.

In the second quarter of 2009, Southern Company's industrial sales dropped a frightening 17.6 percent from 2008, and total sales finished the year down 6.8 percent—the largest drop in annual energy demand in the company's history. But industrial sales stabilized in the third quarter, there was incremental improvement the remainder of the year, and then 2010 saw a return to growth in energy sales. Throughout the recession, Ratcliffe and his leadership team took the long view in making decisions, convinced that investments would be needed to ensure adequate power supply once the economy improved; to reduce emissions and develop solutions to climate change; to demonstrate the viability of coal gasification and carbon capture technologies; and to expand energy efficiency programs and install more than 4 million smart meters by 2012.

Despite one of the most difficult financial markets in U.S. history, Southern Company shareholder value increased by $3.9 billion during Ratcliffe's tenure as CEO. In the months preceding his retirement in late 2010, Ratcliffe, the unselfish leader, received one award after another—the William S. Lee Award for Leadership from the Nuclear Energy Institute, which cited him for his "unparalleled" preparation; the EEI Distinguished Leadership Award, which had been presented only once before; and the Ethics Advocate Award from Georgia State University for addressing issues of workplace ethics, trust, and diversity. But what Ratcliffe was most proud of was "the level of cooperation and communication across the entire Southern Company, between companies and between functions." He had continued a movement Franklin started in the critical months following the spin-off—bringing the system together into a cohesive, more effective unit. "The quality of the people in leadership positions is better than ever in my history," he said. "We have people who've been in multiple functions, they've been in multiple companies, and they are committed to Southern Company's success," he said. "It's a better team, and there's more team dynamic than ever."

LESSONS LEARNED

Fashionable young investors paid little notice when Southern Company first announced a return to its roots. Earnings growth of 5 or 6 percent appeared to be something less than paltry to New Agers addicted to the adrenalin rush stimulated by double-digit, even triple-digit, growth. Allen Franklin's message sounded like an old sentimental song their grandparents might hum.

"The business we know best." *(yawn)*

"The region we know best." *(yawn)*

"The customers we know best." *Boring!*

But those notes were sweet music to the ears of Southern Company's traditional stockholder base, which had not abandoned the company through a chaotic decade that required successful energy companies to reinvent themselves every couple of years. Those older, conservative investors were thrilled to hear that the Southern Company they had known and depended on was finally back. And they did not have to wait too long before a few former thrill seekers joined them. Everyone was looking for safe havens when fashionable portfolios plummeted during the post-Enron financial pandemic.

Southern Company and investors learned that being a little boring is not necessarily a bad trait. Franklin's conservative fiscal strategy suddenly seemed to be the essence of wisdom. So did the company's decision to refocus on the customers, region, and business it knew best, underscoring a lesson straight out of Marketing 101: The more you understand your market, the less risky it is to participate in that market and the greater opportunity you have of being successful in that market. Old school was back in style.

But less than a decade later, Franklin's lessons in market knowledge and fiscal conservatism had to be revisited when a burst in a real estate bubble ushered in the Great Recession of 2008-09. The prolonged crisis called into question several huge investments Southern Company was making for the future—building new nuclear generation, developing cleaner options for burning coal, and installing smart-grid technologies.

Southern Company does not make big bets like these with a roll of the dice. The stakes may be high, but the decisions are based on methodical research and a rigorous analysis of the market, changing energy-demand drivers, and available options for meeting future growth. The planning process includes tedious discussions of multiple scenarios—what can go wrong—and the political and social issues big decisions must take into consideration.

That disciplined process enabled David Ratcliffe to keep an unflinching focus on the long term. With a calm resolve, he confronted the challenge of declining revenues by prudently cutting costs but remained unshaken in his confidence about prospects for the company and its customers. "The Southeast is still an excellent place to live and do business, and we continue to aggressively pursue implementation of smarter, more efficient technologies across our business," he told stockholders.

Southern Company stayed the course even as other utilities began pulling back on financial commitments, especially those required to build new nuclear and new coal. Despite the drop-off in revenues and the size of the capital investments, Southern Company stockholders remained confident in the company's conservative financial policies and the integrity of its business strategy. As a result, the market price of Southern Company stock experienced far less volatility than most stocks as, week after week, headlines shouted some of the worst stock market developments in Wall Street history.

Another lesson was that the tenets of Southern Style have proven to be as important as any legacy a CEO could inherit or pass on. Because of those tenets, Southern Company refused to emulate Enron, and in the wake of Enron's bankruptcy and other high-profile failures, the principles of Southern Style grew ever more laudable. Those values have run like a river through the company's history since its creation to serve the region to which it has remained forever committed. And those strengths were still as critical as ever to the company's business success.

Franklin and Ratcliffe can point to yet another lesson: Sometimes "no" or "go slow" is the right approach, and leaders must have the fortitude to put up an unpopular defense and the conviction to not waver and fold under political pressure. That lesson applied to both the rush toward utility deregulation and the rush to implement climate-change regulations. Although harshly criticized, Franklin said no to many deregulation proposals, buying enough time for the California experiment to fail and prove to critics and regulators that the utility business was different from other industries. What had worked well for more than a century did not need to be scrapped. Basic utility economics and state regulatory principles had not changed, and the most reliable and economical service could be delivered by utilities that coordinated generation, transmission, and distribution functions under the same roof.

While Southern Company won a major victory in the battles over industry restructuring, the jury is still out on whether the company's position will prevail on the climate-change debate. After its typical thoughtful response to that issue, Southern Company was again criticized, this time for slowing down legislation to set aggressive targets for reducing carbon dioxide emissions. But at the same time, it was also working diligently to speed up the research needed to produce better scientific and technological solutions to address the problem. By testing carbon-capture alternatives and developing a new process for burning coal more cleanly, Southern Company was able to start building a coal plant in 2010 that would produce 65 percent less carbon emissions than a traditional coal plant. Whether Southern Company will have enough time to demonstrate the technology and avoid unrealistic new environmental regulations, however, was an unanswered question in 2011.

Other lessons from this era also will have to wait for time and experience to determine the outcome of the big bets Southern Company is making for the future. Company leaders will be dealing with decisions to build new nuclear, new coal, and smart grid for years to come. In carrying out these long-term strategies, they will be challenged and perhaps changed by the challenges. And from these experiences, they will pass on lessons to the next generation of leaders.

The fact that Southern Company has not only thrived over the years but also helped transform the economy of an entire region is a product of the type of leaders who have emerged to shepherd the company through critical crossroads. At times, it seemed as if fortune put the right person in charge for each decisive point in the company's history. But in reality, the credit goes to hard work and foresight. Good leaders rise to the occasion to deal with the crisis at hand, and in naming their successors, they look ahead to see what trials are approaching. Each CEO also has been bolstered by a solid network of supporters—strong directors, management council members, system executives and managers, and a work force with a great diversity of specialized skills and a commitment to common goals and values. That type of talent and dedication has been Southern Company's defining denominator down through the decades.

Southern Company is building the first new nuclear units in the United States in more than three decades. Plant Vogtle units 3 and 4 are scheduled for completion in 2016 and 2017. CEO Tom Fanning (at right) leads Southern Company in making the big bets ahead. *GPC Archives, SCS Communication Files*

A CENTURY HAS PASSED SINCE JAMES MITCHELL created the first holding company in Southern Company's lineage. The leaders who followed him laid a foundation on which a solid enterprise could emerge and endure. The challenges they faced included every conceivable threat—natural disasters, financial ruin, federal invasions, a hostile takeover, a "death sentence," and numerous attempts to pull the business apart and scramble the pieces. The leaders learned to guide their utilities through essential transformations and make hard decisions at critical crossroads—big bets when it mattered most.

Looking for the right leader to guide the company through the challenges inherent in the big bets ahead, David Ratcliffe and Southern Company's board of directors turned to Tom Fanning upon Ratcliffe's retirement at the end of 2010. An energetic, enthusiastic executive, Fanning had earned the nickname "Rocket Man" while blazing a trail through fifteen jobs in eight business units during his 30-year career at Southern Company. After working in every area of corporate finance, he helped launch Southern Energy's entry into international markets in the late 1980s, was involved in the successful start-up of SouthernLINC Wireless, and then restructured the information technology organization in the mid-1990s as Southern Company's first chief information officer. He served as chief financial officer of two operating companies and as Gulf Power president and CEO before being named Southern Company's chief financial officer in 2003 and chief operating officer in 2008.

From 1998 to 2000, Fanning served as Southern Company's first senior vice president of strategy, but through his jobs that followed, he continued to hold the unofficial title of "chief strategy officer," responsible for managing Southern Company's strategic-planning process, meaning he analyzed and validated decisions that, as a CEO, he would execute. For more than a decade, he had been asked to carry that strategic-planning role with him simply because he could accumulate and assimilate more data and translate it into action quicker than anyone else on the team. Ratcliffe described him as "one of the smartest individuals I've ever worked with" and a leader with "impeccable moral fiber, character, and integrity" and "contagious enthusiasm—let's go take the hill, we can do this!"

At times, Fanning seemed to possess many qualities of previous great Southern Company leaders. In addition to the charm and enthusiasm of a Wendell Willkie, he had the analytical mind of an Allen Franklin. Most notably, he radiated the workaholic energy of a James Mitchell.

Fanning might need all those qualities to deal effectively with bets that require capital commitments equivalent to almost half the entire asset base accumulated throughout the company's history. For the three years 2011–13, capital requirements will approach $17 billion. And it's likely that same pace of spending will be required beyond 2013 as the company completes construction of plants Vogtle and Ratcliffe and continues transitioning its generating fleet to meet future needs of a growing Southeast economy.

The bets are real—and big.

Southern Company was still in the early phase of new nuclear construction when dreadful news arrived in March 2011 from more than 7,000 miles away. A 9.0 earthquake and tsunami severely damaged several nuclear power facilities near Okuma, Japan, creating a severe and tragic nuclear accident. Southern Company remained committed to building Plant Vogtle's units 3 and 4, which have designs and safety features more advanced and vastly different from the affected reactors in Japan. Questions raised by the accident, however, presented new challenges to the company in its role as leader of the industry in deploying new nuclear technologies.

Questions also surround other company investments. Can Fanning and his team persuade regulators and policy-makers to set realistic environmental targets so Southern Company can continue its transition toward a more diversified energy mix in a reliable and cost-effective manner? Can the company maintain or increase its research and development work to meet these evolving challenges? What additional hurdles will Mississippi Power have to clear in building a plant featuring the most advanced coal-processing and carbon-capture technologies? Will smart-grid investments pay off in greater reliability and better customer service, and can the technology be secured against "cyber" threats? Through all these challenges, can Southern Company continue delivering attractive financial returns to investors while maintaining one of the industry's lowest-risk profiles?

Those questions will have to be answered by Fanning and his team, and perhaps even the next set of leaders, because none are short-term matters. But the questions are no greater in scope or complexity than those faced by many other leaders throughout the company's history, even all the way back to 1911 when James Mitchell started building giant dams in an impoverished South and sketched out a regional power network, a dream that led to the formation of Southern Company.

One hundred years later, in 2011, Tom Fanning assembled executives from across Southern Company to discuss the challenges facing the company at yet another important crossroads. In advance of that forum, Fanning sent the leadership team some required reading—lessons learned from several of the company's past big bets and challenged them to "Honor the past . . . build the future," a message that echoes Harllee Branch's belief that future leaders should remember the courage, trials, and triumphs of leaders past. In 1957, former CEO Branch wrote: "The experience of our predecessors, their dedication, and their resoluteness . . . must never be forgotten. They constitute the precedents, the guideposts, and the inspiration which, if steadfastly emulated, will enable us not only to sustain but to strengthen and enlarge the heritage which they have left to us."

Branch's message still rings true today. The challenge to strengthen and enlarge that heritage has been handed down to a new generation of leaders who will take the company forward into the next chapter of its history. Southern Company leaders can more clearly face the next big bets because they have inherited strategies and systems tried and tested over many decades. They are heirs to valuable lessons passed on by their founders and forerunners. And they have been bequeathed values and principles that can nurture success no matter which path the future takes.

Power pioneers brought electric transportation to urban areas: Pensacola's street railway system (top) in the 1920s and Montgomery's "Lightning Route" in 1939 on its last run. *Gulf Power Communication Files, APC Archives*

1600s   English scientist William Gilbert coins the term "electricity" in 1600; early experiments are with static electricity.

1700s   Dutch instrument-maker Pieter van Musschenbroek invents in 1746 the Leyden jar, used to store a small charge of static electricity.

James Watt perfects early steam engines in 1782 and coins the word "horsepower" to measure output. The capacity of early electric generators is measured in "horsepower" until the twentieth century, when the standard becomes "watts" in honor of the Scottish inventor.

Benjamin Franklin flew his famous kite in 1752 to prove lightning is electricity. *Library of Congress*

EARLY 1800s   Italy's Alessandro Volta manufactures the first practical commercial battery in 1800; "volt" becomes the term for measuring electromotive force or pressure.

English chemist Humphry Davy invents the first arc lamp in 1808.

The first U.S. energy utility, Gas Light Company of Baltimore, is formed in 1816.

In 1819, Denmark's Hans Christian Oersted creates a magnet using electrical current, a basic principle leading to the invention of the electric motor.

In 1831, English physicist Michael Faraday generates electricity using a magnet and spinning copper plate.

The first dynamo to generate electricity is built in 1832 using Faraday's principles.

Thomas Davenport invents the first electric motor in 1834.

1870s   Belgium's Z. T. Gramme develops the first effective dynamo capable of producing electricity for industrial or commercial use in 1870.

The first U.S. outdoor electric lights are installed at Cornell University in 1875.

Arc lighting technology is demonstrated at the 1876 Centennial Exposition in Philadelphia; Charles F. Brush makes it commercially feasible in 1879 in an outdoor lighting project for Cleveland's Monumental Park.

Thomas Alva Edison invents the incandescent light bulb in 1879. The "Electric Age" begins; Edison will invent more than 1,000 uses of electricity over the next fifty years.

Edison the great inventor
Thomas Edison National Historical Park

1880   The "Great White Way," a mile of arc lighting, is installed along New York's Broadway.

The first industrial use of hydroelectric power occurs at a factory in Grand Rapids, Michigan.

1882   Woodstock Iron Company in Anniston generates Alabama's first street lighting and industrial use of electricity.

Savannah's first electric utility, Brush Electric Light & Power, is formed.

Arc lighting in Savannah
GPC Archives

In Georgia, the first electric street lights are installed in Macon.

Edison Electric Illuminating Company's Pearl Street plant in New York City becomes the nation's first central generating station, distributing electricity to fifty-nine customers using direct current (DC); Thomas Edison becomes the most influential advocate for DC power developments.

In South Carolina, Charleston's first electric street lights appear.

The first commercial hydroelectric plant opens on the Fox River near Appleton, Wisconsin.

1883 Georgia Electric Company of Atlanta, predecessor of Georgia Power, organizes and begins building its first generating plant.

First electric street lights are installed in Savannah and Montgomery.

The nation's first electric tramway is installed in Richmond, Virginia.

1884 Atlanta's first electric street lights are installed.

England's Charles Parsons invents the steam turbine.

1885 The National Electric Light Association, the industry's first association, is formed.

1886 Nation's first electric streetcar begins service in Montgomery, Alabama.

Charleston Electric Light Company is incorporated; it is the first in a lineage of companies that two decades later will be consolidated into South Carolina Power.

Montgomery's street railway system *APC Archives*

First commercial alternating current (AC) is generated in Great Barrington, Massachusetts.

George Westinghouse founds Westinghouse Electric Company and becomes the most influential advocate for AC power developments.

Nationwide, up to fifty small hydro plants are either operating or under construction; the early hydro plants generate DC power that is distributed short distances from the site.

1887 Pensacola Electric Company, a forerunner of Gulf Power, is incorporated and begins constructing its first power plant.

1888 First electric street lights are installed in Pensacola.

1889 The first commercial, long-distance transmission of direct current is sent from Oregon's Willamette Falls to the city of Portland.

National Association of Regulatory Commissioners is formed to regulate railways and later extends oversight to utilities.

Atlanta's first electric street railway line begins operations.

1891 Henry M. Atkinson takes over ownership of Georgia Electric Light Company of Atlanta and replaces it with a newly formed company of the same name.

Georgia Electric Light constructs a plant on Davis Street and provides Atlanta's first "around-the-clock" service for commercial and industrial use.

Henry Atkinson
GPC Archives

Biloxi Electric Light power plant *MPC Communication Files*

1892   General Electric Company is created from the merger of Edison General Electric Company and Thomson-Houston Electric Company.

1894   Biloxi Electric Light Company is incorporated; it is the first in a lineage of companies that later will become part of Mississippi Power.

1895   The first hydro generator producing alternating current is installed at Niagara Falls, New York. In a "battle of the currents," industry leaders debate the merits of AC and DC.

Atlanta hosts the Cotton States and International Exposition, with Atkinson serving as the event's "chief of electricity." Prominent Atlantans install electric lights in their homes, the first residential service from Georgia Electric Light.

1896   George Westinghouse transmits alternating current long-distance from Niagara Falls to Buffalo. AC soon becomes the industry standard for generating and transmitting power long distances, a development that accelerates the building of giant hydro projects and large-scale steam plants.

1897   Atkinson fends off the first of many municipal takeover threats; "private vs. public" power will become a recurring theme in industry debates about utility ownership.

1898   Industry leader Samuel Insull proposes state regulation as a solution to the problem of how to govern rates and service standards; nine years later, Wisconsin, New York, and Massachusetts become the first states to install utility regulatory commissions.

1899   Atkinson's company and Joel Hurt's Atlanta Railway and Power Company wage competitive warfare over control of the city's power and railway business; the two-year clash is called the "second battle of Atlanta."

1900   Westinghouse manufactures the first public utility steam turbine generator.

1901   The Atkinson-Hurt feud ends with Atkinson buying out Hurt's interests. Preston S. Arkwright is named a vice president of Georgia Electric Light and facilitates its consolidation with Atlanta Railway and Power.

Columbus Power Company builds the North Highlands Dam on the Chattahoochee River.

Preston S. Arkwright
GPC Archives

Georgia Railway and Electric work crew *GPC Archives*

Savannah Electric Company is formed by the merger of Brush Electric Light & Power, Edison Electric Illuminating Company of Savannah, and various streetcar and railway businesses.

1902   Georgia Railway and Electric Company is chartered January 28 to merge the two enterprises previously controlled by Atkinson and Hurt; Arkwright is elected president of the new company and Atkinson is chairman.

Alabama's first major hydroelectric plant, built by Montgomery Light & Power on the Tallapoosa River, sends electricity over a twenty-five-mile transmission line to Montgomery.

1903   Georgia Railway and Electric buys Atlanta Gas Light Company, which has 11,000 customers, eight times more than Atkinson and Arkwright have in electric customers. The company also buys Atlanta Steam Company and provides heat to Atlanta's downtown buildings by using exhaust steam from power plants.

To promote its streetcar business, Georgia Railway and Electric builds the Ponce de Leon Amusement Park.

In Mississippi, Biloxi Electric Light is purchased by Biloxi Electric Railway & Power Company.

1904 Atlanta's first hydropower comes from a plant built by the Atlanta Water and Electric Power Company on the Chattahoochee River at Bull Sluice (later named Morgan Falls); Georgia Railway and Electric buys the plant's entire output.

1905 Biloxi Electric Railway & Power is acquired by Gulfport and Mississippi Coast Traction Company.

1906 William P. Lay, Alabama's promoter of the Coosa River, incorporates the first Alabama Power Company December 4 in Gadsden.

William P. Lay *APC Archives*

Muscle Shoals Hydro Electric Power Company is formed in northwest Alabama and acquires Tennessee River sites that years later will become Wilson and Wheeler dams. Numerous other companies interested in developing Alabama waterways are formed during the next two years.

Morgan Falls Dam *GPC Archives*

Pensacola Electric Company acquires the city's and Escambia County's street railway systems.

1907 President Theodore Roosevelt signs a bill authorizing Alabama Power to construct Lock 12 Dam on the Coosa River; Lay begins a five-year search for construction funds. Because the conservation movement produces a national debate over waterpower rights, Lock 12's dam permit will become the last one issued on navigable rivers until 1920.

Savannah River Power Company organizes and develops a small hydro plant near Anderson, South Carolina, and acquires land for a proposed dam at nearby Clark's Hill.

Across the street from its amusement park on Ponce de Leon Avenue, Georgia Railway and Electric builds a baseball stadium that becomes home to the Atlanta Crackers.

1908
The first Georgia Power Company is formed by C. Elmer Smith and other promoters who create the firm while trying to bail out the financially struggling North Georgia Electric Company, which owns waterpower sites in northeast Georgia, including Tallulah Falls, and has a 2,000-kilowatt hydro plant near present-day Buford Dam.

1910
C. Elmer Smith buys the properties of North Georgia Electric and begins constructing Tallulah Falls Dam the following year; Smith also controls Atlanta Water and Electric Power, Etowah Power Company, and Savannah River Power.

1911
Energy pioneer and developer James Mitchell arrives in Alabama and conceives a plan for bringing divergent interests together to develop the state's vast waterpower resources to transmit power across a large southeastern market.

Alabama Power Development Company, one of the companies eventually pulled into Mitchell's plan, completes a small hydroelectric plant at Jackson Shoals near Talladega and begins constructing a steam plant at Gadsden.

Willis Carrier invents air-conditioning. GE unveils an electric refrigerator invented by a French monk.

1912
Mitchell forms Alabama Traction, Light & Power, the first holding company in Southern Company's lineage. Incorporated January 5 in Montreal, Canada, and largely funded by British investors, Alabama Traction buys Alabama Power, Muscle Shoals Hydro-Electric Power, Alabama Interstate Power, Alabama Electric Company, Wetumpka Power Company, Alabama Power Development Company, and nearly a dozen other energy companies in Alabama.

James Mitchell *APC Archives*

Georgia Railway & Power Company is created when Atkinson agrees to combine his interests with those of C. Elmer Smith, who is in financial trouble over the cost of the Tallulah Falls Dam construction.

President William H. Taft vetoes a bill authorizing Alabama Power to build a dam at Coosa River's Lock 18; the company will be unable to get any new dam permits approved during the next eight years as Congress continues to debate waterpower rights.

1913

Plant Gadsden, Alabama Power's first steam plant, is placed in service.

In a Georgia lawsuit contesting land titles, the state supreme court rules in favor of Georgia Railway & Power, allowing the delayed construction at Tallulah Falls to move forward.

With five units completed and operating, Tallulah Falls becomes the third-largest hydroelectric plant in the United States.

Plant Gadsden substation transformers
APC Archives

Workers on incline railcar at Tallulah Falls *GPC Archives*

1914

Georgia Railway & Power makes its first interconnection with Southern Power Company (later named Duke Power). Through other interconnections in the region, power is exchanged across four states, a network later known as the "Great Southern Grid."

On the Coosa River, Lock 12 (later named Lay Dam) is completed.

Alabama Power begins serving Birmingham Railway, Light & Power, its largest wholesale customer.

Alabama Traction and Alabama Power are pushed near bankruptcy when the outbreak of World War I cuts off funds from British investors.

Survey crew for the Lock 12 transmission line *APC Archives*

1915

Numerous Alabama utilities owned by Alabama Traction are consolidated into Alabama Power. The company fends off another bankruptcy threat by winning what becomes known as the "mosquito lawsuits," filed by residents near Lay Dam.

Georgia Railway & Power completes work on Mathis Dam, a storage reservoir that forms Lake Rabun in north Georgia.

1916

First unit of the Warrior Steam Plant (later named Plant Gorgas) is completed in Alabama.

Georgia Railway & Power expands service to several north Georgia communities by purchasing Gainesville Railway and Power Company and Franklin Light and Power Company.

Thirty-three states have installed utility regulatory agencies; along with approving franchises and rates, the commissions charge utilities with an "obligation to serve."

1917

The United States enters World War I; the War Department selects Muscle Shoals as a site for manufacturing nitrates needed for explosives.

1918

Mitchell donates his company's properties at Muscle Shoals, where the government builds two nitrates plants and begins work on a hydro development (later named Wilson Dam). The government also builds a steam plant at Sheffield and funds construction of unit 2 at Alabama Power's Plant Gorgas, with provisions for the company to buy the unit back after the war.

Plant Gorgas after unit 2 construction
APC Archives

Alabama Power furnishes the electricity needed to make nitrates at Muscle Shoals just prior to the end of World War I.

1919

Georgia Railway & Power builds Burton Dam in north Georgia.

1920

James Mitchell dies and Thomas W. Martin becomes president of Alabama Traction and Alabama Power. Martin launches Alabama Power's first rural electrification and industrial recruitment programs.

Georgia Railway & Power builds the state's first radio station, initially used for communication with crews in north Georgia; two years later, the radio equipment is sold to the *Atlanta Constitution* and later donated to the Georgia Institute of Technology.

Tom Martin at Jordan Dam *APC Archives*

President Woodrow Wilson signs into law the Federal Water Power Act, which creates the Federal Power Commission, responsible for issuing licenses and regulating hydro projects on the nation's rivers.

1921 The first interconnection is completed between Alabama Power and Georgia Railway & Power.

Lindale substation near Rome, site of first Alabama-Georgia interconnection *GPC Archives*

Industrialist Henry Ford offers to buy partially built Wilson Dam and other war-surplus facilities at Muscle Shoals, including the Gorgas unit promised to Alabama Power. Martin makes a competing bid, launching the first of many battles for Muscle Shoals assets.

Savannah Electric Company, Savannah Power, and Chatham County Traction Company merge to form Savannah Electric and Power Company.

Workers at camp during Mitchell Dam construction *APC Archives*

1922 Alabama Power starts the first radio station in Alabama and donates the facilities the following year to what is now Auburn University.

Georgia Railway & Power completes Tugalo Dam in north Georgia.

1923 Mitchell Dam, Alabama Power's second major hydro development on the Coosa River, begins commercial operation.

First interconnection is completed between Alabama Power and Columbus (Georgia) Electric Power Company.

Pressing the government to honor its wartime agreement, Martin is able to buy Gorgas unit 2, but the battle over Muscle Shoals assets continues for another decade.

Savannah Lighting Company, last of the city's electric utility competitors, is merged into Savannah Electric and Power.

1924

Southeastern Power & Light, the second holding company in Southern Company's lineage, is incorporated September 2, replacing Alabama Traction, Light & Power. With Tom Martin as president and Eugene A. Yates as vice president and general manager, the new company begins expanding across the Southeast.

Mississippi Power Company is incorporated November 24 as a subsidiary of Southeastern Power & Light; Barney Eaton becomes its first president.

Gulf Electric Company is incorporated August 11 as a subsidiary of Southeastern Power & Light with a goal of acquiring utilities in south Alabama and the Florida Panhandle; its properties are later consolidated into Alabama Power and Gulf Power.

Eight southern power companies join Alabama Power in making an unsuccessful bid for Muscle Shoals. Alabama Power buys the Sheffield Company and begins serving the Tri-Cities in the Muscle Shoals area but still is unable to buy Wilson Dam.

Barney Eaton *MPC Communication Files*

1925

Mississippi Power officially begins operating January 1 by acquiring Gulfport and Mississippi Coast Traction Company.

Georgia Railway & Power completes the Terrora and Yonah plants in north Georgia, but a severe drought forces power cuts to customers; discussions begin with Martin on a possible merger with Southeastern Power & Light.

Gulf Power Company is organized October 29 as a subsidiary of Southeastern Power & Light.

The government completes construction of Wilson Dam; Alabama Power buys the power output while congressional debates continue over Muscle Shoals assets.

Congress asks the Federal Trade Commission to investigate the so-called "power trust," partially based on the claim that General Electric controls most of the nation's utilities; the probe later absolves GE but raises questions about the rise of large holding companies.

1926

Southeastern Power & Light acquires Georgia Railway & Power April 1, reorganizes it as Georgia Power Company that fall, and begins other utility acquisitions in the state. Arkwright, who continues as president, coins "a citizen wherever we serve" as Georgia Power begins moving into new territory.

Georgia Power seal and motto
GPC Archives

Completion of the Nacoochee Dam makes the north Georgia hydro group of six dams and powerhouses an engineering sensation—the largest stair-stepped waterway development in the nation.

Gulf Power officially becomes an operating utility February 6 when it acquires Chipley Light & Power Company; Francis B. Carter becomes its first president. Service to Panama City begins in March, Pensacola Electric is merged into Gulf Power in May, and the company begins expanding to other towns in west Florida.

Pensacola Electric supplies and store room *Gulf Power Communication Files*

A 1926 hurricane shut down Gulf Power's only power plant *Pensacola Historical Society*

A September hurricane severely damages Gulf Power's plant on Barrack and Main streets; it takes two months to restore service.

Mississippi Power acquires utility systems in seventeen additional communities.

South Carolina Power Company is incorporated December 17 as a subsidiary of Southeastern Power & Light; Benjamin A. Hagood is its first president.

Twelve utilities join Alabama Power in a new but unsuccessful bid for Muscle Shoals.

Alabama Power marketing manager A. B. Collins creates cartoon character Reddy Kilowatt, which will become a mascot for electric utilities nationwide.

1927

Georgia Power completes the consolidation of numerous railway and power properties in Georgia, including those in Athens, Rome, Milledgeville, Brunswick, and Macon; operations in the 30,000-square-mile territory are organized into geographical divisions.

Early Reddy Kilowatt sketch
APC Archives

South Carolina Power becomes an operating company by acquiring several of Charleston's gas, electric, and railway businesses.

Alabama Power becomes a statewide utility with the consolidation of properties held by Houston Power Company and Gulf Electric Company, which serve the southern third of the state.

Mississippi Power's territory expands to include most major cities and towns in the eastern half of the state, from the Gulf to the Tennessee border; inside that footprint, the company will extend service to nearly 200 communities during the next three years.

Martin Dam begins operations on the Tallapoosa River; at 168 feet high, the dam creates one of the largest artificial reservoirs in the world.

Forms for the construction of draft tubes at Martin Dam *APC Archives*

1928

Southeastern Power & Light acquires Augusta-Aiken Railway & Electric Company and Georgia-Carolina Power Company; the properties are merged into Georgia Power and South Carolina Power.

Georgia Power also acquires Central Georgia Power Company and Macon Railway & Light Company.

South Carolina Power acquires the Edisto Public Service Company, serving communities south of Charleston. Stuart Cooper is named president early in the year but is replaced by F. P. Cummings in November.

Alabama Power completes a new hydro plant near Tallassee (later named Yates Dam).

The Federal Trade Commission launches a new, seven-year investigation of the nation's electric utilities, with emphasis on the financial structures and activities of large holding companies.

President Calvin Coolidge vetoes a bill to make Muscle Shoals a public power venture.

Preston Arkwright becomes the 1928–29 president of National Electric Light Association.

Francis Carter resigns as Gulf Power president; Tom Martin picks up the title in addition to his other duties.

1929

Southeastern Power & Light is taken over by Commonwealth & Southern (C&S), a new conglomerate incorporated May 23; B. C. Cobb is named chairman and Tom Martin president. In addition to Southeastern's five operating companies, C&S includes Tennessee Electric Power Company, Consumers Power Company, Central Illinois Light Company, Southern Indiana Gas & Electric, Ohio Edison Company, and Pennsylvania Power Company.

Georgia Power sells Atlanta Gas Light, as well as gas operations in Athens, Brunswick, and Decatur, to Central Public Service Corporation of Chicago.

Jordan Dam, on the Coosa River, is completed and begins operations.

Jordan Dam School: Building dams included setting up schools for children of workers who lived in the construction camps. *APC Archives*

The stock market crashes in October, accelerating a worldwide economic collapse that brings on the Great Depression.

1930

Southeastern Power & Light is dissolved following its merger into C&S.

Columbus Electric & Power, serving seventy Georgia towns, is consolidated into Georgia Power. The acquisition includes four hydro plants—the Flint River, North Highlands, Goat Rock, and Bartlett's Ferry dams.

Georgia Power buys the Langdale and Riverview dams on the Chattahoochee River from private groups and extends service to several south Georgia communities.

The first unit of Plant Atkinson, near Atlanta, begins operating.

Alabama Power completes a hydro facility on the lower Tallassee River (later named Thurlow Dam).

L. A. Magraw is named president of South Carolina Power.

Henry Atkinson and his grandsons at Plant Atkinson *GPC Archives*

1931   Its earnings and load declining, C&S reduces dividends on its common stock and discontinues work on several plants, including Furman Shoals in Georgia (later site of Lake Sinclair).

Robert W. Williamson becomes president of Gulf Power.

Another Muscle Shoals bill is vetoed by President Herbert Hoover, who opposes the government entering the electricity business in competition with private utilities.

1932

Martin resigns as C&S president effective June 28 but remains Alabama Power president; Cobb becomes both chairman and president of C&S.

Eugene A. Yates is named executive coordinator of the Southern Group, C&S's six operating companies in the South; he also becomes president of South Carolina Power.

C&S discontinues paying dividends on its common stock after March 1 as electricity sales fall during the Depression.

President Hoover's attempt to reach a public-private compromise on Muscle Shoals dies in congressional committee hearings.

Arkwright becomes president of the newly formed National Electric Cookery Council.

Samuel Insull declares bankruptcy, sending into receivership one of the nation's larger utility empires, Commonwealth Edison.

1933

Attorney Wendell Willkie becomes president of Commonwealth & Southern January 24.

President Franklin D. Roosevelt takes office March 4, stops a panic run on banks, and summons a special session of Congress to begin enacting numerous New Deal measures.

FDR (left) visiting Wilson Dam with (L-R) senators Kenneth McKellar, Clarence Dill, and George Norris and Roosevelt's daughter, Mrs. Anna Dall
Landrum Collection of Historical Prints

On May 18, President Roosevelt signs the Tennessee Valley Authority Act into law. TVA takes over Wilson Dam at Muscle Shoals, begins building a series of other dams on the Tennessee River, and becomes a major competitor for utilities operating in the Tennessee Valley.

Established in June, the Public Works Administration (PWA) begins providing grants and low-interest loans to municipalities that want to build public power projects or take over private utility operations.

Alabama Power develops the "Objective Rate Plan," an incentive-pricing program to induce customers to use more electricity and reverse the declining trend in electric load.

The newly created Edison Electric Institute (EEI) replaces the National Electric Light Association as the group representing America's investor-owned utilities.

1934

Tupelo, Mississippi, previously served by Mississippi Power, becomes the nation's first city to receive TVA power.

Willkie negotiates C&S's first major sale to TVA; Mississippi Power turns over facilities and service in nine counties, and Tennessee Electric Power turns over a site that will become Norris Dam near Knoxville. But Alabama Power property transfers to TVA and fourteen municipalities are delayed by a stockholder lawsuit known as the Ashwander case.

Parade celebrating Tupelo's contract with TVA *TVA Archives*

With Cobb's retirement, C&S eliminates the title of chairman and gives CEO duties to Willkie; operating company executives replace bankers on the C&S board.

In the depths of the Depression, C&S net earnings are in the red $1.55 million; the company cuts its preferred stock dividend in half.

Trying to "sell" the company out of its troubles, Willkie launches a marketing push—promoting electric appliances and cutting rates for customers increasing power usage under the "Objective Rate Plan." By year-end, sales increase nearly 10 percent and will increase more than 14 percent the following year.

Gulf Power buys Florida Public Utilities Company, near Pensacola, and South Carolina Power buys South Carolina Public Service Company.

Samuel Insull, ex-utility tycoon, is found innocent of fraud in a nationally sensationalized trial.

Samuel Insull brought to trial
Bettman/CORBIS

1935

On August 26, FDR signs into law the Public Utility Holding Company Act, which mandates the breakup of large conglomerates and the regulation of approved holding companies by the Securities and Exchange Commission; C&S joins a group of utilities in contesting PUHCA's constitutionality.

By executive order, President Roosevelt creates the Rural Electrification Administration (REA) to provide loans to cooperatives organizing to serve rural areas and small towns.

With backing from Willkie, Barney Eaton saves Mississippi Power from bankruptcy by working out agreements with preferred stockholders who have filed numerous lawsuits.

Georgia Power rural electrification lines in the 1930s *GPC Archives*

Plaintiffs in the Ashwander case secure a favorable court ruling to stop Alabama Power from selling any of its facilities to TVA and municipalities.

Alabama Power files a separate lawsuit against PWA contesting grants and loans used by municipalities to build competing and duplicating electric-distribution systems.

The Federal Power Act gives the Federal Power Commission authority to regulate interstate-electricity commerce.

Yates becomes president of Gulf Power in addition to his other roles at C&S.

Electrical appliances of the 1930s
GPC Archives

December closes with the most intense ice storm in the first half of the twentieth century shutting down service in Alabama and Georgia. Crews work around the clock to repair thousands of line breaks; service is out for ten days in Atlanta, stretching through the first week of 1936.

Fallen branches interrupted streetcar service in Atlanta during a 1935-36 ice storm.
GPC Archives

1936 The U.S. Supreme Court rules against plaintiffs in the Ashwander case; Alabama Power turns over the Wheeler Dam site to TVA and begins settling property sales to several municipalities in north Alabama.

Willkie leads nineteen utilities in filing a new lawsuit, known as the "TEPCO case," to contest the constitutionality of TVA and, in an initial victory, secures an injunction to stop TVA expansion during the course of the trial.

The Rural Electrification Act formalizes REA and provides funding for its programs; C&S initially cooperates closely with new rural cooperatives before REA becomes a competitive threat.

Nevada's Boulder Dam is completed and becomes a modern-day marvel; later named Hoover Dam, it remains one of the nation's larger dams.

C&S leads the industry in appliance sales with eight subsidiaries ranking among the top twelve utility merchandisers nationwide.

A tornado devastates downtown Gainesville April 6, killing 200 and injuring 1,200. The storm destroys Georgia Power district offices and nearby electric facilities.

Ernest L. Godshalk becomes president of South Carolina Power.

1937 The U.S. Supreme Court rules against Alabama Power in its lawsuit against PWA, and a district court in the TEPCO case overturns the injunction against TVA expansion.

Georgia Power inaugurates electric bus service to replace some trolleys.

C&S shows signs of recovery with net income increasing to $15.1 million.

At an average price of 3.28¢ per kilowatt-hour, C&S rates are one-third below the national average; the Southern Group utilities have some of the nation's lowest rates and the highest average residential power usage.

The Bonneville Project Act creates the Bonneville Power Administration to market electricity generated at federal hydro projects in the Northwest; it becomes a model for creating similar power administrations in other regions of the country.

Competition with TVA resulted in duplicate power lines and meters for some houses. *APC Archives*

1938   The U.S. Supreme Court upholds the constitutionality of PUHCA
March 28; Commonwealth & Southern registers with the SEC.

In the TEPCO case, a federal district court rules the TVA Act valid;
utilities appeal the decision to the Supreme Court.

C&S income decreases nearly 22 percent to $11.9 million as a result of
another economic recession and increasing competition from REA;
seventy-five rural cooperatives now operate within C&S's service
territory.

1939   The U.S. Supreme Court rules against utilities in the TEPCO case
January 30.

Willkie agrees to sell the
entire Tennessee Electric
Power Company to TVA for
$78.6 million; the sale closes
August 15, and TEPCO is
dissolved.

C&S also agrees to sell TVA
additional properties in
Alabama and Mississippi for
$13 million. Mississippi
Power settles with TVA in
December, turning over
facilities in eleven additional
counties. Combined with the
first sale, TVA takes over the
entire northern half of
Mississippi Power's service
territory.

Wendell Willkie (L) receives check from David
Lilienthal for the sale of Commonwealth &
Southern property to TVA. *TVA Archives*

Hostilities in Europe escalate into World War II as Hitler invades
Poland and the British and French declare war on Germany. U.S.
defense spending boosts power sales; C&S begins building power plants
for the first time since the start of the Depression.

1940   In July, Alabama Power closes on the forced sale of its Northern
Division to TVA; the company loses eleven counties and portions of
two others.

The SEC notifies C&S and its subsidiaries that they are in violation of
PUHCA and must move toward a single integrated structure.

Willkie wins the Republican Party nomination for president, resigns
from C&S, but fails to unseat FDR in the election.

Wendell Willkie (head of table) at his last Commonwealth & Southern board meeting. Directors included Tom Martin (fifth from right on right side of table), Preston Arkwright (sixth from right), and Eugene Yates (second from right on left side of table). *GPC Archives*

Justin R. Whiting becomes president of Commonwealth & Southern.

Fueled by national defense spending and the rebounding economy, C&S power sales increase by 13.3 percent.

1941   The SEC issues a 317-page report March 19 that gives C&S three options for restructuring; another SEC order April 8 requires the holding company to move to a single class of stock. Both actions begin a series of SEC hearings that will extend over the next six years.

Following the December 7 attack on Pearl Harbor, more than 1,000 C&S employees join the armed services, and the company accelerates power plant construction.

WWII heroes (L-R): Alvin W. Vogtle Jr. who later became CEO of Southern Company; Yvonne Lacoste, only Mississippi Power female employee to enter military service; and Owen L. Buford, Georgia Power employee who died in action. *GPC Archive, MPC Communication Files, GPC Archives*

First units go on-line at Alabama Power's Plant Chickasaw, near Mobile, and Georgia Power's Plant Arkwright, near Macon; another unit is installed at Plant Atkinson.

For the first time since TVA threatened its territory in 1933, C&S's Southern Group is able to sell new securities at low interest rates and retire high-interest bonds.

Southeastern Fuel Company, a C&S subsidiary that owns coal supplies and mining rights in Alabama, is consolidated into Alabama Power.

1942 Because of materials shortages, the War Production Board halts construction projects of Mississippi Power and Gulf Power.

Additional units are installed at plants Arkwright and Chickasaw.

Italian physicist Enrico Fermi directs experiments in Chicago that produce the first controlled nuclear chain reaction.

1943 Mississippi Power and Gulf Power are allowed to resume plant construction; to help fill the interim shortfall in capacity, the Southern Group leases a 30-megawatt floating power plant and places it in operation in Pensacola.

New units are added at plants Gorgas, Chickasaw, and Arkwright.

Despite aggressive energy-conservation campaigns, power sales increase nearly 15 percent, driven by multiple factory shifts and families sharing homes in urban war-production areas.

1944 C&S develops a formalized pension plan that goes into effect July 1 at all subsidiaries.

At the height of the war, more than 4,000 C&S employees serve in the armed forces.

Plant Crist control room *Gulf Power Communication Files*

Following the unexpected death of Barney Eaton, Lonnie P. Sweatt becomes president of Mississippi Power.

The Flood Control Act gives the secretary of the interior jurisdiction over electric power sales from Corps of Engineers projects.

The Rural Electrification Act is reauthorized and extended indefinitely.

1945

Southern Company is incorporated November 9 in anticipation that the SEC may allow the Southern Group to become a separate holding company and is initially incorporated in Delaware under the name of "Southeastern Power Holding Corp." An amended certificate filed later changes the name to "The Southern Company."

Japan's surrender brings World War II to an end; a total of 72 C&S employees died in action. By the close of the year, 1,223 employees serving in the military are back on the job, and 2,500 are still in uniform or employed elsewhere.

Plant Eaton *MPC Communication Files*

First units are completed at Plant Eaton, near Hattiesburg, Mississippi, and a Pensacola plant (later named Plant Crist); a unit is added at Plant Atkinson.

The Donner Estate purchases Savannah Electric and Power; private owners will retain control of the utility for more than four decades.

The National Association of Electric Companies is formed to represent the industry's interests in Washington, D.C. (will merge with EEI in 1978).

1946

Commonwealth & Southern files a new reorganization plan for creating Southern Company and divesting its northern subsidiaries.

With net income at $31.8 million, more than double the previous year's, C&S begins making payments on preferred dividends that are in arrears.

A drop in industrial load and military spending is more than offset by a 13 percent increase in residential power use and a 16 percent increase in commercial sales; demand is stimulated by a postwar economic boom. Utilities can begin promoting appliance sales again; consumers want refrigerators, air-conditioning, fluorescent lighting, and new electrical appliances of all types.

Southern Company's first board meeting is held March 29.

On October 9, Southern Company's first operating directors are selected. There are four representatives from the Southern Group—Eugene A. Yates, Tom Martin, Preston Arkwright, and E. L. Godshalk; three from the Northern Group—Justin Whiting, G. H. Bourne, and Jacob Hekma; and three outside directors—Percy H. Clark, Beauchamp Smith, and Pearson Winslow. Yates is named chairman and Bourne president of the proposed company.

In December, Georgia Power's legendary president, Preston Arkwright, dies and is succeeded by W. E. Mitchell.

The Atomic Energy Act restricts ownership and use of fissionable materials to the federal government and creates the Atomic Energy Commission to oversee the government's nuclear operations.

1947

On August 1, the Securities and Exchange Commission approves the formation of Southern Company as the parent of Alabama Power, Georgia Power, Gulf Power, and Mississippi Power. The SEC mandates the sale of South Carolina Power.

Southern Company's board eliminates the position of chairman August 21 and elects Eugene Yates president.

On September 1, Southern Company officially becomes the parent of the four operating companies and little-known subsidiary Savannah River Electric Company.

The first 10 million shares of Southern Company common stock are issued and held by Commonwealth & Southern, which technically owns Southern Company until C&S can be dissolved.

Southern Company leases office space in the William-Oliver Building in Atlanta.

In compliance with SEC requirements that Southern Company divest its non-electric business lines, Alabama Power sells its gas properties in Phenix City and bus transportation service in Tuscaloosa.

As an indication of the growing boom, C&S power sales increase 16 percent, 126,487 new customers are added, and twenty-six new generating units are under construction or being designed. Mississippi Power adds another unit at Plant Eaton.

A major hurricane hits the Mississippi coast September 19; new two-way radios prove to be invaluable during service restoration.

Georgia Power president W. E. Mitchell resigns in February and is replaced by Preston Arkwright Jr., who dies unexpectedly in November and is succeeded by C. B. McManus.

1948

Southern Company issues its first dividend of 15¢ a share March 29, payable to C&S, which still holds its stock.

In response to an SEC ruling that Southern Company requires more equity capital, C&S provides $20.2 million in additional funding, $10.2 million of which comes from the sale of South Carolina Power May 18 to South Carolina Electric & Gas.

Southern Company and its subsidiaries serve 809,342 customers within a 94,000-square-mile territory. The companies own and operate 1,500 megawatts of generating capacity, 46 percent of which is hydro and the rest steam generation; some 2,200 megawatts of additional generation is under construction, most of it steam.

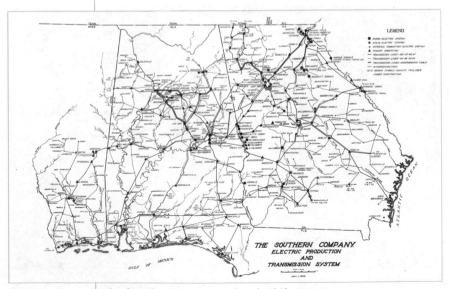

Southern Company service territory in 1948 *GPC Archives*

Southern Company holds its first annual meeting of stockholders in Wilmington, Delaware, May 26.

First unit of Georgia Power's Plant Mitchell near Albany goes commercial; new units are added at plants Atkinson and Arkwright.

Gulf Power and Georgia Power sell gas properties in Pensacola, Columbus, and Americus.

James F. Crist becomes president of Gulf Power.

Golf legend Robert T. (Bobby) Jones joins Southern Company's board of directors.

Bobby Jones *GPC Archives*

1949

Southern Company common stock trades over the counter for the first time July 19; the stock is listed for the first time on the New York Stock Exchange September 30.

Quarterly dividend increases to 20¢.

Southern Company appoints its first transfer agents: Guaranty Trust of New York and Trust Company of Georgia in Atlanta. The board also selects the company's first registrars: Bankers Trust of New York and Citizens and Southern in Atlanta.

Commonwealth & Southern stock was canceled and the first shares of Southern Company common stock were distributed in 1949. *GPC Archives*

Commonwealth & Southern is dissolved September 30; on October 1, its common stock is dispensed to shareholders—4,035,491 shares to Consumers Power, 792,686 to Central Illinois Light, 2,020,400 to Ohio Edison, and 11,785,665 to Southern Company.

In a realignment of Southern Company's board, three directors previously associated with C&S are replaced by operating company CEOs Jim Crist, C. B. McManus, and Lonnie Sweatt.

Southern Services, Incorporated, is formed to provide engineering, planning, and power coordination services for Southern Company and its subsidiaries; H. J. Scholz becomes its first president.

Southern Company completes its first public offering of common stock—1.5 million new shares sold by Lehman Brothers.

First two units of the new Plant Gadsden in Alabama are completed; units are added at existing plants Mitchell, Crist, and Eaton and at Mitchell Dam.

Georgia Power sells its bus transportation properties in Macon and Augusta.

James M. Barry becomes president of Alabama Power; Martin continues as chairman.

Despite protests from private utilities, TVA is authorized for the first time to build steam plants specifically for commercial power sales.

Sperry Corporation introduces Univac I, the first commercial electronic computer.

1950

Throughout the new decade, earnings, power sales, and new plant construction will continue to increase rapidly, and Southern Company will sell new common stock shares every year but one.

On January 23, Yates is named chairman and McManus president of Southern Company; McManus also continues to serve as Georgia Power president.

Following a favorable ruling on Southern Company's tax status by the Georgia Supreme Court, the board decides to domesticate the company in Georgia but continues to maintain an office in New York to handle financing and relations with the financial community.

Southern Company buys Birmingham Electric Company from Electric Bond & Share and transfers the assets and customers to Alabama Power.

Dedication of Plant Yates *GPC Archives*

First two units of Plant Yates, near Newnan, Georgia, come on-line; they are the system's first 100-megawatt units.

Georgia Power sells its transit system in Atlanta.

The Southeastern Power Administration is created to market government-generated power in the Southeast; Southern Company's operating companies submit proposals to purchase and distribute power from federal hydro dams to cooperatives and public bodies at cost.

At one of the new federal hydro projects—Clark Hill Dam, near Augusta, Georgia—the government condemns and takes 40,000 acres owned by Savannah River Electric; the subsidiary is folded at a loss to Southern Company.

1951

Southern Company launches its first national advertising campaign, designed to attract new industry to the Southeast; the company also stages information meetings in nine national financial centers. By year-end, the company has 115,417 stockholders of record.

An early Southern Company ad
GPC Archives

Control room at Plant McManus *GPC Archives*

First unit begins operating at Plant Sweatt, near Meridian, Mississippi; Alabama Power installs its first 100-megawatt unit at Plant Gorgas; units are added at Plant Chickasaw and Bartlett's Ferry Dam.

Georgia Power negotiates for power purchase and distribution rights at Clark Hill Dam, but co-ops seeking direct access to the power press the government for duplicate transmission lines into the area, spurring a tug-of-war that makes national headlines.

Meridian mayor Laurence Paine and Lonnie Sweatt dedicated the first unit of Plant Sweatt in 1951. *MPC Communication Files*

In January, McManus begins a six-month leave of absence to head the Defense Electric Power Administration, an appointment made by the secretary of the interior to help coordinate energy needs of the defense industry during the Korean War. Harllee Branch Jr. becomes president of Georgia Power.

1952

All remaining assets of the dissolved Commonwealth & Southern are transferred to Southern Company following a series of legal actions that delayed transfer of the final 234,335 shares of common stock.

The merger of Birmingham Electric into Alabama Power becomes effective.

First unit of Plant McManus, near Brunswick, Georgia, begins operating; additional units come on-line at Martin Dam and plants Gorgas, Yates, Crist, and McManus; annual construction expenses approach $100 million for the first time.

Southern Company joins a utility coalition studying the generation of electricity from atomic energy.

Barry is named chairman of the executive committee, a new Southern Company position based in Birmingham; Lewis M. Smith becomes president of Alabama Power.

This sign invited Hattiesburg moviegoers to the new comfort of air-conditioning.
MPC Communication Files

1953

A new electric "heat pump" developed by Alabama Power is marketed by the operating companies to provide summer cooling and winter heating, making it possible for new homeowners to go "total electric."

First units come on-line at Gulf Power's River Junction Steam Plant (later named Plant Scholz) and Georgia Power's Sinclair Dam; a unit is added at Plant Sweatt.

On November 12, Alabama Power files an application with the Federal Power Commission for a preliminary permit to build a series of new dams on the Coosa River.

The Atomic Energy Commission approves Southern Company's participation in a nuclear research program headed by Dow Chemical Company and Detroit Edison Company; twenty-six utilities and industrial companies join in the project.

Start-up of Plant Scholz and Sinclair Dam *Gulf Power Communication Files, GPC Archives*

1954   Southern Company joins Middle South Utilities in forming the Mississippi Valley Generating Company, which plans to build a plant to provide power to the Atomic Energy Commission; Yates and Middle South's Edgar Dixon sign the contract November 11. Because the power would be fed into TVA's system, opposition to the contract flares into a national controversy known as "Dixon-Yates."

Edgar Dixon and Eugene Yates at congressional hearings on their joint contract with the government
Bettman/CORBIS

First two units of Georgia Power's Plant Hammond, near Rome, come on-line, as do the first two units of Alabama Power's Plant Barry, near Mobile.

An analog computer system called the "Early Bird" is invented by Southern Services engineer Donald Early. Installed to coordinate and dispatch power from all of Southern Company's plants, it is hailed as the world's most advanced system of its type.

Donald Early (L) demonstrated his "Early Bird" marvel to Clark Nichols, C. B. McManus, Harllee Branch Jr., and E. C. Gaston. *GPC Archives*

The Atomic Energy Act opens the door to private development of commercial nuclear power under license and control of the Atomic Energy Commission.

The industry's nuclear research is reorganized under the name "Atomic Power Development Associates," with thirty-three member companies now participating.

1955

President Dwight Eisenhower pulls the plug on the "Dixon-Yates" contract. When political opponents block the government from refunding expenses that are contractually due, Southern Company and Middle South file a lawsuit to recover those costs.

Southern Company raises its dividends on common stock to 22.5¢ per share.

In Georgia, units are added at Plant Hammond and Goat Rock Dam.

Southern Company joins the Power Reactor Development Company, which is planning to build a nuclear plant in Michigan (later named Enrico Fermi Atomic Power Plant).

Branch becomes the 1955–56 chairman of EEI.

Lansing T. Smith becomes president of Gulf Power.

1956

A new subsidiary, Southern Electric Generating Company, is organized in May with plans to build four 250-megawatt units near Wilsonville, Alabama, that will be co-owned by Alabama Power and Georgia Power. Crist is named president of SEGCO, replacing Scholz, who headed the planning phase of SEGCO in his role as service company president.

Georgia Power buys Georgia Power & Light Company from Florida Power Corporation March 1; the acquisition adds twenty south Georgia counties to the company's territory.

In a resolution of the Clark Hill conflict, Georgia Power retains wheeling rights to the dam's electricity and successfully works out contracts with public power groups given preference to the energy.

Branch becomes president of Southern Company; McManus becomes vice chairman. John I. McDonough is named president of Georgia Power.

Quarterly dividend increases to 25¢ per share.

"Live Better . . . Electrically" is the theme adopted as part of the industry's promotional efforts.

Gulf Power used the industry's theme to promote electric appliances.
Gulf Power Communication Files

1957 Southern Company celebrates its tenth full year of operation. During the past decade, the company has added more than 2,000 megawatts of capacity and the number of customers has more than doubled to 1,453,000. Average residential power use is up from 1,886 kilowatt-hours to 3,474; average price per kwh is down from 2.31¢ to 2.07¢.

Quarterly dividend increases to 27.5¢ per share.

First unit of Mississippi Power Gulf Coast plant (later named Plant Watson) goes into service; units are added at Plant Yates and Goat Rock Dam.

First barge of coal is unloaded at Plant Watson.
MPC Communication Files

In September, Alabama Power receives a federal license to begin four new dams and enlarge Lay Dam on the Coosa River. Also granted is a license to build a new dam and install powerhouses at existing federal dams on the Warrior River.

The nation's first commercial nuclear reactor begins operating in Shippingport, Pennsylvania. Southern Company commits $2.4 million in funding and $15 million in loan guarantees to continuing nuclear research.

The Price-Anderson Act reduces liability in the event of a nuclear plant catastrophe.

Southern Company closes its Delaware office and moves the corporate secretary function to its new Atlanta offices at 1330 West Peachtree Street; the company continues to maintain a small New York office but moves most of its finance staff to Atlanta.

Yates has a heart attack and dies October 5; McManus becomes chairman; Branch continues as president. Walter Bouldin becomes president of Alabama Power; E. C. Gaston becomes president of Southern Services.

1958

Work starts on the Coosa-Warrior developments in Alabama and continues through the next decade, making the project one of the larger hydro developments undertaken by private enterprise.

Units are added at plants Yates and Gorgas.

Branch and Scholz attend the Second International Conference on the Peaceful Uses of Atomic Energy, held in Geneva; in addition to supporting nuclear research, Southern Company begins nuclear reactor training programs for its engineers.

The Advertising Federation of America honors Southern Company's national advertising program for promoting the South's progress and economic development; 186 new industrial plants are added in the four-state region during 1958.

Quarterly dividend increases to 30¢ per share.

Southern Company's national ads promoted economic development in the service territory. *GPC Archives*

A. J. (Jack) Watson Jr. becomes president and CEO of Mississippi Power; Sweatt continues as chairman.

Company CEOs testify in Washington against a proposed bill to allow TVA to issue bonds with no restriction on its expansion into territories served by investor-owned utilities.

EEI creates the "Medallion Home" program to promote all-electric homes.

1959

Alabama Power receives the industry's Edison Award for undertaking the Coosa-Warrior hydro developments. Georgia Power completes Oliver Dam, near Columbus on the Chattahoochee River; units are added at plants Barry, McManus, and Crist.

A nuclear engineering department is created within Southern Services.

The operating companies promote a new home-rewiring program to accommodate new appliances, conveniences, and total-electric living.

Quarterly dividend increases to 32.5¢ a share.

President Eisenhower signs the TVA Revenue Bond Act into law, setting TVA free of congressional appropriations and control and allowing it to raise future construction funds through selling bonds. The act also places a "fence" around TVA, limiting its expansion to a five-mile perimeter around its existing territory.

Ruble Thomas participated in early nuclear research and later headed the service company's nuclear organization.
GPC Archives

The U.S. Court of Claims rules that Southern Company and Middle South Utilities are entitled to $1.9 million in damages from the canceled "Dixon-Yates" contract, but the Department of Justice appeals to the Supreme Court.

1960

First two units of the SEGCO plant (later named Plant Gaston) begin commercial operation; a second unit is added at Plant Watson.

Quarterly dividend increases to 35¢ a share.

SEGCO owned and operated coal mines during early years of its operations.
GPC Archives

McManus retires as chairman of Southern Company; the position is unfilled as Branch takes on CEO responsibilities.

1961

First units in the Coosa-Warrior developments are placed in service at the Lewis Smith and Weiss dams; units are added at plants Crist and Gaston.

The U.S. Supreme Court reverses a judgment by the Court of Claims and dismisses all damage claims related to the "Dixon-Yates" contract; Southern Company's portion of the write-off is half a million dollars.

The Alabama state legislature declares August 13 "Thomas W. Martin Day" in honor of Alabama Power's longtime leader.

Alvin W. Vogtle Jr. is named president of SEGCO; R. L. Pulley becomes president of Gulf Power.

The Enrico Fermi nuclear plant in Michigan is completed and undergoes start-up tests.

As co-ops move into urban markets, Alabama Power and Mississippi Power try to block two REA loans—$20.4 million in Alabama and $16 million in Mississippi—from being used to build generating and transmission facilities in areas the companies already serve. The projects are contested in hearings and state courts during the next seven years.

Quarterly dividend increases to 37.5¢ a share.

1962

Alabama Power installs the first unit at the Bankhead Dam on the Warrior River, near Tuscaloosa; Georgia Power redevelops the powerhouse at North Highlands Dam on the Chattahoochee River, near Columbus; units are added at plants Gaston and Watson and at the Lewis Smith and Weiss dams.

Plant McDonough featured a unique coal-car-unloading operation. *GPC Archives*

Southern Services is reorganized December 21 as a subsidiary of Southern Company; it previously had been owned by the operating companies.

Quarterly dividend is 40¢ per share.

1963

First unit is installed at Plant McDonough, near Atlanta; other units are added at the North Highlands and Bankhead dams.

A U.S. Department of Commerce study reports that the southern region leads the country in more than 75 percent of all economic indices; over the past ten years, 1,555 new industrial plants, creating 124,000 new jobs, have located in Southern Company's service territory.

Southern Company officers and Atlanta-based employees of the service company move to Lenox Towers, across the street from Lenox Square, one of the nation's first all-electric shopping malls.

Southern Company's quarterly dividend increases to 42.5¢.

Bouldin becomes the 1963–64 chairman of EEI.

Edwin I. Hatch is elected president of Georgia Power; McDonough continues as chairman and CEO.

The first Clean Air Act focuses on research, creation of state control agencies, and interstate pollution issues; specific pollution-control policies will be enacted seven years later.

1964   Southern Company's dividend is raised to 45¢, the tenth increase in ten years.

Alabama Power completes Logan Martin Dam on the Coosa River, near Gadsden; new units are installed at plants McDonough and Mitchell.

The four operating companies revise rate schedules to pass on a reduction in the federal income tax.

Legendary Alabama Power chairman Thomas W. Martin dies December 8 at age 83; he had been associated with the company since 1911. Clyde A. Lilly Jr. becomes president of Gulf Power; Pulley continues as chairman.

1965   First unit of the Greene County Steam Plant, near Demopolis, Alabama, comes on-line; the new plant is owned jointly by Alabama Power (60%) and Mississippi Power (40%). Georgia Power completes the first unit of Plant Branch, near Milledgeville, and Gulf Power completes the first unit of Plant Lansing Smith, near Panama City.

Greene County Steam Plant *MPC Communication Files*

Southern Services begins to centralize and coordinate system fuel procurement.

Mississippi's Chancery Court of Hinds County upholds a PSC ruling allowing cooperatives to build facilities duplicating those of Mississippi Power; while the company appeals to the state supreme court, co-ops in the state form a larger coalition and obtain an additional $22 million in loans from REA.

In Alabama, the courts release the Alabama Electric Cooperative to begin work on a generating plant in southwest Alabama. Another legal fight breaks out when AEC-member cities Troy and Luverne become wholesale customers of Alabama Power, a move supported by the courts and PSC.

Quarterly dividend increases to 48¢.

A major blackout in the Northeast raises concerns about reliability.

1966

Southern Company splits its common stock two-for-one; in October, dividends are set at 25.5¢ a share, an increase when adjusted for the split.

Alabama Power completes the H. Neely Henry Dam on the Coosa River, near Ragland; unit additions are made at plants Branch, Lansing Smith, and Greene County.

A nineteen-week strike by the International Brotherhood of Electrical Workers (IBEW) against Alabama Power begins August 16; non-union employees move to generation and distribution jobs critical to keeping the lights on.

Turbine runner at Neely Henry Dam *APC Archives*

Various models of line trucks used in the 1960s *GPC Archives*

A United Mine Workers of America strike closes the coal-mining operations of Alabama Power and SEGCO for seven weeks.

Southern Services begins developing procedures for standardizing customer accounting across the system, the first step toward centralizing computer operations.

Hatch becomes CEO as well as president of Georgia Power upon McDonough's retirement. William R. Brownlee becomes president of Southern Services; Gaston continues as chairman and CEO.

An accident shuts down unit 1 of the Enrico Fermi nuclear plant; although the unit is repaired and restarted, it will be mothballed in 1972.

1967

The IBEW strike against Alabama Power ends January 7.

Southern Company announces plans to build its first nuclear plant—Plant Hatch, near Baxley, Georgia.

Alabama Power completes Bouldin Dam on the Coosa River, near Wetumpka, and the first phase of a redevelopment of Lay Dam; units are added at plants Branch and Lansing Smith.

Branch initiates "Project Look Ahead," a study that leads to dozens of coordinated policies, practices, and technological developments.

Mississippi Power employee Winona Latimer helped sell electric cooking on a Biloxi television program.
MPC Communication Files

Southern Services creates an aviation department and purchases the system's first aircraft.

Dividend increases to 27¢.

Gaston retires, and Brownlee assumes CEO duties at the service company.

1968

Alabama Power and Georgia Power file for rate increases—a sign of things to come as the declining-cost utility business is hit with inflation, higher labor and fuel costs, and new expenses for environmental controls.

Georgia Power is granted a rate increase of $2.3 million; Alabama Power begins collecting $6 million in higher rates under bond, pending an appeal of an adverse commission order.

For the first time, Southern Company's three-year construction budget exceeds $1 billion.

First unit of Alabama Power's generating facility at Holt Lock and Dam on the Warrior River comes on-line; additional units are installed at plants Branch and Watson and at Lay Dam.

Educating investors: Five of the thirty-eight security analysts who toured Southern Company operations in 1967. *GPC Archives*

The REA-loan legal battles end when the U.S. Supreme Court refuses to review unfavorable state court decisions from Mississippi and Alabama; Mississippi Power loses four major wholesale customers, and Alabama Power loses three.

Quarterly dividend increases to 28.5¢ a share.

In response to the threat of "reliability legislation," Southern Company helps create the National Electric Reliability Council to self-regulate the industry's transmission exchanges and promote a reliable power supply nationwide.

1969

The century's most intense storm, Hurricane Camille, strikes the Gulf Coast and devastates Mississippi Power's operations; service is restored to those who can accept it fifteen days later with the help of crews from sister companies and six other utilities.

Alabama Power's rate increase of $6.9 million goes into effect.

Southern Company's quarterly dividend increases to 30¢.

A research department is created at Southern Services to conduct the system's most challenging environmental studies.

Hurricane Camille destruction near Gulfport *MPC Communication Files*

The National Environmental Policy Act requires environmental-impact studies in the permitting process for new power plants.

Alabama Power announces plans to build the system's second nuclear facility—Plant Farley, near Dothan.

Generating facilities placed in service include the system's largest— a 490-megawatt unit at Plant Branch and a 350-megawatt unit at Plant Barry; combustion turbines are added at plants Arkwright and Greene County.

Vogtle becomes president of Southern Company; Branch remains chairman and CEO. Joseph M. Farley becomes president of Alabama Power; Bouldin remains chairman. Lilly becomes president of Southern Services; Brownlee continues as chairman. Robert R. Ellis Jr. becomes president of Gulf Power.

1970

The 1970 Clean Air Act amendments create the Environmental Protection Agency and require utilities to reduce air emissions; the first national environmental-awareness event, "Earth Day," is held April 22.

Southern Company joins with eighteen regional utilities in forming the Southeastern Electric Reliability Council to set standards for a reliable power supply in the Southeast.

The "Early Bird" is replaced with a digital computer system that will coordinate economic dispatch of electric power across the service area.

Mississippi Power wins the industry's Edison Award for its response to Hurricane Camille. The company's first rate increase of $1.9 million is approved, helping to offset losses from the natural disaster.

With annual system expenses climbing 20 percent for the first time, Georgia Power seeks an $11 million increase in its wholesale rates, Alabama Power files for a $19.9 million increase in retail rates, and Mississippi Power files for a $3 million retail increase. Rate hearings will dominate the decade as inflation and expenses continue to increase.

Units are added at plants Hammond and Crist; combustion turbines are added at plants Atkinson, Gaston, and Watson.

The Atomic Energy Commission's licensing procedures are amended to consider antitrust actions when public power groups are denied participation in the ownership of investor-owned nuclear power plants.

Vogtle is named CEO as well as president of Southern Company; Brownlee retires and Lilly becomes CEO as well as president of Southern Services.

1971   Southern Company and the Atlanta staff of Southern Services move into a new corporate headquarters in north Atlanta that houses the Data Center, a new mainframe computer providing centralized data processing for customer accounting and many financial, engineering, telecommunications, and other applications across the system.

Data Center operations in Atlanta during early 1970s *GPC Archives*

Branch retires; Vogtle continues as CEO and president of Southern Company.

In compliance with President Richard Nixon's wage and price freeze, Southern Company postpones a decision to increase its dividend in October.

Retail rate increases are awarded to Alabama Power ($16.9 million), Georgia Power ($26 million), and Mississippi Power ($3 million). Gulf Power files for its first increase.

First unit of Georgia Power's Plant Bowen near Cartersville goes into service, and a new unit is added at Plant Barry; they are the system's first 700-megawatt units.

Plant Bowen *GPC Archives*

A line inspector on new 500-kilovolt transmission lines *GPC Archives*

The system's first 500-kilovolt transmission line is built to connect Plant Bowen to the Atlanta load.

Southern Services' research group begins studying solvent refining, a new process for "cleaning" coal of its pollutants before it is burned.

1972   Southern Company has the highest peak-hour demand among the nation's investor-owned utilities.

For the third consecutive year, expenses rise 20 percent; fuel costs increase 22 percent.

Units are added at plants Bowen and Gorgas; combustion turbines are added at Plant McManus.

Alabama Power is granted a $26.9 million retail rate increase; Georgia Power, $17.9 million; and Gulf Power, $3.7 million. Mississippi Power is denied an increase. All four companies receive small increases in wholesale rates.

Victor J. Daniel Jr. becomes president of Mississippi Power; Watson continues as chairman and CEO.

The Federal Water Pollution Control Act regulates utility discharges into water.

1973   Unable to proceed with a bond sale, Georgia Power is granted an interim $11 million emergency increase and a permanent increase of $67.9 million.

Units are added at plants Crist and Watson.

Southern Company builds a solvent-refining pilot plant at Wilsonville, Alabama, and begins testing new methods of removing pollutants from flue gas at Plant Scholz. Plant Crist becomes the site of the nation's largest program for evaluating flue-gas analyzers, instruments for monitoring power plant emissions.

The Electric Power Research Institute is created to coordinate large-scale industry research projects and share funding among electric utilities, manufacturers, government, and third-party participants. Pledging $8.7 million for the first two years of operations, Southern Company becomes one of the largest contributors to EPRI.

Quarterly dividend is raised to 33.5¢ a share.

Watson retires and Daniel becomes CEO, as well as president, of Mississippi Power.

Vogtle becomes the 1973–74 chairman of EEI.

An Arab oil embargo leads to gas rationing, 55-mph speed limits, and an "energy czar" in the White House.

Utilities order forty-one nuclear reactors, a single-year record.

Oil dependent and unable to get a rate increase, Savannah Electric and Power is near bankruptcy; John McIntosh is named chairman and CEO and works for several years to restore financial health to the company while fending off threats of takeover.

1974

The Energy Supply and Environmental Coordination Act gives the federal government power to prohibit utilities from burning natural gas or oil. Coal-burning utilities also feel the sting; Southern Company's fuel expenses jump by more than 83 percent.

Earnings fall to $123 million, close to the dividend payout level.

Southern Company announces $2.1 billion in construction cutbacks for the next three years; energy sales increase only 1 percent, far below historical averages of 10 percent.

Units are added at plants Gaston, Bowen, and Yates.

Three operating companies receive emergency interim retail rate relief— Alabama Power ($7.5 million), Georgia Power ($35 million), and Gulf Power ($17.2 million). Mississippi Power's $3.4 million rate increase is denied but is billed under bond while appeals work through the courts. All four companies file for new wholesale rate increases.

Gulf Power imports low-sulfur coal from South Africa and Australia in an attempt to meet stringent state air-quality standards.

The Nuclear Reorganization Act establishes the Nuclear Regulatory Commission (NRC) as an independent agency to regulate civilian use of nuclear materials.

1975

Earnings rebound to $238 million; Southern Company's quarterly dividend is raised to 35¢.

The system's first nuclear unit at Plant Hatch begins commercial operation.

Georgia Power agrees to sell 30 percent of Plant Hatch to Oglethorpe Electric Membership Corporation, a group of thirty-nine rural cooperatives.

Georgia governor Jimmy Carter at the Plant Hatch Visitors Center *GPC Archives*

Plant Hatch construction *GPC Archives*

Alabama Power postpones its planned Barton Nuclear Plant, which later will be canceled. Construction moves forward on a coal plant in Jackson County, Mississippi (later named Plant Daniel) and a new nuclear plant near Waynesboro, Georgia (later named Plant Vogtle).

Rate cases are stacking up from regulatory lag: Mississippi Power seeks a new $14 million increase while still fighting legal battles over a "zero order" in 1974; Gulf Power files for a supplemental increase before being awarded $20 million of its 1974 request; Georgia Power receives two temporary increases before being awarded $116 million in permanent relief, less than 40 percent of its previous year's request; and Alabama Power receives $54 million but files for a new increase before the end of the year.

Flue-gas-scrubbing research at Plant Scholz *Gulf Power Communication Files*

The last of three scrubbers being tested at Plant Scholz becomes operational.

A Plant Crist fire takes a unit out of service four months.

Hurricane Eloise hits Fort Walton Beach; power to 55,000 affected Gulf Power customers is restored in six days.

Southern Company begins a Dividend Reinvestment and Stock Purchase Plan for stockholders; it will become an important future source of equity capital.

Thirteen nuclear projects nationwide are canceled following a fire at TVA's Browns Ferry plant.

Break at Bouldin Dam *APC Archives*

A break at Bouldin Dam causes extensive damage; Alabama Power and its insurers file suit against contractors in attempts to recover the cost of repairs, estimated at $65 million.

Robert W. Scherer becomes president and chief operating officer of Georgia Power; Hatch continues as chairman and CEO.

1976

A new corporate identity is adapted by all Southern Company affiliates; for the first time, the parent company and its subsidiaries have a common triangular logo.

Southern Services' name is changed to Southern Company Services (SCS).

First unit of Georgia Power's Plant Wansley, near Carrollton, begins commercial operation.

Gulf Power cancels plans to build a plant at Caryville and agrees to buy half interest in Mississippi Power's Plant Daniel, which will burn low-sulfur coal from Utah and Colorado—the system's first coal purchases from western states.

Quarterly dividends are 36.5¢.

A new corporate identity was adopted in 1976, giving Southern Company and its subsidiaries a common logo. *SCS Communication Files*

After the Alabama PSC rejects a $106.8 million rate filing in its entirety, Alabama Power receives half the request through two circuit court orders while appeals are pending, then files a new $173.9 million request in October. Mississippi Power receives a $6 million increase, less than half its prior year's request. Wholesale rate increases contribute $14 million to net income, although four settlements are still pending.

The Resource Conservation and Recovery Act creates standards for disposing of hazardous and nonhazardous wastes.

New load-management programs go into effect, including Southern Company's first time-of-day rates and experiments with radio-control systems used to turn off air-conditioning units and water heaters during peak-demand periods.

Gulf Power's "Good Cents" is one of the industry's first programs to promote building standards to achieve home energy-efficiency goals; the program eventually will be marketed to utilities nationwide.

1977

Georgia Power sells portions of four of its power plants and some of its transmission facilities to three public-power groups—Oglethorpe Electric Membership Corporation, the Municipal Electric Authority of Georgia, and the City of Dalton.

An SCS plane crash, outside Washington, D.C., kills Clyde A. Lilly, SCS president; William B. Lalor, SCS executive vice president; and pilots Thomas R. Taylor III and Ronald Golden.

First unit of Plant Farley, the system's first rated at 860 megawatts, is placed in commercial service. First unit of Plant Daniel comes on-line.

Nuclear reactor on its way to Plant Farley *APC Archives*

Plant Daniel's second unit under construction in 1978 *MPC Communication Files*

A successful test burn of solvent-refined coal is conducted at Plant Mitchell.

New Clean Air Act amendments disallow tall stacks as a compliance strategy and force reductions in emissions.

Completion of a four-year test program at Plant Scholz results in major improvements in scrubber technology.

Quarterly dividend increases to 38.5¢.

Georgia Power constructs test houses to study solar-assisted water and space heating and other new energy-efficient features.

Retail rate-case settlements for Alabama Power, Georgia Power, and Gulf Power total $198.8 million, with another $38.1 million in requests still pending or being appealed.

System companies receive $59.2 million in wholesale rate increases; another $78.3 million in requests are still pending or being appealed.

Alabama governor George Wallace initiates a complaint case against Alabama Power, calling its rates excessive; evidence later presented in hearings proves otherwise.

A blackout in New York City heightens anxiety about the energy crisis and power reliability.

The Federal Energy Regulatory Commission (FERC) is created to replace the Federal Power Commission as the regulator of wholesale energy and hydro licensing.

President Jimmy Carter creates the Department of Energy; James Schlesinger becomes DOE's first secretary.

William B. Reed becomes president of SCS.

1978

First unit completed at Plant Miller, twenty miles northwest of Birmingham; a unit is added at Plant Wansley.

An outside audit confirms Alabama Power and SCS are well managed and low cost.

After a negative rate-case ruling by the state supreme court, Alabama Power's financial condition deteriorates; while pleading for emergency relief, the company halts all construction in December. Gulf Power is granted $10.8 million in rate increases.

FERC awards the operating companies $7.9 million in wholesale rates, with $65 million in requests still pending.

Alabama Power is the first utility to participate in DOE's new commercial solar-energy program; the company's new Montevallo District office will become a solar and energy-conservation demonstration building.

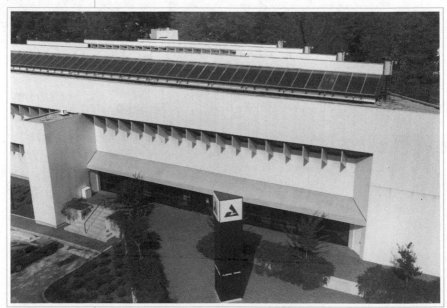

Solar-powered Montevallo district office *APC Archives*

SCS became a DOE partner in designing a clean coal plant in 1978. Signing contracts were SCS executive Dr. William B. Harrison (L) and Secretary of Energy James R. Schlesinger; observing were Kentucky energy secretary David Drake (L) and Georgia senator Herman Talmadge. *GPC Archives*

President Carter signs several energy bills: The National Energy Conservation Act requires utilities to provide customers free conservation service; the Public Utility Regulatory Policies Act requires utilities to buy electricity from qualified cogenerators and independent power producers (IPPs); the Natural Gas Policy Act partially deregulates gas prices at the wellhead; and the Power Plant and Industrial Fuel Use Act limits use of natural gas in electric generation (repealed in 1987).

Hatch retires and Scherer becomes CEO and president of Georgia Power. Edward L. Addison is named president of Gulf Power.

1979

The nation's most significant nuclear accident occurs March 28 at Three Mile Island (TMI) near Harrisburg, Pennsylvania, resulting in a major overhaul of nuclear regulations and safety standards and sending the cost of nuclear construction soaring.

The Nuclear Regulatory Commission orders extensive testing of piping supports in all nuclear plants to ensure they can withstand severe earthquakes; plants Hatch and Farley are out of service all summer and into the fall.

In response to TMI, Southern Company establishes a task force April 3 to conduct a ten-month study of safety designs and operating procedures at its nuclear plants; the review produces twenty recommendations to further enhance safety.

Southern Company joins other utilities in creating: a nuclear "watchdog" (Institute for Nuclear Power Operations), a nuclear member insurance group (Nuclear Mutual Limited), and an information group that later becomes known as the Nuclear Energy Institute.

Ruble Thomas headed a nuclear safety task force in response to the accident at TMI. *GPC Archives*

Additional hikes in oil prices by OPEC countries create another energy crisis, double-digit inflation, and high fuel prices.

Southern Company maintains its dividend, although earnings fall below the dividend level.

Alabama Power receives $208 million in rate relief but has to file a new request by the end of the year; Georgia Power receives $169 million in higher rates.

First unit of Wallace Dam, the system's first pumped-storage facility, is completed near Eatonton, Georgia.

Hurricane Frederic causes $30 million in damage to electric facilities and leaves 20 percent of the system in the dark; Gulf Power and Alabama Power are hardest hit.

Wallace Dam, system's first pumped-storage plant *GPC Archives*

Computerized energy-efficiency audits are conducted for residential customers; new energy-management programs are developed for industrial and commercial customers.

SCS designs the world's first large-scale plant capable of producing liquid solvent-refined coal; it is expected to cost up to $725 million and be built by DOE in Newman, Kentucky; research continues at Southern Company's SRC plant near Wilsonville.

Liquid solvent-refined coal was produced at Wilsonville in 1979. *GPC Archives*

1980

Southern Company ranks number one in system capacity among all U.S. utilities. By burning 36 million tons of coal during the year, Southern Company also is the nation's third-largest user of coal.

Off-system power sales to neighboring utilities total 4 billion kilowatt-hours; long-term contracts become increasingly important as Southern Company struggles to complete its construction program while demand growth declines. Although no new plants have been initiated since 1974, some 7,000 megawatts of generating capacity are still in the pipeline.

Unit 2 of Plant Farley and Bouldin Dam reconstruction are finished; units are added at Wallace Dam. Gulf Power purchases 25 percent interest in a unit under construction at Georgia Power's Plant Scherer, near Macon.

Mississippi Power receives $16.8 million in rate relief; $40 million is awarded to Gulf Power. In a settlement of two previous cases, Alabama Power is awarded $92.5 million in additional increases beginning July 30, reduced to $80 million after seven months.

Plant Farley *APC Archives*

Quarterly dividend increases to 40.5¢.

Southern Company turns over management of its solvent-refined coal process to International Coal Refining Company, which plans to make the technology a commercial reality; declining fuel prices will eventually render the process commercially infeasible.

Line crews during the 1981 winter storm *APC Archives*

1981

A winter storm affects service to 300,000 customers across four states; hardest hit by the freezing rain and snow, Alabama Power restores service in three days.

Plant Farley has the nation's best-performing nuclear units; unit 2 completes its initial year with the highest operating availability of any reactor of its type, surpassing the record set by unit 1 four years earlier.

Southern Company creates Southern Electric International (SEI) to market engineering, operating, and planning expertise to utilities and industrial concerns. Harold C. McKenzie Jr. is named president of the new subsidiary.

Congress authorizes $50 million to study "acid rain," an emerging environmental concern; Southern Company joins EPRI in researching acid rain in the Southeast.

IBEW ends a nineteen-day strike against Georgia Power.

With expenses still increasing at 20 percent levels, all operating companies continue to seek rate increases. Alabama Power receives a "zero rate order" on a $324.9-million request, but court rulings allow it to begin collecting a portion while the case is under appeal. Mississippi Power is granted $10.9 million, less than one-third of its request, and Gulf Power receives $5.5 million, less than 20 percent of its request. Georgia Power is awarded $265.2 million in a two-step order.

FERC grants Southern Company utilities $53.6 million in wholesale rate increases.

Daniel retires, and Alan Barton is named president of Mississippi Power.

1982

First unit of Plant Scherer comes on-line; all but 8.4 percent of its capacity has been sold to cooperatives and municipalities.

Earnings rebound to $472 million, or $2.38 a share, the best they've been since 1975; Southern Company sells a record 18 million new shares in a public offering to raise $239 million for construction. Dividends increase to 42.5¢.

A one-month strike against Alabama Power ends October 14 with union members signing a new two-year contract.

Following a state supreme court ruling, the Alabama PSC makes permanent a $186 million rate increase for Alabama Power, awards it another $120 million in December, and approves a new rate-stabilization plan that promises to stabilize Alabama Power's financial roller-coaster ride.

FERC approves $35 million in wholesale increases for the operating companies.

Georgia Power, DOE, and the Shenandoah Development Corporation complete the world's largest commercial solar-energy installation, designed to provide energy for a knitwear factory in Shenandoah, Georgia.

Solar installation at Shenandoah *GPC Archives*

At Plant Scholz, Southern Company begins a four-year study of "baghouse" technology to clean exhaust gases.

A new computerized radar network is developed to track storms across the system and aid the companies in preparing for possible outages.

Alabama Power introduces Project Share to help low-income, elderly, and disabled customers pay energy bills; all the operating companies will adopt similar programs.

Baghouse research at Plant Scholz
GPC Archives

James H. "Jim" Miller Jr. becomes president of Georgia Power; Scherer continues as chairman and CEO.

Arthur Gignilliat Jr. becomes president of Savannah Electric and Power; McIntosh continues as chairman.

The Nuclear Waste Policy Act requires DOE to site, build, and operate a national facility for disposing of nuclear wastes.

1983

Off-system sales increase to 12 billion kilowatt-hours.

Southern Company signs ten-year unit-power agreements to sell major blocks of capacity off-system to the Jacksonville Electric Authority, Florida Power & Light, and Texas-based Gulf States Utilities.

Harris Dam begins commercial operation in east central Alabama as the system's thirty-third hydro plant.

Georgia Power defers work on the Rocky Mountain pumped-storage plant in northwest Georgia.

The system's three-year construction budget is up to $7.2 billion, driven largely by increasing costs at Plant Vogtle.

Dividends are at 45¢ a share.

Through the new rate stabilization plan, Alabama Power receives two small adjustments; three major rating agencies upgrade the creditworthiness of the company's securities.

Georgia Power reaches a $195.4 million negotiated settlement in its rate proceedings; Gulf Power files an appeal after receiving $3.4 million, less than 10 percent of its request; Mississippi Power receives an $18.6 million increase in a court resolution of a three-year-old request.

Harris Dam *GPC Archives*

Southern Company makes progress on a coal liquefaction process at Wilsonville and conducts a test burn of synthetic liquid coal at Plant Sweatt.

Alvin Vogtle retires, and Ed Addison is named Southern Company president and CEO. Doug McCrary becomes president of Gulf Power.

1984

Southern Company stock is at $18.88, its highest level in eleven years. Dividends increase to 48¢ a share.

Estimates for completing Plant Vogtle are up to $7.2 billion, reflecting the high cost of labor, inflation, and numerous post-TMI design changes required by NRC. MEAG buys an additional 5 percent share of the plant, making its ownership 22.7 percent.

Georgia Power begins an eighteen-month "Readiness Review" to address licensing issues early and avoid problems some utilities are having in getting an operating license once their nuclear plants are built.

A unit is added at Plant Scherer.

Off-system sales reach 18.8 billion kilowatt-hours.

Gulf Power receives a rate increase of $4.7 million, 25 percent of the amount requested.

The Alabama Electric Cooperative asks the NRC to impose antitrust sanctions against Alabama Power after the co-op group fails to negotiate a 6 percent purchase of Plant Farley.

System researchers study fuel cells at the University of Alabama and a hospital in Gainesville, Georgia. Southern Company joins a group developing a fluidized bed combustion boiler in Paducah, Kentucky, the world's largest demonstration of this scrubber technology.

Southern Company participates in a five-year, $400 million study of acid rain headed by EPRI.

McIntosh retires; Gignilliat becomes president and CEO of Savannah Electric and Power.

1985

The cost of Plant Vogtle is adjusted upward to $8.4 billion.

The state senate passes a bill requiring the Georgia PSC to phase in the impact of Plant Vogtle on customer rates, and the PSC begins holding hearings on phase-in options. Meanwhile, Georgia Power is forced to refund a portion of a 1983 rate increase.

Hurricane Elena strikes the Gulf Coast on Labor Day; service is restored in seven days to some 270,000 affected customers of Alabama Power, Gulf Power, and Mississippi Power. In

Construction at Plant Vogtle *GPC Archives*

December, Mississippi Power is granted a $6.8 million rate increase to help offset the storm's damages.

With earnings up to $829.6 million, or $3.20 per share, the dividend rate is increased to 51¢ in the fourth quarter.

At 27.1 billion kilowatt-hours, off-system sales represent 21 percent of Southern Company's total power sales.

Liming acidic lakes by helicopter was one response to acid rain. *GPC Archives*

Southern Electric Investments is created to invest in energy technologies; the new subsidiary invests $6.1 million in a factory making photovoltaic cells.

The system sets a new winter peak of 19,204,000 kilowatts and a new summer peak of 21,287,800.

Units are added at Plant Miller and the Mitchell and Bartletts Ferry dams.

Southern Company takes a lead role in forming Living Lakes, Incorporated, a five-year program to help restore acidic lakes and streams in the eastern United States.

A. W. "Bill" Dahlberg III becomes president of SCS and also oversees Southern Electric International upon McKenzie's resignation.

1986

Plant Vogtle cost estimates are up to $8.87 billion; $226 million will be taken as a write-off because it exceeds a cost cap that Georgia Power has pledged to the PSC and because of buyback arrangements with co-owners.

A stockholders lawsuit charges directors with negligence related to Plant Vogtle and Rocky Mountain construction; the legal dispute will end with a settlement in 1992.

Gulf States Utilities files a lawsuit against Southern Company seeking release from its unit-power contracts; Southern Company appeals the dispute to FERC.

Southern Company increases its dividend to 53.5¢, but it will be the last increase for six years because of write-offs, lawsuits, and Plant Vogtle rate-making problems.

The Mississippi PSC approves a new Performance Evaluation Plan that will stabilize rate making and financial problems for Mississippi Power; two small retail rate increases go into effect under the plan. Alabama's rate-stabilization program is extended three more years.

Amendments to the Clean Water Act and the Resource Conservation and Recovery Act present new environmental compliance challenges for Southern Company.

The nuclear power industry faces another crisis of confidence following the worst accident in nuclear power history at Chernobyl, north of Kiev in the Ukraine.

Containment dome being lifted atop unit 1 at Plant Vogtle *GPC Archives*

1987

Plant Vogtle unit 1 begins commercial operations May 31.

The write-off related to Plant Vogtle's "cost cap" reduces Southern Company's earnings by 79¢ a share. In October, the PSC grants Georgia Power a $464 million rate increase to be phased in but disallows $951 million in plant costs as imprudent. Georgia Power appeals the decision hoping to avoid another write-off.

Southern Company reaches an agreement to purchase Savannah Electric and Power Company with an offer of 1.05 shares of Southern Company stock for each share of Savannah Electric stock.

Off-system sales increase to 21.5 billion kilowatt-hours even without the Gulf States Utilities contract, which is still under legal dispute.

Georgia Power agrees to transfer majority ownership of the Rocky Mountain project to Oglethorpe Power Corporation.

Unit 3 of Plant Scherer begins commercial operation.

Computer trading and investor panic drive the Dow Jones Industrial Average down 22.6 percent in one of history's worst days on Wall Street; Southern Company stock drops $2 a share to close at $20 October 19.

Bob Scherer is named the 1987–88 chairman of EEI.

In addition to serving as Georgia Power chairman, Scherer resumes duties as president when Miller retires.

1988

Savannah Electric becomes the fifth operating company effective March 3, following approvals from stockholders, FERC, and the SEC. Savannah Electric's plants Riverside, Kraft, and McIntosh join Southern Company's generation fleet.

Plant Riverside on Savannah's waterfront *GPC Archives*

The U.S. attorney for the northern district of Georgia and the Internal Revenue Service begin a criminal investigation, alleging Southern Company's operating subsidiaries engaged in inappropriate tax accounting for spare parts used in power plants. The companies respond that their tax accounting practices are proper. As the investigation moves forward, the U.S. attorney looks into other issues, resulting in Georgia Power pleading "no contest" to a misdemeanor charge related to fund raising for a PSC candidate.

The Georgia PSC halts the second phase of Georgia Power's Plant Vogtle-related rate increase, awaiting outcome of the IRS investigation. (The following February, the PSC agrees to allow the next phase to take effect.)

Georgia Power voluntarily shuts down Plant Hatch to correct problems identified in an INPO audit.

Southern Company decides to form a new subsidiary, Southern Nuclear Operating Company, to manage its nuclear operations. While awaiting SEC approval, the nuclear corporate staffs in Alabama and Georgia form project teams.

Southern Company signs a new long-term power sales contract with Florida Power and expands agreements with JEA and FP&L.

Following a FERC ruling that its off-system sales agreements are valid, the company files a counterclaim against Gulf States Utilities, charging breach of contract. Through 1988, Southern Company excludes $149 million from earnings in the event some of the amounts due from Gulf States are not collectible.

In resolving a dispute that dates back to 1971, Alabama Power agrees to sell the Alabama Electric Cooperative 8.16 percent of units 1 and 2 of Plant Miller instead of a portion of Plant Farley. (The deal closes in 1992.)

Southern Company adopts a new incentive-pay program to stimulate productivity and launches studies to prepare for anticipated competition and deregulation.

DOE selects four SCS proposals totaling $71 million; three projects will test processes for removing NOx and one will test equipment for reducing SO_2 at coal-fired plants.

DOE awards the company's research group an $8 million grant to study another advanced coal-cleaning technology at Wilsonville called hydrocarbon agglomeration.

NRC requires utilities to develop plans for funding the eventual decommissioning of power reactors; Alabama Power and Georgia Power establish external trust funds and start setting aside internal reserves earmarked for that purpose.

Public Service of New Hampshire files the first utility bankruptcy in more than fifty years.

Bill Dahlberg becomes president of Georgia Power; Bob Scherer continues as chairman. H. Allen Franklin is named president of SCS.

1989
Unit 2 of Plant Vogtle begins commercial operation; units are added at plants Miller and Scherer.

The Georgia PSC allows Georgia Power to recover $218 million over a ten-year phase-in period. Still at issue are disallowances that threaten to force another write-off.

Unit 2 of Plant Farley sets a world record for continuous operation—453 days—for pressurized water reactors; Hatch's two units also set records for boiling-water reactors by being on-line 251 days.

An SCS plane crashes April 10, killing Gulf Power senior vice president Jake Horton and SCS pilots Mike Holmes and John Major; the National Transportation Safety Board and other investigators will never be able to determine a definitive cause of the crash.

The continuing U.S. attorney's investigation in Atlanta expands to include issues from a separate IRS investigation in Pensacola; the SEC launches a similar investigation. On October 31, Gulf Power pleads guilty to two offenses related to illegal political contributions; the company is fined $500,000.

President George H. W. Bush discussed acid rain legislation with energy leaders; Southern Company CEO Ed Addison is right of the president. *GPC Archives*

A December chill results in a new winter peak demand of 20.8 million kilowatts; the new summer peak is 24.4 million kilowatts.

More than 1,000 system employees travel to the Carolinas and Virgin Islands to help respond to destruction caused by Hurricane Hugo.

A more competitive utility environment is emerging from the growth of independent power producers; SEI begins competing for IPP and cogeneration projects.

Georgia is considered to have one of the nation's most competitive electricity markets because large customers can choose their energy providers; Georgia Power captures 73 percent of the customer-choice revenues during the year.

Farley becomes president and CEO of Southern Nuclear; Elmer B. Harris becomes president of Alabama Power; Dahlberg becomes president and CEO of Georgia Power upon Scherer's retirement; Paul J. DeNicola becomes president of Mississippi Power upon Barton's retirement; Jeff Hamburg becomes president of SEI.

Alabama Power's rate-stabilization plan is extended through 1994. The Performance Evaluation Plan used to set Mississippi Power's retail rates is reaffirmed when the state legislature supports the PSC's authority to establish the plan.

1990

After the state supreme court upholds a Plant Vogtle disallowance, Southern Company takes a $218 million write-off, reducing its earnings 69¢ per share, which is below the dividend level.

New Clean Air Act Amendments end a decade-long legislative debate over acid-rain controls; the law requires major reductions in SO_2 and NOx but also sets up a nationwide emission-allowances trading program to provide compliance flexibility.

The U.S. Attorney's office drops its criminal investigation of tax accounting for spare parts; a civil tax audit of Georgia Power continues.

The dispute with Gulf States Utilities is settled with Southern Company receiving cash, common stock, and deferred payments valued at $300 million. Unit 4 of Plant Scherer, which previously was earmarked for Gulf States, is sold to Florida utilities for $810 million.

The SEC approves the formation of Southern Nuclear, which begins managing operations at the system's three nuclear plants.

Unit 1 of Plant Hatch sets another world record for boiling-water reactors by operating 423 consecutive days.

Gulf Power receives a rate increase of $14.1 million, reduced in the first two years by $2.3 million as a penalty for "mismanagement" related to illegal political contributions.

Nearly $100 million in expenses are reduced in 1990 through coal contract renegotiations, volume procurement, inventory controls, and other efforts. Over the next three years, the company will take nearly a billion dollars out of its capital budgets in an attempt to offer more competitive prices.

DOE awards Southern Company a $46 million contract for researching clean-coal gasification at the Power Systems Development Facility in Wilsonville.

1991

Unit 4 of Plant Miller begins commercial operation, bringing to an end an ambitious construction program that has challenged Southern Company for the past two decades.

In the final rate case related to Plant Vogtle, Georgia Power is granted a $117 million increase, a settlement that recovers some costs deferred during previous hearings.

Southern Company begins implementing a decade-long compliance plan for new clean-air rules; the first phase involves installing low-NOx burners at eight plants and switching to low-sulfur coal.

The availability of Southern Company's coal-fired units reaches 91.2 percent, a new system record.

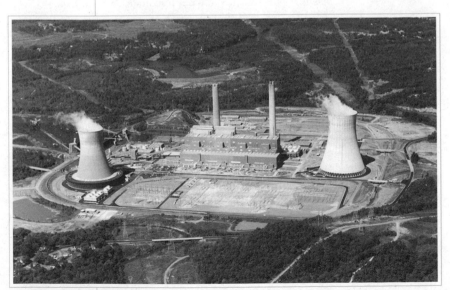

Plant Miller was the last traditional coal plant completed by Southern Company.
APC Archives

The SEC concludes its investigation of Southern Company with no further action beyond a consent order signed by Gulf Power agreeing to make no political contributions.

A new stockholder derivative action lawsuit is filed against officers and directors of the company charging breach of fiduciary duty and violation of the federal Racketeering Influenced and Corrupt Organizations Act. The four-year legal dispute will end with a dismissal by a trial court and an appellate court ruling in 1996.

DeNicola is named executive vice president of Southern Company and group executive responsible for representing the three coastal companies and SEI on Southern Company's board; David M. Ratcliffe becomes president of Mississippi Power; Pat McDonald becomes president of Southern Nuclear; J. R. Harris becomes interim president of SEI upon Hamburg's departure.

1992

With earnings improving, Southern Company raises its dividend rate to 55¢, its first increase since 1986.

Southern Company's stock price reaches a record high of $39 December 23.

The spare parts accounting audits end with Georgia Power agreeing to pay $21 million in back taxes and interest.

Southern Company refinances $2.4 billion in securities to save $45 million in annual interest costs; over the next three years, another $5 billion will be refinanced to save an additional $166 million.

Peak demand hits 24.1 million kilowatts; operating companies develop integrated resource plans that include interruptible rates, time-of-use rates, and other demand-side options to reduce peaks and maximize use of the system's energy-supply network.

Georgia Power reduces its work force by 900 employees. The system's core business work force is at 28,872, down from the construction-era peak of 32,557 in 1985.

Southern Company forms a fossil/hydro business unit to bring non-nuclear plant operations under common management; Bill Guthrie leads the new effort as the system's first chief production officer.

The Energy Policy Act promotes competition, energy efficiency, and alternative fuel use; it grants IPPs and other market players access to utility grids for wholesale power transactions but leaves the question of retail access for states to decide.

After a decade of minimally contributing to earnings, SEI shows improved success with an IPP project in Oahu, Hawaii, a cogeneration project in King George, Virginia, and a repowering project in the Republic of Slovakia.

In Atlanta, Georgia Power opens the Technology Applications Center, where customers can see emerging electric technologies and test manufacturing applications.

Southern Company College is created to enhance managers' competitive, financial, and leadership skills.

Pat McDonald is named president and CEO of Southern Nuclear upon Farley's retirement; Tom Boren becomes president of SEI.

1993

Earnings reach a record level of $1 billion. Southern Company ranks in the top quartile of U.S. electric utilities in terms of return on common equity. The board raises dividends to 57¢ a share.

Alabama Power helps attract a Mercedes-Benz manufacturing plant to Tuscaloosa County; the economic boost is estimated at $7 billion and 15,000 new jobs.

SEI wins power plant contracts in Argentina, Chile, Nevada, and New York and becomes 50 percent owner of Freeport Power in the Grand Bahamas.

In an agreement with the Georgia Department of Natural Resources, Georgia Power helps create a state park at Tallulah Gorge; the partners agree to jointly manage and protect 3,000 wooded acres surrounding the gorge and hydro dam.

Georgia governor Zell Miller (L) and Georgia Power CEO Bill Dahlberg at dedication of Tallulah Gorge State Park *GPC Archives*

Georgia Power builds an Electric Vehicle Research Center in Atlanta to test and promote the development of EVs.

Addison becomes the 1993–94 chairman of EEI.

George Hairston becomes president of Southern Nuclear upon McDonald's retirement.

Little River Canyon National Preserve *APC Archives*

Alabama Power sells 8,500 acres of land to help create the Little River Canyon National Preserve, the first site in the state to be designated a part of the National Parks system; proceeds help establish the Alabama Power Foundation to provide charitable donations and grants for education, health, human services, and the arts.

1994

Southern Company common stock splits two for one; the adjusted dividend rate is 29.5¢ per share.

Southern Communications is organized as a new subsidiary to build and operate a wireless communication network across the service territory; in addition to meeting system dispatch radio and cell phone needs, the company will market services to external customers; Roy Barron is named president.

Southern Company reduces its work force by 1,000; human resources, accounting/finance, information technology, and volume procurement are among the administrative functions restructured systemwide to achieve efficiencies and eliminate duplicate efforts.

Marketing forms a "key accounts" group to provide specialized energy services to the system's 2,000 largest commercial and industrial customers.

California regulators shake up the industry by announcing the nation's first retail deregulation plan; industrial customers will be the first group to choose their energy providers, and all customers will be given choice by 2002. The threat of retail access accelerates as nearly half of the states adopt some form of electricity restructuring.

Six combustion turbines are added at Savannah Electric's Plant McIntosh.

The Mississippi PSC approves an enhanced version of its Performance Evaluation Plan; the tool continues to stabilize rates and Mississippi Power's finances.

SEI becomes part-owner of PowerGen, the electric supplier serving Trinidad and Tobago, and acquires Mobile Energy Services Company, a cogeneration and chemical-recovery complex near Mobile, Alabama.

Southern Company joins the government-industry Climate Challenge program and commits to reducing, offsetting, or sequestering nearly 12 million metric tons of CO_2 emissions by 2000.

Dahlberg becomes president of Southern Company; Addison continues as chairman and CEO. Franklin becomes president of Georgia Power; DeNicola is named president of SCS; Travis J. Bowden becomes president of Gulf Power upon McCrary's retirement.

1995

Fortune magazine ranks Southern Company as "most admired" among the nation's electric utilities.

Net income reaches $1.1 billion, and the dividend is raised to 30.5¢.

Dahlberg becomes chairman, president, and CEO of Southern Company upon Addison's retirement March 1; Dahlberg outlines goals for becoming "America's Best Diversified Utility" and introduces "Southern Style" to define behaviors expected of all employees.

An additional 1,000 employees leave the work force as restructuring continues, reducing overhead costs by 20 percent.

SWEB offices near Bristol, England *GPC Archives*

Southern Electric International acquires SWEB, a utility serving 1.3 million customers in southwestern England.

Southern Company is among 110 utilities, investment houses, and energy traders receiving FERC approval to trade in wholesale energy markets nationwide. SEI opens a 24/7 trading facility; power marketing is expected to become a $100 billion annual business.

Hurricane Erin affects 215,000 Gulf Power customers August 3; the storm is eclipsed October 6 by Hurricane Opal, which knocks out power to more than 1 million customers in Florida, Alabama, and Georgia.

Dwight Evans is named president of Mississippi Power, replacing David Ratcliffe, who becomes Southern Company's senior vice president for external affairs; Bob Dawson becomes president of Southern LINC, the new name for Southern Communication.

1996

Southern Company becomes the nation's largest generator of electricity; its rates are 16 percent below the national average.

Georgia Power is the "Official Power Source of the Centennial Olympic Games;" 2,000 employees become Olympic volunteers, many of them assisting in the opening and closing ceremonies.

Employee volunteers at the Centennial Olympic Games *GPC Archives*

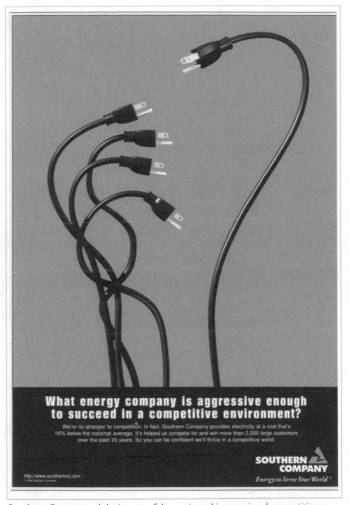

What energy company is aggressive enough to succeed in a competitive environment?

We're no stranger to competition. In fact, Southern Company provides electricity at a cost that's 16% below the national average. It's helped us compete for and win more than 2,200 large customers over the past 20 years. So you can be confident we'll thrive in a competitive world.

http://www.southernco.com

SOUTHERN COMPANY
Energy to Serve Your World™

Southern Company ad during era of domestic and international competition
SCS Communication Files

Southern Company launches a national advertising program and re-brands itself; all companies adopt the new red triangle logo.

Southern Electric International is renamed Southern Energy and becomes one of the top ten power marketers with offices in twelve domestic and foreign markets.

In northern Chile, Southern Energy builds a 160-megawatt plant for EDELNOR (Empresa Electrica del Norte Grande, S. A.), of which it owns 65 percent.

Electricity futures begin trading on the New York Mercantile Exchange.

Quarterly dividend increases to 31.5¢ a share.

Fearing that "stranded" investments will drive up residential power bills, the Georgia PSC approves a new rate plan allowing Georgia Power to accelerate depreciation on high-cost power plants; the Alabama legislature passes a law to prevent new competitors from "cherry picking" large industrial loads.

Georgia Power appeals a PSC order disallowing a portion of its Rocky Mountain project investment, but the company will have to take a $21 million write-off after the case is settled two years later.

Southern Energy's power plant operations in the Philippines *GPC Archives*

1997

Southern Energy closes on its 80 percent acquisition (later increased to 100 percent) of Consolidated Electric Power Asia (CEPA), which has assets in China and the Philippines; Southern Energy also acquires 26 percent of Berlin-based BEWAG and a small interest in Brazilian energy company CEMIG.

Quarterly dividend is increased to 32.5¢.

For the third straight year, *Fortune* ranks Southern Company as the most-admired U.S. electric utility.

Southern Telecom is formed to provide dark fiber optic and wholesale telecommunications services to businesses in the Southeast.

Southern Energy forms a joint venture with Vastar Resources, creating Southern Company Energy Marketing to offer electricity and natural gas in competitive markets.

Southern LINC has 60,000 wireless units operating in the Southeast.

Although revenues jump nearly 22 percent, Southern Company earnings decline 14 percent; England's windfall-profits tax on SWEB operations reduces earnings by $111 million.

Southern Company's wholesale energy marketing arm in the Southeast, Southern Wholesale Energy, has 4,000 megawatts of generating capacity under contract.

EPA revises the national ambient air-quality standards for ozone and particulate matter, requiring further reductions in NOx emissions at fossil-fuel power plants.

New England Electric becomes the first utility to divest generation assets; ISO New England becomes the first independent system operator for regional transmission grids.

Ed Holland is named president of Savannah Electric upon Gignilliat's retirement.

1998   Southern Company common stock closes the year at $29.06, a new year-end record; dividends are raised to 33.5¢.

The operating companies hold the top five positions in a nationwide survey measuring satisfaction among large customers.

Southern Energy acquires plant assets in New England and announces plans to acquire generating capacity in California, Texas, New York, and Wisconsin.

Southern Company Energy Marketing is the nation's second largest power marketer.

Southern Energy's trading floor operations in Atlanta *GPC Archives*

Clean-coal research facility in Wilsonville *GPC Archives*

To offset carbon dioxide emissions, Southern Company begins researching new clean-coal technologies at its Power Systems Development Facility in Wilsonville, Alabama, and announces a program to plant 20 million trees.

Scottish Power's purchase of Pacificorp becomes the first foreign takeover of a U.S. utility; UK's National Grid announces plans to purchase New England Electric System.

Charles McCrary is named chief production officer and head of the fossil/hydro group with the retirement of Guthrie.

1999

Within a dot.com market bubble, Southern Company stock falls 19 percent, ending the year at $23.50 even though earnings increase more than 30 percent to a record $1.3 billion; the company tries to shore up its stock price by repurchasing 50 million shares.

Southern Energy buys a 9.9 percent interest in China's Shandong International Power Development Company.

Southern Energy sells the power-supply system of SWEB, announces plans to sell its holdings in Argentina and Chile, and files for Chapter 11 on Mobile Energy Services in response to the closing of a pulp mill, its primary customer.

FERC issues rules encouraging utilities to form regional transmission organizations, which Southern Company explores with neighboring utilities for several years.

Southern LINC grows to nearly 200,000 customers.

Through environmental controls and compliance strategies since 1990, Southern Company has reduced its SO_2 emissions by 30 percent and its NOx emissions by 40 percent; it also has reduced, avoided, or offset 33 million metric tons of CO_2 emissions.

EPA initiates a lawsuit against Alabama Power, Georgia Power, and SCS for alleged violations of new source review provisions of the Clean Air Act; the civil action alleges that routine maintenance, repair, and replacement projects conducted at various plants were actually major modifications subject to new source permitting. The action is expanded in 2001 to include Savannah Electric; the lawsuits will be contested for more than a decade.

Franklin becomes president and chief operating officer of Southern Company; Ratcliffe becomes president and CEO of Georgia Power. Upon the retirement of Boren, Marce Fuller becomes president and CEO of Southern Energy. Upon the retirement of DeNicola, Dahlberg assumes the duties of president and CEO of SCS in addition to his role as chairman and CEO of Southern Company.

Georgia Power rates decrease by $262 million January 1; the rate order allows the company to continue accelerating amortization or depreciation of assets and to earn above a 12.5 percent return through an arrangement that shares benefits with customers.

To address one-hour ozone nonattainment, Georgia and Alabama adopt new rules that require additional NOx controls on power plants in the Atlanta and Birmingham areas by 2003.

2000

In April, the board announces a decision to split the company into two businesses: Southern Company will continue as a regulated utility operating in the Southeast, and Southern Energy will spin off as a separate diversified energy company.

A lawsuit alleging race discrimination is filed against Georgia Power, Southern Company, SCS, and Southern Company Energy Solutions.

Plant Dahlberg *SCS Communication Files*

In preparing for the spin-off of Southern Energy, Southern Company completes an initial public offering of 66.7 million shares (19.7 percent) of the new company.

Southern Company's common stock closes the year at a record $33.25, increasing its market value by $7 billion in a single year. The stock boost is aided in part by the bursting of the stock market bubble, which sends investors scurrying to conservative, risk-averse companies.

The first eight combustion turbines at Plant Dahlberg, near Commerce, Georgia, begin commercial operations.

Because DOE has yet to resolve issues for permanently disposing of spent nuclear fuel, a new dry-storage facility is completed at Plant Hatch; a similar facility is under construction at Plant Farley.

The "Y2K Bug" scare is a nonevent; the industry and Southern Company survive through a massive, multiyear reprogramming and computer-patching effort.

Mike McClure (R) managed Southern Company's response to the "Y2K Bug" challenge. *GPC Archives*

The California experiment with retail deregulation is derailed by spiraling energy prices, brownouts, and threats of blackouts; the fiasco will cause other states to pull back in the rush to deregulate retail markets.

The fossil/hydro group is renamed Southern Company Generation.

2001   Southern Company completes the spin-off of Southern Energy—renamed Mirant Corporation—by distributing 272 million shares of Mirant stock to Southern Company shareholders April 2. Mirant's stock soars above $46 within a month.

Allen Franklin becomes chairman, president, and CEO of Southern Company; Dahlberg retires from Southern Company and becomes chairman of Mirant.

Southern Power Company is created as a new subsidiary to own, manage, and finance wholesale generating assets in the Southeast; McCrary becomes president in addition to his role as president of Southern Company Generation. Southern Power has 800 megawatts of capacity at year-end, and the competitive generation business contributes $153 million to system earnings.

Alabama Power wins EEI's Emergency Response Award for power restoration after a severe windstorm.

Southern Company is the highest-rated utility on the American Customer Satisfaction Index.

Units are added at Plant Dahlberg.

In the race-discrimination lawsuit against Georgia Power, Southern Company, SCS, and Southern Company Energy Solutions, a district court ruling denies the plaintiffs' motion for class certification. (The ruling will be reaffirmed three years later by an appeals court judge.)

The September 11 terrorist attacks in New York and Washington, D.C., push the nation into a deeper recession.

In December, Enron declares bankruptcy in the midst of stunning revelations about its accounting tricks; Mirant struggles to stay afloat as Enron's dramatic fall threatens to take down the entire energy-marketing and IPP sector.

McCrary is named president and CEO of Alabama Power upon the retirement of Harris; Paul Bowers becomes president of Southern Company Generation and Southern Power; Mike Garrett is named president and CEO of Mississippi Power upon Evans's move to Southern Company as executive vice president of external affairs; Anthony James becomes president of Savannah Electric upon Holland's move to Southern Company as executive vice president, general counsel, and chief compliance officer; Andy Dearman is named executive vice president and chief transmission officer.

2002

Despite a recession, Southern Company achieves earnings of $1.32 billion, or $1.86 per share. At $20.3 billion, Southern Company ranks tops in market value in the S&P 500 Electric Index.

Southern Company enters the retail gas business in Georgia; Southern Company Gas serves 200,000 customers.

In the new "electric and gas utility" category, Southern Company is rated "America's Most Admired" by *Fortune* for the second consecutive year.

Plant Franklin *SCS Communication Files*

The first unit of Plant Franklin begins operating in Smiths, Alabama; units are added at plants Wansley and Smith.

Mirant begins selling assets in an attempt to shore up its credit ratings and survive the recession and fallout from Enron's collapse; by July, its stock is trading under $4.

In a biomass project, Alabama Power burns switchgrass at Plant Gadsden, which helps the plant reduce emissions.

Tom Fanning is named president of Gulf Power upon Bowden's retirement. Jerry Stewart is named chief production officer.

The Sarbanes-Oxley Act passes Congress in response to a number of corporate failures and scandals; the new law brings about major changes in financial reporting, compliance programs, and corporate-information transparency.

2003   Southern Company earnings reach $1.47 billion; the board increases dividends to 34.25¢ per share.

Construction at Plant Harris *SCS Communication Files*

Southern Power completes two units at Plant Harris, near Autaugaville, Alabama, and begins operations at Plant Stanton, near Orlando, Florida; the additions increase the company's competitive generation capacity to 4,800 megawatts.

In August, more than 50 million people in the Northeast lose power in the nation's worst blackout; Southern Company's transmission personnel take quick action to keep the cascading problem from affecting customers in the Southeast.

Southern Company is rated "America's Most Admired" by *Fortune* for the third consecutive year.

Mirant files for bankruptcy protection under Chapter 11 and begins work on a reorganization plan.

Southern Company spends nearly $1 billion on equipment to reduce NOx emissions as part of the effort to address ozone nonattainment in the Atlanta and Birmingham areas.

Franklin is named the 2003–04 chairman of EEI.

Susan Story is named president of Gulf Power when Fanning becomes Southern Company's chief financial officer.

2004 Quarterly dividend is raised to 35¢ a share.

Hurricane Ivan disrupts service to 1.6 million system customers across four states; service is restored within two weeks to all who are able to safely receive power.

Hurricane Ivan damages at Pensacola Beach *Gulf Power Communication Files*

Southern Company joins NuStart Energy Development, a consortium to demonstrate and test a new licensing process for constructing advanced nuclear power plants.

Georgia Power gets a 4.2 percent rate increase, its first since 1991.

Georgia Power acquires from Southern Power two units under construction at Plant McIntosh; in approving the transfer, the PSC disallows $16 million of the costs, which reduces Southern Company's net income by $9.5 million.

Southern Company pays $39 million in additional taxes and interest related to an IRS audit of Mirant's 2000 and 2001 tax records; the company seeks reimbursement as a creditor in Mirant's Chapter 11 proceedings.

In cooperation with DOE and the Orlando Utilities Commission, Southern Company begins work on a commercial-scale coal-gasification facility in central Florida.

Southern Power completes a third unit at Plant Franklin.

Ratcliffe becomes chairman, president, and CEO of Southern Company upon Franklin's retirement. Garrett becomes president of Georgia Power. Anthony Topazi becomes president of Mississippi Power. Barnie Beasley becomes president and CEO of Southern Nuclear upon Hairston's retirement.

Ratcliffe redefines "Southern Style" into three core values: superior performance, unquestionable trust, and total commitment.

2005

Hurricane Katrina leaves nearly one million Southern Company customers in the dark, two-thirds of them in Alabama. Damage to Mississippi Power reaches historic proportions and disrupts service to all 195,000 of its customers; service is restored in 12 days.

For their response to Hurricane Katrina, Mississippi Power, Alabama Power, and Gulf Power receive EEI Emergency Response awards; Emergency Assistance awards also go to Alabama Power, Georgia Power, and Gulf Power.

Southern LINC is rebranded as SouthernLINC Wireless.

President George W. Bush and Mississippi governor Haley Barbour (R) praised the company's response to Hurricane Katrina.
MPC Communication Files

Hurricane Katrina's damages near Mississippi Power's headquarters
MPC Communication Files

Southern Company sells Southern Company Gas to an affiliate of Cobb EMC.

Quarterly dividend increases to 37.25¢.

Southern Power acquires 680-megawatt Plant Oleander in central Florida.

President George W. Bush signs the Energy Policy Act of 2005, which contains mandatory reliability standards, measures to increase energy efficiency and fuel diversity, and incentives for nuclear power developments. The act also repeals the Public Utility Holding Company Act of 1935 but gives FERC greater authority to protect consumers and prevent utility-market manipulations.

Alabama Power receives a favorable ruling from a federal district court in Birmingham in EPA's lawsuit related to alleged new source review violations; the following year, Alabama Power and EPA reach a settlement on claims involving Plant Miller. (A similar case against Georgia Power and Savannah Electric has been administratively closed since 2001.)

Southern Company joins the FutureGen Industrial Alliance, a national effort to develop the first near-zero-emissions coal plant.

Legal matters related to the race-discrimination lawsuit against Georgia Power, Southern Company, SCS, and Southern Company Energy Solutions come to a close October 17 when the U.S. Supreme Court declines to hear an appeal by plaintiffs.

Southern Company begins a ten-year, $6 billion environmental program that will reduce SO_2, NOx, and mercury emissions 70 percent below current levels. Gulf Power constructs the nation's first comprehensive mercury research center at Plant Crist.

Mercury research facility at Plant Crist *Gulf Power Communication Files*

In bankruptcy court, Mirant's creditors file a complaint against Southern Company and seek monetary damages in excess of $2 billion for alleged actions that forced Mirant to breach its fiduciary duties to creditors; Southern Company files a response denying the charges and prepares to defend the fairness of its actions in court.

Ronnie Bates is named president and CEO of Southern Power.

2006

Savannah Electric merges with Georgia Power July 1.

Southern Nuclear files for an early site permit for two new units at Plant Vogtle, a preliminary step in the NRC's evaluation of proposals to build new nuclear plants.

Southern Power buys generating capacity at Progress Energy facilities in Arcadia, Florida, and Salisbury, North Carolina; with the acquisitions, Southern Power has 6,700 megawatts of competitive generation.

Complying with a proposed FERC agreement, Southern Company splits its competitive generation business into two segments: Southern Power continues to own and operate generating units that supply energy in competitive markets, while wholesale power sales from operating company units are incorporated into the system's traditional business.

The system sets four peak records over eight summer days; the highest is on August 10 at 38,056 megawatts.

The quarterly dividend is raised to 38.75¢ a share.

Mirant emerges from Chapter 11 under new management and is re-listed on the New York Stock Exchange; Mirant's complaint against Southern Company is transferred from a district court in Texas to the Northern District court in Georgia.

2007

Taking another step toward building two new nuclear units at Plant Vogtle, Southern Nuclear files an application with the NRC for a combined construction and operating license on behalf of the plant's co-owners.

Peak demand records are set on five consecutive days, reaching 40,870 megawatts on August 22.

Plant Vogtle *GPC Archives*

Southern Company's quarterly dividend rate moves up to 40.25¢ per share.

Uncertainties about new Florida regulations on carbon emissions cause Southern Power to cancel plans to build a 285-megawatt, integrated gasification combined cycle (IGCC) plant near Orlando.

EPA's new source review lawsuit against Alabama Power is returned to district court for further consideration following an appeal of the district court decision and a U.S. Supreme Court ruling in a similar case against Duke Power.

2008

Southern Company begins work on one of the nation's first carbon capture and sequestration projects at Mississippi Power's Plant Daniel.

Fanning becomes chief operating officer with responsibility for non-nuclear generation, transmission, and research and environmental affairs. Bowers replaces Fanning as CFO. C. Alan Martin is named president and CEO of Southern Company Services, with responsibility for SouthernLINC Wireless in addition to various service company functions.

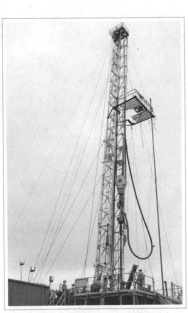

A Georgia Power base-rate increase of $99.7 million goes into effect, as does a special tariff of $222 million to recover costs related to environmental compliance.

Carbon storage testing near Plant Daniel
MPC Communication Files

System operating companies begin installing advanced metering equipment that will automate readings, provide customers and the companies with comprehensive data, and speed power restoration. Southern Company plans to install 4.5 million "smart meters" by 2012.

Southern Company raises its quarterly dividend rate to 42¢ per share.

Ratcliffe becomes the 2008–09 chairman of EEI.

James H. "Jim" Miller III is named president and CEO of Southern Nuclear upon Beasley's retirement.

For the ninth consecutive year, Southern Company is rated the nation's top energy utility in the American Customer Satisfaction Index.

In what will become the most challenging economic recession since World War II, stock prices plummet. Initially, the Southeast is impacted less than the rest of the nation.

2009

Industrial sales fall 11.8 percent as the economic recession continues throughout 2009. Despite the challenges, Southern Company contains costs to report earnings of $1.65 billion, or $2.07 a share, compared with 2008 earnings of $1.74 billion, or $2.26 a share. Southern Company's common stock closes the year at $33.32.

Mississippi Power announces plans to build a 582-megawatt IGCC plant in Kemper County, Mississippi; the new design and carbon capture technology could reduce carbon emissions by 65 percent; the plant is later named Plant Ratcliffe.

Southern Company raises its quarterly dividend to 43.75¢ per share.

DOE selects Southern Company to manage and operate its National Carbon Capture Center at Wilsonville, Alabama, to test various technologies for capturing carbon dioxide from coal plants.

An energy company in China is the first to implement a commercial application of TRIG—Transport Integrated Gasification—a clean-coal technology Southern Company helped develop.

The NRC awards an early site permit for Vogtle units 3 and 4. The permit is part of a streamlined licensing process to reduce regulatory uncertainty and resolve many safety and environmental issues related to nuclear construction.

Southern Power breaks ground on a 720-megawatt, gas-fueled plant near Grover, North Carolina, and on a 100-megawatt biomass plant near Austin, Texas. The subsidiary also buys the West Georgia Generating Company, a 600-megawatt facility near Thomaston, Georgia.

As part of President Barack Obama's economic-stimulus program, Southern Company is awarded $165 million to invest in its smart energy grid program.

2010

Southern Company makes international headlines when President Obama announces that DOE nuclear loan guarantees will be awarded to the first new nuclear power units to be built in the U.S. in more than thirty years. The conditional commitments are to be applied to future borrowings related to construction at Plant Vogtle.

More than 500,000 photovoltaic modules are installed at Southern Company's Cimarron Solar Facility. *First Solar*

On January 6, Southern Company sets its third all-time winter peak of the week. At 37,224 megawatts, the new peak even surpasses the summer peak of 2009.

In conjunction with Turner Renewable Energy and First Solar Incorporated, Southern Company builds one of the nation's largest solar power projects, a 30-megawatt photovoltaic plant in New Mexico.

Southern Company raises its quarterly dividend to 45.50¢ per share.

Tom Fanning becomes president of Southern Company August 1 and chairman and CEO upon Ratcliffe's retirement December 1. Anthony Topazi becomes chief operating officer, and Ed Day replaces him as president of Mississippi Power. Art Beattie becomes Southern Company chief financial officer, replacing Paul Bowers, who becomes chief operating officer, then president and CEO of Georgia Power upon Garrett's retirement. Susan Story is named president and CEO of SCS, and Mark A. Crosswhite replaces her as president and CEO of Gulf Power.

In September, EPA dismisses five of its eight remaining claims in its new source review lawsuit against Alabama Power. (All remaining claims are dismissed by a federal judge in March 2011.)

William O. (Billy) Ball becomes chief transmission officer of Southern Company upon Dearman's retirement. Oscar C. Harper is named president and CEO of Southern Power upon Bates's retirement. Doug Jones becomes Southern Company's chief production officer upon Stewart's retirement.

SOUTHERN COMPANY GROWTH: VITAL STATISTICS

	1950	1960	1970	1980	1990	2000	2010
Assets ($ in millions)	148	1,707	3,098	11,467	19,955	31,362	55,032
Revenues ($ in millions)	136	319	738	3,763	8,053	10,066	17,456
Net Income ($ in millions)	16.3	46.1	100.7	344	822[∞]	1,313[‡]	1,975
Earnings Per Share (in dollars)	1.06	2.06	1.94	2.23	2.60[∞]	2.01[‡]	2.37
Dividends Per Share (in dollars)	0.80	1.40	1.215	1.56	1.07	1.34	1.8025
Stock Price (in dollars)	11.375	48	26.25*	12.25	13.85	33.25*	38.23
Capacity (in megawatts)	1,904	4,778	10,883	23,223	29,532	32,807	42,963
Peak Demand (in millions of kw)	N/A	4.76	11.82	19.55	26	31.4	35.59
Sales (in billions of kwh)	9.5	22.8	57.5	92.5	145	177	197
Customers (in thousands)	1,049	1,576	2,037	2,565	3,283	3,944	4,417
Stockholders (in thousands)	98.8	122	109	345	263	160	160
Employees (in thousands)	9.9	13	16	27.9	30.3	26	25.9
3-Year Construction Budget ($ in millions)	243	454	2,000	4,200	3,400	10,700	13,796
Average Rates (¢/kwh)	1.38	1.38	1.25	4.04	5.47	5.42	8.53
Residential Rates (¢/kwh)	2.29	1.96	1.69	4.81	7.07	7.29	10.93

* Stock split 2-for-1 in 1966 and 1994

∞ Following a write-off that year, earnings were $604 million, or $1.91 per share.

‡ In anticipation of Mirant's spin-off, earnings of continuing operations were reported at $944 million, or $1.52 per share.

SOUTHERN COMPANY DIRECTORS

Gloster B. Aaron	1/26/46 – 10/9/46	Dan MacDougald	11/18/47 – 4/13/53
Donald H. Aiken	1/26/46 – 10/9/46	Robert T. Jones Jr.	5/11/48 – 12/18/71
Eduardo Andrade	1/26/46 – 10/9/46	L. P. Sweatt	3/22/49 – 5/23/62
Preston S. Arkwright	10/9/46 – 12/2/46	C. B. McManus	6/29/49 – 5/23/62
E. L. Godshalk	10/9/46 – 9/22/47	Gordon D. Palmer	10/27/49 – 7/11/56
Jacob Hekma	10/9/46 – 2/17/49	James F. Crist	10/27/49 – 1/1/66
G. H. Bourne	10/9/46 – 10/27/49	Earl M. McGowin	1/22/51 – 11/18/71
Justin R. Whiting	10/9/46 –10/27/49	J. M. Barry	8/22/52 – 5/23/62
Pearson Winslow	10/9/46 – 12/13/50	Harllee Branch Jr.	5/27/53 – 7/1/71
Percy H. Clark	10/9/46 – 7/22/57	H. J. Scholz	5/26/54 – 1/16/61
E. A. Yates	10/9/46 – 10/5/57	Leo W. Seal	5/26/54 – 5/22/63
Beauchamp E. Smith	10/9/46 – 1/20/64	James V. Carmichael	5/26/54 – 11/28/72
W. H. Brantley Jr.	10/9/46 – 6/19/64	M. G. Nelson	5/26/54 – 1/20/75
Thomas W. Martin	10/9/46 – 12/8/64	Peyton T. Anderson	5/26/54 – 4/9/77
W. E. Mitchell	1/14/47 – 5/28/47	Alfred M. Shook III	7/23/56 – 5/9/77
Preston S. Arkwright Jr.	5/28/47 – 11/6/47	John J. McDonough	7/22/57 – 2/1/66

L. T. Smith Jr.	10/28/57 – 5/23/62	Herbert Stockham	4/17/78 – 5/26/99
E. C. Gaston	1/16/61 – 12/1/67	Alan R. Barton	1/1/82 – 5/24/89
R. L. Pulley	5/23/62 – 11/1/66	Douglas L. McCrary	11/1/83 – 5/22/91
A. J. Watson Jr.	5/23/62 – 9/1/73	Charles H. Chapman Jr.	1/16/84 – 4/17/90
Alvin W. Vogtle Jr.	5/23/62 – 11/1/83	Gloria M. Shatto	1/16/84 – 6/13/99
W. C. Vereen Jr.	5/23/62 – 12/8/83	A. W. Dahlberg III	1/21/85 – 4/1/01
J. D. Lewis	5/22/63 – 4/14/72	William J. Cabaniss Jr.	3/6/85 – 11/15/88
Joseph L. Lanier	4/20/64 – 4/18/68	Earl D. McLean Jr.	5/10/85 – 5/24/95
Walter Bouldin	7/20/64 – 8/1/70	L. G. Hardman III	3/14/86 – 9/13/03
Edwin I. Hatch	4/19/65 – 4/1/78	Vincent J. Whibbs Sr.	4/23/86 – 3/9/92
Leonard H. Jaeger	1/17/66 – 11/1/70	Virginia A. Dwyer	9/17/86 – 3/9/92
Clyde A. Lilly Jr.	4/18/66 – 4/28/77	William P. Copenhaver	9/17/86 – 5/24/95
Robert H. Radcliff Jr.	11/1/66 – 11/14/87	Jack Edwards	11/14/87 – 5/26/99
William R. Brownlee	1/15/68 – 1/1/71	Arthur M. Gignilliat Jr.	4/18/88 – 5/22/91
William J. Cabaniss	5/21/68 – 5/24/72	John M. McIntosh	4/18/88 – 5/25/94
Joseph M. Farley	8/1/70 – 10/31/92	H. Allen Franklin	7/18/88 – 6/30/04
Robert F. Ellis, Jr.	11/1/70 – 3/20/78	Elmer B. Harris	3/1/89 – 1/11/02
William S. Morris III	1/18/71 – 9/19/85	Paul J. DeNicola	7/17/89 – 5/26/99
William J. Rushton III	7/19/71 – 5/26/99	Louis J. Willie	3/11/91 – 5/25/94
William W. McTyeire Jr.	1/17/72 – 9/6/83	Alston D. Correll	5/25/94 – 9/22/00
A. F. Dantzler	4/17/72 – 5/9/85	Bruce S. Gordon	10/17/94 – 2/21/06
H. G. Pattillo	4/17/72 – 5/26/93	John C. Adams	5/24/95 – 5/26/99
Frank P. Samford Jr.	5/24/72 – 3/5/85	Gerald J. St. Pe'	5/24/95 – 5/26/10
H. H. Callaway	1/15/73 – 5/14/73	Zack T. Pate	5/27/98 – 5/23/07
William A. Parker Jr.	5/23/73 – 5/27/98	David J. Lesar	5/26/99 – 9/22/00
Victor J. Daniel Jr.	9/1/73 – 12/31/81	Dorrit J. Bern	5/26/99 – 7/21/08
Crawford Rainwater	3/11/75 – 4/23/86	Thomas F. Chapman	5/26/99 – 5/26/10
John W. Langdale	4/18/77 – 2/8/87	Donald M. James	12/13/99 – Present
William B. Reed	5/25/77 – 6/8/84	Daniel P. Amos	10/16/00 – 2/21/06
Robert W. Scherer	5/25/77 – 5/24/89	J. Neal Purcell	2/17/03 – Present
Edward L. Addison	4/17/78 – 2/28/95	David M. Ratcliffe	12/8/03 – 11/30/10

Francis S. Blake	5/26/04 – 10/7/09
Juanita Powell Baranco	2/21/06 – Present
William G. Smith Jr.	2/22/06 – Present
H. William Habermeyer Jr.	2/20/07 – Present
Jon A. Boscia	12/7/07 – Present
Warren A. Hood Jr.	12/7/07 – Present
Veronica M. Hagen	12/8/08 – Present
Henry A. Clark III	10/19/09 – Present
Larry D. Thompson	5/26/10 – Present
Dale E. Klein	7/19/10 – Present
Steven R. Specker	10/18/10 – Present
Thomas A. Fanning	12/1/10 – Present

Spanning nearly a century of power and innovation: Construction crews erected a transmission tower in Alabama in 1918 using only manpower and mule power; while, at right, line crews used the latest tools and technology in the twenty-first century to restore power to customers in record time following storms.
APC Archives, Gulf Power Communication Files

THIS BOOK WAS BORN AS AN IDEA OF TWO Southern Company leaders, Allen Franklin and Tom Fanning, who identified the need to record the landmark decisions, events, and developments that led to Southern Company's formation as well as the lessons learned as it evolved into the company it is today. The project was tabled for several years because of financial considerations but was reactivated in late 2010 by Fanning. Its publication in 2011 marks the one hundredth anniversary of James Mitchell's first "big bet" for Southern Company.

The authors are indebted to two other former Southern Company CEOs who understood the importance of the company's history and took steps to preserve it. In 1999, Bill Dahlberg initiated the Southern Company Oral History Project to videotape interviews with eighteen retired executives of Southern Company and its subsidiaries. Observations and perspectives from these interviews were used extensively in several chapters. Additionally, in 1982, Harllee Branch Jr. came out of retirement to research key dates in the company's history and record his memories of its early leaders. Branch's notes were passed on to the authors twenty years ago by John

Vezeau, an employee who worked with Branch on that first "corporate history project." At the time, neither Vezeau nor the authors knew they would be undertaking this book years later.

Successful completion of the project was enabled by the support of Dave Altman and Carrie Kurlander, the former and current corporate communication vice presidents of Southern Company, who allocated the resources necessary to research, write, and produce the book and provided direction and encouragement to the authors.

In producing the book, we were fortunate to have the services of Jim and Mary-Frances Burt, a design team based in Macon, Georgia, who have extensive experience in the book publishing industry. Burt&Burt Studio produced a high-quality design, provided valuable counsel during the production process, and coordinated innumerable details under very tight schedules.

A great debt is also due Leah Rawls Atkins—noted Alabama historian and author of *Developed for the Service of Alabama—The Centennial History of Alabama Power Company, 1906–2006*. Atkins provided advice to the authors and often acted as a consultant during research. She also edited the *Big Bets* manuscript and provided suggestions on the draft.

Special thanks goes to Elena Mappus, who was invaluable in the final stages of production, coordinating proofreading support, overseeing indexing services, and orchestrating many project management details needed to transform the finished manuscript into a book.

We also would like to recognize the contributions of Ken Willis, an Atlanta communications consultant, who provided research and writing support in 2005 on the Harllee Branch era. Portions of his draft were used in chapters 7 and 8.

During the research process, invaluable assistance was provided by Alabama Power archivist Bill Tharpe and Georgia Power archivist Margaret Calhoon. They pulled boxes of files, publications, correspondence, and other historical records and located numerous images used in the book. At the Georgia Power archives, the authors were aided by Jim Huddelston, who shared his knowledge of the company's early leaders; Brandi Williams, who offered her photographic expertise; Lynn Speno, who shared her draft biography on Henry Atkinson; and Ann Foskey, who scanned images and located files.

Important records also were located by various records management and corporate communication organizations. We appreciate the assistance of Gail

Ann McCreary and Tammy Frierson at Mississippi Power and Laura Bolt and Jamie Suber at Georgia Power. At Gulf Power, John Hutchinson and Scott Harrington made available historical documents. And Swann Seiler and John Kraft provided help in locating records on Savannah Electric.

Photographic searches and scans were provided by a number of individuals. In addition to those already mentioned, we would like to thank Billy Dugger at Mississippi Power; Jim Conway at Gulf Power; Rick Ward, Christina Wedge, and Sarah Dorio at Georgia Power; and Vicki Gardocki, Matt Carmack, and Jennifer Higgins at Southern Company.

Many other company associates assisted the authors. DeWitt Rogers at Troutman Sanders provided a legal and editorial review of the manuscript. Teresa Taylor at Mississippi Power was helpful in researching Hurricane Camille. Yvette Camp spent several days pulling newspaper articles for the authors from the files of the *Atlanta Journal-Constitution*, where she was assisted by archivist Richard Hallman.

We'd like to thank certain personnel at various industry, academic, and public libraries, including Susan Farkas at the Edison Electric Institute; Janine D'Addario and Luis Acosta at the Library of Congress; Meg Nakahara at the NBC News archives; Louise Huddleston at University of North Alabama's Collier Library; Pat Bernard Ezzell at the Tennessee Valley Authority; Bill Clifton and Robyn A. Minorof of the Pensacola Historical Society; and Maurella Power at the Biloxi Public Library.

We also want to thank Pat Heys for her constant support and her exceptional proofreading skills. During the review and editing process, Anna Weinstein and Bob Giles provided copyediting expertise. Chuck Chandler, Beverly O'Shea, Gayle Peeples, Betty Bell, Kathy Roberts, Charon Clymer, Carla Caldwell, and Victoria Vogt provided proofreading support. Jennifer Nichols checked many of the facts in the timeline and proofread the book. And in the final proofreading stage, the authors enlisted the eyes of numerous communication colleagues, including Jo Alice Driggers, Jim Barber, Mark Williams, Terri Cohilas, Kirk Martin, Barry Inman, Katherine Thompson, Lee Birdsong, Lynnmarie Cook, Amy Fink, Amoi Geter, Jeannice Hall, Lori Kasserman, Margaret White, and Lynn Williams. Exceptional administrative support was provided at various stages of the project by Janice Tomasello, Prakhara Harter, Alice Patterson, Donna Barron, Jillian Bowen, Earline Adams, and Jamille Chinnis. And finally, we thank Bob Land for helping us bring the project to an end with his indexing skills.

Long coal haul: To meet environmental regulations, Southern Company began transporting low-sulfur coal from mines in Colorado and Utah in 1978. *GPC Archives*

ENDNOTES

ABBREVIATIONS USED IN ENDNOTES

ABC	Atlanta Business Chronicle
AC	The Atlanta Constitution
AG	The Atlanta Georgian
AJ	The Atlanta Journal
AJC	The Atlanta Journal-Constitution
APC	Alabama Power Company
BAH	The Birmingham Age-Herald
BN	The Birmingham News
BPH	Birmingham Post-Herald
C&S	Commonwealth & Southern Corporation
EEI	Edison Electric Institute
GPC	Georgia Power Company
MPC	Mississippi Power Company
MS	Manuscript
NYHT	New York Herald-Tribune
NYT	The New York Times
PJ	The Pensacola Journal
PNJ	Pensacola News Journal
SCHC	Southern Company History Collection
SCOHC	Southern Company Oral History Collection
SCS	Southern Company Services
SMN	Savannah Morning News
SoCo	Southern Company or The Southern Company
SPL	Southeastern Power & Light
WP	The Washington Post
WSJ	The Wall Street Journal

Company annual reports and newsletters referenced in the endnotes are located in the archives and corporate communication files of Southern Company and its subsidiaries. The employee publications include: Alabama Power, *Powergrams;* Georgia Power, *Snap Shots, Bright Spots, Round the House, Citizen, This Week,* and *The Citizen;* Gulf Power, *Gulf Currents* and *Contemporary;* Mississippi Power, *Power Lines/Powerlines* and *Dialogue;* and Southern Company, *Southern Highlights, Highlights,* and *Inside.*

PROLOGUE

vii description of Cherokee Bluffs: Harvey H. Jackson III, *Putting Loafing Streams To Work: The Building of Lay, Mitchell, Martin, and Jordan Dams, 1910–1929* (Tuscaloosa, 1997), 117 [hereafter cited as Jackson, *Loafing Streams*]

viii construction challenge: Thomas W. Martin, "Remarks at Martin Dam Dedication," November 7, 1925, reprinted in *Laying of the Cornerstone and Dedication of Martin Dam* (APC brochure, 1925), 55–56 [hereafter cited as *Cornerstone and Dedication*]

viii Mitchell's sacrifice: Thomas W. Martin, "Address at Dedication of Mitchell Dam," December 19, 1921 (APC brochure, 1921); John R. Hornady, *Soldiers of Progress and Industry* (New York, 1930), 67–69 [hereafter cited as Hornady, *Soldiers*]

CHAPTER 1

1 "He was a man...": "Henry C. Jones, Power Pioneer," *Powergrams* (December 1925), 16

1 "Electrified...": W. P. Lay, untitled tribute to Mitchell, *Powergrams* (September 1920), 12

1 Brady: Obituary of Paul T. Brady, *NYT*, May 10, 1928

1–2 Mitchell to Alabama: Thomas W. Martin, *The Story of Electricity in Alabama Since the Turn of the Century* (Birmingham, 1952), 23–24, 28 [hereafter cited as Martin, *Story of Electricity*]; W. E. Mitchell, *James Mitchell, an Industrial Pioneer*, APC brochure, 1930, 6 [hereafter cited as Mitchell, *Industrial Pioneer*]

2 Progressive era: Richard C. Wade, "Expanding Resources 1901–1945," in *The Almanac of American History*, ed., Arthur M. Schlesinger, Jr. (New York, 1993), 400–401 [Wade's essay hereafter cited as Wade, "Expanding Resources"; historical event and date references from almanac listings cited as Schlesinger, *Almanac*]

2 "I had sought...": "Henry C. Jones..." 16

2–3 background on Jones: Ibid., 13–16; Martin, *Story of Electricity*, 16

3 "stupendous..." and Mitchell's response to bluffs: "Henry C. Jones..." 16; Henry Jones, untitled tribute to Mitchell, *Powergrams* (September 1920), 14, 17

3 Washburn/Jones plans: Martin, *Story of Electricity*, 19–21

3 role of Massey Wilson: Thomas W. Martin, *Address to Joint Session of Alabama Legislature*, Montgomery, August 11, 1961

3 Wilson moved out of state: Leah Rawls Atkins, *Developed for the Service of Alabama: The Centennial History of the Alabama Power Company, 1906–2006* (Birmingham, 2006), 25 [hereafter cited as Atkins, *Centennial History of Alabama Power*]

3 "pleasant and...": Martin, *Story of Electricity*, 25

3 incentives for developers: Ibid., 22–23, 25

4 economic problems in the South: Thomas W. Martin, *Forty Years of Alabama Power Company* (Birmingham, 1952), 10–12 [hereafter cited as Martin, *Forty Years*]

4 Lay's background: Hornady, *Soldiers*, 31–44, 57–67; Milford W. Howard, "Tribute Paid to River Developer," *BN*, May 19, 1929; *In Honor of William Patrick Lay* [brochure produced for dedication of Lock 12, November 23, 1929]

4 "anywhere..." and "it would all...": W. P. Lay, "The Story of the Early Days of the Alabama Power Company" (undated report in APC Archives)

4 "Well do I...": Lay's untitled tribute, *Powergrams* (September 1920), 12

4–5 Washburn's interest in Muscle Shoals: Martin, *Story of Electricity*, 21; William M. Murray Jr., *Thomas W. Martin: A Biography* (Birmingham, 1978), 48–49 [hereafter cited as Murray, *Martin Biography*]

5 fifteen groups: Thomas W. Martin, *Statement Before Alabama Legislative Joint Committee Investigating Public Utility Companies*, Montgomery, May 20, 1931.

5 "Some of these..." (Martin observations attributed to Mitchell): Ibid.; Martin, *Story of Electricity*, 29

5 "the most satisfactory...": James Mitchell, "Alabama Traction, Light & Power Company, Limited," (undated report, ca. 1912), APC Archives [hereafter cited as Mitchell, "Alabama Traction"]

5 plan in form of map: Richard A. Peacock, "The Southern Company," working paper, April 8, 1966, APC Archives [hereafter cited as Peacock MS]; Harllee Branch Jr., *Alabama Power Company and The Southern Company*, (New York, 1967), 7

5 "There is no record...": Martin, *Story of Electricity*, 29

6–8 Mitchell's many careers: unless otherwise noted, compiled from "An Autobiography of James Mitchell," *Powergrams* (September 1920), 1–2, 28; Editorial, *Powergrams* (September 1920), 3, 12; Mitchell, *Industrial Pioneer*, 1–11; Martin, *Forty Years*, 14–15; Martin, *Story of Electricity*, 25–28; Murray, *Martin Biography*, 29–31

6 "how one red...": Mitchell, *Industrial Pioneer*, 3

6 "He was always...": W. N. Walmsley, "Cherished Memories of Pioneer Days with Mr. Mitchell," *Powergrams* (September 1920), 5 [hereafter cited as Walmsley, "Cherished Memories"]

7 "indefatigable worker...": Mitchell, *Industrial Pioneer*, 4–5

7 "one of the great...": Ibid., 6

7 "A super amount...": Hugh L. Cooper, untitled tribute to Mitchell, *Powergrams* (September 1920), 8 [hereafter cited as Cooper tribute]

7 Pearson: Gil Cooke, "An Extreme Power Engineer," *IEE Power & Energy* (November/December 2003), 60–65

7 "I've wanted...": Walmsley, "Cherished Memories," 6

7 Sir Edward Mackay Edgar: "Edgar05," News Letter Number Five, Society of Edgar Families (Melbourne), users.chariot.net.au/~tucker/hope/edgar051.htm

8 "sun in the financial solar system": Ron Chernow, *The House of Morgan, An American Banking Dynasty and the Rise of Modern Finance*, (New York, 1990), 3 [hereafter cited as Chernow, *House of Morgan*]

8–9 marketing the company to Sperling: unless otherwise noted, discussion based on prospectus and letters, including Mitchell, "Alabama Traction"; James Mitchell to Messrs. Sperling and Company, January 10, 1912, APC Archives; Sperling and Company to Clients, January 10, 1912, APC Archives

8 "an exceptionally...": Murray, *Martin Biography*, 35

9 "most trustworthy...": Sir E. Mackay Edgar , untitled tribute to Mitchell, *Powergrams* (September 1920), 7

9 "attacked the complicated problems...": Lawrence Macfarlane, untitled tribute to Mitchell, *Powergrams* (September 1920), 7

9 bonds bought by English investors: Philip H. Willkie, "The Story of the Commonwealth & Southern" (senior thesis, Princeton University, 1940), 38 [hereafter cited as Willkie MS]

9–10 background on Mitchell's team: "Our New General Manager," *Powergrams* (January 1923), 3; "A Brief History of Our Chief Engineer," *Powergrams* (October 1920), 3; "A Little Chat About Our Assistant General Manager," *Powergrams* (August 1920), 3; "A. C. Polk, Construction Manager," *Powergrams* (December 1921), 7, 32; W. W. Freeman to James Mitchell, July 2, 1912,

APC Archives; Martin, *Story of Electricity*, 32, 98, 166, 175-176; B. C. Forbes, "Mitchell, the Man Who Saves Millions for Investors," *Forbes* (June 15, 1925), 315–318

10–11 Electric Bond & Share: Douglas W. Hawes, *Utility Holding Companies*, (New York: 1987), 2.5–2.7 [hereafter cited as Hawes, *Utility Holding Companies*]

11 S. Z. Mitchell's partners: Federal Trade Commission, *Utility Corporations*, 70th Congress, 1st Session, 1931, S. Doc. 92, Part 30, 41

11 competitive move by Bonbright: Atkins, *Centennial History of Alabama Power*, 31–32; R. H. Mangum, "History of SPL," (working paper, ca. 1930, APC Archives), 70–71 [hereafter cited as Mangum MS. Several versions exist; the draft referenced appears in file No. 1.1.1.71.41]

11 "handsome, if not extravagant": Lawrence Macfarlane to Thomas W. Martin, December 18, 1912, APC Archives

11 stock swap and Mitchell properties: Martin, *Story of Electricity*, 31–32 [Included in the Mitchell brothers' holdings were the Alabama Power Development _Company, Anniston Electric & Gas Company, Decatur Light Power and Fuel Company, Huntsville Railway, Light, & Power Company, Alabama Power and Light Company, Little River Power Company, Etowah Light & Power Company, and Asbury Electric Power Company.]

11 "I now commit…": Ibid., 31

11 "To make money…": Ibid.

12 "Within 20 years…": Ibid., 33; *Cornerstone and Dedication*, 52

12 "What a dream…": Martin, *Story of Electricity*, 33

12 buying land and Nora Miller's help: "Mrs. Nora E. Miller, Mother of Cherokee Bluffs, Passes," *Powergrams* (August 1924), 4–5; Martin, *Story of Electricity*, 68

12 trouble with Benjamin Russell: Charles H. Baker to Tyson, Wilson, & Martin, December 4, 1911, and Thomas W. Martin to Charles H. Baker, December 30, 1911, APC Archives

12 "While perfect strangers…": Benjamin Russell, untitled tribute to Mitchell, *Powergrams* (September 1920), 12

13 restraining orders: Eugene A. Yates, "Preliminary Report on Coosa and Tallapoosa Developments," July 2, 1912, APC Archives

13 one-third the cost: Sperling and Company to Clients, January 10, 1912, Mitchell Correspondence Files, APC Archives

13 Martin and Macfarlane reviewed laws: Mangum MS, 63–64

13–15 building the first dam: unless otherwise noted, Lock 12 construction is summarized from Jackson, *Loafing Streams*, 14–36

14 statistics on sand, cement, rocks: James Mitchell, *Memorandum Relating to Water Power Developments of Alabama Power Company* (Birmingham, 1914), APC Archives

14 "Liquidation in all lines…": James Mitchell to W. W. Freeman, June 6, 1913, APC Archives

14 appeal to S. Z.: James Mitchell to W. W. Freeman, June 10, 1913, and W. W. Freeman to James Mitchell, June 11, 1913, and July 16, 1913, APC Archives

14 "Defer unnecessary…": Mitchell to Freeman, June 6, 1913

15 $300,000 over budget: Frank Washburn to James Mitchell, December 20, 1913, APC Archives

15 "It is perfectly…": James Mitchell, "General Criticism Arising from My Recent Visits to Lock No. Twelve," December 30, 1913, APC Archives

15 "unusual degree…": James Mitchell to Frank Washburn, January 31, 1914, APC Archives

16 "octopus," "water power trusts": "Do Not Let the New Octopus Monster Grab the Inexhaustible Store of White Coal in Our Southern States," *Southern Farming*, January 4, 1913; Murray, *Martin Biography*, 46

16 ten groups and GE pawn: Hubert Bruce Fuller, "The Water-Power War," *The World's Work*, December 1913, 199–200

16 "I think this is…": *Veto Message Relating to the Building of a Dam Across the Coosa River, Ala.*, 62nd Congress, 2nd Session, 1912, S. Doc. 949, 1–2

16 "The secretary…": J. W. Worthington to James Mitchell, January 19, 1913, Alabama U.S. Congress Senators Correspondence Files, APC Archives

16 nitrates plant in Canada: J. W. Worthington to James Mitchell, November 7, 1912, and November 28, 1912, APC Archives; "Food Supply Chief Concern: Five Thousand People Listen to Address by Mr. Frank S. Washburn," *Nashville Banner*, November 24, 1913

17–18 mosquito lawsuits and role of Gorgas: Martin, *Forty Years*, 20–21; Benjamin Russell, "Remarks at Martin Dam Dedication," November 7, 1925, *Cornerstone and Dedication*, 40–41

18 "The new reservoir…": Martin, *Story of Electricity*, 46–47

18–19 financial crisis: unless referenced, summarized from Martin, *Story of Electricity*, 42–45; Alabama Traction, Light & Power Company, *Second Annual Report* (Montreal, June 22, 1915), 2, and *Fifth Annual Report* (Montreal, June 1, 1918), 1–3

18 "We realized…" (paraphrased): Martin, *Story of Electricity*, 44

19 "We are under…": James Mitchell to L. A. Osborne, Vice President, Westinghouse Electric, April 20, 1915, APC Archives

19 "We couldn't possibly…": B. C. Forbes, editor, *America's Fifty Foremost Business Leaders* (New York, 1948), 313 [hereafter cited as Forbes, *America's Fifty*]

19 "forever indebted…": Martin, *Story of Electricity*, 45

20 first customers: Ibid., 35–36

20 "The getting of new…": Alabama Traction, Light & Power Company, *First Annual Report: 1913* (Montreal, May 15, 1914), 3

20 Theodore Swann: Willkie MS, 41–42

20 difficulty with Birmingham Railway: Murray, *Martin Biography*, 38; Mitchell, "Alabama Traction"; James Mitchell to Frank Washburn, January 14, 1914, APC Archives; W. W. Freeman to James Mitchell, July 16, 1913, APC Archives; "Friel Prepares to File Complaint

on UG&E Activity," *BN*, February 16, 1914; "Friel Complains of Power Monopoly in this District," *BAH*, February 16, 1914

20 Anniston Steel and other industries: J. J. Willitt, "Some of my Recollections of James Mitchell," *Powergrams* (September 1920), 14; Willkie MS, 49; James Mitchell to W. N. Walmsley, August 15, 1916, APC Archives

21 money problems during war: James Mitchell to W. N. Walmsley, May 2, June 22, June 23, June 25, and October 23, 1917, and James Mitchell to Thomas W. Martin, July 26 and October 5, 1917, APC Archives

21 coal famine and purchase of coal lands: Martin, *Story of Electricity*, 54–55; Mangum MS, 101

21 discussions with Atkinson: James Mitchell to Thomas W. Martin, October 10, 1917, and James Mitchell to W. N. Walmsley, December 20, 1918, APC Archives; Thomas W. Martin to W. N. Walmsley, October 13, 1917, APC Archives

22 Mitchell's views, plans, and surveys of Muscle Shoals: Mitchell, "Alabama Traction"; "A Condensed History of Muscle Shoals," *Powergrams* (March 1922), 1–2

22 "The proposed combination…": Thurlow to Eugene Underwood, November 29, 1913, APC Archives

23 "condemn the property" and valuation: Thomas W. Martin, "Memorandum of interview between Col. Charles Keller and Messrs. James Mitchell and Thos. W. Martin at Col. Keller's office in the War Department," February 14, 1918, APC Archives

23 "In times like these…," assets donated, "any surplus power…": James Mitchell to Col. Charles Keller, Corps of Engineers, February 18, 1918, APC Archives; Murray, *Martin Biography*, 48–50

23 "generous and…": "An Appreciation of Patriotism," *Powergrams* (May 1921), 12–13

23 construction at Muscle Shoals: George W. Norris, "Shall We Give Muscle Shoals to Henry Ford?" *Saturday Evening Post*, May 24, 1934, 30–31

23 Warrior unit expansion and contract: J. S. Sutherland, "The Story of Gorgas," *Powergrams* (April 1922), 12–13; Alabama Traction, Light & Power, *Fifth Annual Report of the Board of Directors* (Montreal, June 1, 1918), 3–4; Martin, *Story of Electricity*, 101–102

24 first ammonia nitrates: Alabama Traction, Light & Power, *Sixth Annual Report of the Board of Directors* (Montreal, June 1, 1919), 4

24 "deep lines in his face …": Mitchell, *Industrial Pioneer*, 8

24 doctor's advice: James Mitchell to J. W. Worthington, February 9, 1917, APC Archives

24 Mitchell's work habits: Frederick Darlington, "Two Distinguished Engineers Pay Tribute to Mr. Mitchell," *Powergrams* (September 1920), 9; Walmsley, "Cherished Memories," 6

24 *Lusitania* and Mitchell on passenger list: "Lusitania Sunk by a Submarine, Probably 1,260 Dead; Twice Torpedoed off Irish Coast…," *NYT*, May 8, 1915; Murray, *Martin Biography*, 30

24 fifteen-page: James Mitchell to Frank Washburn, May 8, 1914, APC Archives

25 handling of Freeman's transition: James Mitchell to Frank Washburn, September 2 and September 14, 1913, APC Archives

25 "He shed his coat…": L. P. Sweatt Jr., "James Mitchell, the Man," *Powergrams* (September 1920), 11

25 "Never you mind…": Cooper tribute, 8

25 Atkinson attempts to meet with Mitchell: Henry Atkinson to Howard Duryea, Office Engineer, Alabama Power, June 17, 1919, and Henry Atkinson to James Mitchell, July 8, 1919, APC Archives

26 Mitchell's death: "James Mitchell Dies of Paralysis at 54," *NYT*, July 24, 1920

26 "His personality…": *Powergrams* (September 1920), 10

26 "His fairness…" and "He is mourned…": Ibid., 7

26 "He could visualize…": Ibid., 4

26 "A creative genius…": Ibid.,15

26 "His failing health…": Ibid., 3

26 impact of Westinghouse: Leonard S. Hyman, *America's Electric Utilities: Past, Present, and Future* (Arlington, VA, 1983), 63–65 [hereafter cited as Hyman, *America's Electric Utilities*]; Energy Information Administration, "The Changing Structure of the Electric Power Industry: History of U.S. Electric Power Industry," www.eia.doe.gov/cneaf/electricity/page/electric_kid/ap pend_a.html [hereafter cited as EIA History website]

28 "We have retained…": James Mitchell to Frank Washburn, April 27, 1912, APC Archives

CHAPTER 2

31–32 Martin's itinerary in London and return passage: various receipts, brochures, invitations, schedules, and notes in "London Trip" folder, Thomas W. Martin files, Thomas W. Martin Memorial Library, Southern Research Institute

32 "London mission successful…": Niel A. Weathers to E. A. Yates, July 22, 1924, APC Archives

32 "It seems proper…": Martin, *Story of Electricity*, 60

32–33 "foreign ownership" and "swell the dividends": Preston J. Hubbard, *Origins of the TVA: The Muscle Shoals Controversy, 1920–1932* (Nashville, 1961), 57–58, 115, 119 [hereafter cited as Hubbard, *Origins of TVA*]

33 "Red Menace" scare: Wade, "Expanding Resources," 401–402, 438–445

33 expansion of markets: Alabama Traction, Light & Power, *Eleventh Annual Report of the Board of Directors* (Montreal, March 15, 1924), 1–3; Chester Morgan and Donald M. Dana, Jr., *A Priceless Heritage: The Story of Mississippi Power Company* (Gulfport, Mississippi, 1993) 6, 7 [hereafter cited as Morgan and Dana, *Priceless Heritage*]

34 industry mergers and "superpower" trends: Rose C. Feld, "More Power for You through Superpower Plan," *Powergrams* (June 1924), 1–3; "Superpower to Increase National Production," *Powergrams* (February 1924), 1–2, 38 and part II in March 1924 issue, 5–6, 41; Hyman, *America's Electric Utilities*, 75–83

34–36 Making of Tom Martin: unless otherwise noted, compiled from Murray, *Martin Biography*, 5–11, 19–34; Forbes, *America's Fifty*, 309–317; "Address of Thomas

W. Martin Presented at Joint Session of Alabama Legislature," Montgomery, Alabama, August 11, 1961, APC Archives; Hubert F. Lee, "South's Man of the Year," *Dixie Business*, 2, 19; "Thomas Wesley Martin," obituary, *Powergrams* (December 1964), 2–5; interview with Joseph M. Farley, March 24, 1999, SCOHC

34 "work and more work": Forbes, *America's Fifty*, 316

35 "As Alabama grows…": Martin, *Story of Electricity*, 93–94

36 recession and retrenchment: Wade, "Expanding Resources," 401–402

37 social and economic changes: Modern World History Index website, "America's Economy in the 1920s," www.historylearningsite.co.uk/America_economy_1920's.htm; Kingwood College Library website, "American Cultural History 1920–1929," kclibrary.nhmccd.edu/decade20.html

37 first dam under new law: Alabama Traction, Light & Power, *Tenth Annual Report of the Board of Directors* (Montreal, May 1, 1923), 3

37 "well nigh ideal site": W. O. Crosby to O. G. Thurlow, December 31, 1920, APC Archives

38 construction at Cherokee Bluffs: "Cherokee in Embryo as Mitchell Dam is Completed," *Powergrams* (August 1923), 16–17; Martin, *Story of Electricity*, 65 70

38 Martin Dam dimensions: Ibid., 68

38 largest manmade reservoir: J. A. Douglas, "Cherokee Bluffs," *The Auburn Engineer* (Auburn, Alabama, January 1926), 6

38 3,000 workers, 1,600 graves, 100-foot high bridge, 40,000 acres: Jackson, *Loafing Streams*, 130, 123, 154

38 "Next to the manufacture…": Martin, *Story of Electricity*, 93

38 "Some Eastern cotton…" and first mill: Ibid., 95

38 forty mills in 1924: Willkie MS, 59

38 five thousand agricultural customers: APC, *1926 Annual Report*, 7

38 Martin's support of agriculture industry: Forbes, "How Alabama Power…"

39 100,000 stockholders: Ibid.

39 interconnections with Georgia utilities: Wade H. Wright, *History of the Georgia Power Company: 1855–1956* (Atlanta, 1957), 177–178 [hereafter cited as Wright, *History of GPC*]

39 wheeling power to Carolinas: "South Saved by Super Power," *United States Investor*, January 1926

39 $112 million: E. A. Yates, "Report on Power for Southeastern Power Committee," June 1920, APC Archives

39 operating committee coordination: W. E. Mitchell, "Interconnection of Power Systems in the Southeastern States," address to the Pacific Coast Convention of the American Institute of Electrical Engineers, October 13–17, 1924, Pasadena, California

39 "These early…": Martin, *Story of Electricity*, 60

40 "Service from hydroelectric…": Milo S. Long, "Southwestern Power System: Alabama and Mississippi," January 18, 1922, APC Archives

40 Yates: Harllee Branch Jr., "Corporate History Project," part 3, November 25, 1985, SCHC [hereafter cited as Branch, "History Project" part 3]

40 customers nearly doubled in 1923: Alabama Traction, *Eleventh Annual Report*, 2

41 formation of Southeastern Power & Light: Martin, *Story of Electricity*, 60–61; SPL, *Minutes of Meeting of Associates* and *Minutes of a Special Meeting of the Board of Directors*, September 2, 1924, in Augusta, Maine, and *Minutes of a Special Meeting of the Board of Directors*, in New York City, September 2, 1924, included with incorporation papers, APC Archives

41 "At the meeting…": E. A. Yates to Thomas W. Martin, September 3, 1924, APC Archives

41 October 6 meeting in Maine: SPL, *Minutes of Special Meeting of Stockholders*, October 6, 1924, Augusta, Maine, APC Archives

41 transfer of stock: "Extract of Minutes for Special Meeting of Board of Directors of Southeastern Power & Light," October 10, 1924, Montreal, APC Archives

41 New York office: "The New York Office Personnel," *Powergrams* (July 1926), 10–12

41 Mitchell looking at Mississippi: Atkins, *Centennial History of Alabama Power*, 146

41 Polk: S. S. Simpson, "The Function of the Dixie Construction Company and the Men Who Make it Function," *Powergrams* (March 1925), 12–13

41 Barry: "Two New Executives Named," *Powergrams* (January 1927), 15, 54

41–42 "The distribution systems…" and "This should prove…": A. C. Polk and J. M. Barry, "Mississippi Project," March 1924, APC Archives

42 negotiations for Gulfport and Mississippi Coast Traction: Morgan and Dana, *Priceless Heritage*, 7–11

42 purchase of Mississippi Power: Ibid., 9; E. A. Yates to W. J. Henderson, June 7, 1924, and E. A. Yates to Niel Weathers, July 24, 1924, APC Archives

42 Eaton: Morgan and Dana, *Priceless Heritage*, 6–8

42 "There is not a…": Ibid., 15–16

42 "a Mississippian…": Ibid., 19–20

43 "Mr. Couch has been…": E. A. Yates to F. E. Gunter, December 3, 1924, and E. A. Yates, notes on conference held in Birmingham on the Gulfport and southern Mississippi situations, December 1924, APC Archives

43 "attract new industries…": MPC, "Our Policies" advertisement, MPC Corporate Records

43 Barry's assessment: J. M. Barry, "Report to Mr. T. W. Martin on Mississippi Situation," January 5, 1925, APC Archives

44 "declaration…" and celebration in Iuka: Morgan and Dana, *Priceless Heritage*, 24–26

44 "northeast-southwest exchange": Ibid., 29–32

44 growth through 1930: Ibid., 33–34

44 Consumers Power/Gulf Electric formation: Thomas W. Martin, "Gulf Electric Company," document on merger of properties into Gulf Electric, June 9, 1925, APC Archives

81 board and incorporation information: C&S, *Report to the Stockholders*, 1, 4; "Cobb and Martin Head Utility Group," *NYT*, May 29, 1929

81 Voting control of four top stockholders: House Committee on Interstate and Foreign Commerce, *Relation of Holding Companies to Operating Companies in Power and Gas Affecting Control*, 73rd Congress, 2nd Session, House Report No. 827, Part 3, 1935, 233–234 [hereafter cited as House Report No. 827, Part 3]; "$1,200,000,000 Deal to Merge Utilities," *NYT*, January 8, 1930

81 "the largest charter…": "Will Hold Utilities…" *NYT*, May 24, 1929

81 C&S assets: C&S, *Notice of Annual Meeting of Stockholders*, July 14, 1931, and *Report to the Stockholders*, 29–33

81 stock price jumps: New York Curb Market listings, *NYT*, May 24, 1929; July 3, 1929; July 26, 1929

81 private offers and conversion ratios: "Terms Forecast for Big Utility Deal," *NYT*, May 30, 1929

81–82 broker promotion of C&S stock: numerous advertisements, *WSJ*, June 4, 1929, the prior week and afterward

82 trading on the Philadelphia Exchange: "Com. & Southern Stirs Interest," *WSJ*, June 8, 1929

82 trading on the Curb Market: "Superpower Board Votes…" *NYT*, June 6, 1929

82 New York utilities: "Three New York Power Companies in Huge Merger," *AJ*, June 18, 1929

82 586,800 shares: "Rush of Buying Follows J.P. Morgan Merger News," *AC*, June 14, 1929

82 95 percent of shares exchanged, 30 million: "Holding Company Reports Earnings," *NYT*, September 4, 1929

82 warning signs: David M. Kennedy, *Freedom from Fear: The American People in Depression and War, 1929–1945* (New York, 1999), 34–37 [hereafter cited as Kennedy, *Freedom from Fear*]

82 Black Thursday panic: Ibid., 38; "Worst Stock Crash Stemmed by Banks; 12,894,650-Share Day Swamps Market; Leaders Confer, Find Conditions Sound," *NYT*, October 25, 1929

82 Morgan's role during panic of 1929 and 1907: Ibid.; Chernow, *House of Morgan*, 121–129

82 cash and speculative climate: Ibid., 303–307; Kennedy, *Freedom from Fear*, 35–37

82–83 "chords from…" and scene at close: "Weird Roar Surges from Exchange Floor During Trading in a Record Smashing Day," *NYT*, October 25, 1929

83 rally: "Wall Street Optimistic After Stormy Day; Clerical Work May Force Holiday Tomorrow," *NYT*, October 25, 1929; "Stocks Gain as Market is Steadied; Bankers Pledge Continued Support; Hoover Says Business Basics is Sound," *NYT*, October 26, 1929

83 special $1 dividend: "U.S. Steel to Pay $1 Extra Dividend," *NYT*, October 30, 1929

83 "the fundamental…": "President Hoover Issues a Statement of Reassurance on Continued Prosperity of Fundamental Business," *NYT*, October 26, 1929

83 Tragic Tuesday: "Stocks Collapse in 16,410,030-Share Day, But Rally at Close Cheers Brokers; Bankers Optimistic, to Continue Aid," *NYT*, October 30, 1929; Chernow, *House of Morgan*, 315–319; Kennedy, *Freedom from Fear*, 38–39

83 16 million record: Ibid., 38

83 Martin in NY office: Atkins, *Centennial History of Alabama Power*, 165

83 Cobb at Bras Coupe Lake: Bush, *Future Builders*, 261

83 "Let's not make any…": Ibid., 238

84 C&S stock at $10: "Transactions on the NYSE," *NYT*, December 31, 1929

84 $30 billion: Schlesinger, *Almanac*, 454

84 merging intermediate holding companies: "$1,200,000,000 Deal to Merge Utilities," *NYT*, January 8, 1930

84 "Many corporations have…": "Senators Stirred by Market Break," *NYT*, October 25, 1929

84 merger plans: C&S, *Plan of Merger and Consolidation*, January 7, 1930, and related notices to stockholders from B. C. Cobb and Thomas W. Martin, SCHC

85 Yates leading Allied Engineers: "To Absorb Three Concerns: Allied Engineers, Unit of Commonwealth and Southern, Formed," *NYT*, April 4, 1930; B. C. Cobb memo to management, Circular Letter No. 3, May 7, 1930, APC Archives

85 description of Northern and Southern Groups: C&S, *1930 Report to Stockholders*, 33–45

85–86 simplification of corporate structure, elimination of subsidiaries: C&S, *Outline of History and Development* (New York, February 26, 1935), SCHC, 7–12 [hereafter cited as C&S, *Outline of History*]; C&S, *1930 Report to Stockholders*, 12; C&S, *1931 Report to Stockholders*, 5, and *1932 Report to Stockholders*, 5

86 sixteen companies controlling 80 percent: Hausman and Neufeld, *Rise and Fall*, 14

86 top three: Bush, *Future Builders*, 323

86 "the desire for commercial…": FTC, *Summary Report*, 8

86 unethical practices: Ibid., 7–12; Hausman and Neufeld, *Rise and Fall*, 15–16, 18–20; Hawes, *Utility Holding Companies*, 2.12–2.14; Tate, *Keeper of the Flame*, 127–128, 130–131; Hyman, *America's Electric Utilities*, 77–83

86 Martin's influence on service company policies: Martin, *Story of Electricity*, 146

86 Martin's scrapbook: Murray, *Martin Biography*, 87

87 New York apartment: Ibid., 87–88

87 Southern Group coordination: C&S, *Outline of History*, 36–39

87 Middlemiss role: Howard Duryea to Messrs. Martin, Thompson, & McWhorter, June 22, 1932, SCHC

87 Public Light and Power: "Plans to Acquire Utilities in the South," *NYT*, October 17, 1929

87 Columbus and other acquisitions: C&S, *Outline of History*, 86–87; Wright, *History of GPC*, 254–255

87 "we have passed the worst": Kennedy, *Freedom from Fear*, 58

87 recovery by summer: Ibid., 39–40

87 Allied Engineers dissolved, Yates named Southern Group sponsor: B. C. Cobb memo to management, Circular Letter No. 35, November 7, 1931, and Circular Letter No. 32, November 7, 1931, APC Archives

87–88 completion of construction: C&S, *1930 Report to Stockholders*, 6–7

88 advantages of Southern Group integration: C&S, *Outline of History*, 38–39

88 "I don't know…": *Official Report of Proceedings Before the Securities and Exchange Commission*, Philadelphia, Docket No. 59–20, September 1, 1942, 1634 [hereafter cited as *SEC Proceedings*]

88 "among the finest"; "In all my life…": Bernard C. Cobb to T. W. Martin, November 24, 1929, Thomas W. Martin Library, Southern Research Institute

88 "congenial as two…": Crist, *They Electrified the South*, 54

88–89 Martin's management style, quirks: "Looking Back: Remembering Thomas Martin" and "There Will Never Be Another Like Him," *Powergrams* (June 1990), 6–7, 8–9; Forbes, *America's Fifty*, 309–317; "Martin Profile," *Alabama Sportsman*; Lee, "South's Man of the Year," 2, 19

88–89 Cobb's management style, quirks: Bush, *Future Builders*, 168, 242–243, 249–253, 256, 260–261, 269; Crist, *They Electrified the South*, 54–55

89 "happened to have…": *SEC Proceedings*, September 11, 1942, 2557

89 Cooke connection: Bush, *Future Builders*, 111–112 [E. W. Clark & Co. was a one of the Eastern money firms that partnered with Hodenpyl to finance some of its early deals, including the takeover of Tennessee Electric Power. Enoch Clark, founder of the company, had a partnership with Jay Cooke, the tycoon given major credit for financing the Civil War for the Union government. Clark and Cooke had long gone their separate ways by the time Cooke's own financial empire fell in 1873 with an over-commitment to the Northern Pacific Railroad, a collapse that set off the worst financial panic of the nineteenth century.]

90 "as much warmth as…": Crist, *They Electrified the South*, 54

90 separate Northern-Southern camps: Bush, *Future Builders*, 256

90 Cummings replaced with Northerner: C&S, *1931 Report to Stockholders*, 1 (Cummings's replacement was S. Sloan Colt, president of Bankers Trust Company in New York)

90 net income and power sales drop: C&S, *1930 Report to Stockholders*, 5; C&S, *1931 Report to Stockholders*, 3–4

90 unemployment rates: Kennedy, *Freedom from Fear*, 87

90 more than a billion kilowatt hours: C&S, *1930 Report to Stockholders*, 6; C&S, *1932 Report to Stockholders*, 4

90 Cobb keeping Insull waiting: Bush, *Future Builders*, 269

91 "nothing good ever…": Crist, *They Electrified the South*, 54–55

91 Martin brooding: Murray, *Martin Biography*, 88

91 "For the information…": B. C. Cobb memo to management, Circular Letter No. 2–K, June 28, 1932, APC Archives

91 "I was unable…": Martin, *Story of Electricity*, 144

91 six bankers on board: C&S, *1932 Report to Stockholders*, 2

92 dividend cut: Ibid., 5

92 preferred dividend reduced: C&S, *1934 Report to Stockholders*, 5–6

92 U.S. Steel and others cut wages: Kennedy, *Freedom from Fear*, 87

92 Insull empire, its fall, Morgan's role: Thomas P. Hughes, *American Genesis: A Century of Invention and Technological Enthusiasm, 1870–1970* (New York, 1989), 226–231, 238–240; Chernow, *House of Morgan*, 502–505; Tate, *Keeper of the Flame*, 130; Amity Shlaes, *The Forgotten Man* (New York, 2007), 22–23 [hereafter cited as Shlaes, *The Forgotten Man*]

92 Insull support of Martin in Muscle Shoals battle: *Congressional Record*, 74th Congress, 1st Session, Volume 79, Part 10, 1935, H 10547

93 PSC concerns causing Martin to return to Alabama: Atkins, *Centennial History of Alabama Power*, 183–184

93–94 Willkie's background: Ibid., 284–288; Steve Neal, *Dark Horse* (New York, 1984), 1–28 [hereafter cited as Neal, *Dark Horse*]; Crist, *They Electrified the South*, 57–59

93 "We should not let…": Bush, *Future Builders*, 286–287

94 "Gentlemen, I am…": Ibid., 282

94 Willkie removing bankers: Ibid., 276; Morgan and Dana, *Priceless Heritage*, 82

94 Cobb's retirement, chairman's post eliminated: C&S, *1934 Report to the Stockholders*, 7

95 unemployment 25 percent: Kennedy, *Freedom from Fear*, 163

95 auto production down one third: Ibid.

95 50 percent unemployment in Detroit: Ibid., 87

95 banking holiday in Michigan: Bush, *Future Builders*, 294–295

95 cotton prices and 40,000 farms in Mississippi: Morgan and Dana, *Priceless Heritage*, 37

95 $117 per capita income: Kennedy, *Freedom from Fear*, 163

95 10 to 15¢ an hour: Goldfield, *Cotton Fields*, 180

95 Atlanta shops closing, "back to the farm" movement: Ibid.

95 "We've got to…": Morgan and Dana, *Priceless Heritage*, 46

96 Objective rate plan: C&S, *Outline of History*, 65–68; C&S, *1935 Report to Stockholders*, 6–7; Atkins, *Centennial History of Alabama Power*, 191

96 500 sales force: Bush, *Future Builders*, 28

96 leading nation in appliance sales, 80 percent: C&S, *1934 Report to Stockholders*, 6

96 appliance prices: Morgan and Dana, *Priceless Heritage*, 49

96 "You are not selling…": "Let's Do Our Part," *Snap Shots* (January 1932), 4

96 $200,000 in appliance sales: "$201,837 in Appliances Sold …," 1–2

96 "Home Town Electrical" contests: "Senator George Cites Georgia's Power Progress," *Snap Shots* (December 1936), 1, 3; "Woodbine, Reidsville, Baxley and Americus Are Chief Winners in Home Town Contest," *Snap Shots* (November 1936), 1, 5; "Louisville Leads Whole State in Residential Use of Service, *Snap Shots* (February 1935), 5

96 "Squalor is…": Tarleton Collier, "One Sees the Stars, Another Mud. The Fuller Life in Georgia," *AG*, January 28, 1935

97 Five Point Campaign: Morgan and Dana, *Priceless Heritage*, 47

97 "loading…": Ibid., 49

97 "Fellows…" and "So we…": Ibid., 50

97 sales up in 1934: C&S, *1934 Report to the Stockholders*, 4

97 rate decreases: C&S *Outline of History*, 67

97 rates below 3¢, power use above 1,200 kilowatt-hours: C&S, *1940 Report to Stockholders*, 6

97 national ranking in appliance sales: C&S, *1936 Report to the Stockholders*, 5

97 $1.55 million earnings deficit: C&S, *1935 Report to Stockholders*, 3

97 "wrecking crew" process: Crist, *They Electrified the South*, 55–56

97 "One of my hardest…": Tina Luckett, "Herbert J. Scholz," *Southern Highlights* (November 1976), 9

98 Lansing Smith: Jowers, "One Sunny Day Last May…," 11–12; Gulf Power, *Tradition*, 9

98 Gaston, "those who know…": Glen Kundert, "Ernest C. Gaston," *Southern Highlights* (August 1977), 7

98 "Everybody got…": Morgan and Dana, *Priceless Heritage*, 40

98 "My salary was…": Crist, *They Electrified the South*, 56

98 salary increases in 1935: Employee Relations section of Mississippi Power's entry in competition for the 1935 Charles A. Coffin Award, MPC Corporate Records

98–99 MPC financial crisis in 1934: Morgan and Dana, *Priceless Heritage*, 43–46

98 "The offer hinges…": [paraphrased] Ibid., 44

99 "Wendell L. Willkie Month": "Willkie Month Proves to be Victory Month," *Power Lines* (January 1936), 1

99 Willkie's travels, work habits: Bush, *Future Builders*, 289–303

99 "That's dandy" and "Right now": Ibid., 290, 292

99 "Hell, no…": Ibid.

99 wearing no watch: interview with James Samuel Eaton, Volume 2, 1985, MPC Oral History Program, MPC Corporate Records

99 "That's dandy, I approve…": Ibid., 293

100 replacing "money changers" with operations men: Ibid., 276; C&S, *1934 Report to Stockholders*, 2; "Sidney Mitchell, Utilities Leader, Leaves Business," *AJ*, March 28, 1933

100 "We take no…": Wendell L. Willkie, "Argument Presented to Interstate & Foreign Commerce Committee," March 14, 1935, reprinted in brochure form, SCHC, 25–26

100 "They neither control…": House Committee on Interstate and Foreign Commerce, *Public Utility Holding Companies Act, Hearings on H.R. 5423*, 74th Congress, 1st Session, 621

100 "He was extremely…": Preston S. Arkwright, "Fit to Survive," address to group leaders of Georgia Power's employee information program, Atlanta, September 27, 1940

100 "dangerous man," "sins of wildcat…,": "Roosevelt Would End Racketeering Career of the Power Trust," *AG*, September 27, 1932

100 "Insull monstrosity": McCraw, *TVA*, 34

101 "birch rod…": Ibid., 33

101 concessions: Preston Arkwright, "Muscle Shoals Memorandum," to B. C. Cobb, April 12, 1933, GPC Archives; House Committee on Military Affairs, *Muscle Shoals Hearings*, 73rd Congress, 1st Session, April 11 to April 15, 1933, 107–108 [hereafter cited as *Muscle Shoals Hearings*]

102 "If anything is wrong…": Preston S. Arkwright, *What About Holding Companies?* [reprint of speech ca. 1934], GPC Archives, 6

102–03 utility contributor to bubble: Hausman and Neufeld, *Rise and Fall*, 14

103 more than 50 utilities losing $1.7 billion: Hawes, *Utility Holding Companies*, 2.12

103 $16 billion in value lost: Ibid., 2.14

103 "Too late…": "Report of National Power Policy Committee on Public-Utility Holding Companies," contained in U.S. Senate Report, *Public Utility Act of 1935*, 74th Congress, 1st Session, Senate Report No. 621, 57

103 public mood turning against utilities: Bush, *Future Builders*, 277

CHAPTER 5

105-06 celebration in Tupelo: numerous accounts in the *Tupelo Journal*, including: "New Year May Bring Cheap Muscle Shoals Power," October 13, 1933; "TVA Director Tells World of Tupelo's Signing for Cheap Electric Power from Muscle Shoals," November 7, 1933; "City Beautiful Is Basking in Limelight Since Signing for Cheap Electric Power," November 10, 1933; "City Signs Contract Friday for First Power Line from Huge Plant at Muscle Shoals," and "Celebration Is Attended by Thousands," November 19, 1933, special edition

105 "Everyone was talking…" and other Kirpatrick quotes in chapter: Frankie Kirpatrick, interviews in September 2004

106 "Tupelo's contract…": Morgan and Dana, *Priceless Heritage*, 62

106 "Tupelo is going to…": "TVA Director Tells World of Huge Line," *Tupelo Journal*, November 7, 1933

106 "ultimate complete electrification…": "TVA Foresight and Farmer Cooperation," *Tupelo Journal*, November 10, 1933, special edition

106 Morgan's impressions: Arthur E. Morgan, "A Birch Rod in the National Cupboard," *Survey Graphic*, March 1934, 139

106 "When the moon…": Harry Rutherford, "Tupelo First TVA City," TVA Files, Lee County Public Library

106 "greatest one-day…": "Hundreds to Take Part in Huge Parade," *Tupelo Journal*, November 19, 1933

106 Mississippi municipal votes: Morgan and Dana, *Priceless Heritage*, 62

107 Guild's plans for Cove Creek: *Muscle Shoals Hearings*, 171

107 "including some…": "Cooperative Plan to Put Electricity Within Reach of All, Says TVA Head," *AC*, November 11, 1933

107 ten Alabama towns: "More Power Than Is Needed," *NYT*, November 13, 1933

107 "standard for all…": "TVA Director Tells World of Huge Line," *Tupelo Journal*, November 7, 1933; Shlaes, *The Forgotten Man*, 188; "Federal Contract Cuts Power Rates," *NYT*, November 19, 1933

108 Morgan's background: McCraw, *TVA*, 36–39; North Callahan, *TVA: Bridge over Troubled Waters* (New Jersey, 1980), 93 [hereafter cited as Callahan, *TVA*]; Roy Talbert, Jr., *FDR's Utopian: Arthur Morgan of the TVA* (Jackson, Mississippi, 1987), 36–38, 45–47, 55–58 [hereafter cited as Talbert, *FDR's Utopian*];

108 "Only as men…": Ibid., 58

108 "Your new undertaking…": McCraw, *TVA*, 47

108 Morgan and Roosevelt's first meeting: Talbert, *FDR's Utopian*, 84–86

108 "chiefly about a designed…": Arthur E. Morgan, "Bench Marks in the Tennessee Valley: The Strength of the Hills," *Survey Graphic*, January 1934, 43

108 "The president wanted…": Ibid.

108 "the kind of thing…": McCraw, *TVA*, 39

108 Morgan's tour and impressions of the valley: Callahan, *TVA*, 41–43; Arthur E. Morgan, "Roads to Prosperity in the TVA," *Survey Graphic*, November 1934, 548–550

108 "pick up…": Arthur E. Morgan, "Remarks at Swarthmore College," January 13, 1935, Swarthmore, Pennsylvania, GPC Archives

108 "relative aimlessness…": Arthur E. Morgan, "Planning for the Use of the Land," *Survey Graphic*, May 1934, 236

109 "the greatest social…": William Hard, "Our Greatest Experiment: Is the Tennessee Valley Authority a Millennium or a Monster?" *Redbook*, August 1935, article in TVA Files, APC Archives

109 "worst mistake": Callahan, *TVA*, 99

109 Harcourt Morgan: Ibid., 40; McCraw, *TVA*, 41–42

109 Lilienthal: Ibid.,, 43–46; Talbert, *FDR's Utopian*, 78; Callahan, *TVA*, 96–97

109 disagreement over Willkie's letter: Ibid., 41; McCraw, *TVA*, 47; David E. Lilienthal, *Journals of David E. Lilienthal, Volume I, The TVA Years 1939–1945* (New York: 1964), 39 [hereafter cited as Lilienthal, *Journals*]

109 "had power…": Davidson, *Tennessee II*, 223–224

110 "an open…": Richard Lowitt, "The TVA, 1933–45," *TVA: Fifty Years of Grassroots Bureaucracy*, ed., Erwin C. Hargrove, and Paul K. Conkin (Chicago, 1983), 38 [hereafter cited as Lowitt, "The TVA"]

110 Willkie-Morgan's meeting: Talbert, *FDR's Utopian*, 137; Morgan and Dana, *Priceless Heritage*, 61

110 Morgan-Lilienthal different views over yardstick: McCraw, *TVA*, 54–57

110 "regional reconstruction" and "reawakening…": Lowitt, "The TVA," 39

110 planned community, education, cooperatives: Talbert, *FDR's Utopian*, 116–122; Callahan, *TVA*, 30–38; Morgan, "Roads to Prosperity," 552, 575–576; Arthur E. Morgan, "Building a Labor Policy," *Survey Graphic*, October 1935, 529–532, 575–576

110 "entirely free of politics": Talbert, *FDR's Utopian*, 84

110 165 municipalities: "Cooperative Plan to Put Electricity Within Reach of All, Says TVA Head," *AC*, November 11, 1933

110–11 power policy: Morgan, "A Birch Rod…," 110; McCraw, *TVA*, 57–59

111 "You fellows…": Lilienthal, *Journals*, 711–712

111 "I was…": Ibid.; McCraw, *TVA*, 63

111 PWA grants and loans: Martin, *The Story of Electricity*, 109

111 Lilienthal's ultimatum: McCraw, *TVA*, 65

111 Corinth's grant: Morgan and Dana, *Priceless Heritage*, 63

112 "It's tough…": Ibid., 63–64

112 terms of first sale: MPC, *1934 Annual Report*; McCraw, *TVA*, 65

112 "To a fully…": Wendell L. Willkie, "Our Co-Operation with TVA," *Electrical World*, March 31,1934

112 "The agreement…": "Tennessee Given Georgia's Rates by TVA Agreement," *Snap Shots* (January 1934), 1

112 Hickok's assignment: Kennedy, *Freedom from Fear*, 161–162

112 "A Promised Land…": Lowett, "The TVA," 49

112 closing on first sale, delays: Bush, *Future Builders*, 327; McCraw, *TVA*, 67–69, 112

112 65 percent of book: Ernest R. Abrams, *Power in Transition* (New York, 1940), 229 [hereafter cited as Abrams, *Power*]

113 Ashwander lawsuit and initial favorable ruling: McCraw, *TVA*, 89–90, 111–112

113 "An absolute and…": Ibid., 115

113 "under the circumstances…": Wendell L. Willkie to Forney Johnston, August 14, 1934, SCHC

113 claim that Georgia market reprieved at Alabama's expense: George Ashwander, et al. vs. Tennessee Valley Authority et al., in the Circuit Court for the Eighth Judicial Circuit of Alabama, *Copy of Bill of Complaint*, APC Archives, 14–15

113 lawsuit against Ickes: Abrams, *Power*, 30

113 $10 million in PWA grants: McCraw, *TVA*, 86

113 TVA arguments in court: Wendell Willkie, "Political Power: The Tennessee Valley Authority," in *This Is Wendell Willkie* (New York, 1940), 129–130, originally published in *Atlantic Monthly*, August 1937 [hereafter cited as Willkie, "Political Power"]

113 "to skim the cream" and "prevent TVA…": Lilienthal, *Journals*, 54

113 300 municipal applications: Lowitt, "The TVA," 41

113 "won with…," and "the promise…": "Buying Votes for the TVA," *Snap Shots* (April 1935), 4

114 increase in power consumption: McCraw, *TVA*, 74

114 "proof of the mismanagement…": Ibid., 73

114 Roosevelt visit to Tupelo: "President Sees the Nation Developing All Its Power After Model of Tennessee," *NYT*, November 19, 1934; "75,000 Hear Roosevelt," *Tupelo Daily News*, November 19, 1934; "President Roosevelt in Tupelo" and "He is the One Man," editorials, *Tupelo Daily News*, November 19, 1934

114 "not come by…" and "People's eyes…": "Roosevelt's Two Speeches During Trip on Sunday," *AJ*, November 19, 1934

115 "My God, what a racket!" and "That is true…": John E. Rankin, "What the Government Is Doing in the Way of Public Power in the Tennessee Valley Area," remarks to the Public Ownership League of America, Washington, D.C., February 25, 1935, reprinted in the *Congressional Record–Appendix*, March 13, 1935, 3710–3713

115 "write-down" and "Thus we see…": Wendell L. Willkie, "Government and the Public Utilities," reports to the joint meeting of the Economic Club of New York and the Harvard Business School Club, New York, January 21, 1935, reprinted in *Vital Speeches of the Day*, Vol. I, No. 10, 292–299

115 "If TVA was to be…" and rate comparisons: Willkie, "Political Power," 146, 133; Wendell L. Willkie, "Government and Private Ownership," remarks to American Statistical Association, New York, September 26, 1934; Wendell L. Willkie, "The Other Side of the TVA Program," remarks to the Rotary Club of Birmingham, November 7, 1934

115–16 "Whenever a household…": C&S, *1935 Report to Stockholders*, 9 [repeated in numerous Willkie speeches]

116 "Tennessee River…": Morgan and Dana, *Priceless Heritage*, 78

116 comptroller general critique: Lowitt, "The TVA," 46–47

116 "impossible to sell…": George Bryant, Jr., "Lilienthal Admits TVA Could Not Operate if Current Is Sold on Production Cost Basis–Dependence on Subsidy Indicated," *WSJ*, May 24, 1935

116 "seemed to sustain…": Edward H. Collins, "The Week in Finance," *NYHT*, May 27, 1936

116 "If a private…": Herbert Corey, "The Lawless Honesty of TVA," *Nation's Business*, July 1935

116 "One would suppose…": Hard, "Our Greatest Experiment"

116 "The real lesson…": Wendell L. Willkie, "'Lessons' of the TVA," *The Financial World*, June 3, 1936, reprint in GPC Archives

116 "define the limits…": Wendell L. Willkie, *The Utilities and the TVA Situation*, reprint of address over Station WEAF and the Red Network of the National Broadcasting Company, March 5, 1936, APC Archives; also reprinted in *Powergrams* (March 16, 1936)

116 "Self-seeking ambition" and "selfish rivalry": Talbert, *FDR's Utopian*, 112

116 Morgan's attempt to oust Lilienthal: Ibid., 159–162

117 creation, funding and background on REA: Morgan and Dana, *Priceless Heritage*, 85–88; McCraw, *TVA*, 86–87; Abrams, *Power*, 32–38

117 nine of ten farms without electricity: "A Brief History of 'Rural Electrification' in America," Georgia Electric Membership Cooperative, www.georgiaemc.com/history.html

117 "Let me say…": *Congressional Record*, 75th Congress, 2nd Session, Volume 80, Part 5, April 9, 1936, H5283

117 half of Georgia Power's rural customers: "Why Company Built Few Rural Lines During Depression," *Snap Shots* (May 1937), 4

117 initial cooperation: Martin, *Story of Electricity*, 77; Leslie N. Sharp, "Seeing the Light: The Georgia Power Company and the REA During the Depression," working paper drafted in 2001, manuscript in GPC Archives [hereafter cited at Sharp, "Seeing the Light"]

117 Arkwright's success: Ibid.; "REA Magazine Praises 'Good Neighbor' Policy," *Snap Shots* (September 1936), 1; "Company's Rural Electrification Policy Commended by Georgia Newspapers," *Snap Shots* (September 1936), 4; "For a Broadened 'Arkwright Plan,'" editorial, *Electrical World*, December 5, 1936

118 "If some of the…": *Rural Electrification in Alabama* (Birmingham, September 1936), APC Archives

118 more than half of cooperatives: *Era of Rural Electrification in Alabama* (Birmingham, 1951), APC Archives

118 agreement ending early: "Roosevelt's Power Pooling Conference," editorial, *Jackson* [Tennessee] *Sun*, September 29, 1936

118 "The present status…": Wendell L. Willkie to Franklin D. Roosevelt, May 21, 1936, GPC Archives

118 nineteen utilities lawsuit: McCraw, *TVA*, 116–117 [The nineteen utilities included Tennessee Electric Power Company, Franklin Power & Light Company, Memphis Power & Light Company, South Tennessee Power Company, Birmingham Electric Company, Mississippi Power Company, Appalachian Electric Power Company, Georgia Power Company, Carolina Power & Light Company, Tennessee Public Service Company, Holston River Electric Company, Alabama Power Company, Kentucky & West Virginia Power Company, Inc., Kingsport Utilities, Incorporated, Kentucky-Tennessee Light & Power Co., West Tennessee Power & Light Company, Mississippi Power & Light Company, East Tennessee Light & Power Company, and Tennessee Eastern Electric Company. Georgia Power later dropped out, having filed a similar lawsuit against TVA in Georgia.]

118 "They have seen…": Willkie, "Political Power," 139

119 notification of contract expiration: Wright, *History of GPC*, 277

119 1,300 miles of transmission lines, Wheeler Dam almost complete, four others: C&S, *1936 Report to Stockholders*, 5

119 plans for eleven dams: Willkie, "Political Power," 130–131

119 "prohibiting any future agreement…": McCraw, *TVA*, 96

119 Morgan's appeal to Roosevelt, election concerns: Ibid.; Callahan, *TVA*, 104

119 "You, and you alone…": Willkie to Roosevelt, May 21, 1936

119–20 power pool proposal and concepts: McCraw, *TVA*, 91–93

120 Arkwright-Roosevelt relationship and Georgia Power service to Warm Springs: Wright, *History of GPC*, 284–296; Franklin D. Roosevelt to Thomas W. Martin, November 5, 1926, and Preston Arkwright to E. A. Yates, November 11, 1929, GPC Archives

120 meeting between FDR, Willkie and Arkwright: Preston Arkwright, "Memorandum of Conference with President Roosevelt in the Executive Offices in the White House," August 25, 1936, GPC Archives

120 "That is election day" and interchange that follows: Ibid.

121 "A political ploy" and 15 percent C&S stock increase: McCraw, *TVA*, 97

121 "effort to dispose…": "The President's Proposal for Pooling Power," editorial, *Chattanooga Times*, September 20, 1936

121 "This is the decisive…": "Roosevelt's Power Pooling Conference," editorial, *Jackson Sun*, September 29, 1936

121 "nice idea," and "take the ball…": McCraw, *TVA*, 94–95, 98

121 Willkie's views on pool: Ibid., 95; "Georgia Power President for TVA Accord," *NYHT*, November 22, 1936; C&S, *1936 Report to Stockholders*, 6

121 $6 million potential savings: Willkie, "Political Power," 138–139

121 Morgan's views, memo, and Lilienthal's quotes: McCraw, *TVA*, 98–99

121–22 "Weapons did not seem…" and Wehle's account of conference and negotiations: Ibid., 100–103

122 October 7 extension: "Memorandum of Agreement Between Tennessee Valley Authority and Commonwealth & Southern Corporation," GPC Archives

122 "For God's sake…": McCraw, *TVA*, 103

122 Gore injunction: Lowitt, "The TVA," 42–43

122 "The securing of…": "FDR Calls Halt on Power Talks," *AC*, January 27, 1937

122–23 "I am unable…": Ibid.; "Willkie Replies to President in Power Pool Plan Ban," *Powergrams* (February 1, 1937), 1

123 fifty lawsuits: Davidson, *Tennessee II*, 307

123 nineteen utilities lawsuit court proceedings: Ibid., 310–311; Crist, *They Electrified the South*, 79–83

123–24 "The trial came…" and other Branch recollections: Harllee Branch Jr., interview on October 28, 1993, SCHC

124 "I didn't know…": Crist, *They Electrified the South*, 81–82

124 Sweatt's testimony remote: Morgan and Dana, *Priceless Heritage*, 68

124 formula for peace: Wendell L. Willkie to Franklin D. Roosevelt, November 23, 1937, SCHC

124 "What has the government…": "Peace with the Utilities," editorial, *NYT*, December 2, 1937

124 "too honest…": "A Document Is Discovered," editorial, *NYHT*, December 2, 1937

125 APC-Ickes ruling: McCraw, *TVA*, 120–121

125 district court ruling on TEPCO: Ibid., 119; Davidson, *Tennessee II*, 311

125 "lock, stock, and barrel" offer: "Federal Power Policy Again Inspires Debate," *NYT*, January 23, 1938

125 "join hands…": "Gov. Browning Ready to Act," *NYT*, January 22, 1938

125 C&S stock below $2 a share: "New York Stock Exchange Listing," *NYT*, January 21–28, 1938

125 $88 million below par: "Jubilee Service by a Public Utility System," C&S advertisement, *AJ*, January 13, 1938

125 north Alabama cities funded by PWA: APC, *1937 Annual Report*, 17–18; APC, *1938 Annual Report*, 9–10

125 Sweatt losses and threatened losses in Mississippi: Morgan and Dana, *Priceless Heritage*, 72–76

125 "just like chicken…": Allen Arno Mills, interview by Donald M. Dana, Jr., Oral History Program, Volume I, 1986, MPC Corporate Records

125 NGEMC competition: Wright, *History of GPC*, 277–278; Bob Scherer interview, July 6, 1999, SCOHC; "Agreement with NGEMC in North Georgia Ends Duplication of Service" and "We Enter 1939 Free From Controversies," *Snap Shots* (January 1939), 1, 4

126 hostilities on both sides: Bush, *Future Builders*, 334–335; Scherer interview, July 6, 1999

126 "conspiracy…" and bitter TVA board disputes: Callahan, *TVA*, 108–109; Robert S. Allen and Drew Pearson, "The Daily Washington Merry Go Round," *AJ*, January 19, 1937

126 "hearings" in FDR offices and related quotes: "Removal of a Member of the Tennessee Valley Authority; Message from the President of the United States," Senate Document No. 155, 75th Congress, 2nd Session, 1938 (transcript of March 11, 18, and 21, 1938 hearings)

126 "deceptive publicity…" and other Morgan's accusations: Abrams, *Power in Transition*, 217, 223; "headline" and "Arthur Morgan Reviews Dispute within TVA," *AJ*, May 26, 1938

126 Harcourt Morgan's and Lilienthal's responses: Robert Humphreys, "Obstruction Laid to Ousted Chief in Counterblast," *AG*, May 26, 1938; David E. Lilienthal, "Statement Before the Joint Congressional Committee to Investigate the TVA," May 26, 1938, copy in GPC Archives

126 "I doubt if in all…": Ibid.

127 101 witnesses, 15,470 pages of testimony, 588 exhibits: Lowitt, "The TVA," 45–46

127 Lilienthal's changes to board minutes: Davidson, *Tennessee II*, 322

127 "If you can persuade…": "Text of President Willkie's Statement to TVA Probers," *AG*, November 24, 1938

127 "For a man…" and "It is a pleasure…": "Mr. Willkie Goes to Bat," *Snap Shots* (December 1938), 1, 5

127 "His greatest offense…": "The difficult Mr. Willkie," editorial, *NYHT*, November 25, 1938

127 final agreement: McCraw, *TVA*, 135–136; "TVA Pays $78,600,000 for Tennessee Power Company," *AJ*, February 5, 1939

127 "In short…": Wendell Willkie, "Idle Money-Idle Men," in *This Is Wendell Willkie* (New York, 1940), 94 [originally published in the *Saturday Evening Post*, June 17, 1939]

127 sales price close to offer five years earlier: George Carmack, ed., *Knoxville News-Sentinel*, June 14, 1940 interview published in *This Is Wendell Willkie* (New York, 1940), 150

127 Willkie's negotiations with Krug: Douglas Clark, "Territorial Integrity," paper excerpting statements concerning the intention of TVA to refrain from further invasions, compiled March 7, 1941, APC Archives

127 "We have offered…": Ibid.

128 "It appears that…": C&S, *1939 Report to Stockholders*, 22

128 1939 TVA Act amendment: Abrams, *Power in Transition*, 232–234

128 check amount and date: Bush, *Future Builders*, 338

128 closings in Mississippi and Alabama: Peacock MS, 38–39

128 "Thanks Dave…": Bush, *Future Builders*, 338

128 C&S ad and "To numerous friends…": C&S, "Tonight, at Midnight…" advertisement, SCHC

128 financial stability of TVA settlement: Martin, *Story of Electricity*, 113–115; C&S, *1940 Report to Stockholders*, 7 and *1941 Report to Stockholders*, 3–4

128 four shifts: Arthur E. Morgan, "Building a Labor Policy," *Survey Graphic*, October 1935, 529

128 sixteen dams in twelve years: Richard Lowitt, "Tennessee Valley Authority," in *Encyclopedia of Southern Culture*, Charles Reagan Wilson and William Ferris, eds. (Chapel Hill, North Carolina, 1989), 365

129 other TVA achievements: Ibid., Lowitt, "The TVA," 49–53; Callahan, *TVA*, 80–87, 122, 131–135

129 "Never before…": Davidson, *Tennessee II*, 227

129 criticisms of TVA: Lowitt, "Tennessee Valley Authority," 46–47, 57, 61; W. V. Howard, *Authority in TVA Land* (Kansas City: 1948), 52–61, 86–100, 128–131, 145–158, 163–172

129 "If you were discontented…": Davidson, *Tennessee II*, 333

129 Southern territory lost to TVA: Morgan and Dana, *Priceless Heritage*, 77; APC, *1940 Annual Report*, 8

129 "They came in there…": Ishmael (Red) Howard, interview by Donald M. Dana, Jr., Oral History Program, Volume I, 1987, MPC Corporate Records

130 duplicated systems dismantled and salvaged: Morgan and Dana, *Priceless Heritage*, 77; E. K. Leary, "Report of the Dismantling of the Distribution Systems at Decatur, Hartselle and Courtland by the Decatur District Crews," APC Archives

130 "The last work…": Crist, *They Electrified the South*, 84

130 public-private developments and percentages: EIA website; *The Government Power Issue* (Birmingham, September 1961), APC Archives; Foundation for Water & Energy Education website, "Time Line of Electricity, Hydroelectricity, and the Northwest," www.fwee.org/timeline.html

130 conservation movement: Conkin, "Intellectual…," 8–9; Library of Congress, "The Evolution of the Conservation Movement," memory.loc.gov/ammem/amrvhtml/conshome.html

131 "There is far more…": Willkie, "Political Power," 143 [and other Willkie speeches]

131 public power support in 1933 compared to 1937: "Public Ownership Sentiment Declines," *Snap Shots* (April 1938), 4

131 "The contest between…": Shlaes, *The Forgotten Man*, 10

132 "We are at a crossroads.:.": Preston Arkwright, "Self Reliance," address to the University of Georgia alumni, May 4, 1935, reprinted in *Snap Shots* (July 1935), 1, 5

132 bill to "TVA-ize the rest of the nation": J. Fred Essary, "Utilities Open Fire on New Power Plan," *Baltimore Sun*, June 4, 1937; John D. Battle, testimony to Senate Subcommittee on Agriculture, July 1, 1937, reprinted as *TVA's Seven Sisters* by the National Coal Association, APC Archives; Ellis W. Hawley, *The New Deal and the Problem of Monopoly: A Study in Economic Ambivalence* (Princeton: 1966), 340 [hereafter cited as Hawley, *The New Deal*]

133 "The gift…": Martin, *Story of Electricity*, 98, 107

CHAPTER 6

135 snowstorm: "11-Inch Snow Falls in City, 15 Lose Lives in Delta Flood," *WP*, January 24, 1935; "Forecasts of Weather Over the Nation and Region," *NYT*, January 23, 1935; "Six Dead as Snow, Worst Since 1888, Cripples the City," *NYT*, January 24, 1935; "Ice Derails Train, Killing Engineer," *NYT* January 24, 1935; "33 Dead in Storm in City and Near By," *NYT*, January 25, 1935

135 northwest gate entrance: William Bushong, White House historian, e-mail to authors, November 10, 2004

135 Willkie's dress habits: Bush, *Future Builders*, 281–282

136 FDR's relentless attacks: Arkwright, "What's the Use of Quitting Now?"

136 three punitive taxes: "New Taxes," *Snap Shots* (September 1933), 1

136 "abolition of the evil…": *Congressional Record*, January 4, 1935, 89–92; EEI, "The Public Utility Bill of 1935: A Chronological Record," EEI Library

136 correction, "evils of holding companies": Ibid.; "Roosevelt Skips a Word, But It Was Only an Error," *NYT*, January 5, 1935

136 "grotesque…": Wendell L. Willkie, "Horse Power & Horse Sense," *Review of Reviews*, August 1936, 38

136 Willkie's cooperation with Cohen: McCraw, *TVA*, 82

137 "Our discussions…" and other quotes during meeting: Lilienthal, *Journals*, 46–47

138 "Fraud, deceit…" and "taken sums…": C&S, *Outline of History*, 83

138 "only to find out…": Arkwright, "What's the Use of Quitting Now?"

138 "Why don't you…" and "Mr. Willkie, I should be…": Willkie, "Horse Power & Horse Sense," 38

138 Wheeler-Rayburn Act introduced: Hawley, *The New Deal*, 331–332

138 Wheeler's comment to Willkie: Bush, *Future Builders*, 326

138-39 Bonbright praise of C&S: Shlaes, *The Forgotten Man*, 191

139 "Its sponsors say…": "The Attack on Holding Companies," *Snap Shots* (February 1935), 4

139 "cause an overturning…,": "DANGER!" *Snap Shots* (March 1935), 1

139 provisions of the bill: Ibid.; Hawes, *Utility Holding Companies*, 2.14–2.16; Hawley, *The New Deal*, 332; Hausman and Neufeld, *Rise and Fall*, 25–26

139 "common control…": "Report of National Power Policy Committee on Public-Utility Holding Companies," contained in U.S. Senate Report, *Public Utility Act of 1935*, 74th Congress, 1st Session, Senate Report No. 621, 55 [hereafter cited as "NPPC Report"]

139 "This in effect…": House Committee on Interstate and Foreign Commerce, *Public Utility Holding Companies, Hearings on H.R. 5423*, 74th Congress, 1st Session, 647, 637 [hereafter cited as *Hearings on H.R. 5423*]

140 $3.5 billion drop: Shlaes, *The Forgotten Man*, 238

140 "No objection is made…": C&S, *Outline of History*, 22

140 pyramiding schemes: Hausman and Neufeld, *Rise and Fall*, 18–19; William Z. Ripley, *Main Street and Wall Street* (Lawrence, Kansas, 1926), 296–302 [hereafter cited as Ripley, *Main Street and Wall Street*]

140 "There is no end…": Ripley, *Main Street and Wall Street*, 292, 298

140 Standard Gas & Electric example: *Congressional Record*, House of Representatives, 1935, 10544; Energy Information Administration, U.S. Department of Energy, *Public Utility Holding Company Act of 1935: 1935–1992* (Washington DC, January 1993), 2.6 [hereafter cited as EIA, *PUHCA*]

140 C&S flat structure, $96 million: C&S, *Outline of History*, 83-84

140 "loading fixed capital accounts" and Willkie's response: Ibid.

141 "sitting on both…": "NPPC Report," 56

141 "Nothing of this kind…": C&S, *Outline of History*, 84–85, 87

141 House commending C&S corporate simplification and services at cost: House Report No. 827, Part 3, 216, 226

141 "If the bill…": *Hearings on H.R. 5423*, 635

141 "We did not build…": Ibid., 724

141 "There is not…": Ibid., 645

141 "Are you going…": Ibid., 611

141 "would be in bankruptcy…": Ibid., 644

141 "If you were to abolish…": Ibid., 680

141 "I want to say…": Ibid., 697; "Mr. Arkwright's Testimony," *Snap Shots* (Atlanta: May 1935), 4 [quotes slightly differ]

141 state commissions opposing Title II: Hausman and Neufeld, *Rise and Fall*, 25–26

142 800,000 notes: Neal, *Dark Horse*, 31

142 Hearst press: M. L. Ramsay, "Power Spies on Women Voters," *AG*, May 30, 1928; M. L. Ramsay, "Million Hear Power Talks in Year," *AG*, June 1, 1928; "Reveal Power 'Interest' in Col. Schools," *AG*, June 1, 1928; "Probe Discloses Boast of Bravado by Trust," and "Power Lobby Censor Derides Fear," *AG*, June 24, 1928

142 FTC reports on utility propaganda: Federal Trade Commission, *Utility Corporations: Summary Reports, Pursuant to Senate Resolution No. 78, 70th Congress, 1st Session*: "Efforts by Associations and Agencies of Electric and Gas Utilities to Influence Public Opinion," 1934, Doc. 97, Part 71A, and "Publicity and Propaganda Activities by Utilities Groups and Companies with Index," 1935, Doc. 97, Part 81-A

142 "The power trust…": Hyman, *America's Electric Utilities*, 85

142 "the most decided…": "House Defeats Roosevelt, 216 to 146, on 'Death Sentence' in Utilities Bill; New Test in a Vote of Record Today," *NYT*, July 2, 1935

142 "the richest and most ruthless…": Neal, *Dark Horse*, 31-32

142 Black: "BLACK, Hugo Lafayette," Biographical Directory of the U.S. Congress, bioguide.congress.gov/scripts/biodisplay.pl?index=B000499

142-43 Black's investigation of utility lobby: unless otherwise indicated, summarized from William A. Gregory and Rennard Strickland, "Hugo Black's Congressional Investigation of Lobbying and the Public Utilities Holding Company Act: A Historical View of the Power Trust, New Deal Politics, and Regulatory Propaganda," *Oklahoma Law Review*, Volume 29, 1976, 543–576

143 $1.5 million: Hawes, *Utility Holding Companies*, 2.16

143 250,000 telegrams: Gregory and Strickland, "Hugo Black…," 553

143 3¢ a signature: *Congressional Record*, August 5, 1935, 11823

143 "Hell, no…": Gregory and Strickland, "Hugo Black…", 557

143 "no fake…": "Arkwright Gives Lobby Probe Data," *Snap Shots* (September 1935), 1

143 "creatures…": numerous references in *Congressional Record*, House of Representatives and U.S. Senate, June 3, 1935, through August 22, 1935

143 Hopson: Crist, *They Electrified the South*, 71–75

143 more than 260 companies: *Congressional Record*, U.S. Senate, June 5, 1935, 8507

143 $1 billion pyramid controlled with $50,000: *Congressional Record*, House of Representatives, 1935, 10544

143 thirty-five kinds of securities: Senate Committee on Interstate Commerce, *Hearings, Public Utility Holding Company Act of 1935*, 74th Congress, 1st Session, April 1935, 200

143 $875,000 lobbying campaign: Gregory and Strickland, "Hugo Black …", 565

143 "Its size…": "Black Describes Lobby Inquiry–Tells Radio Audience 'You Will Pay Bill' in Increased Utility Rates," *Washington Evening Star*, August 9, 1935

144 "the holding…": "Congress Leaders Press Big Bills to Assure Clean-up by Saturday," *NYT*, August 21, 1935

144 chunks of gavel, "vote, vote!": "Utility Bill 'Truce' Is Voted by House," *NYT*, August 23, 1935

144 sixty switch vote: "Utility Vote Switches," *NYT*, August 23, 1935

144 PUHCA passage: "'Compromise' Voted on 'Death Clause' by House, 219 to 142," *NYT*, August 23, 1935

144 Norris last person standing: "Utilities Measure Sent to President," *NYT*, August 25, 1935

144 C&S stock below $2: "New York Stock Exchange Listing," *NYT*, August 26, 1935

144 PUHCA restrictions: "Legislative History of PUHCA," in report from Ellen L. Wilkinson to DeWitt R. Rogers, August 14, 1991, SCHC; EIA, *PUHCA*, 3.9–3.11

144 "Tens of thousands…": "An Appeal to Reason," *Powergrams* (January 6, 1936), 5

144 "Take the people…": "Willkie Given Standing Ovation at U.S. Chamber of Commerce Meeting," *Powergrams* (May 28, 1936), 2

145 $25 billion: Turner Catledge, "New RFC Loans, Easing Taxes, Using Social Security Fund; Studied to Spur Business," *NYT*, November 10, 1937

145 1937 recession stimulating policy debate: Kennedy, *Freedom from Fear*, 350–361; Hawley, *The New Deal*, 386–395

145 "For the sake…" and "to modify laws…": "One Way to Revive Business," editorial, *NYT*, November 10, 1937

145 Morgenthau and Farley arguments: Kennedy, *Freedom from Fear*, 352

145 "It arises too much…": McCraw, *TVA*, 157

145 "an outfit who…": Neal, *Dark Horse*, 33

145 "Every time…": Kennedy, *Freedom from Fear*, 352

146 SEC request in August 1938: Hawley, *The New Deal*, 337

146 "not wise policy…": Hawes, *Utility Holding Companies*, 2.15

146 SEC notices of violation: Preston S. Arkwright to Justin R. Whiting, March 11, 1940, GPC Archives

146 "Keep these…": Preston S. Arkwright to Wade Wright, March 9, 1940, GPC Archives

146 "The tearing to pieces…": C&S "Statement by Wendell Willkie," March 6, 1940, APC Archives

146 "We expect to do…": C&S, *1939 Report to the Stockholders*, 6

146 Willkie-Jackson radio debate: Walker, "A Biographical Introduction," 31; Neal, *Dark Horse*, 45–46

146 "Willkie so utterly…": Shlaes, *The Forgotten Man*, 351

147 other debates, articles, speculation on candidacy: Ibid., 46–48; Bush, *Future Builders*, 346; Walker, "A Biographical Introduction," 32–33

147-49 Willkie's nomination, campaign, envoy experience, death: summarized from Neal, *Dark Horse*, chapters 8–19; page numbers of specific references as follows – "The lights of liberty…" (75); "We want Willkie!" (99, 106, 110, 112); "Our way of life…" (121); bicycle ride, "Everything's dandy" (197); "Go home and…" (195); "a godsend…" (314); "Willkie! Willkie! Willkie!" (245); "the only man…" (270)

147 Willkie's resignation and reaction: Crist, *They Electrified the South*, 58

148 "I say that…": Shlaes, *The Forgotten Man*, 374–375

149 "This corporation's personnel…": C&S, *Wendell L. Willkie: In Memoriam*, October 8, 1944, board resolutions excerpted in *1944 Report to the Stockholders*, 2

149-50 Whiting and his personality quirks: Bush, *Future Builders*, 347–350; Crist, *They Electrified the South*, 61; C&S, news release on Whiting's election, July 17, 1940

150 integrating Citizens Light & Power: C&S, *1940 Report to the Stockholders*, 9

150 317–page report and options for C&S: Ibid., 10–11

150 C&S stock below $1 and less than a dime: "New York Stock Exchange Listings," *NYT*, March 19, 1941, and March 17, 1942

150 "It must come…": C&S, *1940 Report to the Stockholders*, 11

150-51 "The territory we serve…": Bush, *Future Builders*, 354 [narrative rephrased as quote]

151 "The times are…": C&S, *1940 Report to the Stockholders*, 11

151 "The present scattered…": Edward C. Eicher, remarks to the annual convention, EEI, June 5, 1941, GPC Archives

151 first plan for splitting the northern utilities: C&S, *1941 Report to the Stockholders*, 16

151 "Is it not reasonable…": J. F. Crist to the President, October 27, 1942, SCHC

152 5,000 pages: C&S, *1942 Report to the Stockholders*, 8

152 Yates: Branch, "History Project," part 3

152 new capacity in north: C&S, *1937 Report to the Stockholders*, 6–7

152 power policy committee meeting, projected power shortages and response: Eugene A. Yates, "Draft of Testimony for the Securities Exchange Commission," 1942, APC Archives, 12–13

152 FPC study and 100,000 kilowatts of capacity: Ibid., 13

153 military ordering curtailments, power pooling in thirteen states: C&S, *1941 Report to the Stockholders*, 14–15

153 Middlemiss to OPM offices in Atlanta: "Official Report of Proceedings before the Securities and Exchange Commission," Philadelphia, Docket 59–20, June 24, 1942, 520, 523

153 curtailments ending December 5: Ibid., 519

153 "operation of the…": C&S, *1941 Report to the Stockholders*, 15

153 "We believe...": Ibid.

153 wartime industry buildup: Eugene A. Yates, "Remarks at Dedication of Yates Dam, Tallassee, Alabama, June 15, 1947, APC Archives, 5–6

153 Hattiesburg growth: Morgan and Dana, *Priceless Heritage*, 102; Goldfield, *Cotton Fields*, 183

153 Mobile's population: Ibid.

153 boom from other military towns in the South: Ibid., 182–184

153 twenty-six different units: C&S, *1947 Report to the Stockholders*, 11

153 450,000 kw of capacity: "Corrected Transcript of Testimony of E. A. Yates before the Securities and Exchange Commission, Washington, D.C., August 25, 1948, APC Archives, 10

153-54 generation additions: C&S, *Report to the Stockholders*, annual property addition updates in 1941–1947 reports

154 floating power plant: Gulf Power *Tradition*, 8; Eugene A. Yates to C&S executives, November 6, 1944, GPC Archives

154 conservation campaigns and demand growth: C&S, *1943 Report to the Stockholders*, 8

154 "These are the days...": MPC, *Thoughts on Electric Service to Our Customers* (Gulfport, February 1, 1943), 4

154 "The stress of war...": Preston A. Arkwright, "War and Customer Service," Georgia Power employee meetings during January 1943

154 20 percent of work force, 4,090 employees, fatalities and other statistics: C&S, *1945 Report to the Stockholders*, 9

154 pension plan: C&S, *1943 Report to the Stockholders*, 7, and *1944 Report to the Stockholders*, 8

154 Whiting and law firm battle with SEC: Bush, *Future Builders*, 357–358

155 sixth plan: Ibid.; C&S, *1945 Report to the Stockholders*, 10–12

155 SEC authorize action on Northern properties: A. K. Callahan to M. R. Ferrer, May 12, 1953, enclosure including Arthur Andersen & Company's "Chronology of Compliance by the Commonwealth & Southern Corporation with the Requirements of Section 11 (b) of the Public Utility Holding Company Act of 1935," April 16, 1953, SCHC [hereafter cited as PUHCA Chronology]

155 SEC stipulations: C&S, *1946 Report to the Stockholders*, 7–9

155 initial sale of gas and transportation properties: C&S, *1947 Report to the Stockholders*, 5–6

155 reasons for SEC decision on South Carolina: Eason Balch interview, February 25, 1999, SCOHC

155 "I was determined...": Crist, *They Electrified the South*, 93

155 negotiations on the sale of South Carolina Power: Ibid., 93–95

155 "It was one...": Murray, *Martin Biography*, 144

155-56 sense of vindication, "Condemned...": Martin, *The Story of Electricity*, 144–145

156 FDR policies, contradictory paths: Hawley, *The New Deal*, 472–476, 489

156 Martin's belief that C&S played its part: Martin, *The Story of Electricity*, 143–144

156-57 contributions of C&S: Peacock MS, 42

157 214 holding companies, 922 subsidiaries, 1,054 nonutility companies: Hawes, *Utility Holding Companies*, 2.18

157 seventy-two in 1949: "Holding Company Act Enforcement Nearing Completion, SEC Reports," *Electrical World*, November 26, 1949, 14

157 eighteen in 1958: Hyman, *America's Electric Utilities*, 88

157 Birmingham Electric: SoCo, *1950 Annual Report*, 3–4

157 Georgia Power and Light: SoCo, *1956 Annual Report*, 6

157 fate of Hopson: Hausman and Neufeld, *Rise and Fall*, 30; Crist, *They Electrified the South*, 74–75

157-58 fate of Insull: Ibid., 69–70; Huges, *American Genesis*, 240–243

158 more conservative characteristics by being first sanctioned: Farley interview, March 24, 1999

159 repeal of the act: "PUHCA Repeal: A Door Opens," *Electric Perspectives*, January–February 2006, 32–44

CHAPTER 7

161 incorporation in 1945: Certificate of Incorporation, November 9, 1945 [Incorporation papers and all board minutes referenced are located in Southern Company Corporate Secretary Files]

162 Smith: Crist, *They Electrified the South*, 92–93; Balch interview, February 25, 1999

162 $3.4 million savings, capacity and capital needs: Yates, "Draft of SEC Testimony," 15–17

162 "required more than...": Ibid., 16–17

162 "It is a very..." and other quotes from SEC hearings: *SEC Proceedings*, Philadelphia, Docket 59-20, 1942–1943, dates of testimonies —Collier (May 3, 1943), Robinson (September 9, 1942), Sweatt (December 7, 1942), Parks (December 14, 1942), McManus (December 1, 1942), transcripts in GPC Archives

162 extent and impact of McManus testimony: SoCo, Resolution of the Board of Directors, January 16, 1961

162 "as efficiently as...": Ibid.

163 "According to the record...": Crist, *They Electrified the South*, 93; C&S, *1947 Report to the Stockholders*, 5–6

163 Yates named president: SoCo, Board of Directors Minutes, August 27, 1947

163 Yates: "Our New General Manager," *Powergrams* (February 1923), 3, 17; Crist, *They Electrified the South*, 105–110; "Eugene A. Yates," *Southern Highlights* (July 1976), 17–21

164 "Mother Goose Yates...": Branch, "History Project," Part 3, November 25, 1985

164 "We cannot afford...": Thomas W. Martin to Justin Whiting, February 22, 1947, Martin personal files, Thomas W. Martin Library, Southern Research Institute

164 size of Southern at formation: C&S, *1948 Annual Report*, 32–39

164 first dividend: Ibid.

164-66 the fight to make Southern Company "southern": unless otherwise indicated, compiled from Murray, *Martin Biography*, 142–145; John Temple Graves II, "Chapter One: Epochal Decision," part of a Martin biography manuscript and supporting notes from interviews conducted by Graves [ca. 1961], various drafts in Thomas W. Martin Library, Southern Research Institute [hereafter cited as Graves MS]

164 Bourne's initial election: SoCo, *Minutes of the Board of Directors*, October 9, 1946

165 initial service company agreement: SoCo, *Minutes of the Board of Directors*, November 18, 1947

165 "I have decided…": recounted in memo from Bill Brantley to John Temple Graves, January 13, 1959, notes with Graves MS

165 "We will not…": Ibid.

165 "He is highly…": Thomas W. Martin to Justin Whiting, February 22, 1947, Thomas W. Martin Library, Southern Research Institute

165 "well known…": Ibid.

166 Whiting's concession: Justin R. Whiting to Thomas W. Martin, March 17, 1947, Martin personal files, Thomas W. Martin Library, Southern Research Institute

166 Yates named president, Bourne and Crist vice presidents: SoCo, *Minutes of the Board of Directors*, August 21, 1947

166 role of Stetson: Graves MS; board resolution contained in *Minutes of the Board of Directors*, January 18, 1960

166 "We have done nothing but…": Yates, 1948 SEC testimony

166 C&S stock range, volume and record trading: "Trading Centers in a Utility Stock," *NYT*, July 20, 1949; "Huge C&S Sales Dominate Market," *WSJ*, July 20, 1949; "Stocks Achieve New Seven-Week High," *AC*, July 19, 1949

166-67 early "when distributed" stock prices: "The Southern Company: Daily Record of Common Stock Transactions," SoCo Corporate Secretary's Files [hereafter cited as "Daily Record of Common Stock Transactions"]

167 "It was a new…": Crist, *They Electrified the South*, 96

167 security analysts tour: "Security Analysts' Inspection Trip of The Southern Company System," July 17–24, 1949, notebook compiled by Jim Crist, SCHC

167 "We in the East…": Ibid.

168 "I returned…": Ibid.

168 "Management is…": Ibid.

168 "This type…": Ibid.

168 "the first of its…": "Reciprocity Note," *NYT*, July 29, 1949

168 final dissolution of C&S: SoCo, *1949 Annual Report*, 2–3; PUHCA Chronology; "Southern Co. Common Near for Stock Buyers," *AJC*, September 30, 1949

168 NYSE début: "Daily Record of Common Stock Transactions"

168 domestication in Georgia: SoCo, *1949 Annual Report*, 3

168 northern director resignations: SoCo, *Minutes of the Board of Directors*, October 27, 1949

168 C&S (New York) contract terminated, Southern Services formed: SoCo, *Minutes of the Board of Directors*, November 29, 1949 and April 4, 1949

169 "All the investments…": Yates, "Dedication Remarks"

169 $168 million and 600,000 kilowatts: E. A. Yates to Stockholders of The Southern Company, October 28, 1949, and August 10, 1949, SCHC

169 consulting twelve investment groups: Yates, 1948 SEC testimony

169 "We approached…": Crist, *They Electrified the South*, 96

169 success of first offering and bid price: Ibid.; SoCo, *1949 Annual Report*, 3

169-70 "good old days": Stephen Budiansky, "Home, Hearth and Heretics," *U.S. News & World Report*, October 25, 1993, 28–35; "American Cultural History," Kingwood College Library, kclibrary.nhmccd.edu/decade50.html

170 45-degree angle, growth, rates: SoCo, *1951–1953 and 1957–1959 Annual Reports*

170 three-year construction: SoCo, *1950 Annual Report*, 5–6

170 2 million kilowatts and sales increase: SoCo, *1957 Annual Report*, 1–3

170 construction budget increases, stock sales: SoCo, *1950–1959 Annual Reports*

171 corporate office description: James McGuire interview, [ca. July 1980], SCHC

171 "The Southern Company's…": SoCo, *The Southern Company and the Territory It Serves* (Atlanta, October 1949), 4

171 "Better Service…", "Business is up…", and "Power of the South…": SoCo Ad Files, SCHC

171-72 "Better Home Towns" program: "Better Home Towns Program Proves Popular," *Bright Spots* (November 1944); Wright, *History of GPC*, 305–309

172 "the businessman, the farmer…": MPC, "A Time for Greatness," Open Letter to Mississippians, MPC Corporate Records

172 "Helping Develop Alabama": APC, *1955 Annual Report*, cover logo treatment; logo with slogan appears on numerous other annual reports during the 1950s and 1960s

172 "Research Turns…": SoCo Ad Files, SCHC

172 1,000 new industries: "Southern Company in Growth Territory," *Financial World*, May 28, 1958, 13

172 military impact on the South: Harllee Branch Jr., "The Newer South," address to Augusta Kiwanis Club, January 25, 1954, and "The Resurgent South," address to Association of Stock Exchange Firms, Atlanta, May 9, 1960; Goldfield, *Cotton Fields*, 182–184

172 air-conditioning: Robert J. Samuelson, "The Chilling of America," *Newsweek*, June 10, 1991, 42; Robert Friedman, "The Air-Conditioned Century, *American Heritage*, August/September 1984, 20–32; "The Cooling of America," *Southern Highlights* (August 1985), 1–6

172 "greater use…": SoCo, *1951 Annual Report*, 3

173 "The officers started…": Bell interview, February 15, 1999

173 Birmingham Electric: SoCo, *1950 Annual Report*, 3–4; *1952 Annual Report*, 12

173 Georgia Power and Light: SoCo, *1956 Annual Report*, 6; Wright, *History of GPC*, 346–347

173 customer base doubled: SoCo, *1957 Annual Report*, 1

173 retirement date extended: SoCo, *Minutes of the Board of Directors*, various January minutes 1949–1957

173 "He watched them…": Crist, *They Electrified the South*, 106

173 "When he pulled…": Branch, "History Project," part 1

173 "Hotel clerks…": Crist, *They Electrified the South*, 106

173-74 chewing out editor: Branch, "History Project," part 1

174 "warm and…": Ibid.

174 "a beautiful mind…": William H. Brantley, "Remarks at Memorial Exercises Honoring Eugene A. Yates," Atlanta, April 7, 1958, SCHC

174 Barry's and McManus's duties: SoCo, *Minutes of the Board of Directors*, August 22, 1952

174 Barry: "Our Assistant Chief Engineer," *Powergrams* (November 1921), 3; Crist, *They Electrified the South*, 119–122; Martin, *The Story of Electricity*, 149–150

174 "among the men…": "James M. Barry," *Southern Highlights* (April 1977), 14–15

175 McManus: "C. B. McManus," *Southern Highlights* (February 1979), 12–13; Wright, *History of GPC*, 355–356; Crist, *They Electrified the South*, 112–117

175 Scholz: Ibid., 151–153; "Herbert J. Scholz," *Southern Highlights* (November 1976), 8–11

175 Early: "Edward Donald Early," *Southern Highlights* (January 1977), 7–8

175 "world's first…": Grady L. Smith, "The 'Early Bird,' World's First Incremental Cost Computer for Delivered Power," *Powergrams* (August 1954), 7–10

175 $400,000 savings: Gene Smith, "Computer to Get New Power Role," *NYT*, July 6, 1958

175-76 nuclear research: "Brackett Reports on Work at Atomic Power Plant," *Snap Shots* (Atlanta: March 1955), 6; SoCo, April 25, 1955, October 22, 1956, and July 22, 1957, *Board of Directors Minutes*; SoCo, *1961 Annual Report*, 21; H. J. Scholz, Remarks at "March of Progress" Conference, Mississippi Agricultural & Industrial Board, Gulfport, July 17, 1953

176 "Ruble brought…": Bob Usry interview, June 13, 1999, SCHC

176 Yates concerns about future leadership needs: Branch interview, November 12, 1991

176 Branch: "Harllee Branch Jr. … A Career," and other articles contained in special issue of *Southern Highlights* (Issue 3, 1971), 1–19; Wright, *History of GPC*, 356–360

176 Bouldin: "Walter Bouldin, Industrial Statesman, Retires," *Southern Highlights* (Issue One, 1970), 12–13

176 "impeccable judgment": Joseph M. Farley interview, February 26, 1999, SCOHC

176 "most brilliant": Branch, "Some Southern Company Profiles," 1985, SCHC [hereafter cited as Branch, "Profiles"]

176 Hatch background: "Portrait of a Leader: Edwin I. Hatch," *Southern Highlights* (Issue Five, 1971), 2–4; Crist, *They Electrified the South*, 131

177 federal dams and power politics behind "preference customers" issue: Carey E. Brown, "Hydro Power in a Sound National Water Policy as Viewed by Engineers Joint Council," Association of Edison Illuminating Companies, White Sulphur Springs, Virginia, October 19, 1955, EEI Library

177 "We do not oppose…": C. B. McManus, "Statement before President's Water Resources Policy Commission," Atlanta, July 31, 1950, GPC Archives

177 "Were it not…": C. B. McManus, "Remarks at Plant Yates Dedication," Whitesburg, Georgia, October 14, 1952, GPC Archives

178-84 Dixon-Yates scandal: unless otherwise footnoted, summarized from two detailed accounts: Jason L. Finkle, *The President Makes a Decision* (Ann Arbor, Michigan, 1960) and Aaron Wildavsky, *Dixon-Yates: A Study in Power Politics* (Westport, Connecticut, 1962) [hereafter cited as Finkle, *The President Makes a Decision* and Wildavsky, *Dixon-Yates*]

178 alternative to taxpayer expense: Herbert Murphy, "TVA Turning-Point: Fulton Plant Decision Could Have Far-Reaching Implications," *Barron's*, September 14, 1953

179 "It seemed expedient…": Wildavsky, *Dixon-Yates*, 54

179 "From bitter…": Crist, *They Electrified the South*, 108

180 AEC complaints: William M. Blair, "President Revives TVA Power Issue by Order to AEC," *NYT*, June 18, 1954

180 "those bastards": Wildavsky, *Dixon-Yates*, 6

180 Friends of TVA response under Hill: "Clapp Condemns Power Unit Plant," *Chattanooga Times*, July 3, 1954

180 "hatchet men": "U.S. Hires 'Hatchet Men' To Kill TVA, Hill Says," *AC*, July 7, 1954

180 "a fair and reasonable contract": "Answers to Questions Taxpayers Ask About the 'Dixon Yates' Contract," (1955), EEI Library

180 "like a hammer…": Wildavsky, *Dixon-Yates*, 20

181 "The president will rue…": Ibid.

181 "bad business…": Ibid., 101

181 attack on Eisenhower-Jones friendship: James Reston, "Mitchell Spurns a Rule," *NYT*, August 18, 1954; "Says Ike Favored Bobby Jones on Atom Power Pact," *AC*, August 17, 1954; Joseph A. Loftus, "President Scorns Mitchell Attack on AEC Contract," *NYT*, August 18, 1954

181 "get the complete record…": Joseph A. Loftus, "Ike, Defending Jones, Opens AEC Pact Files," *AC*, August 18, 1954

181 "It would come as…": "Ridiculous, Golfer Jabs at Mitchell," *AC*, August 17, 1954

181 "carrying guilt…": "Jones Power Role Splits Senate Dems," *New York World Telegram*, August 17, 1954

181 "I have known…": Jack Bell, "Mitchell Slap at Ike Draws Biparty Fire," *AJ*, August 17, 1954

181 "Who is Dixon…": "The Congress: Broader than Dixon Yates," *Time*, November 22, 1954

181 "A few months ago…": Robert M. Bleiberg, "Dixon-Yates: The Dispute Is and Indictment of Public, Not Private Power," *Barron's*, November 1, 1954

181 "bobbing up…": "The ABC's of 'Dixon Yates,'" *U.S. News & World Report*, November 19, 1954

182 "Meet the Press" summary: "Dixon and Yates Defend Contract," *NYT* December 6, 1954

182 "Well, certainly…": Eugene Yates, interview by Richard Wilson and panel, *Meet the Press*, NBC, December 5, 1954 [audiotape in the U.S. Library of Congress; transcript in SCHC]

182 "looking somewhat…": "Meet the Dixon Yates," *St. Louis Post-Dispatch*, December 6, 1954

182 advertising campaign: SoCo, "Straight Talk about the Dixon-Yates Proposal," SCHC

182 "The whole thing…": James Reston, "The AEC in Politics," *NYT*, November 19, 1954

182 "The trail of double…": Wildavsky, *Dixon-Yates*, 284

182 "The Dixon-Yates thing…": "The Congress…"

182 "to withdraw…": EEI, "Chronology of Principle Events in Atomic Energy Commission's Contract with the Mississippi Valley Generating Company," [ca. 1956], EEI Library

182 "We cannot withdraw…": Ibid.

183 "Who is…": Finkle, *The President Makes a Decision*, 183

183 "This man participated…": Ibid., 184

183 contract cancellation: Russell Baker, "Dixon Yates Pact is Killed by President as Memphis Pledges Own Power Plant," *NYT*, July 11, 1955

183 book of political cartoons: Untitled collection of reprints, SCHC

184 "Our actions…": "Statement Issued by Edgar H. Dixon," July 11, 1955, EEI Library

184 "good will…: The White House, "Statement by Murray Snyder," July 12, 1955, EEI Library

184 "no injustice…": Ibid.

184 "criminal conspiracy": Bill Crider, "Do You Remember Dixon & Yates?" *The Charlotte Observer*, October 21, 1956

184 "Nixon, Dixon, and Yates": Ibid.

185-87 Coosa and SEGCO developments: compiled from SoCo, *1957 Annual Report*, 9–13; *1969 Annual Report*, 21–22, 28–29; Graves MS, Chapter 7; Crist, *They Electrified the South*, 165–167; APC, *Coosa and Warrior Rivers Projects* (Birmingham, April 1958); APC, *1953–1964 Annual Reports* (Birmingham, various publication dates 1954–1965); Harvey H. Jackson III, *Rivers of History: Life on the Coosa, Tallapoosa, Cahaba, and Alabama* (Tuscaloosa, 1995), 208–222

185 Eisenhower power policies: Davis, "Our Controversial Natural Resources"; Douglas McKay, "Partnership in Water Development," National Reclamation Association, Lincoln, Nebraska, October 24, 1955, EEI Library

185 150 resolutions: APC, *Resolutions and Other Expression Endorsing the Proposed Coosa River Development* (Birmingham, May 1954), APC archives

185 all but one Alabama delegation supported Coosa: Clarence A. Davis, "Remarks by Under Secretary of the Interior," Lane County Republican Women, Eugene, Oregon, September 25, 1955, EEI Library

185 "a mammoth…": APC, *1958 Annual Report*, 16

185 "Yates saw…": Crist, *They Electrified the South*, 166

186 "turning it over…": Joseph A. Fox, "Power Issue Proves Political Powerhouse," *The Washington Evening Star*, May 12, 1955

186 "That very much…": Farley interview, February 26, 1999

186 "If you keep…": Ibid. (quote based on Farley's recall of the exchange)

187 status of SEC hearings: U.S. Department of Energy, Energy Information Administration, *Public Utility Holding Company Act of 1935: 1935–1992* (Washington, D. C., January 1993), 9–12

187 "The flap ended…": Farley interview, February 26, 1999

187 Yates funeral arrangements: "Eugene A. Yates, Sr., Dies at his Home in New York," *Snap Shots*, October 1957

187 "It was appropriate…": Branch, "History Project," part 1

188 more conservative characteristics by being first sanctioned: Farley interview, March 24, 1999; McGuire interview, July 1980

188 edits made to annual reports questioned: "Official Report of Proceedings Before the Securities and Exchange Commission," Philadelphia, Docket 59-20, June 14, 1943, transcript in GPC Archives

188 SEC approaching Branch about restructuring: Branch interview, November 12, 1991; McGuire interview, July 1980

189 "Our future is committed…": Walter Sanders, "Remarks at Plant Yates Dedication," Whitesburg, Georgia, October 15, 1952, GPC Archives

189-90 "further from the cash register": Farley interview, February 26, 1999

190 $1.9 million claim: "U.S. Court Upholds Dixon-Yates Pact," *AC*, July 16, 1959

190 "not entitled…": "Conflict of Interest," *WP*, January 12, 1961

190 amount of loss: SoCo, *Minutes of the Board of Directors*, October 16, 1961

190 Yates legacy: Harllee Branch Jr., interview on March 16, 1999, SCOHC; Thomas W. Martin, "Remarks at Memorial Exercises Honoring Eugene A. Yates," Atlanta, April 7, 1958, SCHC

190 125,000 stockholders: SoCo, *1958 Annual Report*, 2

CHAPTER 8

193 "Ladies and gentlemen…": Harllee Branch Jr., "Statement Before House Committee on Public Works," [ca. July 1958], SCHC, [hereafter cited as Branch, 1958 House Statement]

193 $750 million and territory threat: "TVA Revenue Bonds," *Snap Shots* (September 1958), 4

194 "a tense talkative man," and "a devoted worrier…": "Branch of Southern Company," *Fortune*, May 1957

194 25,000 square miles: Branch, 1958 House Statement

194 "This new area…": Ibid.

194 $1.7 billion, 75 percent from steam: EEI, "An Analysis of the TVA Power Business," July 1957, EEI Library

195 bill passed in Senate, tied up in House: "TVA Self-Financing Bill Fails to Pass," *Snap Shots* (September 1958), 5; "New TVA Bills," *Snap Shots* (February 1959), 4

195 "Why tack on…": "Representative Vinson Asks Limit on TVA Service Area," *Snap Shots* (March 1959), 5; U.S. House of Representatives, *Tennessee Valley Authority*, Hearings Before the Committee on Public Works on H.R. 3460 and H.R. 3461, 86th Congress, 1st Session, March 10 and 11, 1959, 115, 108 [hereafter cited as 1959 House Hearings on TVA]

195 "If this is a true…": Ibid., 127

196 "There was chaos…": Ibid., 147

196 "We have lived…": Ibid., 153

196 4,239 miles and 255,621 customers: Ibid., 154

196 "specifically and unquestionably…": Ibid., 164

196 "We hope and…": Ibid., 166

196 TVA could more than double: "TVA Bills Represent a Program for Vast Expansion of Public Power," editorial, *The Roanoke Times*, August 18, 1957; "TVA Self-Financing Bill Tied up in House Committee," *Snap Shots* (August 1958), 4

196 June Senate arguments: U.S. Senate, *Revenue Bond Financing by TVA*, Hearings Before a Subcommittee of the Committee on Public Works on S. 931 and H.R. 3460, 86th Congress, 1st Session, June 9 and 10, 1959, 38–49, 210–225

196 "We were willing…": Ibid., 42

196-97 provisions of new law: "Eisenhower Signs TVA Bond Bill," *NYT*, August 7, 1959; "TVA Granted Authority to Issue Revenue Bonds," *Snap Shots* (September 1959), 6

197-98 Branch background: unless otherwise noted, summarized from "Harllee Branch Jr. … A Career," and other articles contained in special issue of *Southern Highlights* (Issue 3, 1971), 1–19; Wright, *History of GPC*, 356–360; various biographical summaries in Harllee Branch Jr. File, SCHC

198 "I'll give…"; "My function…": Branch interview, November 12, 1991

198 "You got to fight…": "Branch of Southern Company," *Fortune*, May 1957

199 Savannah River Electric: SPL, "Interim Board Report," October 15, 1926, GPC Archives; "$45,000,000 Project Proposed at Clark Hill," *Snap Shots* (August 1946), 1, 8; "Clark Hill: Shall Private Enterprise Be Left Out?" *Round the Home* (April 1948), 2

199 "For the past twenty…": "Statement of the Honorable Walter Harrison," in *Truth About the Clark's Hill Project*, Clark's Hill Authority of South Carolina, [ca. 1946], 26

199 $653,000 loss: SoCo, *Board of Directors Minutes*, January 22, 1951

199 forty-four munis and thirty-seven co-ops: Wright, *History of GPC*, 342

199 "preference" policies: Ralph A. Tudor, "Partnership with Government in Power Production," *Civil Engineering*, October 1955, 86–89; Douglas McKay, "Partnership in Water Development," National Reclamation Association, Lincoln, Nebraska, October 24, 1955, EEI Library

199 "machine gun burst…": Mike Edward, "Power Probe Here Stirs Fiery Charges," *AJ*, September 2, 1955

200 "propagandizing…": Ibid.

200 "a privileged class…": Harllee Branch Jr., "A Privileged Class for America," Rocky Mountain Electrical League, Jackson Hole, Wyoming, September 12, 1955

200 "fraud, bad faith…": "Fraud in Sale of Power Charged by Democrats," *NYHT*, October 12, 1955

200 "moot": Ibid.; "Chudoff Says Power Policy Ignores Laws," *Chattanooga Times*, October 13, 1955

200 "Actually, we are…": Harllee Branch Jr., "Statement to the Press," October 12, 1955, EEI Library

200 "inadequate" White House meeting: Harllee Branch Jr., "Statement to the Press," October 13, 1955, EEI Library

201 "maybe next year…": "Georgia Utility Denied Voice in Probe," *New York Journal of Commerce*, October 19, 1955; "House Group Bars Critic as Witness," *NYT*, October 19, 1955

201 "fair-minded Americans…": Ibid.

201 editorial headlines: "Unfair Tactics by Public Power Proponents," *SMN*, October 31, 1955; "Witch Hunting for Alleged Skeletons," *Pueblo, Colorado Chieftain*, October 22, 1955; "Biased Hearing," *WP*, October 20, 1955

201 "If the subcommittee…": Ibid.

201 "no evidence…": Earl Chudoff, "Biased Hearing," *Washington Post and Times Herald*, October 26, 1955

201 "We are gratified…": Harllee Branch Jr., "Statement Regarding Chairman Chudoff's Letter to the *Washington Post*," October 26, 1955, EEI Library

201 Clark Hill outcome: Wright, *History of GPC*, 342–343

201 "Would it be all right…" and Yates's response: Branch interview, November 12, 1991

201-02 selection of Branch, dialogue as told by Branch: Ibid.; Branch interview, March 16, 1999

202 board resolution and incentives for Yates to move: SoCo, *Board of Directors Minutes*, April 13, 1953

202 Martin opposing Branch selection: Branch, "History Project," part 3

202 Martin's ego: Crist, *They Electrified the South*, 19

202 "Martin was very…": Branch interview, November 12, 1991

202 Crist led to believe he had the job: Ibid.

203 Crist: "James F. Crist: A Southern Company Historian," *Southern Highlights*, June 1978, 16–18; SoCo, *Board of Directors Minutes*, October 6, 1965, Southern Corporate Secretary Records

203 "Although he never…": Branch, "History Project," part 3

204 textiles down to 18 percent: Harllee Branch Jr., "Remarks at 1969 Southern Company Stockholders Meeting," Gulfport, Mississippi, May 28, 1969 [hereafter cited as Branch, "Remarks at 1969 Stockholders Meeting]

204 diversification of industry: SoCo, *1964 Annual Report*, 8–25

204 "The last half...": SoCo, Ad Files, SCHC

204 slogan coined by Martin: APC, press release on Advertising Federation of America award, October 7, 1958, APC Archives

204 growth in industries, investments, and jobs: compiled from Branch, "Remarks at 1969 Stockholders Meeting" and SoCo, *1969–1971 Annual Reports*

204 "Now people...": SoCo, *1964 Annual Report*, 23

204 "The Deep South carried...": cited in SoCo, *1963 Annual Report*, 6

204 "Those of us...": Thomas W. Martin, "Remarks at Presentation of Public Relations Award to The Southern Company," Advertising Federation of America, Deep South Seventh District, Montgomery, Alabama, October 7, 1958

204 10 percent or more: SoCo, *1960–1969 Annual Reports*

204 5 percent in 1961: SoCo, *1961 Annual Report*, 1, 3

204 wiring retrofits: SoCo, *1960 Annual Report*, 14

204 more than half a million: nine-year total in *1968 Annual Report*, 5; balance reported in SoCo, *1969 Annual Report*, 2

205 peak load shift to summer: Branch, "Remarks at 1969 Stockholders Meeting"

205 first 2,600 heat pumps: SoCo, *1960 Annual Report*, 14

205 200,000th all electric customer: SoCo, *1971 Annual Report*, 6

205 growth in home use: Ibid., 3; SoCo, *1957 Annual Report*, 6

205 "The load growth...": Grady Baker interview, June 29, 1999, SCOHC

205 construction additions: SoCo, *1957–1971 Annual Reports*

205 trophy to free enterprise: Harllee Branch Jr., "The Functions of Private Enterprise in Water Resource Development and Conservation," National Conference on Water Resources Policy, St. Louis, January 25, 1956

205 "Every dollar...": "Private Power in TVA's Backyard," *Business Week*, October 17, 1964

205 "The Coosa River development...": "H. Nelly Henry Dam," Powergrams, October 1968, 24

206 Edison award: "H. Neely Henry Dam," *Powergrams* (October 1968), 1

206 "most comprehensive...": SoCo, *1969 Annual Report*, 20

206 "the country's most...": "Private Power in TVA's Backyard"

206 Ringgold and Chickamauga exceptions: "TVA Granted Authority to Issue Revenue Bonds," *Snap Shots* (September 1959), 6

206 "second battle of Chickamauga" and "lost handsomely": Scherer interview, July 6, 1999

206 "When he came...": Balch interview, February 25, 1999

206 $365 million: V. J. Daniel, Jr., "Government–Our Biggest Competitor," Southern Company Biennial Meeting of System Executives, Sea Island, Georgia, October 4, 1965

206 $38 million and $20.4 million co-op loans: SoCo, *1961 Annual Report*, 21

207 "There is no economic...": Harllee Branch Jr., "Power by Stealth!" reprinted in *Powergrams* (January 1962), 2

207 background on Mississippi co-ops: Morgan and Dana, *Priceless Heritage*, 88–90; Allan John Watson, Jr., interviews with Donald M. Dana, Jr., and Chester Morgan, MPC Oral History Program, 1988, MPC Corporate Records

207 "Branch proposal": Morgan and Dana, *Priceless Heritage*, 91–95

207 "the horrible...": Ibid., 94

207-08 Branch's office: Tom Nunnelly interview, January 19, 2005; Dwayne Summar interview, February 4, 2005

208 service company reorganization: SoCo, *1962 Annual Report*, 5; McGuire interview, July 1980; James F. Crist, "Remarks to the New York Society of Security Analysts," September 15, 1965

208 customer accounting centralization: SoCo, *1966 Annual Report*, 10–11

208 fuel procurement centralization: "Southern Services' Fuel Department–Meeting the Crisis by Planning for the Future," *Southern Highlights* (Issue Two, 1970), 4–5

208 nuclear plant decision: SoCo, *1967 Annual Report*, 12; *1969 Annual Report*, 4–5; SoCo, *1958 Annual Report*, 16; Branch interview, March 16, 1999

208 "Project Look Ahead": Nunnelly interview, January 19, 2005; Summar interview, February 4, 2005; "Project Look Ahead: A View of Better Ways," *Southern Highlights* (Issue Two, 1970), 9–13

209 Data Center formation, 225 employees: "Simplifying by Unifying," *Southern Highlights* (Issue One, 1971), 2–5

209 environmental department and projects: William B. Harrison, "A Researcher's View of the Environment," *Southern Highlights* (Issue Two, 1970), 13–16

209 digital power coordination computer: Robert O. Usry, "The Power Pool: Economic Dispatch," *Southern Highlights* (Issue Two, 1971), 9–13

209 reliability issues: SoCo, *1970 Annual Report*, 23–24; William R. Brownlee, "Reliability: How We're Improving a Valuable Commodity," *Southern Highlights* (Issue One, 1970), 7–9

209 new building: "Moving Day Arrives: A New Home," *Southern Highlights* (Issue Two, 1971), 2–5

210 Branch's involvement in design: Summar interview, February 4, 2005

210 Branch advising King: Harllee Branch Jr., Obituary, *NYT*, August 19, 2000

210 "unthinkable," "unwise," "It would damage...": "Southern Co. Rejects Alabama Boycott Bid by Rev. King's Group," *WSJ*, May 13, 1965

210 Alabama labor strike: Farley interview, July 26, 1999; Bill Whitt interview, July 13, 1999

210 10 percent labor increase: SoCo, *1970 Annual Report*, 2

210 fuel increases: SoCo, *1970 Annual Report*, 2 and *1971 Annual Report*, 3

211 "the highest cost…": SoCo, *1967 Annual Report*, 2

211 9 percent interest: SoCo, *1970 Annual Report*, 4

211 20 percent operating expenses: Ibid., 2

211 first rate requests: SoCo, *1968 Annual Report*, 2, 26

211 other requests: SoCo, *1969 Annual Report*, 6–7, *1970 Annual Report*, 4–6, and *1971 Annual Report*, 2–3

211 utility economics: Ibid., 9; SoCo, *Working Toward Tomorrow Today, Costs More than Yesterday* (Atlanta, 1972)

211 "There probably has not…": Summar interview, February 4, 2005

212 public power growth: U.S. Department of Energy, "History of the Electric Power Industry," www.eia.doe.gov/cneaf/electricity/page/electric_kid/append_a.html

212 "missing opportunities…," and "I do not…": Philip Sporn, "Electric Power's Future Begins at 80," 29th annual Convention of the EEI, New York, June 6, 1961

212 "must reading" and "what you can do…": Harllee Branch Jr., to All Southern Company Officers and Principal Executives of System Companies, June 12, 1961, SCHC

212 monitoring federal issues: McGuire interview, July 1980

212 growth in generation and transmission technology: C. A. Lilly, Jr., "Growth Keeps Us Young," Southern Company Biennial Meeting of System Executives, October 4, 1965

212 "optimum top transmission…": Ibid.

213 benefits of unified system: "Private Power in TVA's Backyard"

213 $30 million savings: "The Power Pool," 11

213 "As a collection…": Summar interview, February 4, 2005

213 "We make a fetish…": "Private Power in TVA's Backyard"

214 Branch's "low profile" preferences: Summar interview, February 4, 2005

214 "analyze not where…": Branch interview, November 12, 1991

CHAPTER 9

Unless otherwise noted, Harry Bell quotes are from an interview November 12, 2004. Norman Yandell and Wallace Major quotes are from interviews November 11, 2004. Winona Latimer quotes are from an interview December 15, 2004. George East quotes are from an interview November 8, 2004. Buck Ladner quotes are from an interview December 14, 2004.

217 rainstorm off Africa: "The Lady Was a Killer," *Power Lines* (Vol. 43, No. 7, 1969, *Special Issue: Camille*), 3 [hereafter cited with headings of referenced articles as *Power Lines Special Issue*]

217 storm developments into hurricanes: Bob Sheets and Jack Williams, *Hurricane Watch: Forecasting the Deadliest Storms on Earth* (New York, 2001), 10–11, 148–150 [hereafter cited as Sheets and Williams, *Hurricane Watch*]

218 repairs on Watson Unit 4: D. H. Taquino, Jr., "Plant Jack Watson," *Power Lines* (June–July 1969)

218 "Sis" Dambrink: Teresa Taylor to authors, December 15, 2004; "Miss E. Dambrink," obituary, *Daily Herald*, August 26, 1969

218 Latimer: Adele Winona Latimer, interview with Donald M. Dana, 1988, MPC Oral History Program

218 Watson: Allan John Watson, interview with Donald M. Dana and Chester Morgan, 1988, MPC Oral History Program

219 sales more than double: MPC, *1968 Annual Report*, 16–17

219 2,300 at open house: "Open House Is Successful," *Power Lines* (April/May 1969), 2

219 "to the fortunes…," and "continue to keep…": Morgan and Dana, *Priceless Heritage*, 170

219 850 employees: "Mississippi's Edison Award: Recognition for a Response to Tragedy," *Southern Highlights* (Issue One, 1970), 15

219 1923 sleet storm: George H. Middlemiss, "The Sleet Storm," *Powergrams* (March 1923), 2, 11

219 "A glowing tribute…": Ibid., 11

220 1926 hurricane: "Pensacola Fortunate as 120-Mile Hurricane Rages," "Monetary Damage to City Probably Now Over Two Million," and "Pensacola Has 'Tidal Wave,'" *PJ*, September 22, 1926; Gulf Power, *Tradition*, 5–6

220 1936 tornado: Lawrence Sadgett interview, January 6, 1999, SCOHC, "Terrific Tornado Levels Large Gainesville Area," *Snap Shots* (April 1936), 1, 5

220 1947 hurricane: U.S. Corps of Engineers, "Report on Hurricane Survey of Mississippi Coast," U.S. Army Engineer District, Mobile, Alabama, January 25, 1965, MPC Library, A.9–A.11; "Hurricane Destroys Electric Service to Nearly 40% of Company's Customers," *Power Lines* (September 1947), 1–9

220 "That bridge…" and "We didn't…": Watson interview, 1988

220 first formal plan: W. J. Carr to Robert H. Short, November 15, 1962, Hurricane Files, MPC Library

220 Hurricane Betsy: Watson interview, 1988; Sheets and Williams, *Hurricane Watch*, 296–297, 299

221 "no improvements…": Corps of Engineers, "Report on Hurricane Survey…", 41

221 most intense storm: Sheets and Williams, *Hurricane Watch*, 156, 195

221 showers on Leeward Islands: Dan Ellis, *All About Camille* (Pass Christian, Mississippi, July 2000 and revised September 2001), 1 [hereafter cited as Ellis, *All About Camille*]

221 Simpson and storm development: Sheets and Williams, *Hurricane Watch*, 10–11, 32–40; 149–150

221 "The new storm…": Environmental Science Services Administration's Weather Bureau, "Hurricane Camille August 14–22, 1969," preliminary report published

September 1969 by the U.S. Department of Commerce, copy in MPC Library, 5 [hereafter cited as ESSA's Camille Report]

221 preliminary planning: Harry Bell interview, February 15, 1999, SCOHC; "Mississippi's Edison Award...,"14; Harry Bell, "Restoration of Electric Service Following Hurricane Camille," address to the 48th Annual Conference of State Utility Commission Engineers," Denver, Colorado, June 23, 1970 [hereafter cited as Bell, 1970 Speech]

221 "full-fledged hurricane": ESSA's Camille Report, 7

222 Cuba landfall: "The Lady Was a Killer," *Power Lines Special Issue*, 3

222 "Headed for the...": ESSA's Camille Report, 9

222 "sure the storm...": Sheets and Williams, *Storm Watch*, 151

222 "The thing was solid...": Charles L. Sullivan, *Hurricanes of the Mississippi Gulf Coast: 1717 to Present* (Gulfport, 1969), 93 [hereafter cited as Sullivan, *Hurricanes*]

222 26.72 reading and "This shook everybody...": Sheets and Williams, *Hurricane Watch*, 151

222 "Estimated at 160...": ESSA's Camille Report, 13

223 Sunday preparations: Bell, 1970 Speech; MPC, "Presentation for Edison Award Entry," March/April 1970, MPC Library, 5 [hereafter cited as MPC, "Award Entry"]

223 200,000 evacuated: "The Lady Was a Killer," *Power Lines Special Issue*, 3

223 residents preparing: Jim Lund and Richard Glacier, "Coast Area Preparing if Camille Should Hit," and "Hurricane Precautions," *Daily Herald*, August 16, 1969; MPC, "Award Entry," 3

223 26.62 readings and 190 mph: Sheets and Williams, *Hurricane Watch*, 152–153

223 "No one had seen...": Ibid., 153

224 storm surge warning: ESSA's Camille Report, 15

224 storm surge description: Ellis, *All About Camille*, 5; Sheets and Williams, *Hurricane Watch*, 72–74

224 SPLASH predictions of storm surge: Ibid., 152

224 generation taken off line: Charles F. Stanford, "Generation, Transmission System Heavily Damaged," *Power Lines Special Issue*, 13

224 "feeble minded" and "bedridden...": Ellis, *All About Camille*, 30–31

224 conditions at 9 p.m.: "The Lady Was a Killer," *Power Lines Special Issue*, 4; ESSA's Camille Report, 17

225 Watson units tripping and taken off-line: Stanford, "Generation, Transmission System Heavily Damaged," *Power Lines Special Issue*, 15

225 faults monitored up to 10:58 p.m.: MPC "Award Entry," 7

225 200-mph winds: "40 Injured in Shelter 'Cave-In' as Wind, Rain, Tides Stun Coast," *Daily Herald*, August 18, 1969

225 26.84: Sheets and Williams, *Hurricane Watch*, 295

225 reports of 230 mph: "Hurricane Camille: Storm of the Century," N5YCN–Amateur Radio Around the World website, www.angelfire.com/ms3/n4ycn/camille.html

225 instruments destroyed: "Hurricane Camille 1969," Category 3 Marketing website, category3.net/camille.htm

225 "The strangest green...": "It Was a Dark and Stormy Night...," *Powerlines*, June 1985, 6-8

226 22.6 feet: Sheets and Williams, *Hurricane Watch*, 153

226 above twenty-four feet: *The Story of Hurricane Camille* (Gulfport: 1969), special publication of Gulf Publishing Company, Biloxi Public Library, 4 [hereafter cited as *Story of Camille*]

226 tidal surge at Biloxi: Roger A. Pielke, Jr., Chantal Simonpietri and Jennifer Oxelson, "Thirty Years After Hurricane Camille: Lessons Learned, Lessons Lost," Hurricane Camille Project Report, July 12, 1999, sponsored by National Science Foundation, [hereafter cited as "Thirty Years" Report]

227 plant status: Stanford, "Generation, Transmission System Heavily Damaged," *Power Lines Special Issue*, 15

227 "I got a feel...": Watson interview, 1988

227-28 Camille damage: unless noted, summarized from: Robert McHugh, Richard Glacier, and Ted O'Boyle, "Gulf Coast Begins Tremendous Task of Digging Out from Awesome Blow," *Daily Herald*, August 19, 1969; "Hurricane Stuns Mississippi Coast as 200,000 Flee," *NYT*, August 18, 1969; Hurricane Dead Reported at 101; Toll May Grow" and "What the Hurricane Did," *NYT*, August 19, 1969; "Storm Toll 170: A Luxury Project Yields 23 Bodies," *NYT*, August 20, 1969

227 twenty miles of rails: ESSA's Camille Report, 2

227 "stacked like...": Philip D. Hearn, *Hurricane Camille: Monster Storm of the Gulf Coast* (Jackson, Mississippi, 2004), 117 [hereafter cited as Hearn, *Camille*]

227 damage to oil and gas operations: George W. Cry, "Louisiana–August 1969: Special Weather Summary of Hurricane Camille," ESSA Office for State Climatology, Louisiana State University, Baton Rouge, 93 [hereafter cited as Cry, "Louisiana Report"]

227 Ship Island sliced: Gregory Durrschmidt, "Paradise Lost," *Weatherwise*, July/August 1999

227 nearly 100 vessels: Sullivan, *Hurricanes*, 100

228 8,000 cattle, 150,000 orange trees: Cry, "Louisiana Report," 94

228 Dauphin Island, Mobile, and Pensacola damage: Hearn, *Camille*, 128; "Deadliest Hurricane in History, Camille Slams into Gulf Coast" and "Coast Slashed: Rampage Cost to Hit Millions," *BPH*, August 18, 1969; "Killer Camille Left Death, Destruction Everywhere Her Ill Winds Touched," *BPH*, August 24, 1969

228 172 killed and 9,000 injured: Hearn, *Camille*, 123

228 sixty-eight square miles destroyed in Harrison: Sullivan, *Hurricanes*, 112; "Hurricane Camille," Harrison County Library

228 homes destroyed or damaged: Ibid.

228 700 businesses: Sheets and Williams, *Hurricane Watch*, 155

228 "Restoration began...": Bell, 1970 speech

228 31,000 of 135,000 customers: MPC, "Award Entry," 9

228 477 megawatts to 69 megawatts: "Mississippi's Edison Award...," 15

228 waterfront and Highway 90: Pielke and others, "Thirty Years" Report, 9–11

229 psychological impact and physical obstacles to employees: MPC, "Award Entry," 10–11

229 general office conditions: "Rising Above an End-less...," *Power Lines Special Issue*, 30–31

229 Usry's role: R. O. Usry, "Memorandum for File: Activities of the Southern System Power Pool in Conjunction with Hurricane Camille," August 20, 1969, MPC Library

230 "I didn't know...": Latimer interview, 1988

230 Magnolia Hotel standing 100 years: Jim Lund, "Biloxi: How Bad Was It? Unbelievable!" *Daily Herald*, August 19, 1969

230 damage at Pass Christian: Ted O'Boyle, "Only Courage Left Along Beachfronts," *Daily Herald*, August 20, 1969; Bonnie Elias, "Pass Christian Bodies Recovered," *Daily Herald*, August 20, 1969; Ellis, *All About Camille*, 23–30

230 sixteen members of one family: Hearn, *Camille*, 21

230 at least eight at Richelieu: Ibid., 112

231 large diesel barge: Ellis, *All About Camille*, 71

231 85 percent of employees at work: MPC, "Award Entry," 11

231 "It's unbelievable...": Ibid.

231 housing arrangements: Watson interview, 1988; John Pearson Stephens, interview with Donald M. Dana, 1989, MPC Oral History Program

231 600: cutline to photograph, *Citizen* (December 1987), 7

231 "I slept on...": GPC, untitled news release [ca. August 1969], copy in MPC Library

231 Military restored: MPC, "Award Entry," 12

231 Williams declaring martial law: Sullivan, *Hurricanes*, 112; "Martial Law Set for Area," *Daily Herald*, August 20, 1969

232 Nixon declares "disaster area": "Governor Joins Vice President, Others for Disaster Inspection," *Daily Herald*, August 20, 1969

232 15,000 people homeless: "Hurricane Camille 1969," United States Hurricane website, www.geocities.com/hurricanene/hurricanecamille.htm

232 conditions: "Mississippi Faces Epidemic Threat After Hurricane," *NYT*, August 21, 1969; and numerous articles in the August 20, 1969, *Daily Herald*

232 "almost defy...": "Damage Defies Imagination, Agnew Declares," *Daily Herald*, August 21, 1969

232 "It's disastrous...": "Camille Strewed Havoc on Miss. Utility Systems," *Electrical World*, August 25, 1969, 43

232 statistics on damages: Bell, 1970 speech; "Mississippi's Edison Award...," 14

232 restoration priorities: Bell interview, February 15, 1999; "Power Crews on the Job Day, Night," *Daily Herald*, August 21, 1969

232 "The first day...": GPC, untitled news release, August 1969

233 "We had maps...": Bell interview, February 15, 1999

233 spirits sagging: "An Editorial," *Daily Herald*, August 21, 1969

233 forty bodies discovered by pilot: Vernon Guidry, "Dead Shifts to Sea," Associated Press, appearing in *Daily Herald*, August 23, 1969

233 "Faith, Hope, and Charity": Ellis, *All About Camille*, 41

233 "Over all this...": "Meeting the Challenge," editorial, *Daily Herald*, August 20, 1969

233 "I didn't see...": GPC, untitled news release, August 1969

234 700 outside help by 20th; 1,350 by peak day: Bell, 1970 speech

234 "Are you sure..." and "Bob, you just...": Bell interview, February 15, 1999

234 1,350 total: "Mississippi's Edison Award...," 15

234 571 from sister companies: Ibid.

234 statistics from other crews: "Good Neighbors Lend a Hand" and "Those Who Served in an Hour of Need," *Power Lines Special Issue*, 22, 36–42

234 step three restoration: Bell, 1970 speech; Weathersby, "Distribution System Interruptions Extensive," *Power Lines Special Issue*, 19–20

234 Woodall fatality: MPC, "Information Bulletin for Restoration Personnel," Number 4, August 27, 1969, MPC Library

234 "Just one more...": MPC, "Award Entry," 13

234 "The employees...": Bell interview, February 15, 1999

235 "We averaged...": GPC, untitled news release, August 1969

235 "We gather...": *Story of Camille*, 18

235 "If anyone has...": Ibid., 25

235 "a new spirit...": "Courage Is Our Banner," *Daily Herald*, August 25, 1969

235 $1.3 million: "Nixon Praises Aid to Mississippians," *Daily Herald*, August 25, 1969

235 70 percent and 60 percent: Weathersby, "Distribution System Interruptions Extensive," *Power Lines Special Issue*, 20

235 425 miles of conductor: "Logistical Support Is Vital Factor in Restoration," *Power Lines Special Issue*, 26

235 400 linemen and Cooper's role: H. L. Welch to H. H. Bell, September 22, 1969, Camille Restoration Files, MPC Library

235 other housing and food service: Bell, 1970 speech; "Logistical Support...," *Power Lines Special Issue*, 24–28

236 "a reasonable length...": MPC, "Information Bulletin...," August 27, 1969

236 "a symbol...": "Rising above an Endless...," *Power Lines Special Issue*, 31

236 "tallest building...": Ibid.

236 "We were exhausted...": Cagle interview, December 2004

236 additional repairs: C. F. Stanford and R. E. Weathersby, "Report of Storm Damage and Restoration to Mississippi Power Company Facilities After Hurricane Camille," address to Southeastern Electric Exchange, Washington, D.C., October 6–7, 1969

236 $10 million cost: Morgan and Dana, *Priceless Heritage*, 174

236 $59 million: Economic History Services website, eh.net/hmit/ppowerusd/

236 5,000 customers: Bell, 1970 speech

236 1,242 loss: MPC, *1969 Annual Report*, 2

236 most since TVA sale: Morgan and Dana, *Priceless Heritage*, 174

236 I-10 and impact on tourism: Ellis, *All About Camille*, v

237 comeback taking years and the gaming industry: Ibid., v–vi; Hearn, *Camille*, x

237 Nixon visit: *Story of Camille*, 26–27

237 "When a people…": "Hail to the Chief!" *Power Lines Special Issue*, 33

237 "I feel a deep…": "Letters and Comments," *Power Lines Special Issue*, 35

237 "Your men…": Ibid.

237 "being in the highest…": "Mississippi Power Company Wins Coveted Edison Award," *Power Lines* (July 1970), 2

237 "I don't believe…": Morgan and Dana, *Priceless Heritage*, 175–176

238 "It taught us…": Kerry Moore Ezell, interview with Donald M. Dana, 1992, MPC Oral History Program

238-39 Bell's team and summary of lessons learned: J. E. Lipsey to H. H. Bell and other management team members, May 25, 1970, contains minutes of meeting on hurricane recommendations conducted in Gulfport on April 28, 1970, MPC Library

239 wireless radios: "Southern Communications Ready to Unveil a LINC to the Wireless Future," *Southern Highlights* (December 18, 1995)

239 "Another storm…": "Thirty Years" Report, 1

239-40 Frederic: F. Neal Wade, "Not Since the Battle of Mobile" and Judy Stone," "The First Days," *Powergrams* (October 1979), 2–7; APC, *Public Relations Storm Plan*, G–1; "Frederic's Fury Batters World's Whitest Beaches," and other articles contained in special edition of *Contemporary* (October 1979)

240 "storm of the century": "The Blizzard of '93," *Highlights* (Issue Four, 1993), 3; Lynn Williams, "Snowed Under," *Powergrams* (May 1993), 15–20

240 Ivan: SoCo, *2004 Annual Report*, 16–17; "In the Eye of the Storm," and other articles of "POWEREdition," insert in *Gulf Currents* (November 11, 2004); "Hurricane Season 2004 Laid to Rest Nov. 30," and other articles in "POWEREdition," insert in *Gulf Currents* (December 2, 2004); APC, "Alabama Power Company Update #24," September 23, 2004; "Hurricane Ivan Worst Storm in Southern Company History," *The Citizen* (October 2004), 3

240 general summary of Katrina: National Hurricane Center website, "Historical Hurricane Tracks," www.nhc.noaa.gov/HAW2/english/history.shtml#katrina

240 200 miles in diameter: "Hurricane Size Comparison," *AJC*, August 30, 2005

240 category 5, 145 mph: "Katrina Comes Ashore," *AJC*, August 30, 2005

240 category 3, 125 mph: John Pain, Associated Press, "Report: Katrina Hit Land as Category 3," *AJC*, December 21, 2005

241 economic damage, oil and gas industry crippled: Eduardo Porter, "Damage to Economy Is Deep and Wide," *NYT*, August 31, 2005; Jad Mouawad and Vikas Bajaj, "Gulf Oil Operations Remain in Disarray," *NYT*, September 2, 2005; Jennifer Bayot, "First Estimate Puts Storm's Economic Toll at $100 Billion," *NYT*, September 3, 2005

241 eight of twelve casinos: Campbell Robertson, "Coastal Cities of Mississippi in the Shadows," *NYT*, September 12, 2005

241 "crumpled-up litter…": "Katrina Clobbers the Coast," *TIME: The Year in Review* (New York, 2005), 20

241 Katrina much worse: Shaila Dewan, "For Biloxi, Devastation and Death Are Too Close," *NYT*, August 31, 2005

241-42 impact on SoCo: unless specified, summary and statistics from SoCo, *2005 Annual Report*, 20–25; Mark Williams, "Katrina Cuts Wide Swath," *Highlights* (September 9, 2005), 1, 4; MPC, *Today's Dialogue*, numerous updates posted from August 28, 2005 through September 15, 2005, sotoday.southernco.com/mpc/storm_watch.html

241 637,000 in Alabama: APC, *Powergrams Extra* (September 5, 2005), 1

241 80 percent, twenty-one buildings: MPC, *Dialogue* (November 23, 2005), 1, 3

241 "We are strong…": "Message from Anthony Topazi" *Dialogue Storm Update* (September 1, 2005), MPC Corporate Communications Department

242 2,400 workers positioned, worst-case scenario planning, 11,000 workers and restoration efforts: Dennis Cauchon, "The Little Company That Could," *USA Today*, October 10, 2005

242 restoration statistics: Ibid.; SoCo, *2005 Annual Report*, 24

242 SouthernLINC role: Williams, "Katrina Cuts…", September 9, 2005, 4

242 "associate that date…": MPC, News Release, "Mississippi Power Restoration Update," September 6, 2005

242 27,000: MPC, *Today's Dialogue* (September 10, 2005), posted online, sotoday.southernco.com/mpc/katrina_0910.html

243 "Recovery, Rebuilding, and Renewal" commission: SoCo, *2005 Annual Report*, 24

243 New Orleans update, 80 percent, "national disgrace": "Katrina: It Struck the Gulf Coast, but it Wounded a Nation," and "Ordeal in New Orleans," *TIME: The Year in Review* (New York, 2005), 12–19

243 Ratcliffe's testimony in D.C.: SoCo, news release, "Southern Company CEO Shares Details of Successful Hurricane Katrina Response with Senate Committee," November 16, 2005

CHAPTER 10

Unless otherwise noted, Bob Scherer's quotes are from a SCOHC interview July 6, 1999 or from interviews June 3 and 20, 2005; Joe Farley's quotes are from a SCOHC interview February 26, 1999; Eason Balch's quotes are from a SCOHC interview February 26, 1999; Vic Daniel's quotes are from a SCOHC interview February 15, 1999; John Hemby's quotes are from a SCOHC interview June 3, 1999; and Grady Baker's quotes are from a SCOHC interview June 29, 1999.

245 failed stock-bond sale: Gary Hendricks, "Georgia Power Gets No Bids on $190 Million Issues," *AC,* July 18, 1974

245 "We got no bids…": Bill Dahlberg interview, October 15, 2001

246 other failed sales: Tom Henderson, "Negotiated Stocks-Bonds Sale OK'd for Ga. Power," *AC,* July 24, 1974

246 credit rating drop: Hendricks, "Georgia Power Gets No Bids…"

246 Con Ed dividend: "No," *Southern Highlights* (Issue 4, 1974), 5

246 stock drop: Ibid.

246 request of SEC: Henderson, "Negotiated Stocks-Bonds…"

246 five-year maturity: Tom Henderson, "Ga. Power Will Sell $130 Million Bonds," *AC,* July 26, 1974

246 successful bond sale: Tom Henderson, "Georgia Power Sells $130 Million in 5-Year Bonds," *AC,* August 2, 1974

247 $86 million rate increase: Tom Henderson, "Ga. Power to Seek Hike," *AC,* October 18, 1974

247 Pafford quote: Ibid.

247 Carter questions request: "Carter to Question Ga. Power Figures," *AC,* November 21, 1974

247 earnings drop 95 percent: James Hightower, "Ga. Power Faces Crisis," *AJ,* December 12, 1974

247 stock sell-off: Tom Henderson, "Earnings Drop by 95 Pct., Georgia Power Co. Says," *AC,* December 13, 1974

247 "The continuing erosion…": Ibid.

247 cost of coal: Larry Woods, "Classically Caught Between a Rock and a Hard Place," *Atlanta Magazine,* September 1979

248 hearing postponed: James Hightower, "PSC Delays Hearing on Power Rate Hike," *AJ,* December 16, 1974

248 motion to reopen: James Hightower, "Ga. Power Ups Surcharge Plea," *AJ,* December 20, 1974

248 new rate filing: Ibid.

248 Wilson's testimony: James Hightower, "Ga. Power Ups Surcharge Plea," *AJ,* December 20, 1974

248 generation installed: "3.3 Million Kilowatts Added to System Capacity in '74," *Southern Highlights* (Issue 3, 1974), 26

248 soaring electricity rates: "Electric Rates Rise Across the Nation," *Southern Highlights* (April 1975), 12

249 cost curve: Dahlberg interview, October 15, 2001

249 only two previous: "Georgia Power Asks Increase; Alabama Is Granted Relief," *Southern Highlights* (Issue 3, 1971), 20

249 McDonough background: "Looking Back with Pride," *Southern Highlights* (February 1980), 12

249 Hatch background: "Portrait of a Leader," *Southern Highlights* (Issue 5, 1971), 2; "Hatch Presided During Changing Era," *Citizen* (May 1975), 5; Matthew Quinn, "Georgia Power's Edwin Hatch Dies," *AC,* February 6, 1997

250 Hatch's illness: Scherer interviews, July 6, 1999 and June 3, 2005

250 Georgia Power Project: Bill Dahlberg interview, October 4, 2001

250 break to residential customers: James Hightower, "Big Industries Challenge Ga. Power Rate Increase," *AJ,* August 17, 1973

250 Georgia Industrial Group: Ibid.

250 Supreme Court action: James Hightower, "Ga. Power Rate-Hike Hopes Up," *AJ,* ca. November 1973

251 Dow Jones drops: Karma Banque website, karma-banque.com/modules.php?op=modload&name=News&file=article&sid=2651

251 "Fuel prices…": Dahlberg interview, October 15, 2001

251 need for creative leadership: "A Call for Active Leadership," *Southern Highlights* (January 1975), 6; "Corporate Relations Committee," *Southern Highlights* (June 1975), 3

251 "I said, 'Alvin…": Harllee Branch Jr. interview, August 1983, SCHC

251-52 Vogtle background: "A Man Who Persisted," *Southern Highlights* (October 1983), 2; "Reflections of a 42-Year Career," *Inside* (October 1983), 3; Sarah Dunbar, "Alvin Vogtle," *Buckhead Atlanta,* August 9, 1979; "At Tea Time or Tee Time, a Top–Notch Guy," *Southern Highlights* (Issue 1, 1970), 2; "Charisma," *Southern Highlights* (Issue 3, 1973), 6; Branch interview, August 1983

252 "I'll just stand…": "A Man Who…," *Southern Highlights*

252 "Alvin said he…": Ibid.

253 "Alvin was one of…": Ibid.

253-54 Vogtle's management style and personality: Branch, "Profiles;" Tom Nunnelly interview, January 19, 2005; Donna Jonsson interview, January 21, 2005; Summar interview, February 4, 2005; Branch interview, August 1985

253 "One of the amazing…": "Reflections of…," *Inside*

253 "He was the most private…": Branch, "Southern Company Profiles"

254 "the so-called Vogtle…": Jonsson interview, January 21, 2005

254 "Sit down …": Nunnelly interview, January 19, 2005

254 construction halted: "Operating Companies Cut Construction," *Southern Highlights* (Issue 5, 1974), 1

254 "unsettled state": "Southern to Cut Building Program," *AJ,* September 12, 1974

254 short-term debt: "A Man Who…," *Southern Highlights*

254 decision to sell stock: Ibid.

254 stock price in 1974: James Hightower, "Southern Wins Support," *AJ,* September 19, 1974

254-55 17.5 million shares: "The Southern Company Approves Sale of 17,500,000 Shares of Common," *Southern Highlights* (Issue 5, 1974), 28

255 largest equity sale: Hightower, "Southern Wins ..."

255 Vogtle in WWII: Alvin Vogtle, autobiographical POW account, April 13, 1945, GPC Archives; "Over Two Years a POW in Germany," *Powergrams* (July 1959), 34; "Great Escapades," *Southern Highlights* (October 1983), 8

255 details of stock sale: Tom Henderson, "Southern Co. Sells $152.9 Million in Common Stock," *AC*, September 19, 1974

255 "ice-breaking": Henderson, "Southern Co. Sells ..."

255 "the respect of...": Branch, "Profiles"

256 "I can remember...": Dahlberg interview, October 4, 2001

256 $21 million in taxes: Frank Wells and Tom Henderson, "2,300 Layoffs Swell State Jobless Rolls," *AC*, December 28, 1974

256 Putnam County: Ibid.

256 $35 million rate increase: "Georgia Power Makes Further Cutbacks," *Southern Highlights* (January 1975), 3

256 1,500 job cuts: Wells and Henderson, "2,300 Layoffs..."

256 Territorial Act passed: "Governor Signs Territorial Bill," *Snap Shots* (April 1973), 1

257 antitrust laws: Scherer interview, July 6, 1999

257 role of municipals: "Territorial Legislation Bill Signed by Carter," *Southern Highlights* (Issue 3, 1973), IFC

258 Territorial Affairs team: Baker interview, June 29, 1999

258-59 Scherer background: Larry Woods, "Classically Caught Between a Rock and a Hard Place," *Atlanta Magazine*, September 1979; Bob Deans, "Bob Scherer: The Power at Ga. Power," *AC*, January 6, 1986; "The Scherer Years," *Citizen* (May 1989), 3; Scherer interviews, July 6, 1999 and June 3, 2005

258 "I learned early...": Deans, "Bob Scherer..."

259 "I started law school...": "The Scherer Years"

260 Oglethorpe's belief: "Unique Contract Provides Mutual Benefits," *Southern Highlights* (March 1975), 4

260-61 disagreement within Southern: Scherer interview, June 3, 2005

262 Plant Hatch sale: Beau Cutts and Frederick Allen, "U.S.-Backed Loan to Aid Georgia Power," *AC*, January 7, 1975; "Historical Agreement Signed with OEMC," *Citizen* (March 1975), 3; GPC, *1974 Annual Report*, 10

262 hearings begin: Sharon Bailey, "Ga. Power's 'Crisis' Told at Hearing," *AC*, January 21, 1975

262 "Do you know...": Dahlberg interview, October 4, 2001

262-63 Wilson's testimony: "Precedent-Setting Action," *Southern Highlights* (March 1975), 2; Bailey, "Georgia Power's Crisis..."

263 "That was great...": Dahlberg interview, October 15, 2001

263 NYSE halts trading: Bailey, "Georgia Power's Crisis..."

263 $25 million granted: "Precedent-Setting Action"

263 letter-writing campaign: "Advertisements, Petition Back Requested Rate Relief," *Citizen* (February 1975), 1

263 $305 million request: "Precedent-Setting Action"

263 presentation at Capitol: Charles Hayslett, "Georgia Power: Image Low," *AJ*, February 26, 1975

263 "He would arrive...": Summar interview, February 4, 2005

264 Hill & Knowlton study: Ibid.

264 financial condition: "The Utility Game," *Industry Week*, January 25, 1982

264 "Bob Scherer brings...": "New Leaders Bring Fresh Insight to Georgia Power," *Southern Highlights* (April 1975), 2

265 construction cuts: "Making Your Electric Service More Efficient," *Citizen* (May 1975), 3

266 $116 million rate increase: John Huey, "It Was Hottest Potato," *AC*, April 25, 1975

266 "candidate for a funeral": "Scherer Asks Employee Support During Tour of Divisions," *Citizen* (June 1975), 1

266 "Bob kept us going...": Dahlberg interview, October 15, 2001

266 employee dinner meetings: "Scherer Asks..."

267 "We must make...": GPC, *1975 Annual Report*, 15

267 Miller's promotion: Ibid., 14

267 attracting capital: "System Raises More Capital Than Any Other Electric Utility," *Southern Highlights* (January 1976), 17

267 "Twelve months ago...": "We've Met the Challenges and Made Visible Accomplishments," *Citizen* (December 1975), 3

267 additional plant sales: "Agreement Assures Construction of Plant Vogtle," *Southern Highlights* (October 1976), 17

268 earnings increase: GPC, *1978 Annual Report*, 2

268 "winter of our discontent": Alvin Vogtle, "Address to Southern Company Annual Meeting of Stockholders," Mobile, Alabama, May 24, 1978

268 1968 rate increase: Farley interview, February 26, 1999

268 1971 financial trouble: Ibid.

269 visit to see Wallace: Farley interview, February 26, 1999

269 Farley background: Clarke Stallworth, "Joseph Farley: Family Man with a Big Business to Run," *BN*, February 28, 1982; "Farley," *BPH*, March 20, 1984; "Joe Farley," *Southern Highlights* (Issue 4, 1971), 10; Farley interview, February 26, 1999

270 $106.8 million request denied: "Rate Case Chronology," *Powergrams* (January 1989), 8

270 $61 million increase: "Rate Case Chronology"

270 complaint case filed: "Rate Case Chronology"; Farley interview, February 26, 1999

271 Barton nuclear plant: "Alabama Power Cancels Barton Units," *Southern Highlights* (December 1977), 15; Farley interview, February 26, 1999

271 "we were asking...": "Making Money the New-Fashioned Way," *Powergrams* (January 1989), 6

271 "You did not go...": Whitt interview, June 13, 1999

271 PSC meetings moved: Farley interview, February 26, 1999

272 complaint case ends: "Rate Case Chronology"; Farley interview, February 26, 1999

272 appeal to Supreme Court: "Rate Case Chronology"

272 1978 year-end financial condition: "Making Money…"

272 name in phone book: Stallworth, "Joseph Farley:…"

272 "I am so deeply…": Ibid.

273 ROE of 3.7 percent: "Making Money…"

273 James holds meeting: Otis White, "Politics May Pull the Plug at Southern Company," *South Magazine*, February 1980

273 $288 million request: "Rate Case Chronology"

273 Frederic impact: Farley interview, February 26, 1999

273 ROE climbs: "Making Money…"

274 1970 rate increase: "MPC Enters New Era of Electric Service," *Power Lines* (Issue 12, 1975), 51

274 ensuing three requests: "Mississippi Power Company Retail Rate Cases Summary," MPC Library

274 1975 request delayed: Morgan and Dana, *Priceless Heritage*, 193

274 "They knew what…": Bell interview, February 15, 1999

274 "small-town" agenda: Ibid.

275 full testimony: Ibid.

275 collected under bond: Morgan and Dana, *Priceless Heritage*, 190

275 "Citizens for More Power…": Ibid., 191

275 "The meter readers…": Ibid., 193

275 denials overturned by courts: "MPC Rate Cases Summary"

275 1975 rate case: Ibid.

275 1979 rate request: Morgan and Dana, *Priceless Heritage*, 193

275 Allain's role in rate cases: Ibid., 191

276 rates in the early years: C&S, *Outline of History*, 37; Martin, *Story of Electricity*, 16

276 below 2¢: SoCo, *1961 Annual Report*, 24–25; SoCo, *1969 Annual Report*, 8–9

276 83 percent: SoCo, *1974 Annual Report*, 4

276 nuclear from $150 to $600 per KW: EIA website

276 11 percent rate increases: Ibid.

276-77 regulatory lag and ratemaking problems: SoCo, *1973 Annual Report*, 2–3; George B. Campbell, "The Proper Care and Feeding of Capital," *Southern Highlights* (Issue 4, 1973), F4–F7; "George Campbell Reviews the System's Financial Situation," *Southern Highlights* (May 1978), 8–10

277 $29.38: SoCo, *1979 Annual Report*, 25

277 $11.50: Ibid., 1

277 "I think our only…": "Do Your Best Every Day and Never Give Up," *Southern Highlights* (December 7, 1992), 2

277 "unparalleled partnership…": "Unique Contract…," ·*Southern Highlights*

279 "If we had not…": "Do Your Best Every Day…"

CHAPTER 11

Unless otherwise noted, Ed Addison quotes are from a SCOHC interview August 11, 1999. Joe Farley quotes are from SCOHC interviews March 24, 1999, and June 25, 1999. Bob Scherer quotes are from a SCOHC interview July 6, 1999, and interviews on June 1, 3, and 20, 2005. Bill Dahlberg quotes are from interviews August 7, 2001, and January 10 and 28, 2002. Doug McCrary quotes are from a SCOHC interview July 8, 1999.

282 events leading to accident: "Here's What Happened at Three Mile Island," preliminary report from the Atomic Industrial Forum, *Southern Highlights* (April 1979), 6

282-83 events following the accident and responses to it: unless otherwise noted, summarized from nearly 100 articles March 29–April 7, 1979, editions of *NYT* and a twenty-year perspective by Marianne Lavelle, "When the World Stopped," *U.S. News & World Report*, March 29, 1999, 38–39

282 Carter at Plant Hatch: "Unit One Completion Marked at Plant Hatch," *Citizen* (July 1974), 1

283 SoCo and industry response: "Can It Happen Here?" *Southern Highlights* (April 1979), 2, 3; William B. Reed, "The Nuclear Industry Is Presented with its Most Severe Communications Problem," *Southern Highlights* (April 1979), 4–5; "After TMI: The Industry's Efforts," *Southern Highlights* (December 1979), 8–9

284 70,000: "Nation's Largest Anti-Nuclear Rally Held in Washington," *Southern Highlights* (June, 1979), 16

284 government's report, "To prevent nuclear…": "Three Mile Island: The Kemeny Commission Reports," *Southern Highlights* (December 1979), 3–5

284 "This is really like *1984*": B. Drummond Ayres Jr., "Within Sight of Stricken Plant, a Town's Main Street is Empty," *NYT*, March 31, 1979

285 eighty agencies: Harllee Branch Jr., "Free Enterprise: Its Origins, Its Achievements, Its Promises, and Its Problems," speech for Southern Company's Campus Visit Program, SCHC

285 piping support and anchor bolt testing: "A Milestone in Alabama History," *Powergrams* (August 1981), 2–3

285 nuclear industry problems: Leonard Sloane, "The Troubled Utility Stocks," *NYT*, January 24, 1984

285 sixty nuclear units: Lavelle, "When the World Stopped"

285 2,000 new regulations: GPC, *Georgia's Energy Future* (Atlanta, 1984), 5

285 units under construction: SoCo, *1984 Annual Report*, 17–19

285 drop-off in demand growth: SoCo, *1980 Annual Report*, 3

286 need to raise $1 billion: "Southern Company Tells the Whole Story," *Inside* (May 1984), 4

286 potential acid-rain cost: "So Many Questions, So Few Answers," *Southern Highlights* (November 1983), 1

286 FERC policies: Reddy Communications, Inc., *Regulation: The Evolution of Control* (Albuquerque, February 1989) and *The Scope and Status of Structural Changes in the U.S. Electric Utility Industry* (Albuquerque, December 1993)

286 cogeneration: Stuart Diamond, "Cogeneration Jars the Power Industry," *NYT*, June 10, 1984

286 impediments to IPPs: Allen Franklin, "Remarks at the 1989 SCS Management Forum," May 25, 1989

287 "It naturally follows…": "In Defense of Plant Vogtle," *Georgia Trend*, June 1987, 79

288 report on thefts: Thomas D. Baker and J. L. Childers, "Investigative Report," December 22, 1983, through January 23, 1984, Gulf Power Corporate Communication Files

288 amnesty program: Elizabeth Wilson, "Abuse of Power," *Florida Trend*, January 1990, 66–67

288 Horton reimbursing: Ginny Graybiel, "Gulf Power Had Told Horton to Repay Political Donation," *PNJ*, June 20, 1989

288–90 Addison profile: compiled from Jeffrey Lauterbach, "Who Gets the Next Decade at Southern Company?" *Business Atlanta*, April 1982; Cable News Network, "Pinnacle" profile, November 3, 1984; Tess Fraser, "Addison Typifies Success," *PNJ*, February 11, 1985; "The Addison Legacy," *Southern Highlights* (February 23, 1995), 4–5

288 "You just can't…": "Ed Addison: Business Activist," *Southern Highlights*, September 1980, 9

288 "younger…" and "Southern directors…": Lauterbach, "Who Gets…"

290 "His style of…": SoCo, untitled news release, April 18, 1983

290 speculation on Vogtle's choices and internal campaigns: Dwight Evans interview, March 2, 2005, SCHC; Nunnelly and Summar interviews, January 19, 2005, and February 4, 2005

290 "Farley has faced …" and "Everything is done …": Lauterbach, "Who Gets …"

291 board agenda: SoCo, *Minutes of Regular Meeting of Board of Directors*, April 18, 1983

291 Vogtle's style: Addison, Nunnelly, Summar, and Jonsson interviews, August 11, 1999, January 19, 2005, February 4, 2005, and January 21, 2005, respectively

292 "everyone in the…": Jim Miller interview, June 17, 1999, SCOHC

292 Miller background and role at Vogtle: Ginger Kaderabek, "A Parting Salute," *Citizen* (November 1987), 3–9; "Resolution on Retirement of James H. Miller, Jr.," by the GPC board of directors, October 21, 1987

292 "before launching…": "The Reagan Administration Takes a Stand," excerpts of Ruckelshaus testimony in Congress, *Southern Highlights* (April 1984), 8–10

293 cost increase projections: "Headed for the Future," *Southern Highlights* (Summer 1988), 2–5

293 "We need to…" and "the most significant…": "The Answer … Is Change," *Southern Highlights* (July 1985), 11–12

293 new Vogtle costs and schedules: "Update on Plant Vogtle," *Southern Highlights* (September 1985), 8–9

293 up to 12,000 workers, "biggest…": Tripp Cagle, "Where Will All the People Go?" *Citizen* (July 1988), 11; Bob Scherer, "Remarks to the Georgia Power Heritage Preservation Club," June 20, 2005, Atlanta, Georgia

294 phase-in proposals: "Plant Vogtle: A Special Report," *Southern Highlights* (February 1985), 1–5

294 audit reports: "Moving Toward Generation," *Southern Highlights* (Summer 1986), 20–21; SoCo, *1986 Annual Report*, 43–44

294 problems with sales, Rocky Mountain, and lawsuits: SoCo, *1986 Annual Report*, 11–14, 26, 42–46

294–95 Chernobyl accident: "Nuclear Crossroads," "Defense in Depth," "After Chernobyl," and "Success in France," *Southern Highlights* (Summer 1986), 2–20

295 calling for nuclear phase-out: Irvin Molotsky, "Phase-Out of A-Plants in U.S. Is Urged," *NYT*, April 30, 1986

295 stock market drop: Gary Klott, "Dow Falls a Record 41.91 Points," *NYT*, May 1, 1986

295 price tag for Vogtle: "The Final Phase," *Southern Highlights* (Summer 1987), 38–39

295 Unit 1 rate case and outcome: GPC, *1987 Annual Report*, 7, 16; "You Wanted to Know," *Citizen* (June 1987), 12–14; "Georgia Power Files Rate Increase Request with PSC," "Scherer Responds to Vogtle Prudence Audit," and "Company Asks PSC to Reconsider Decision," *This Week* (April 2, 1987, April 16, 1987, and October 8, 1987)

295 "It ate me alive …" and SONOPCO project background: Grady Baker interview, June 29, 1988, SCOHC

296 Farley's nuclear leadership and Southern Nuclear role: "The SONOPCO Project," *Southern Highlights* (Summer 1989), 18

296 Canadian pressure: Edward L. Addison, "Remarks to the Atlanta Kiwanis Club," June 27, 1989

296 clean coal proposals: "A Burning Question," *Southern Highlights* (Autumn 1988), 14

296 "I want them all" and success of program: Charles Goodman interview, April 22, 2005

296 "fast, cheap…," competition: "IPPs: The Rules of the Game Have Changed," *Southern Highlights* (Fall 1990); "IPPs Say They'll Build Next Southern Company Plant," *Southern Highlights* (December 7, 1992), 5

297 Standard Oil contract, "go and sin no more": Victor J. Daniel interview, February 15, 1999, SCOHC

297–99 Gignilliat quotes and recollections of telephone call, meetings, negotiations: Arthur Gignilliat interview, April 5, 1999, SCOHC

298 Branch's attempt to buy Savannah Electric: Harllee Branch Jr. interview with Tom Boren and David Knope, November 12, 1991, SCHC

298 McDonough's investigation: John Hemby interview, June 3, 1999, SCOHC

299 Riley's attempt to force a merger, "It takes two …": John McIntosh interview, April 6, 1999, SCOHC

299 merger announcement and approvals: "A Natural Fit," *Southern Highlights* (Winter 1987), 38–39; SoCo, *1988 Annual Report*, 3

299 "This merger can't…": "Two Faces of Savannah," *Southern Highlights* (Summer 1988), 8

299 customers, employees, plants: Ibid.

300 "I am deeply troubled…": GPC, "Statement of Georgia Power Chairman Bob Scherer Regarding IRS Investigation," August 26, 1988

300 raid: Gail Epstein and David K. Secrest, "Grand Jury, IRS Investigating Alleged Tax Fraud at Georgia Power," *AC*, August 26, 1988

300 "We're right smack dab…": Robert L. Barr, "Transcript of Press Conference," August 30, 1988, [transcription by Brown Reporting, Inc.]

300–01 informant and release of transcripts: Gail Epstein, "Mole in Ga. Power Told IRS of Alleged Tax Fraud" and "Excerpts from Secretly Taped Meetings," *AC*, September 1, 1988

301 "to avoid paying…": Gail Epstein, "Southern Co. Could Owe $200 Million to IRS," *AJ*, August 30, 1988

301 "The information contained…" and "I want to state…": GPC, "Statement of Robert W. Scherer," August 30, 1988

301 "grievous errors…" and "We have found…": GPC, "Remarks of Robert W. Scherer, Chairman and CEO of Georgia Power Company," September 8, 1988

302 Georgia Power plea: "Chronology of Key Events in the Spare Parts Investigations," Troutman Sanders Archives [hereafter cited as "Chronology…"]; Dick Pettys, The Associated Press, "Georgia Power Casts Long Shadow over PSC Race," *Macon Telegraph and News*, November 1, 1998

302 "We don't know the…": Barr, "Transcript …"

302 lawsuit against Gulf Power: "Chronology…"; Michael Burke, "Witness: Utility Execs Reaped Benefits," *PNJ*, May 7, 1987

302 "normal company perquisites …": Michael Burke, "Large Theft Losses Detailed in Gulf Power Lawsuit," *PNJ*, February 11, 1988

302 amnesty program: Ginny Graybiel, "Utility Boss Repaid $10,000 Under Amnesty," *PNJ*, May 25, 1989

303 "Before it was over…": McCrary interview, July 8, 1999

303 McCrary reinforces code of ethics and employee morale: Douglas L. McCrary, "State of the Company Address," January 19, 1989, Gulf Power Corporate Communication Records; Gulf Power Company, "2:05 Employee Bulletin," January 10, 1989

303 audit committee investigation of Baker's memo: Gulf Power Company, "Special Investigation by the Audit Committee," November 14, 1988; "Ex-Security Manager Opened a Pandora's Box of Trouble," *PNJ*, June 25, 1989

303 kickbacks and fraudulent invoices: Michael Burke, "Former Manager at Gulf Power Admits Tax Fraud," *PNJ*, February 12, 1988; Ginny Graybiel, "Ex-Gulf Power Boss Admits Tax Charge Guilt," *PNJ*, April 8, 1988; Michael Burke, "Jurors Return Guilty Verdict Against Leeper," *PNJ*, June 24, 1988

303 warehouse manager sentence, lawsuit dismissed: Michael Burke, "Ex-Gulf Power Manager Gets Jail Term," *PNJ*, May 12, 1988; Ginny Graybiel, "Judge Dismisses Lawsuit," *PNJ*, July 12, 1988; Michael Burke, "Loses Appeal in Gulf Power Suit," *PNJ*, May 12, 1989

303 summoned to Atlanta: Carl Wernicke and Ginny Graybiel, "Missing Man an Enigma to Many," *PNJ*, December 29, 1988

303 grand jury subpoenaed campaign records: Ginny Graybiel, "Grand Jury Scours Campaigns," *PNJ*, January 20, 1989

303 "a hard worker…" and other quotes about Howell: Wernicke and Graybiel, "Missing Man …"

304 account of plane crash: SCS, "Bulletin," April 11, 1989; Gulf Power Company, "2:05 Employee Bulletin," April 20, 1989; Gulf Power Company, "For the Record," April 25, 1989; Mark O'Brien, "Cabin Fire Suspected in Crash," *PNJ*, April 13, 1989

304 Horton, "tireless community worker" and other related quotes: SCS, In Memoriam, employee posting, April 12, 1989; Michael Burke, "Horton Was 'Enthusiastic Leader,'" *PNJ*, April 11, 1989; Ginny Graybiel, "Jake Horton's Tangled Legacy," April 9, 1990

304 "This tragic accident…": Burke, "Horton Was …"

304 McCrary and Bell meeting with Horton: Gulf Power Company, "For the Record," April 25, 1989; Ginny Graybiel and Tony Welch, "Utility Wanted Horton Out," *PNJ*, April 15, 1989

305 internal investigation of invoicing discrepancies: Gulf Power Company, *Minutes of Meeting of Audit Committee*, February 6, 1989

305 "I don't break the law…": Ibid.

305 "This is certainly a sad…": Gulf Power Company, "2:05 Employee Bulletin," April 12, 1989

305 speculation about Horton's death: Ginny Graybiel, "Just Before Death, Gulf Power Officer Wished to Dispel Rumor of Investigation," *PNJ*, April 11, 1989; Curt Anderson, The Associated Press, "Southern Company Probe Takes Bizarre Twists," *Marietta Daily Journal*, April 24, 1989; Ginny Graybiel, "Call Implies Plane Sabotaged," *PNJ*, April 28, 1989; Ginny Graybiel, "Horton Confidant Hires Bodyguard After Threats," *PNJ*, April 20, 1989; Ginny Graybiel, "Cockpit Tape Doesn't Reveal Cause of Horton Plane Crash," *PNJ*, June 10, 1989; National Transportation Safety Board, "Transcript of Cockpit Voice Recorder from Beech King Air-200," June 9, 1989; Ginny Graybiel, "Gulf Power Director Says He Was Kept in the Dark," *PNJ*, June 25, 1989; Bill DiPaolo, "FBI Finds Traces of Acid in Wreck of Plane that Killed Gulf Power Exec," *PNJ*, November 1, 1989

305 "allow accurate…": Gulf Power Company, series of "For the Record" bulletins, May 2–5, 1989; Michael Burke, "Federal Probe Saps Gulf Power, McCrary Says," *PNJ*, January 15, 1989

306 Barton resolution: SoCo *Minutes of Regular Meeting of Directors*, April 16, 1989

306 audit committee review: SoCo, *Report of the Audit Committee to the Board*, October 16, 1989

306 subpoenas, SEC investigation: "Chronology …"

306 national media coverage: "Fatal Subtraction," *Time*, May 22, 1989; Jeffrey Schmalz, "Florida Mystery is Fueled by Intrigues and 4 Deaths," *NYT*, June 18, 1989; Martha Brannigan, "Mystery in Dixie: Murder, Disappearance and Air Crash Intensify Probe of Southern Co.," *WSJ*, April 28, 1989, and "Southern Co. Braces for Holders' Questions on Inquiry," *WSJ*,

May 24, 1989; Sydney P. Freedberg, "Witnesses, Canaries Die Off in 'Southerngate,'" *The Miami Herald*, May 22, 1989; "Roy Jones," *Sports Illustrated*, May 15, 1989

306   "flood of rumor …" and related quotes at annual meeting: Edward L. Addison, "Remarks at Annual Meeting of Stockholders," Savannah, Georgia, May 24, 1989

306   customer lawsuits: "Chronology … "

307   1989 raids: Gail Epstein and David Secrest, "Ga. Power Files Seized in Raid," *AJC*, July 22, 1989; Gail Epstein, "Feds Seize Southern Co. Papers," *AC*, September 14, 1989; SCS, news posting, September 15, 1989

307   Horton's estate lawsuit and SCS response: "Chronology …"; SCS, bulletin posting, January 1990; "Southern Co. Firm Claims Executive Set Plane on Fire," *Northwest Florida Daily News*, January 6, 1990

307   "We consider this…": Robert L. Barr, "Transcript of Press Conference," October 31, 1989

307   123 examples: Robert L. Barr, "Transcript of Gulf Power Plea Bargain Agreement," *PJN*, November 5, 1989

307   "We do not condone…": SCS, bulletin posting, "Joint Statement by Edward L. Addison and Douglas L. McCrary," October 31, 1989

307   fine and mismanagement penalty: Rick Christie, "Southern Co. Unit Enters Guilty Plea to Felony Charges," *WSJ*, November 1, 1989; "Gulf Power Fined a Record $2.4 Million," *PNJ*, August 10, 1990

307   U.S. Attorney ready to prosecute: Ann Woolner, "Unplugging the Prosecution," *Fulton County Daily Report*, June 15, 1990

308   awaiting word: "Georgia Power Holds Its Breath," *Fulton County Daily Report*, May 23, 1990

308   tax probe dropped: Martha Brannigan, "Southern Co. Wins a Victory in Tax Dispute," *WSJ*, May 29, 1990

308   "At the outset …": SCS, "Statement of A.W. Dahlberg," May 25, 1990

308   "Other aspects…": Ibid.

308   Howell and another vendor guilty plea: Ginny Graybiel, "Ray Howell Pleads Guilty," *PNJ*, April 24, 1990; "Howell Chronology," *PNJ*, December 30, 1989; "Ex-Vendor for Unit of Southern Co. Files Guilty Plea in Court," *WSJ*, June 21, 1990

308   Horton estate lawsuit proceeding, organized crime speculation: Ginny Graybiel, "Horton Felt in Danger," *PNJ*, August 30, 1990, and "Probe Widens in Horton Crash," *PNJ*, September 22, 1990; The Associated Press, "Lawyer: Gulf Power Exec Got Death Threats," *Mobile Press Gazette*, August 31, 1990

308   sensational report and response from Southern: M. Rex Smith and Emory Thomas Jr., "Inside the Southern Co.: Discord, Deception, Death," *ABC*, April 8, 1991, and "Southern Co.: Tough Times Are Continuing," *ABC*, December 23, 1991; "Southern: Addison No Tyrant," *PNJ*, April 6, 1991; Jim King and Hank Ezell, "Newspaper Story 'Lies,' Southern Co. Official Says," *AJC*, April 6, 1991

308   derivative lawsuit: "Chronology…" and background materials, Troutman Sanders Archives; SCS, bulletin posting, week of April 10, 1991

309   Addison speech to industry meeting: Edward L. Addison, "Industry Structure Debate and Trends in the United States: Transmission Access and Pricing," EEI Library

309   "It's your job…" and other quotes attributed to Baskin: Addison interview, August 11, 1999

309–10   resolution of various lawsuits and investigations: "Chronology…" and file summaries prepared for 1991–1997 annual meetings, Troutman Sanders Archives

310   London audio expert suggesting a possible struggle: SCS, bulletin postings, May 7 and 8, 1991

310   NTSB final ruling: SCS, bulletin posting, July 21, 1992

310   Vogtle unit 2 write-off and resolution of rate case: SoCo, *1989 Annual Report*, 3, *1990 Annual Report*, 2–3, 41, and *1991 Annual Report*, 4–5

310   Gulf States settlement: SoCo, *1990 Annual Report*, 11

311   Plant Scherer sale terms: Ibid., 8

311   Clean Air Act compliance: Ibid., 23

311   construction completion, "For the first…": Ibid., 5; Edward L. Addison, "Remarks to Annual Meeting of Stockholders," May 23, 1990

311   earnings bounced back, dividend increase: SoCo, *1991 Annual Report*, 5

311   "I think five years from now …": "Addison Talks Past, Present and Future," *Southern Highlights* (January 27, 1992), 2

311   restructure of fossil/hydro: "Guthrie Steering Staff Toward Common Purpose," *Southern Highlights* (January 27, 1992), 5

312   June 1992 meeting, functionalization decisions, philosophy statement, and one-company mindset concepts: "Management Council Approves New Organizational Philosophy," and other articles, *Southern Highlights* (Special Issue, June 22, 1992)

312   2,000 fewer employees: SoCo, *1992 Annual Report*, 7

312   improved productivity measure: "What Was Said," *Southern Highlights* (June 2, 1993), 3

312   cost-cutting results: Edward L. Addison, "Remarks to Annual Meeting of Stockholders," May 27, 1992

312   fossil/hydro transformation: Bill Guthrie interview, June 24, 1999; "Studying How to Be the Best," "Best Practices Result in Recommendations," "IPPs Say They'll Build Next Southern Company Plant," and "Plants Taking Steps to Raise Competitiveness," *Southern Highlights* (May 20, 1993), 4–5; "Transformation Process Making Big Impact Quickly," *Southern Highlights* (January 17, 1995), 2; Bill Guthrie Retirement Dinner Presentation, May 28, 1998

312   "They think we're…": "IPPs Say They'll…"

312   "When you reach …": "The Addison Legacy," *Southern Highlights* (February 23, 1995), 5

313   $1 billion and dividend increase: Ibid., 3; SoCo, *1993 Annual Report*, 16–17

313   improvements in competitive outlook: SoCo, *1993 Annual Report*, 5–16, and *1994 Annual Report*, 4–13

313   most admired utility ratings: *Fortune* (March 6, 1995), 88

313 "Southern Company defined …": Gregory E. David, "Power Surge," *Financial World*, February 1, 1994, 30

313–14 financial support: Tom Walker, "Southern Co.'s Stock Off $3 for Week Amid Probe Reports," *AC*, September 3, 1988; Andrew Kilpatrick, "Analyst Says Scandal Hasn't Hurt Southern Co.," *BPH*, May 16, 1989

314 improvements in corporate governance, internal auditing: SoCo, *Report of the Audit Committee to the Board*, October 16, 1989

315 clean coal research benefits: Charles Goodman, "Benefits from Investments in Clean Coal Technology," summary paper prepared for the Department of Energy, March 1, 2001, SCHC

315 3,200 items learned from Unit 1: Tripp Cagle, "One Up, One to Go," *Citizen* (July 1988), 7–11

315 "The question is whether or not …": P. D. Crockett, Keystone Custodian Fund, New York, in memo to The Southern Company, Report on 1949 Analysts Tour, SCHC

CHAPTER 12

Unless otherwise noted, Bill Dahlberg's quotes come from interviews on January 28, 2002, February 19, 2002, or March 11, 2002.

317 dawn raid: Emory Thomas Jr., "Southern Co. Buys Stake in Utility Located in Britain," *WSJ*, July 11, 1995

318 observing work practices: Michael Smith, "Southern Trawl Draws the Net Around UK Utility," *Financial Times*, July 11, 1995

318 "Once the regulator…": Bill Dahlberg, "Address to Georgia Power Leadership Development Association (GPLDA)," Atlanta, July 18, 1995

319 SWEB purchase price: Richard W. Stevenson, "British Utility to Be Acquired by Southern Co.," *NYT*, August 26, 1995

319 "You have to grow…": Dahlberg, GPLDA address

320 "Is retail access inevitable?": Bill Dahlberg, "Address to Southern Company Executive Forum," Braselton, Georgia, March 21, 1995 [hereafter cited as Dahlberg, Executive Forum address, March 21, 1995]

320 "national model": Seth Mydans, "California Nears Competition Among Electricity Providers," *NYT*, April 21, 1994

321 "Southern Beyond 2000": "Dahlberg Aims Southern Beyond 2000," *Southern Highlights* (March 27, 1995), 1

321 three drivers of competition: Dahlberg, Executive Forum address, March 21, 1995

321 expanded incentive plan: "PIP Program Eligibility Increased to 2,500," *Southern Highlights* (March 27, 1995), 5

321 offers to customers: Dahlberg, Executive Forum address, March 21, 1995

321 "the most extensive restructuring …": "FERC Issues Open-Access Proposal," SCS, bulletin, March 30, 1995

322 "drive costs down…": Dahlberg, Executive Forum address, March 21, 1995

322 four business units: "Dahlberg Aims Southern…"

322 America's Best Diversified Utility: Ibid.

322 "growth engine": Dahlberg, Executive Forum address, March 21, 1995

322 U.S. electricity growth: Allen Franklin interview, December 8, 2005, SCOHC

322 intermediate goals: "Southern Company's Big Goals," *Southern Highlights* (October 1, 1995), 1

323 Southern Style: Dahlberg, Executive Forum address, March 21, 1995

323 "For the body to be…": Bill Dahlberg, "Address to Southern Company Advanced Management Forum," Atlanta, April 20, 1995

323 "Man of the Year": William Smith, "How Bill Dahlberg Shook Up Economic Development's Old Guard," *Georgia Trend*, January 1994

323 most respected CEO: Tom Barry, "Georgia's Most Respected CEO 1996," *Georgia Trend*, May 1996, 23

323 first to head two chambers: Maria Saporta, "Dahlberg Makes History Today in Dual Roles," *AC*, December 16, 1994

324 monetary support of Olympic bid: Bill Dahlberg interview, October 15, 2001

324 Olympic volunteers and sponsorship: "Georgia Power Fact Sheet," GPC, May 2, 1996, SCHC

324 Centennial Olympic Park contribution: Maria Saporta, "Southern Co. Powers Park Plans," *AC*, January 28, 1997

324 plans for friendly takeover: Patrick Harverson, "Southern May Merge with Top UK Power Generator," *Financial Times*, April 18, 1996

324 National Power-Powergen deal: Matthew Rose, "UK Utility Raises Bid for Rival in Latest Rebuff to a U.S. Suitor," *WSJ*, April 23, 1996

325 right to approve purchaser: David Wighton, Patrick Harverson, and Simon Holberton, "UK to Block Bids for Generators with 'Golden Share,'" *Financial Times*, May 3, 1996

325 "The British government…": Bill Dahlberg, "Address to Southern Company Annual Meeting of Stockholders," Duluth, Georgia, May 22, 1996

325 CEPA purchase: SoCo, news release, "Southern Company to Acquire Interest in Asian Power Group," October 9, 1996

325 "some earnings dilution": Matthew Quinn, "Southern Wins Race in Asia," *AC*, October 10, 1996

325 Asia's power needs: SoCo, "Strategic Advantages/Reasoning," talking points for media, October 8, 1996, SCHC

325 "There is no other area…": Agis Salpukas, "A Deal That Brings Together 2 Players in Electric Power," *NYT*, October 12, 1996

325 Wu's need for cash: Dahlberg interview, March 11, 2002

327 sentiment on the board: Ibid.

327 world's largest IPP: Matthew Quinn, "Southern to Buy Asian Electric Firm," *AC*, October 10, 1996

327 ad campaign: "Southern Co. to Launch National Ad Campaign," *WSJ*, January 15, 1997

327   "We cannot succeed…": Bill Dahlberg, "Address to Southern Company Business Forum," Point Clear, Alabama, October 11, 1996

327   "We wake up…": Matthew C. Quinn, "Southern Rolling Out National Ad Campaign," AC, January 16, 1997

327   branding initiative: "New Logo Unifies Southern's Products and Services," Southern Highlights (October 14, 1996), 1

327   Bewag purchase: Agis Salpukas, "Big U.S. Utility Spreads Its Reach to Berlin," NYT, May 14, 1997; SoCo, news release, "Southern Company Agrees to Acquire Stake in Bewag," May 13, 1997

328   "Bewag creates…": Bill Dahlberg, "Address to Southern Company Annual Meeting of Stockholders," Atlanta, May 28, 1997

328   Brazilian purchase: Matthew Quinn, "Southern Co. Joins Group Buying Stake in Brazil Utility," AC, May 29 1997

329   description of farm life: Bill Dahlberg interviews, August 1 and 7, 2001

329   "Mother was a tough lady …": Dahlberg interview, August 1, 2001

329   early Georgia Power jobs and education: Bill Dahlberg interview, September 19, 2001; Dahlberg interview, August 1, 2001

330   "Ego didn't create…": Scherer interview, July 6, 1999

330   "I don't like…": Michael Ensser, Bill Henderson, and Joel Koblentz, "Face to Face: Bill Dahlberg," The Focus (leadership magazine produced by Egon Zehnder International, Dusseldorf, Germany), Fall 1999 [hereafter cited as "Face to Face"]

330   "Everyone was depending…": Dahlberg interview, October 15, 2001

330   "idea people": Hemby interview, June 3, 1999

330   "If we misread…": Dahlberg interview, October 15, 2001

330   "I think it's important…": Marc Rice, The Associated Press, "Long Climb to the Top," Marietta Daily Journal, January 30, 1994

330   Frankl details: Gerald Corey, Theory and Practice of Counseling and Psychotherapy (Belmont, California, 2001), 141

330   "That helped me…": Dahlberg interview, August 7, 2001

331   "The Vogtle project…": Bill Dahlberg, "Address to 1994 Southern Company Annual Meeting of Stockholders," Mobile, Alabama, May 25, 1994

331   Southern Company staff: "Dahlberg Begins Restructuring of Southern Company Staff," Southern Highlights (March 27, 1995), 5

331   "Others have referred…": SoCo, 1996 Annual Report, 1

332   windfall-profits tax: "UK Government Imposes $3.5 Billion Windfall Tax on Electric Utilities," Electric Power Daily, July 3, 1997; Matthew Quinn, "British Tax Bite on Southern Worse than Expected," AC, July 3, 1997; Arthur Gottschalk, "U.S. Utilities Face British Taxes," Journal of Commerce, May 28, 1997

332   25 percent sale of SWEB: "SEI Completes Sale of Stake in SWEB," Energy Daily, July 2, 1996

332   Wu's departure: Matthew Quinn, "Southern Buys Out Hong Kong Partner," AC, July 17, 1997

332   Java disagreement: Matthew Quinn, "Southern, Wu Tangled over Java Plant," AC, July 17, 1997

332   Indonesia's economic crisis: Joseph Albright and Marcia Kunstel, "Result Less than Electrifying Thus Far," AC, June 30 1998

332-33   Wu's guanxi: Margaret Newkirk, "Foreign Projects Broke Mirant," AJC, September 21, 2003

333   CEO's resignation: Matthew Quinn, "Return to Hong Kong," AC, June 21, 1997

333   creation of SCEM: SoCo, news release, "Southern Energy, Vastar to Create Leading Energy Services Company" April 5, 1997

333   SEC approval: Matthew Quinn, "Southern Gets OK to Enter Natural Gas Business," AC, November 16, 1996

333   Providence Energy: Paul Tolme, "Southern Energy and Providence Energy Forming New Electric Company," The Associated Press, January 30, 1997

333   "Our competition…": Matthew Quinn, "Southern's Natural Gas Marketing in the Pipeline," AC, August 29, 1997

334   Duke buys Pan Energy: Ibid.

334   "If Thomas Alva Edison…": Matthew Quinn, "Power Struggle," AC, November 23, 1997

334   Enron ad campaign: Matthew Quinn, "Southern Rolling Out National Ad Campaign," AC, January 16, 1997

334-35   Franklin quotes on Enron: Franklin interview, December 8, 2005

335   China plant investment: Christopher Seward, "Southern Joins in Chinese Power Venture," AC, June 30, 1998

335   "There are not the same development…": "Power Trip," Institutional Investor, February 1999

335   plants in India and Pakistan: Albright and Kunstel, "Result Less…"

335   26 percent sale of SWEB: Matthew Quinn, "Southern Sells Controlling Stake in UK Utility," AC, June 19, 1998

335   35 percent savings on SWEB: Dahlberg interview, March 11, 2002

335-36   State Line purchase: "Southern Company Closes Acquisition of Commonwealth Ed's State Line Plant," Electric Power Daily, January, 5, 1998

336   New England purchase: Matthew Quinn, "Southern to Buy Plants in Northeast," AC, May 28, 1998

336   Wichita Falls plant: Matthew Quinn, "Southern Buying Plant to Aid Texas Presence," AC, September 22, 1998

336   Wisconsin purchase: SoCo, news release, "Southern Energy Inc. Proposes Town of Neenah, Wis., Electric Generating Plant," October 7, 1998

336   California and New York plants: Martha Brannigan, "Southern Co. Unit to Purchase Plants for $1.28 Billion," WSJ, November 25, 1998

336   "You can put together a strategy…": "Face to Face"

336 low financial ranking: "Strategy Execution – BAG," *Southern Highlights*, (October 28, 1998), 2

336 more aggressive strategy: "Sharpen Focus, Expand Growth," *Southern Highlights*, (October 28, 1998), 1

336 "We hit that goal…": "Face to Face"

336-37 request of SEC: Matthew Quinn, "Southern Seeks OK to Expand," *AC*, January 26, 1999

337 $200 million write-down: Matthew Quinn, "Southern Will Take 'Significant' Earnings Charge," *AC*, December 22, 1998

337 underestimated competition: Newkirk, "Foreign Projects…"

337 decision not to raise dividends: Matthew Quinn, "Southern Leaves Dividends Unaltered," *AC*, January 20, 1999

337 "over time" and "Growing the company…": Ibid.

337 "If you're going…": Matthew Quinn, "Southern Sees Natural Gas as an 'Advantageous Addition,'" *AC*, March 11, 1999

337-38 description of El Paso: Howard Buskirk, "Merger Mania Continues as Southern Eyes El Paso, National Grid Targets EUA," *Energy Daily*, January 26, 1999; Matthew Quinn, "Speculation Weds Texas Gas Firm to Southern," *AC*, February 25, 1999

338 size of potential merger: Ibid.; "Southern Talking with El Paso," *Restructuring Today*, February 11, 1999

338 why merger broke down: "Southern, El Paso Merger Off," *Energy Daily*, March 5, 1999; Christine Cordner, "Southern CEO Refuses to Comment on El Paso Merger Rumor," *Bridge News*, March 9, 1999

338 El Paso buys Sonat: Steven Lipin and Carlos Tejada, "El Paso Energy to Acquire Sonat for $3.9 Billion," *WSJ*, March 15, 1999

338 sinking stock price: Robert Luke, "Bargain Hunters Discover Southern," *AC*, April 21, 1999

338 repurchase of shares: SoCo, news release, "Southern Company Reports Increased Asian Earnings, Announces Stock Repurchase Program," April 19, 1999

338 "With our stock price…": Ibid.

338-39 Franklin named COO: Matthew Quinn, "Power Shift: Executive Moves Up at Southern," *AC*, May 20, 1999

339 Boren retires: SoCo, news release, "Southern Company Second Quarter Earnings Increase 16 Percent," July 19, 1999

339 $14 billion in assets: Ibid.

339 "Tom's aggressive guidance…": Ibid.

339 Fuller named CEO: SoCo, news release, "Fuller Named President and CEO of Southern Energy," July 20, 1999

339 1999 financial results: Matthew Quinn, "Southern Co. '99 Earnings Set Record," *AC*, January 21, 2000

339 regulated performance: Bill Dahlberg, "Address to Southern Company Annual Meeting of Stockholders," Atlanta, May 24, 2000

339-40 SEI performance: Allen Franklin, interview by John Defterios, *Ahead of the Curve*, CNNfn, January 20, 2000

340 energy trading sales: SoCo, news release, "Southern Company Energy Marketing Reports Year-end Sales," February 1, 2000

340 "Despite the economic…": SoCo, news release, "Southern Company Reports Record Earnings for 1999," January 20, 2000

340 "We delivered…": Quinn, "Southern Co. '99 Earnings …"

340 utility stocks down: Dahlberg, 2000 Annual Meeting address

340 "The stock market…": SoCo, *1999 Annual Report*, 2

340 "People have so many…": Bill Dahlberg, interview by Beverly Schuch, *CNN Pinnacle*, CNN, April 26, 1998

340 "I'm patient…": Christopher Edmonds, "Southern Looks to Spark Interest in Electric Utilities," TheStreet.com, March 16, 2000, 1:47 p.m. EST

340 "When you execute…": Dahlberg, 2000 Annual Meeting address

341 options considered: Edmonds, "Southern Looks to Spark…"

341 value down $5 billion: Allen Leverett, "Address to Southern Company External Affairs Forum," Washington, D.C., March 1, 2000

341 first-quarter results: SoCo, news release, "Southern Company Reports Strong First-Quarter Earnings," April 17, 2000

341 "We have reached a difficult…": Bill Dahlberg, "Address to Southern Company Executive Forum," Savannah, Georgia, April 17, 2000

341 details of spin-off: SoCo, news release, "Southern Announces Initial Public Offering of Southern Energy," April 17, 2000

341 "From an emotional standpoint…": Maria Saporta, "Wrenching Decision Brings Farewell to Southern Co.," *AC*, February 20, 2001

341 "By executing…": Dahlberg, 2000 Annual Meeting address

342 "Traditional shareholders…": Todd Terrell, notes from interview of Bill Dahlberg by Matthew Quinn, May 17, 2000, SCHC

342 capital needs: Dahlberg, Executive Forum address, April 17, 2000

342 details of IPO: SoCo, news release, "Southern Company and Southern Energy Announce Closing of Southern Energy Initial Public Offering, Changes in Boards," October 3, 2000

342 SEI becomes Mirant: SoCo, news release, "Southern Energy Is Now Mirant," news release, January 19, 2001

342 Fuller's bold prediction: Matthew Quinn, "Southern Energy Takes New Identity," *AC*, January 19, 2001

342 Dahlberg to Mirant: Matthew Quinn, "Dahlberg to Retire from Southern Company," *AC*, February 20, 2001

342 "an active but…": SoCo, news release, October 3, 2000

342 272 million shares: SoCo, news release, "Southern Company Board Approves Mirant Spinoff April 2," February 19, 2001

342 "This is the final step…": Ibid.

343   Some of the things…": Terrell, interview notes, June
      29, 1999

344   eBay to $241: Roger Lowenstein, *Origins of the Crash:
      The Great Bubble and Its Undoing* (New York, 2004),
      101

344   iVillage to $80: Ibid., 124

344   Priceline: Ibid., 117, 124

344   "I am going…": Dahlberg interview, March 11, 2002

344   description of market bubble: Lowenstein, *Origins of
      the Crash*, 103, 120–122

344   eToys comparison to Toys "R" Us: Ibid., 117

344   "The old rules…": Ibid., 103–105

345   "If you have a slowdown…": Franklin interview,
      December 8, 2005

345   "mindless march…": Allen Franklin interview,
      December 2, 2005, SCOHC

CHAPTER 13

*Unless otherwise noted, Allen Franklin's quotes are from
SCOHC interviews on December 2 and 8, 2005; and
David Ratcliffe's quotes are from a SCOHC interview
November 16, 2010.*

348   formula for success: Franklin interview, December
      2, 2005

348-49   Southern Power strategy: Franklin interview,
         December 8, 2005

350-54   Franklin background: Ibid.

352   "you work hard…": "Franklin Is the Same Man at
      Work and at Play," *Citizen* (January 6, 1995), 2–4

353   "Franklin probably knows…": Matthew Quinn,
      "Power Shift: Executive Moves Up at Southern," *AC*,
      May 20, 1999

353   "principal leader": Ibid.

353   "one of the smartest people…": Maria Saporta,
      "Wrenching Decision Brings Farewell to Southern
      Co.," *AC*, February 20, 2000

354   2001 financial performance: SoCo, *2001 Annual Report*,
      10–11

354   "the business we know best…": Ibid., inside front
      cover

355   2002 financial performance: SoCo, *2002 Annual
      Report*, 2–7

356   highest market value: Allen Franklin, "Address to
      Southern Company Annual Meeting of Stockholders,"
      Pine Mountain, Georgia, May 28, 2003

357   end of deregulation: Jennifer Bjorhus, "California
      Electricity Deregulation Brought to an End," *San Jose
      Mercury News*, March 22, 2002

358   Enron's fall: Lowenstein, *Origins of the Crash*, 166–187

358   El Paso and Reliant 70 percent loss: "Defendant, The
      Southern Company Answers the Amended Com-
      plaint," Mirant Corporation vs. The Southern
      Company, Chapter 11 Case No. 03–46590, Jones Day
      Attorneys' filing in the U.S. Bankruptcy Court for the
      Northern District of Texas, Fort Worth Division,
      August 17, 2005, 3

358   Dynegy 95 percent loss: Ibid.

358   sentencing of Enron executives: Greg Farrell, "Case
      Closed: Last Top Enron Exec Sentenced," *USA Today*,
      November 16, 2006; "They Put Ethics in the
      Shredder"; Greg Burns, "Skilling's 24-Year Term a
      Warning to 'Corporate Crooks,'" *AJC*, October 24,
      2006

359   rise and fall of Mirant stock: Patti Bond, "Southern
      Company Spinoff Timing Fortuitous–but Many
      Investors Kept Mirant," *AJC*, July 19, 2003

359   "A lot of companies…": Ibid.

359   2003 financial performance: SoCo, *2003 Annual Report*,
      2–5

360   "There is nobody…": Maria Saporta, "Franklin Con-
      tinues to Hang Close to Dahlberg," *AC*, May 20, 1999

360-62   Ratcliffe background: Mary Welch, "Style Points,"
         Business to Business, January 2007, 49; Jonathan Hayes,
         "Tifton Native Named CEO of Georgia Power,"
         Tifton Gazette, May 21, 1999; Matthew Quinn, "Rat-
         cliffe's Leadership Skills Cited," *AC*, May 20, 1999;
         Ratcliffe interview, November 16, 2010

361   willingness to listen: Maria Saporta, "Franklin Con-
      tinues to Hang Close to Dahlberg," *AJC*, May 20, 1999

361   "He was very objective…": Ibid.

361   "I joined Georgia Power…": *Business to Business*,
      August 1999

361   "Don't bring him…": Saporta, "Franklin Con-
      tinues…"

362   "David's been involved…": "Ratcliffe to Take Helm of
      Southern, Succeeded by Mississippi Power's Garrett,"
      Citizen (December 15, 2003), 1

362   "This company is not broken…": Terri Cohilas, "Rat-
      cliffe Reflects," *Highlights* (February. 2, 2004), 1

363   "Southern Company is…": Mark Williams, "Ratcliffe
      Unveils Modified Southern Style, Target Zero Safety
      Goal," *Highlights* (October 11, 2004), 1

363   "We've evolved…": Ibid.

363   Southern Style simplified: Ibid.

363   fragmented industry: Ratcliffe interview, November 16,
      2010

364   "We will sit down…": Cohilas, "Ratcliffe Reflects"

364   environmental philosophy: Ratcliffe interview,
      November 16, 2010

364   "Everybody is…": Cohilas, "Ratcliffe Reflects…"

364   Ratcliffe principle: SoCo, David Ratcliffe retirement
      tribute video, December 12, 2010

364   "This is a serious…": Welch, "Style Points…"

364   Prism Analysis: Ratcliffe interview, November 16, 2010

365   "The environmental…": George Lammons, "Missis-
      sippi Power President Settles In," *Sun Herald*, May 5,
      1991

365   never expected to be here: *Business to Business*, August
      1999

365   summoning Miller: Ratcliffe interview, November 16,
      2010

365   "Nuclear power is…": Welch, "Style Points…"

366   nuclear consortium: SoCo, news release, "Seven Com-
      panies to Investigate Licensing, Design Certification of
      Advance Nuclear Reactors," March 31, 2004

367 right thing for America: Ratcliffe interview, November 16, 2010

367 oversight committee: Ibid.

368 Nuclear Energy Financing Act: Jeff Beattie, "Georgia PSC Gives Early Cost Recovery to Southern Reactors," *Energy Daily*, March 19, 2009

368 PSC grants certificate: Margaret Newkirk, "Two Nuclear Reactors Get Green Light," *AJC*, March 18, 2009

368 early site permit: "Plant Vogtle Receives Early Site Permit," *Citizen*, (September 2009), 1

368 description of units: Georgia Power, news release, "Georgia Power Signs Contracts for Nuclear Units," April 8, 2008

368 nearly $500 million: SoCo, entry for Platt's 2010 Industry Leadership award, December 2010

368 IGCC research: Ibid.

368 chosen by DOE: SoCo, news release, "Southern Company to Operate Department of Energy's National Carbon Capture Center," May 27, 2009

369 Kemper County plant: Debbie Myers, "Coal Plant Groundbreaking Dec. 16," *Neshoba Democrat*, December 8, 2010

369 loan guarantee: Matthew Wald, "In Bid to Revive Nuclear Power, U.S. Is Backing New Reactors," *NYT*, February 17, 2010

369 Cimarron plant: SoCo, news release, "Southern Company and Ted Turner Acquire Solar Photovoltaic Power Project, March 15, 2010

370 "the largest natural...": David Ratcliffe, interview with Dave Altman, "Goals and Reviews," January 6, 2006

370 Mirant lawsuit: Margaret Newkirk, "Southern Company to Pay Mirant $202 Million," *AJC*, April 3, 2009

370 worst recession since WWII: Rich Miller and Alison Sider, "World Economy Emerging From Worst Recession Since World War II," Bloomberg, August 22, 2009

371 "As we continue...": Terri Cohilas, "Price Increases to Drive Cost Reduction," Highlights (October 2008), 1

371 2008 performance: "Southern Company Reports Solid 2008 Earnings Despite Weak Economy, Mild Weather," PR Newswire, January 28, 2009

371 "Our customers...": "2009 to Be an Economic Challenge: Customers Face Financial Hurricane," *Highlights* (January 2009), 1

371 salary freeze: Ibid.

371 industrial sales: "Southern Company Reports Second Quarter Earnings," PR Newswire, July 29. 2009

371 2009 performance: "Southern Company Reports Solid Earnings Despite a Challenging 2009," PR Newswire, January 27, 2010

371 largest drop in demand: Ibid.

371 industrial sales stabilized: Ibid.

371 2010 return to sales growth: SoCo, news release, "Southern Company Reports 2010 Fourth Quarter and Full-Year Earnings," January 26, 2011

371 shareholder value: SoCo, entry for Platt's 2010 CEO of the Year award, December 2010

371 Ratcliffe's awards: SoCo, David Ratcliffe bio, SCS Corporate Communication Files

373 "The Southeast is still...": "Southern Company Reports...," PR Newswire, January 27, 2010

EPILOGUE

378 $17 billion: SoCo, Fourth Quarter 2010 Earnings Conference Call, January 26, 2011

379 "The experience of our...": Harllee Branch Jr., "Remarks at Memorial Exercises Honoring Eugene A. Yates," April 7, 1958, SCHC

During the 1960s, the operating companies began using helicopters to help speed the construction of transmission lines, such as this aluminum tower being erected in Mississippi. *MPC Communication Files*

INDEX